THE STUDENT PILOT'S
GROUND SCHOOL MANUAL

Ground school supplement to
THE STUDENT PILOT'S FLIGHT MANUAL

Questions · Answers · Explanations

A study guide for the private pilot
certificate and beyond, including
a review of FARs

William K. Kershner

Genie Rae O'Kelley

Daniel J. Kuchta

IOWA STATE UNIVERSITY PRESS / AMES

To Betty
Dave, and
Tillie

William K. Kershner is the author of *The Student Pilot's Flight Manual*, *The Advanced Pilot's Flight Manual*, *The Instrument Flight Manual*, *The Flight Instructor's Manual*, and *The Basic Aerobatic Manual*. **Genie Rae O'Kelley** is chief flight instructor of Volunteer Aviation of Knoxville, Tenn., and is affiliated with the University of Tennessee aviation programs. **Colonel Daniel J. Kuchta** is a retired Air Force officer and former director of the Noncredit Programs Division of Continuing Education, University of Tennessee.

ILLUSTRATED BY WILLIAM K. KERSHNER

© 1989 Iowa State University Press, Ames, Iowa 50010
All rights reserved

Manufactured in the United States of America
⊗ This book is printed on acid-free paper.

No part of this book may be reproduced in any form—by photostat, microfilm, xerography, or any other means—or incorporated into any information retrieval system, electronic or mechanical, without the written permission of the copyright owner.

Authorization to photocopy items for internal or personal use, or the internal or personal use of specific clients, is granted by Iowa State University Press, provided that the base fee of $.10 per copy is paid directly to the Copyright Clearance Center, 27 Congress Street, Salem, MA 01970. For those organizations that have been granted a photocopy license by CCC, a separate system of payments has been arranged. The fee code for users of the Transactional Reporting Service is 0-8138-0822-7/90 $.10.

The Student Pilot's Ground School Manual replaces *The Student Pilot's Study Guide*.

First edition, 1989
Second printing, 1990

International Standard Book Number: 0-8138-0822-7
Library of Congress Catalog Card Number: 89-080018

CONTENTS

The Recreational Pilot's Certificate, v
Acknowledgments, vii

PART ONE
BEFORE THE FLIGHT
1. An Introduction, 1
2. The Airplane and How It Flies, 3
3. Cockpit: Instruments and Systems, 5
4. Preflight Check, 8
5. Starting the Airplane, 21
6. Taxiing, 23
7. Pretakeoff or Cockpit Check, 26

PART TWO
PRESOLO
8. Effects of Controls, 27
9. The Four Foundamentals, 28
10. Elementary Precision Maneuvers, 30
11. Elementary Forced Landings, 32
12. Stalls and Slow Flight, 33
13. Takeoffs and Landings, 35

PART THREE
POSTSOLO MANEUVERS
14. Advanced Stalls, 37
15. Emergency Flying by Reference to Instruments, 39
16. Postsolo Precision Maneuvers, 42
17. Special Takeoff and Landing Procedures, 43
18. High-Altitude Emergencies, 47

PART FOUR
CROSS-COUNTRY AND NIGHT FLYING
19. The Navigation Idea, 48
20. The Chart and Other Printed Aids, 52
21. Using the Radio, 71
22. Weather Information, 82
23. The Cross-Country: Knowing Your Airplane, 93
24. Navigation Planning, 100
25. Flying the Cross-Country, 109
26. Introduction to Night Flying, 112

PART FIVE
THE WRITTEN AND FLIGHT TESTS
27. The Written Test, 115
28. The Practical Test, 131
29. Review of Federal Aviation Regulations, 135

Appendix, 154

Bibliography and Recommended Reading, 163

Answers and Explanations to Chapter Questions, 164

Index, 203

Author's Note

THE RECREATIONAL PILOT'S CERTIFICATE

BACKGROUND

You may decide initially that you'd rather stick to the basics of flying and fly yourself and friends in the local area for enjoyment only. The recreational pilot's certificate is designed for those who do not want or need to fly in a tower-controlled environment or at night and has certain other restrictions that will be listed shortly. Or you may decide after holding a recreational certificate for a while that you want to go on to the private certificate and get the full privileges. This book covers both possibilities.

If you are working on the recreational pilot's certificate, you won't need to be familiar with the material in Chapter 15, Chapter 21 (and the radio communications portion of Chapter 24), and Chapter 26 (night flying). If you decide to move up to the private certificate, the material in these chapters (plus the private FAR requirements in Chapter 29) should be studied in preparation for the written and flight tests.

Only the recreational pilot's certificate (airplanes) will be discussed at this point, however.

THE RECREATIONAL PILOT'S REQUIREMENTS

1. Minimum age is 17 years.
2. Must be able to read, speak, and write English.
3. Must hold at least a current third-class medical certificate issued under FAR 67.
4. Must pass a written test on the subject areas prescribed in FAR 61.97, which includes:
   a. FARs as applicable to the recreational pilot's privileges, limitations, and flight operations; accident reporting requirements of the National Transportation Safety Board; and use of the applicable portions of the *Airman's Information Manual* and the FAA advisory circulars.
   b. Use of aeronautical charts for VFR navigation using piloting with the aid of a magnetic compass.
   c. Recognition of critical weather situations from the ground and in flight and use of aeronautical weather reports and forecasts.
   d. Safe and efficient operation of aircraft, including collision and wake turbulence avoidance.
   e. Effects of density-altitude on takeoff and climb performance.
   f. Weight and balance computations.
   g. Principles of aerodynamics, power plants, and aircraft systems.

FLIGHT PROFICIENCY

The applicant for a recreational pilot's certificate must have logged instruction from an authorized flight instructor in at least the pilot operations listed in this section. In addition, the applicant's logbook must contain an endorsement by an authorized flight instructor who has found the applicant competent to perform each of the following operations safely as a recreational pilot:

1. Preflight operations, including weight and balance determination, line inspection, airplane servicing, power plant operations, and aircraft systems.
2. Airport and traffic pattern operations and collision and wake turbulence avoidance.
3. Flight maneuvering by reference to ground objects.
4. Pilotage with the aid of a magnetic compass.
5. Flight at critically slow airspeeds and the rec-

ognition of and the recovery from imminent and full stalls entered from straight flight and from turns.

6. Emergency operations, including simulated aircraft and equipment malfunctions.

7. Maximum performance takeoffs and landings.

8. Normal and crosswind takeoffs and landings.

AERONAUTICAL EXPERIENCE

An applicant for a recreational pilot's certificate with an airplane rating must have had at least a total of 30 hours of flight instruction and solo flight time, which must include the following:

1. Fifteen hours of flight instruction from an authorized flight instructor, including at least:

   a. Two hours outside the vicinity of the airport at which instruction is given, including at least three landings at another airport that is located more than 25 nautical miles from the airport of departure.

   b. Two hours in airplanes in preparation for the recreational pilot's flight test within the 60-day period before the test.

2. Fifteen hours of solo flight time in airplanes.

THE RECREATIONAL PILOT'S PRIVILEGES AND LIMITATIONS

A recreational pilot may:

1. Not carry more than one passenger.
2. Share the operating expenses of the flight with the passenger.
3. Act as pilot in command of an aircraft only when:

   a. The flight is within 50 nautical miles of an airport at which the pilot has received ground and flight instruction from an authorized instructor certificated under this part.

   b. The flight lands at an airport within 50 nautical miles of the departure airport.

   c. The pilot carries in his or her personal possession a logbook that has been endorsed by the instructor, attesting to the 2 hours instruction outside the vicinity of the airport as discussed in the previous section.

Except for the purpose of obtaining additional certificates and ratings (to be covered shortly), a recreational pilot may not act as pilot in command of an aircraft:

1. That is certificated for more than four occupants.
2. With more than one power plant.
3. With a power plant of more than 180 horsepower.
4. With retractable landing gear.
5. That is classified as a glider, airship, or balloon.
6. Between sunset and sunrise.
7. In airspace in which communication with air traffic control is required.
8. At an altitude of more than 10,000 feet MSL or 2000 feet AGL, whichever is higher.
9. When the flight or surface visibility is less than 3 statute miles.
10. Without visual reference to the surface.

And you definitely won't be able at any time to act as pilot in command:

1. Carrying a passenger or property for compensation or hire.
2. For compensation or hire.
3. In furtherance of a business.

■ Additional Certificates and Ratings

For the purpose of obtaining additional certificates or ratings while under the supervision of an authorized flight instructor, a recreational pilot may fly as sole occupant of an aircraft:

1. For which the pilot does not hold an appropriate category or class rating.
2. Within airspace that requires communication with air traffic control.
3. Between sunset and sunrise, provided the flight or surface visibility is at least 5 statute miles.

In order to fly solo as just discussed, the recreational pilot must meet the appropriate aeronautical knowledge and flight training requirements for that aircraft. When operating an aircraft under the conditions specified in this section, the recreational pilot shall carry the logbook that has been endorsed for each flight by an authorized pilot instructor who:

1. Has given the recreational pilot instruction in the make and model of aircraft in which the solo flight is to be made.
2. Has found that the recreational pilot has met the applicable requirements.
3. Has found that the recreational pilot is competent to make solo flights in accordance with the logbook endorsement.

A recreational pilot may, for the purpose of obtaining an additional certificate or rating while under the supervision of an authorized flight instructor, act as pilot in command of an aircraft on a flight in excess of 50 nautical miles from an airport at which flight instruction is received if the pilot meets the flight training requirements and in that pilot's personal possession is the logbook that has been endorsed by an authorized instructor attesting that:

1. The recreational pilot has received instruction in solo cross-country flight and the training applicable to the aircraft to be operated and is competent to make solo cross-country flights in the make and model of aircraft to be flown.
2. The instructor has reviewed the student's preflight planning and preparation for the specific solo cross-country flight and stated that the recreational pilot is prepared to make the flight safely under the known circumstances and subject to any conditions listed in the logbook by the instructor.

One last item: If this is a review for you, you should note that *student* pilots (whether working on the recreational *or* private certificate) may not fly solo in *uncontrolled* airspace with a visibility of less than 3 statute miles (day) or 5 statute miles (night). The minimum of 1 statute mile visibility in uncontrolled airspace still applies for pilots holding a private certificate and above.

ACKNOWLEDGMENTS

The authors would like to express their appreciation to those who helped in the process of writing this book.

To Dr. G. Davis O'Kelley of the University of Tennessee at Knoxville, whose suggestions and practical proofreading were of much value in keeping the process moving, and to Frederick Grieger, professor in the School of Architecture at the University of Tennessee, Knoxville, who helped set up navigation problems for Chapter 19 and made valuable suggestions for questions, we owe special thanks.

For their help with communications procedures and most useful suggestions for the book, the following people are noted:

Crossville (Tenn.) Flight Service Station: Carroll De Priest, chief, and specialist James Gregory.

Knoxville Flight Service Station: John Wayne Annas, chief, and all the specialists, especially Andrea Edmondson, John R. "Jack" Stevens, James Oliver, T. J. Harrison, and Clayton M. Pyle.

Nashville Flight Service Station: Melvin Bourgeois, Larry Crawford, George Davis, Dick Edwards, and Jim Edwards.

McGhee-Tyson Airport (Knoxville): Billie B. Cox, chief of the Air Traffic Control Facility, and all the supervisors and controllers, especially Billie Solomon, Io'n Wainwright, William E. Shepherd, Raymond E. Johnson, Edward E. Forbes, Ralph Jones, and Tommy E. Platt.

For their help with regulations: James "Pete" Campbell of Union City, Tenn., formerly of the FAA and now an AOPA lecturer, and Lonnie Thurston with the Nashville FAA Flight Standards District Office.

For help with the navigation chapters: Evelyn Johnson, FAA examiner and manager of Morristown (Tenn.) Flying Service; David E. Hiltz, FAA examiner at Knoxville; Robert Cope, aviation instructor, Cleveland State Community College, Cleveland, Tenn.; James Sexton, president, Smoky Mountain Aero, Knoxville; H. D. Beeson, Area State Vocational School, Crossville; and Proctor Upchurch, Crossville.

Instructors at Volunteer Aviation of Knoxville, especially Dennis Almond, Ross Ramsey, Steve Wilkes, Harvey Coker, Michael Swaggerty, and Charles Taylor.

For weather information for later printings, Gordon Carroll, former chief, Knoxville FSS, and Donald L. Rogers/WSEO, Memphis.

Robert Scripture of Safetech, Inc., for furnishing data on the FDF-57-B computer.

Eleanor Ulton and Judy Rickman, who typed manuscript at Sewanee, Tenn.

Most appreciation of all goes to our spouses Betty, Dave, and Tillie for encouragement and practical help on the manuscript.

William K. Kershner
Genie O'Kelley
Daniel J. Kuchta

PART ONE — BEFORE THE FLIGHT

1

AN INTRODUCTION

This book has been written to help you pass the *Private Pilot—Airplane Written Test*, and it is to be used as a supplement to the material in *The Student Pilot's Flight Manual* (hereafter *SPFM*). (Each chapter is aimed at the equivalent chapter in *SPFM*.) Passing the written test doesn't automatically assure that you have the necessary background to be a safe private pilot, so the questions included here are to help you review the material in *SPFM*, with comments and added material inserted to give more detail in certain areas. Some chapters may have a fairly lengthy lead-in with lots of questions and long explanations, while others may immediately burst into not so many questions and fairly short explanations. The authors, in that infinite wisdom given to those who write textbooks, have designed the format to dovetail and review information in *SPFM* without turning to rote learning just to pass the written test. You'll be the final judge on how this works out.

This may be your first encounter with a written test of this nature, so some ideas on how to cope with the questions in this book (*and* those on the FAA written test) should be laid out.

The FAA test contains 50 questions and you are allowed 4 hours to complete it, but the nuts and bolts of the test will be covered in more detail in Chapter 27. A couple of points should be covered here, however.

The FAA has the following advice (quoted material is in italics) concerning taking the written test:

1. *There are no "trick" questions.* Don't look for hidden meanings or wordplays. The test is intended to check your knowledge of the subject, not semantics.

Multiple-choice questions have been chosen because with essay answers the person who could wax eloquent would have the test grader inspired or depressed over his or her discussion of a subject. Well, that turns out to be subjective and, besides, who needs to get poetic over the functions of a magneto? ("My, that boy has a way with words, but unfortunately he thinks a magneto is attached to the tailwheel.")

There are answer choices that seem quite reasonable (but are wrong) if you haven't fully read the question. You may rest assured that this same technique was used in the answer choices in this book, but it is a "friendly" way of warning you of the pitfalls of not carefully reading the test item. It was also a source of nasty chuckles as comments were passed between the writers, such as "They'll all answer number 3 on this one because it looks logical if they don't read it carefully."

True-false answers don't give enough choices; it has been calculated that based on statistics alone an untrained orangutan flipping a coin could make a score of 50. (There is no data on what a *trained* orangutan could do.)

But getting back to the multiple-choice questions, there are usually two of the answers that can be eliminated fairly quickly if you've done your homework on the subject. For instance, question 1302 in this book may bend a little the idea of two not-so-pertinent answers, but it can be considered as an exaggerated example.

1302. The best normal landing is made

1—by starting the rotation at about 1 foot above the surface.
2—by holding the airplane just off the ground as long as possible.
3—on a Sunday afternoon when there are thousands of admirers lining the airport fence.
4—when trying to impress that good-looking person of the opposite sex who's riding with you.

Answers (3) and (4) will be eliminated in your mind as soon as you start flying or read Chapter 13,

SPFM. The worst landings of your career will be made under the conditions cited in (3) and (4). So that leaves answers (1) and (2) from which to choose. Again, after reading Chapter 13, *SPFM* you'd know that starting the transition from the glide to the landing attitude at 1 foot wouldn't allow enough height, and there soon might be a large airplane-shaped hole in the runway. The answer is (2). The whole secret of a normal landing is to try to keep the airplane from landing—as it says in Chapter 13, *SPFM.*

Continuing some FAA quotes on the written test:

2. *Carefully read the entire test item before selecting an answer.* Truer words were never spoken. You'll start reading a question and the answer is so obvious that reading on would be a waste of time. There's the answer! You can bet that the people who wrote the question know that one of the answer choices will just fit a partially read question. You could misread a question such as the following one taken from an earlier FAA written test.

Of the factors listed, which would tend to *decrease* the density-altitude at a given airport?

1—Decreasing barometric pressure.
2—Increasing relative humidity.
3—Increasing ambient temperature.
4—Decreasing ambient temperature.

Well, the answer is (4). The density-altitude is lowered when the air becomes denser, and cooling the air causes this. All the other choices would increase the density-altitude (Chapter 3, *SPFM*). This could be misread, since as a pilot you are always worried about an increase in density-altitude (or the air getting thinner) and so might read increase instead of decrease in the lead-in sentence.

Another problem with written tests in general is the *negative variety* of choices. The question might be as follows.

0000. Which of the following is *not* a part of an airplane control system?

1—Rudder.
2—Stabilator.
3—Frying pan.
4—Aileron.

The "not" is italic and answer (3) is pretty obvious, at least here, but you'll find that you've been thinking in terms of positive answers and could misread the question. Reading test questions can be like proofreading a textbook; you start seeing what you want to see, not what is really there.

3. *Only one of the answers given is completely correct.* For instance, in the questions in Chapter 17, when using the takeoff distance charts, it's required that you find the distances for the ground roll and the total required to clear a 50-foot obstacle. In some of the answers the ground roll is correct and in others the total distance is, but in only one choice are both correct.

4. *If considerable difficulty is experienced with a particular test item, do not spend too much time on it, but continue with other items you consider to be less difficult.* With 50 test items and 4 hours allowed to complete the test, you'll have an average of 5 minutes for each question. Some of the questions will take much less than this, but some of the takeoff or landing distance or computer problems may eat up more time than you think, so if you seem to be in the middle of a mental block, move on to the next question(s). A lot of the time, successfully answering other questions will start your brain functioning for the computer questions; at least it raises your morale so you feel better about it. It has been said before, but the human mind is an amazing thing: it starts working the instant you are born and doesn't stop until you sit down to take an FAA written test.

5. *In solving problems which require computations or the use of a plotter or computer, select the answer which most nearly agrees with the calculated result.* There will be variations in computers and in your measuring distances and courses, so maybe your answer doesn't exactly match an available answer. There will be enough spread between the choices so that you'll be closest to the correct answer if you have used care and correct techniques. The FAA people used a number of different computers and plotters (as we authors did), and the correct answer is an average of the answers found.

If certain FAA test questions involving regulations, air traffic control procedures, and the like are outdated by very recent changes, you'll be given credit for these test items during the time it takes to distribute a revised question.

Okay, read each chapter of *SPFM* and any supplementary material in the co-chapter in this book and then work on the questions. You'll find that maybe the dreaded FAA written test isn't so bad after all.

2

THE AIRPLANE AND HOW IT FLIES

Review Chapter 2, *SPFM* before answering these questions, and read it again after checking the answers and explanations.

201. Which one of the following statements concerning the Four Forces is correct?

1—In straight and level unaccelerated flight, all Four Forces have equal values.
2—In a climb, lift is greater than weight.
3—In straight and level unaccelerated flight, thrust is greater than drag.
4—Lift acts perpendicular to the relative wind, whether the airplane is climbing, flying, flying straight and level, or gliding.

202. The angle between the relative wind and the chord line of the airfoil is the

1—angle of incidence.
2—angle of attack.
3—planing angle.
4—angle of climb or glide.

203. Taking off at higher altitudes and temperatures for a particular airplane (at a given weight) will require

1—more runway because the air is less dense.
2—less runway because the air is less dense.
3—the same amount of runway because the less dense air creates less drag, making up for any power loss.
4—more runway because the air becomes more dense with increase in altitude.

204. What horsepower is required to raise 55 pounds to a height of 6 feet in 3 seconds?

1—1/10.
2—1/50.
3—1/5.
4—1.5.

205. Brake horsepower is

1—horsepower being developed at the crankshaft.
2—horsepower developed by the propeller in moving the airplane through the air.
3—measured as pounds of thrust in older airplanes.
4—always the same as thrust horsepower in newer airplanes.

206. Which one of the following statements is correct in regard to "torque" corrections (U.S.-built engines)?

1—In a climb, left rudder is necessary to keep the airplane straight.
2—In a climb, right rudder is necessary to keep the airplane straight.
3—In a dive, right rudder is necessary to keep the airplane straight.
4—When power is added abruptly, the airplane will tend to roll to the right.

207. The drag resulting from lift being produced is

1—parasite.
2—interference.
3—induced.
4—gyroscopic.

3

208. The retarding force created by airflow at the junction of the wings and fuselage is the result of

1—induced drag.
2—gyroscopic effects.
3—interference drag.
4—skin friction drag.

209. Which of the following statements is correct concerning drag?

1—Induced drag increases as the airspeed increases.
2—If parasite drag is 200 pounds at a straight and level speed of 100 knots, at 200 knots it will be 800 pounds.
3—Skin friction drag decreases with increased airspeed.
4—Induced drag decreases as the airspeed decreases.

210. Gravity always acts

1—opposite to weight.
2—parallel but opposite to lift.
3—perpendicular to the total drag.
4—toward the center of the earth.

3
COCKPIT: INSTRUMENTS AND SYSTEMS

Altimeter note—Nonstandard temperature affects the accuracy of your altimeter. The standard temperature at sea level is 15°C, and the normal lapse rate is −2°C per thousand feet. At 10,000 feet the standard temperature would be 15 − (10 × 2) = −5°C. The altimeter will read *high* if the outside air temperature is *lower* than standard. This means that in air colder than standard the altimeter will read higher than the airplane actually is and terrain clearances wouldn't be maintained. For temperature effects, remember HALT (*H*igh *A*ltimeter because of *L*ow *T*emperature). In other words, HALT, or you might fly into something solid under those conditions. This is more important in IFR work when you are solidly on the gauges. If you know HALT, then it stands to reason that a *higher than standard* temperature will mean the *altimeter will read low*, a safer condition as far as terrain clearance is concerned. When you are working altimeter-temperature problems, remember HALT to get some idea of the answer, then get the details on your computer.

301. True altitude is height above sea level, and absolute altitude is height above the surface. With this in mind, choose the correct answer to the following: An airplane is flying over the ocean at an actual height of 10,000 feet over the water (altimeter setting and temperature unknown). It is flying at its

1—density- and absolute altitudes.
2—pressure and absolute altitudes.
3—true and absolute altitudes.
4—true and density-altitudes.

302. In computing airplane performance, the pilot or engineer uses

1—density-altitude.
2—true altitude.
3—absolute altitude.
4—indicated altitude.

303. Indicated airspeed corrected for instrument and position error is

1—true airspeed.
2—calibrated airspeed.
3—equivalent airspeed.
4—static pressure.

304. Equivalent airspeed corrected for density-altitude effects is

1—calibrated airspeed.
2—indicated airspeed.
3—true airspeed.
4—density airspeed.

305. You are flying at an indicated airspeed of 120 knots at 6000 feet (assume no instrument error). The outside air temperature is +3°C. Your computer is back on the counter at the airport, but using the rule of thumb you can estimate that your true airspeed is approximately

1—140 mph.
2—134 knots.
3—124 mph.
4—144 knots.

306. The job of the pitot tube is to admit what pressure or pressures to the airspeed indicator?

1—Dynamic only.
2—Static only.
3—Static and vertical speed changes.
4—Dynamic and static.

307. You are flying on a solo cross-country in a trainer and realize that the oil pressure gauge is at ZERO. Your best initial move would be to

1—land immediately; the engine will stop within 3 minutes.
2—watch the oil temperature gauge for an increase in temperature as you fly toward an airport or better terrain.
3—pay no attention to it but continue your flight.
4—go immediately to 7700 on the transponder (if you have one) and call MAYDAY on 121.5 kHz.

308. If you are referring to the magnetic compass on a heading of east, an acceleration of airspeed (maintaining a constant altitude) will result in

1—a more northerly indication.
2—a more southerly indication.
3—no change in compass indication, since it is correct on east or west headings.
4—northerly turning error.

309. Which of the instruments in Figure 3-A indicates a slipping turn to the right?

1—A.
2—B and C.
3—A and D.
4—D.

310. A turn of 180° as indicated by Figure 3-B should take

1—120 seconds.
2—60 seconds.
3—90 seconds.
4—180 seconds.

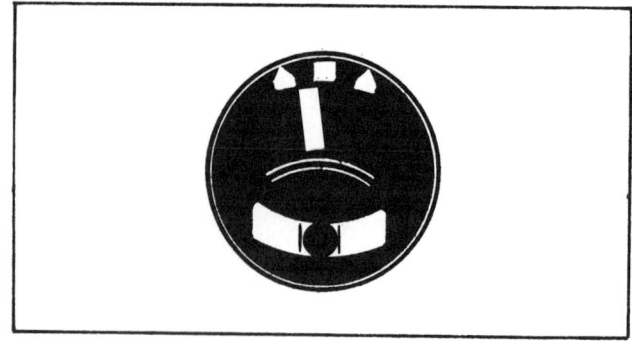

Fig. 3-B.

311. A job of the alternator is to

1—provide a spark to each magneto as needed.
2—provide vacuum for the gyro instruments.
3—run the electrical components and keep the battery charged.
4—alternate the power from the brake system to the electrical system.

312. The majority of turn and slip indicators or turn coordinators in current smaller airplanes are powered by the

1—static pressure system.
2—engine-driven vacuum pump.
3—hydraulic system.
4—electrical system.

313. The vertical speed indicator operates on the principle of

1—change in outside atmospheric pressure.
2—absolute atmospheric pressure.
3—precession.
4—dynamic pressure from the pitot tube.

314. If the engine-driven vacuum pump fails in the average trainer, you would expect to lose the use of the

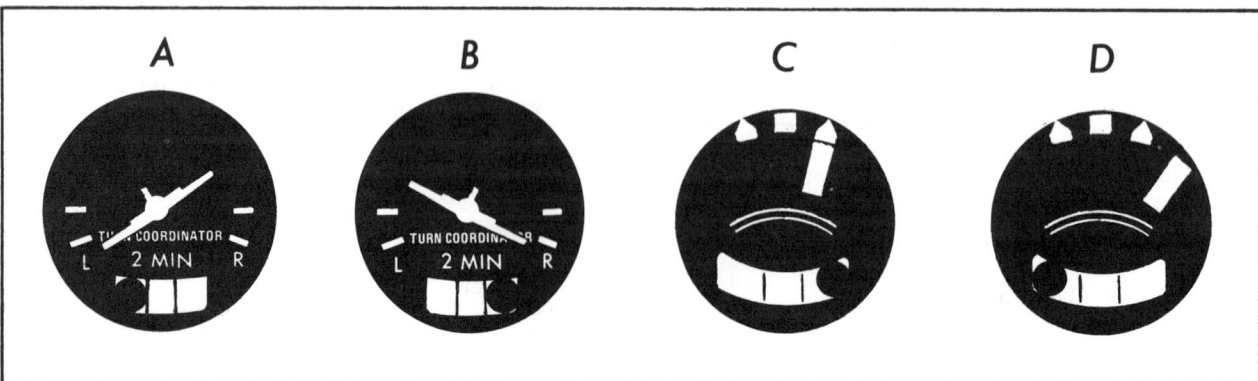

Fig. 3-A.

Chapter 3. Cockpit: Instruments and Systems

1—airspeed and attitude indicators.
2—altimeter and attitude indicators.
3—attitude indicator and heading (directional) indicator.
4—vertical speed indicator and turn coordinator.

315. Based on Figure 3-C, which of the following items is guarded by a *fuse*, not a circuit breaker?

1—Clock.
2—Fuel quantity indicators.
3—Flaps.
4—Oil temperature gauge.

316. At a calibrated airspeed of 150 knots at a density altitude of 10,000 feet, you want to set up a standard rate turn. Using the attitude indicator for bank angle, you would set up a bank of *approximately*

1—15°.
2—25°.
3—35°.
4—10°.

317. Which one of the following items would require the most electrical current when in operation?

1—Landing light.
2—Turn and slip indicator.
3—Flashing beacon.
4—Navigation receiver.

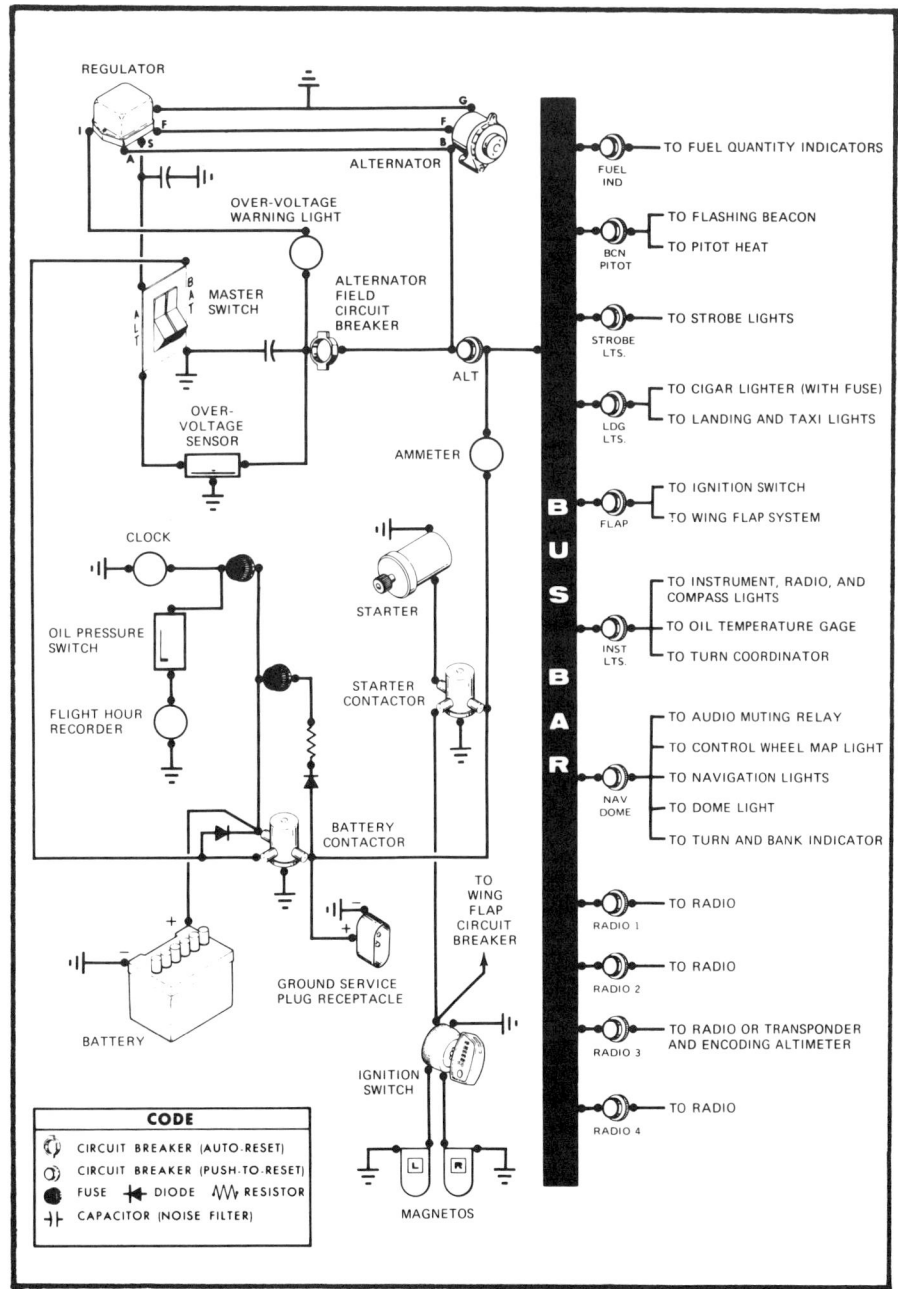

Fig. 3-C.

4

PREFLIGHT CHECK

ADDED NOTES ON ENGINE THEORY, CONSTRUCTION, AND OPERATIONS

There have been cases of certificated private and commercial pilots who have never fully seen the engine of the airplane they've been flying for many hours. (They open the small access door to check the oil and only get a glimpse of the top of the engine crankcase.) The cowlings of many airplanes are designed so that it is impractical for the pilot to open them before every flight; probably the only time the engine is fully seen is when a 100-hour annual inspection is done or the oil is changed.

The point is that you should have a basic understanding of how various things work, so that a lot of the mystery disappears and you aren't sweating out some unknown and unexplained failure. You might avoid a bad situation such as loss of electrical power at night, for instance, by noting that the belt that drives the alternator is getting frayed and should be replaced before it breaks. If you didn't know the function of the belt, you might not be so concerned about replacing it before that long night flight over the Louisiana swamps.

■ Engine Operation

In order to know what to look for in the preflight check or how to analyze engine problems in flight, you should have some basic knowledge of how an engine works. Most general aviation airplane engines are horizontally opposed and air cooled. The horizontally opposed engine is "flat" and has an equal number of cylinders on each side of the crankcase (Fig. 4-A).

The engine uses the "Otto cycle" in operation and works this way: The pistons, enclosed in the cylinders, move *in* and *out* within a limited distance. The burning of the fuel-air mixture pushes the piston in, and it is attached by a connecting rod to an offset section of the crankshaft. Because of that offset section, the back and forth motion of the piston is translated to a rotary motion of the crankshaft, which in turn rotates the propeller either directly or through a gearing system. Most lighter airplane engines have direct drive; that is, the propeller is directly attached to and rotates at the same speed as the engine crankshaft. Higher horsepower engines may have gears that reduce the propeller rotation speed. The engine has four strokes (Fig. 4-B):

1. *Intake stroke*—The piston moves toward the base of the cylinder with the intake valve open (exhaust valve closed), pulling the fuel-air mixture into the cylinder.
2. *Compression*—As the crankshaft rotates, the piston moves away from the base of the cylinder with *both* valves closed so that the fuel-air mixture is compressed.
3. *Power stroke*—The fuel-air mixture is *ignited* in its compressed state, which gives greater power than if it was not compressed, and the piston is moved downward (or inward), rotating the crankshaft and thus turning the propeller.
4. *Exhaust stroke*—As the crankshaft turns, the piston moves up (out) with the exhaust valve open, purging the burned gases out through the exhaust system.

The crankshaft has to make two full revolutions for each cylinder's power stroke, as you can see by analyzing Figure 4-B. This sequence is happening in other cylinders at different times, and each power stroke turns the crankshaft and provides for the intake, compression, and exhaust strokes as needed for the other cylinders.

Fig. 4-A. The Lycoming 0-235 L2C four-cylinder, horizontally opposed, air-cooled engine. This is used in current two-place trainers. (*Avco Lycoming*)

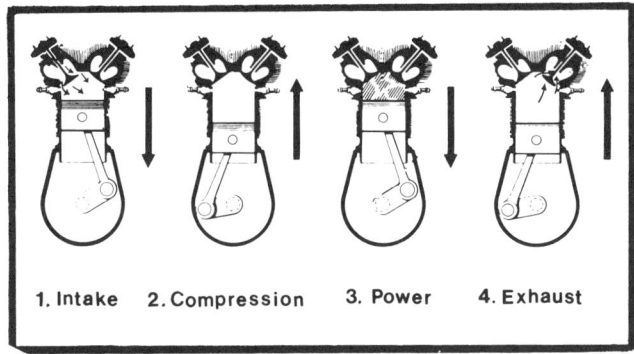

Fig. 4-B. The four strokes. The cylinder is shown as upright rather than horizontal here. (*FAA AC 61-32A*)

■ Engine Components

The pistons, which in most cases are made from aluminum alloy forgings, have rings that fit into grooves cut in them. The rings are made from a good stock of cast iron and have a slightly larger outside diameter than the piston (Fig. 4-C).

Compression rings are designed to prevent the escape of the fuel-air mixture or exhaust gases into the

Fig. 4-C. A—Piston and components: (1) piston, (2) compression rings, (3) oil regulating or oil scraper ring, (4) piston pin (sometimes called "wrist pin"), (5) piston pin plugs, (6) connecting rod (from piston to crankshaft), (7) bushing, (8) connecting rod bolts, (9) connecting rod nuts, (10) connecting rod bearings (replaceable). The line C-C shows where the connecting rod joins the crankshaft. B—Two views of a cylinder. Note the cooling fins. Look at Figure 4-B again.

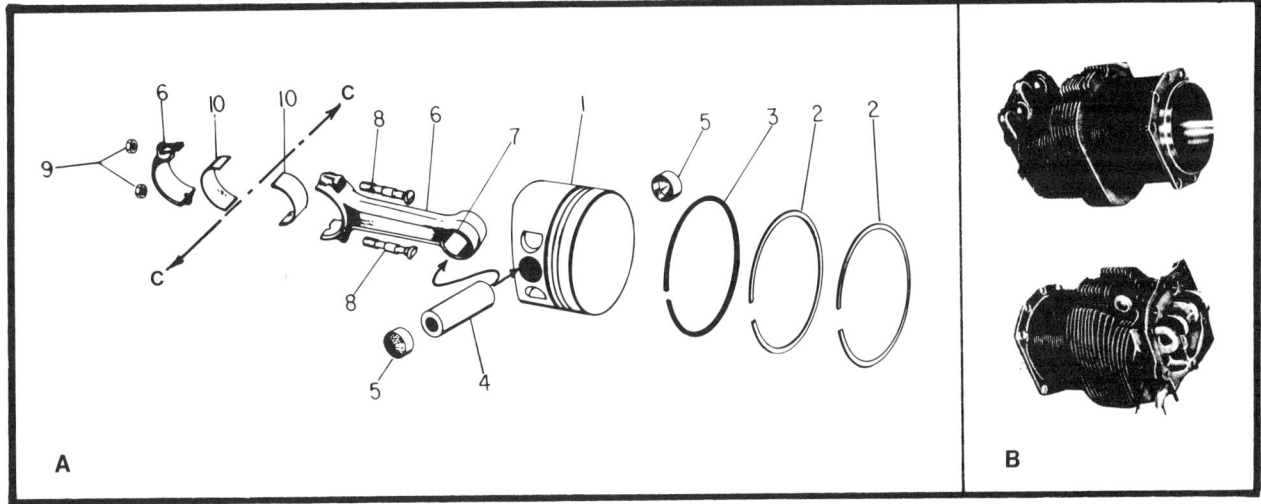

crankcase. There are usually two or more of these per piston, and they are replaceable if worn or broken. The barrel of the cylinder is forged steel; for a certain number of hours from the time the new engine is first started, the rings will be considered to be "seating" or fitting to the cylinder walls. (An operating time of 50 hours is considered a reasonable period for this.) The manufacturer usually recommends that straight mineral oil, which has no additives, be used because this allows more friction so that the slight wear needed for seating is speeded up. Once the rings are seated, ashless dispersant oils are normally used to keep friction to a minimum.

One possible later problem, as the hours pile up on the engine, is that these piston rings get worn or may break, allowing oil from the crankcase to get into the combustion chamber and burn with the fuel-air mixture. That's what was happening in that car in front of you the other day; the driver was laying a smoke screen because oil as well as gasoline was burning. Not only was too much oil being burned but the residue was fouling the spark plugs and gumming up the valves so that they didn't close properly.

Mechanics run compression checks on the 100-hour and annual inspections to check for valve and ring problems. If the airplane you're flying isn't developing the power it should or the oil consumption has gone up radically, rings may be the problem. This can also be checked by an experienced pilot or the mechanic, who (after making sure the ignition is off, the mixture is at idle cutoff, and the airplane is chocked or tied down) pulls the prop through and checks for a cylinder (or cylinders) that doesn't resist the pulling through like the others. Extreme caution is suggested when pulling the prop through, even though the mag switch "says" OFF.

The oil control rings are below the compression rings and regulate the thickness of the oil coating on the cylinder walls.

The camshaft is geared to the crankshaft at the rear of the engine. The camshaft has nodes or cams that are offset around the shaft; as it rotates, the cams move up against pushrods that open the spring-loaded exhaust or intake valves for the various cylinders in the proper sequence. A pushrod extends from the camshaft to the rocker arm, which pushes the valve (exhaust or intake) down and opens it (Fig. 4-D).

Engines are classified by the cubic-inch displacement in the cylinders or the volume of air in all cylinders if the pistons are in the bottom dead center or "withdrawn" position. As an example, suppose the *diameter* of each piston (with rings) of a four-cylinder engine is 5.4 inches (its *bore*) and it *travels* 3 inches (its *stroke*) from full up to full down (or in a horizontally opposed engine, full out to full back) (Fig. 4-E). One cylinder's displacement is the volume of that travel. Volume (V) or displacement = area × distance. (Area = πr^2.)

Radius (r) = 2.7 inches; r^2 = $(2.7)^2$ = 7.3; πr^2 = 22.9 inches = area

Stroke = 3 inches; displacement = 3 × 22.9 = 68.7 cubic inches

There are four cylinders, so the total displacement is 4 × 68.7 = 274.8 cubic inches, and this fictitious engine would have a designation of O-275 because it is a horizontally opposed type. If it had fuel injection, the designation would be IO-275; if it was also turbocharged, the designation would be TIO-275. Another letter G would be included (TGIO-275) if the engine was geared and not a direct drive. It's likely that an engine with this small amount of displacement would

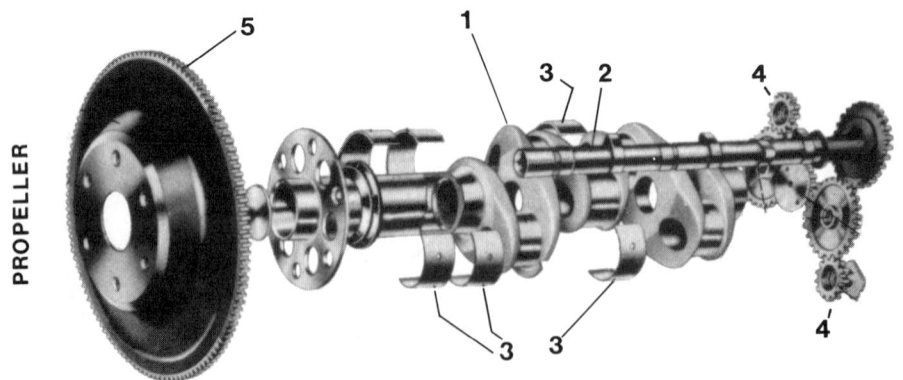

Fig. 4-D. Crankshaft, camshaft, and other parts: (1) crankshaft, (2) camshaft, (3) crankshaft bearing (same as item 10 in Fig. 4-C), (4) magneto gears, (5) starter ring gear.

Chapter 4. Preflight Check

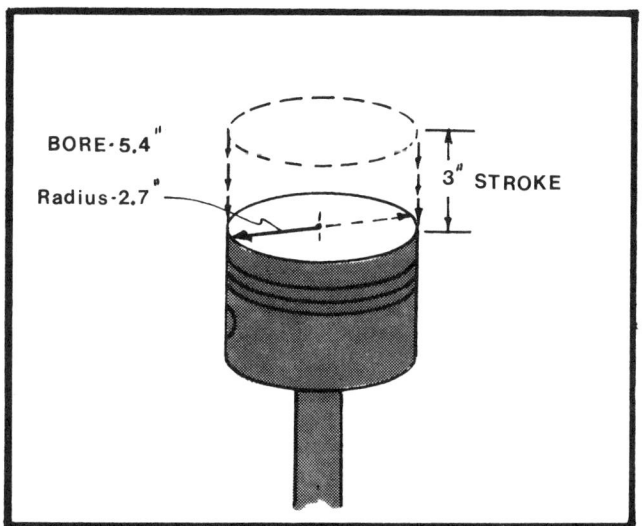

Fig. 4-E. Piston displacement.

not have all the refinements mentioned, but it's an example. The term "compression ratio" is used for reciprocating engines to indicate the ratio of the amount of volume of the mixture when the piston is at the bottom dead center position (fully withdrawn down or back in the cylinder) to top dead center (at the greatest compression). Figure 4-F gives an idea of the relative volumes for a compression ratio of 7 to 1.

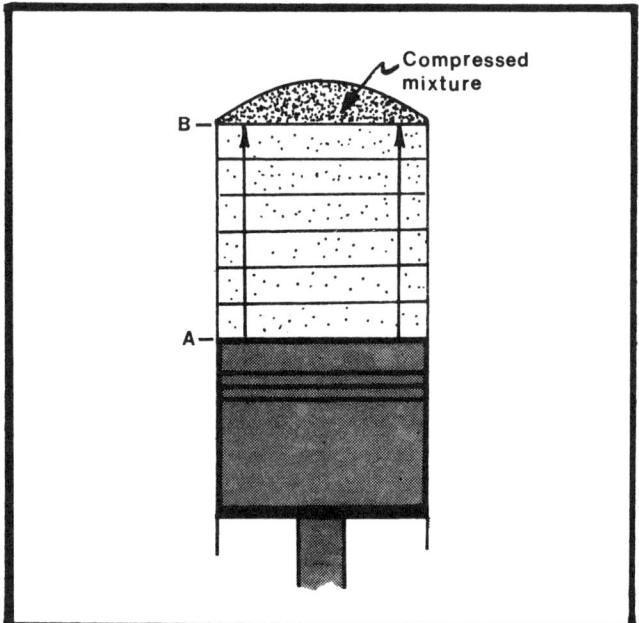

Fig. 4-F. Compression ratio. In moving from the bottom dead center point (A), the piston compresses the fuel-air mixture to one-seventh of its original volume at (B); the compression ratio is 7 to 1. Low-compression engines are considered to be those from 6.5 to 1 to 7.9 to 1. Above that they are considered high-compression types.

TIME BETWEEN OVERHAULS. You'll hear the expression time between overhauls (TBO) as you progress as a pilot, and the tendency is to think that this is a definite time required by regulation until a complete major overhaul of the engine. Also, you might think there would be an immediate failure if the engine was secretly operated past that limit. Not so. The manufacturer sets a *recommended* limit based on inputs of users from around the world and its own experience in overhauling engines returned for that purpose. An engine having a recommended TBO of 2000 hours, for instance, may need overhauling at 1200 hours (if abused and the manufacturer's recommendations for operations neglected), or it may go 2500 hours or more if properly operated and maintained.

Another term you'll hear is *top overhaul*, and this usually consists of removing only the cylinders so that piston rings may be replaced and valves may be replaced or reseated. This is done by some operators between *major* overhauls (in which the engine is totally disassembled). Some manufacturers feel that if the engine is properly maintained and operated, it should go to at least the recommended TBO without the need for a top overhaul. However, local conditions, need for special operations, and use of higher lead content fuels may necessitate a top overhaul.

■ **Carburetion**

The engine has a way to get the fuel-air mixture in, compress it, fire it, and exhaust it, so the next step is to design a method of mixing the fuel and air in the proper amounts. Figure 4-G shows a carburetor, which for horizontally opposed engines is located beneath the crankcase.

The carburetor has a float chamber that stores a small amount of fuel for use in mixing with the incoming air. As the fuel in the chamber is depleted, the float moves down, opening a valve to let in more fuel. This is a repeating process as the engine runs.

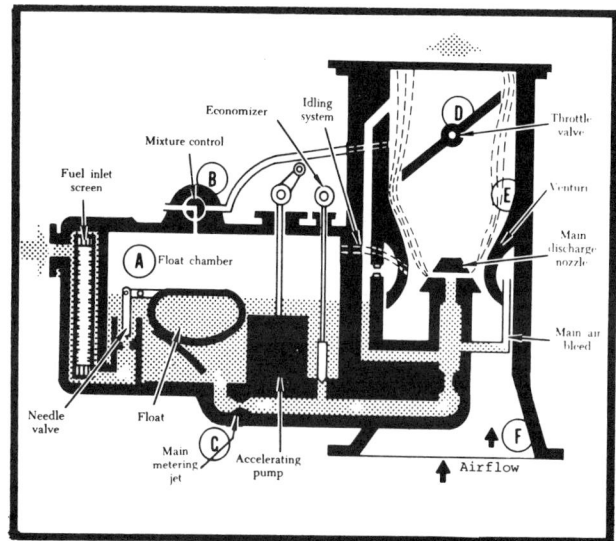

Fig. 4-G. Float-type carburetor. (*FAA AC 61-32C*)

The fuel is vaporized by the main discharge nozzle and mixes with the incoming air (as shown in Figure 4-G) just past the venturi (which speeds up the airflow like the upper camber of an airfoil). As you move the throttle forward, the throttle valve opens more and allows a greater amount of fuel and air to enter the engine and provide more power. The temperature is decreased in the venturi discharge nozzle and throttle valve area by two events: (1) the pressure of the air moving through the venturi is lowered, lowering the temperature, and (2) the vaporization of the fuel lowers the temperature so that a drop of up to 60°F is possible. If the incoming air contains moisture, it may freeze in that area and eventually shut off the air (and fuel) flow, with engine stoppage resulting. Look again at Chapter 4, *SPFM* for the background of carburetor heat and for diagrams of how it works.

FUEL INJECTION. The fuel injection system is normally used for higher powered engines, and later you will get a chance to fly an airplane so equipped. The advantage of this system is that the fuel is injected into the air just as it enters the cylinder, resulting in less chance of carburetor ice and a much better fuel distribution.

When you lean a carburetor-equipped engine, it will become rough (you can feel it), since the air and fuel are mixed at the carburetor and the mixture will vary between cylinders because of the distances involved. One or more cylinders may be leaner than the others, and as you move the mixture control out to lean the engine, those cylinders start losing power earlier. The engine runs rough, and you move the mixture control forward just enough to smooth it out.

Because of the better fuel distribution, the fuel injection normally can't be leaned by feel and you'll use a fuel-flow gauge or an EGT (exhaust-gas temperature) gauge. Fuel-injected engines don't use carburetor heat as such but have an alternate air source (usually from inside the cowling) if induction icing (icing in the air intake area) occurs. Fuel injection is best used in an engine of over 200 horsepower with a constant-speed propeller.

If a tank is run dry in a carburetor system, it normally takes 1–2 seconds for power to be restored after the tanks are switched; a fuel injection system may require 8–10 seconds and special techniques to get power back. It's best never to deliberately run a tank dry with *any* system. Check your *Pilot's Operating Handbook* now for the procedure if you should inadvertently run a tank dry.

■ Ignition

MAGNETOS. There must be a system to ignite the mixture when it's been compressed in the cylinder. The magneto is used in an airplane because it is self-sufficient, as noted in Chapter 4, *SPFM*. Two magnetos are used for two reasons: (1) there is one remaining to keep the engine going if one fails, and (2) two spark plugs provide a smoother burning of the mixture in the cylinder. With one magneto and one spark plug the ignition would start in one corner of the combustion chamber and proceed across, taking some time (milliseconds), whereas *two* separate sparks can each set off a portion of the fuel-air mixture and make for smoother and more efficient combustion. That's one reason why you get a drop in rpm in the mag check when going from BOTH to just LEFT or RIGHT.

The magneto is "timed" so that the spark plug gives ignition to its cylinder at a time that would result in the most efficient burning and best power. The initial thought would be that the spark should occur just at the instant the piston reaches its farthest point up (or out) in the cylinder when the compression is greatest (top dead center, or TDC). The problem in that case is that by the time the burning reached its peak, even though it's burning fast, the piston would have already started down and the peak power wouldn't result. The idea is to time the spark so that the maximum effect of combustion results. Since it takes time for the combustion to propagate, the ignition should be started *before* the piston reaches TDC so that the best "push" is obtained. The mechanic "times" the magneto by setting it to fire at some point, say 25° of crankshaft rotation before TDC, as recommended by the manufacturer. Magnetos get out of time and mechanics have to check them. Timing is critical to smooth operation; for instance, you can imagine what would happen if the timing was accidentally set too early (for instance, 90° before TDC) so that the piston was still moving up when the full force of combustion occurred. Pandemonium would occur in the powerhouse.

It's possible that in flight one of the magnetos might slip out of timing and the engine will run very rough. You might go from BOTH to LEFT *or* RIGHT to find the magneto that is acting properly. Since the airplane is now running on one mag, it would be best to get on to the nearest safe airport for repairs.

In some cases, the magnetos may be timed slightly apart. One is set to give the word to the spark plug at 25° before TDC, and the other fires its plug in the same cylinder slightly later, at 23° before TDC. This may be done to get an even smoother operation; it depends on the engine.

If you get a chance, go out into the hangar or shop some day between flights and observe some of the engine work being done. Most mechanics don't mind good questions as long as it doesn't interfere with their work. There's a sign that mechanics show to airplane owners:

MAINTENANCE CHARGES

1. Our mechanic alone $30.00/hr
2. If you stand around and
                       offer suggestions   35.00/hr
3. If you help   40.00/hr

The pilots come back with a sign that says:

> IT TAKES SIX PEOPLE TO WORK
>
> ON AIRPLANES HERE:
>
> ONE MECHANIC
>
> AND FIVE MORE TO HOLD THE PILOT BACK.

Most engines have each magneto separately geared to the engine accessory section, but some newer models use a common engine drive with both magnetos in the same housing. Advantages of this are a decrease in weight and freeing of one magneto drive that might be used for other accessories. Some argue against having a *single* drive for *both* mags and prefer a separate one for each.

The magnetos and plug leads ("leeds") must be shielded to prevent ignition noise from coming through the radio receivers. If you hear a repetitive crackling noise coming through the radio, you might try checking to see which mag and its ignition components (plugs, leads, etc.) are causing the problem. You can tell the mechanic which is the guilty system and save time in analysis.

SPARK PLUGS. Spark plugs are seemingly simple pieces of equipment, but they can affect the performance of the engine to a great extent. They are subjected to extremely high temperatures when the engine is running.

A great deal depends on the plug "gap" or gaps, that is, how far apart the electrodes are. The spark has to "jump" a certain length to get the optimum ignition—the wider or narrower the gap from that recommended by the manufacturer, the less efficient the result.

Spark plug electrodes are subjected to temperatures of over 3000°F, gas pressures of up to 2000 pounds per square inch, and electrical pressures of up to 15,000 volts.

It's noted in Chapters 4 and 7, *SPFM* that each magneto furnishes ignition (through the spark plugs) to each cylinder, and the wiring route may vary between makes and models. The ignition wiring on one four-cylinder engine used in a current trainer is established so that the right magneto fires the two lower right and two upper left plugs and the left magneto fires the lower left and upper right (Fig. 4-H). Usually though not always, the lower plugs foul more easily, so if you had a bad permanent drop on the left mag, under the just mentioned arrangement you'd probably start a maintenance check, looking at those bottom left plugs first. Of course, the mechanic would know the wiring arrangement, but you should have an idea of the general layout of your airplane ignition system.

Fig. 4-H. In this particular installation the left magneto (1) fires the bottom plugs on the left two cylinders (2) and the top plugs on the right cylinders (not shown). The right mag (not shown) fires the bottom right (not shown) and top left (3). While it's not a part of the ignition system, (4) shows the ground-service plug receptacle for use of an external electrical power source.

Problems occurring in the combustion chamber are *preignition* and *detonation*, and sometimes people get confused between the two.

Preignition, as defined by *The Lycoming Flyer*, is a situation in which the combustion takes place within the cylinder before the timed spark occurs. Usually it's caused by combustion deposits such as lead, which cause local hot spots. It can be caused by a cracked valve or piston or a broken spark plug insulation that sets up a local glow spot. The mixture is not fired at the proper time, the engine runs rough and backfires, and a sudden increase in cylinder-head temperature is noted if you have a CHT (cylinder head temperature) gauge. Older airplanes without mixture control had to be shut down by turning off the ignition, and if the engine was hot it continued running. Also, some model-airplane engines use the principle of preignition by electrically preheating a certain type plug, which is then kept hot by combustion.

Preignition is a serious condition that can cause burned pistons and damaged valves and is similar to early timing of the spark.

Detonation results when limits of compression and temperature are exceeded; this is most likely at higher power settings. Leaning the mixture at high power settings and abrupt opening of the throttle can cause detonation.

Unless it is heavy, the pilot doesn't know it's happening. Light to medium detonation may *not* cause noticeable roughness, observable oil temperature or CHT increase, or loss of power. But after an engine has been detonating, a teardown shows damage to valves, pistons, and cylinder heads.

In *normal combustion* the piston is pushed

smoothly down (or in, in a horizontally opposed engine); with *detonation* the piston acts as if it was being hit by a sledgehammer.

The best temporary in-flight methods for correcting preignition and detonation are to retard the throttle, richen the mixture, open cowl flaps if available, or do all three.

You might remember the causes of detonation by the following three "too's":

Too lean—mixture too lean for higher power settings.

Too hot—climbing at too slow an airspeed and/or too lean a mixture.

Too cheap—lower grade fuel than recommended.

■ **Oil System**

The engine operation would be short-lived without lubrication. The oil used in the engine has three major purposes: (1) to maintain a film between moving parts so that they do not actually make metal-to-metal contact, (2) to carry off heat from the various internal parts as it circulates, and (3) to pick up foreign particles for depositing in a filter.

The oil used in the airplanes you are flying is designed to take care of the three items just mentioned. Without going into laborious details about the theory of oil viscosity (or flow rate ability), the higher the commercial aviation number or SAE (Society of Automotive Engineers) number, the higher the viscosity (thickness). The viscosity of oil varies inversely with heat—the colder the temperature, the thicker the oil. If you choose a low-viscosity (thin oil) for use in hot weather, the viscosity gets even lower as the engine heats up, and metal-to-metal contact results. The use of high-viscosity oil in cold climates would mean that it would be like grease, making the engine difficult to start, and the oil circulation would be very poor. Your *Pilot's Operating Handbook* will note the oil grades to be used for various ambient temperature ranges and, as indicated earlier, will probably note that after the first 50 hours of operation, ashless dispersant oil meeting certain criteria is to be used. It may recommend use of multiviscosity oils.

Some typical light-trainer oil system components are shown in Figure 4-I. This is a wet-sump system, meaning that the oil is contained in the lower part of the engine (the sump) as in most automobiles.

The carburetor for this engine is located as shown in Figure 4-I and gets warmth from the warm oil in the sump. Because of this, the engine is less susceptible to carburetor ice than the dry-sump type, which has the oil in a container separate from the engine and not close to the carburetor. The wet-sump engine *can* have carb ice troubles, and carb heat should be used to check for the presence of ice before the throttle is retarded to lower power settings, such as when starting an approach.

With less availability of 80-octane fuel and more use of grade 100 and 100 Low-Lead, it's important that the oil be changed more often when using these higher grade fuels with their attendant higher lead contents. The old oil, when drained, will carry off impurities, thus lengthening the engine life.

Your instructor may show you the engine oil breather, which is an attachment and hose designed to release pressures that build up in the crankcase because of the high temperature there. The breather usually comes out the top of the crankcase, with the hose running down and out the bottom of the cowling (item 9, Fig. 4-I). During the preflight check in the winter be sure that the breather is not closed by ice (the warm water vapor from the engine will freeze at the breather outlet).

Since lighter airplanes don't have a cylinder-head temperature gauge, the oil temperature gauge becomes very important in indicating whether the engine is being abused in a too slow climb or a too lean setting for the flight condition. As noted at the beginning of this section, part of the job of the oil is to remove heat from the engine components. The *Airframe and Powerplant Mechanics Powerplant Handbook* (DOT-FAA) indicates that the thermal distribution of the heat released by combustion in an engine is approximately as follows:

1. 25–30 percent is converted into useful power.
2. 40–45 percent is carried out with the exhaust.
3. 5–10 percent is *removed by the oil.*
4. 15–20 percent is removed by the cylinder cooling fins.

■ **Engine Cooling**

The principle of the cylinder cooling fins is radiation of heat from the cylinder into the air moving past the engine. The fins present a large surface area and are oriented so that the air moves around and between them, thus removing heat. In a preflight inspection you may note that some of the fins are broken off; this should call for a discussion with your instructor or mechanic because if enough cooling fin area is missing serious heat problems could arise and the cylinder should be changed.

In the spring, birds may build a nest in the cowling, with the result that the cooling flow is shut off or redirected and a hot spot exists, leading to serious damage. Baffles are shaped aluminum plates attached to the engine or cowling to help direct the airflow for best engine cooling. These should be checked for security and proper alignment during the preflight if possible.

Your current light trainer may not have cowl flaps (which are normally located at the bottom rear of the cowling), but probably one or more of the airplanes you fly later will have them.

Engine cooling, from a pilot's standpoint, results from two main sources: (1) rich mixture and (2) airflow past the cylinders. Looking at the airflow idea, there's usually no problem at cruise, and a small opening at the bottom rear of the cowling is sufficient

Chapter 4. Preflight Check 15

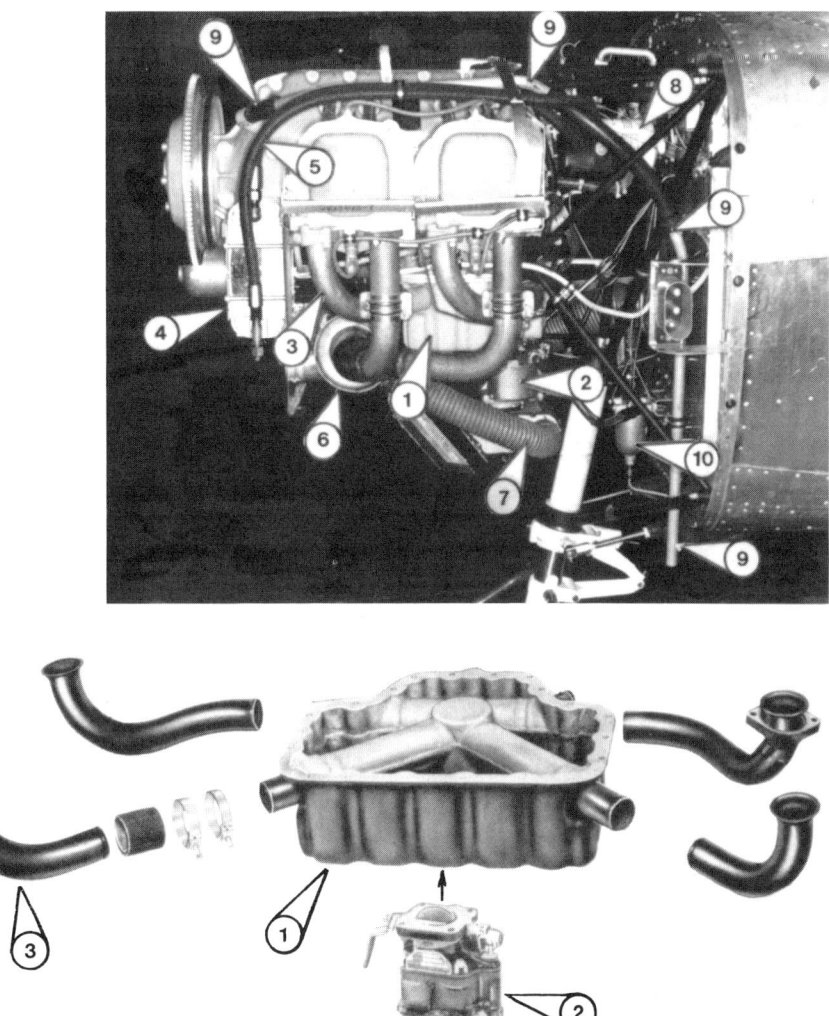

Fig. 4-I. Oil system and other components: (1) oil sump (the bottom picture shows a front view of the sump), (2) carburetor (note its position in relation to the oil sump), (3) intake pipe, (4) oil cooler (radiator), (5) oil line, (6) carburetor heat/cabin heat muff, (7) carburetor heat hose, (8) oil filter, (9) breather pipe, (10) fuel strainer.

for the now warmed ram air to escape; there is a large volume of air moving over the engine each second, carrying off engine heat. Also, the power is back to cruise, so there's a comparatively low heat problem and plenty of air passing by to take care of it.

When the airplane is sitting on the ground with the engine running, there is comparatively little air moving across the cylinders, and the cowl flaps should be fully open to allow the greatest amount of heat escape possible. Some airplanes require that the cowl flaps be set fully open for takeoff and not quite fully open for a cruise climb. After cruise is established, the cowl flaps are closed to cut down on aerodynamic drag and also, particularly in cold weather, to keep the engine from running *too* cool.

You may also fly an airplane using exhaust augmenters, which use exhaust gas velocity to draw air over the engine. The simpler types do not require cowl flaps or other controls to be adjusted by the pilot. The system is automatic; as the exhaust gases are released through the ejector, the hot air is pulled from the engine compartment and sent out with the exhaust.

■ **Exhaust Systems**

The exhaust system should seem simple enough; all that is apparently needed is a pipe to let the burned gases out. The most efficient (and noisiest) system was that of the short-stacks type used earlier on radial engines; it consisted of a short, curved exhaust pipe for each cylinder. This meant that there would be little back pressure in the "system." When the exhaust system requires long pipes or collector rings (as for bigger, cowled radial engines), it is less efficient because of the resistance of the burned gases in the longer system. The exhaust gas just emerging from the exhaust port has to push against this mass to get out. The exhaust system must provide a method of getting the hot waste safely out of the cowling and away from the airframe; this may require a long crossover exhaust pipe system in some airplanes.

The metal of the exhaust system must withstand very high temperatures without burning through at a critical place in the engine compartment. Exhaust systems on each side of horizontally opposed engines may be joined to a single final exhaust stack (Fig. 4-J).

Fig. 4-J. Exhaust system. The exhaust stacks (1) join to one outlet (2). The other end of the carburetor heat/cabin heat muff and the other two stacks can be seen in Figure 4-I. The cabin heat hose is shown at (3). Item (4) is the oil filler cap, admittedly not a part of the exhaust system, but there it is anyway.

EXHAUST GAS TEMPERATURE GAUGE. The exhaust gas temperature (EGT) gauge measures the relative change in the exhaust gas temperature with change in mixture and gives an indication of the best economy and best power mixtures.

One simple system consists of the gauge, wiring, and a probe into one of the exhaust stacks at a point 1.5 inches, or slightly more, from the cylinder head. The gauge may be calibrated in 25°F increments (with no fixed numbers shown) or in a range of 1200°F–1750°F. One manufacturer's engines normally operate in the 1200°F–1600°F EGT range.

Peak EGT—As you slowly lean the mixture from full rich, the fuel-air ratio decreases and the cooling effect of the fuel is lessened. Watching the EGT gauge, you can see the gradual increase in the temperature until at some point it will peak and further leaning causes a decrease in temperature. The peak EGT is where the maximum utilization of the fuel and air occurs; it's a chemically correct mixture. As the leaning continues, the ratio of air to fuel increases and power is lost, and the exhaust temperature decreases for that one examined cylinder. If the mixture control is moved forward, richening the mixture from peak, the EGT will drop again as fuel cooling takes place. More expensive EGT systems have a probe for each cylinder, with a selector to check each.

Operating at peak EGT is only practical in *fuel-injected* engines of over 250 horsepower.

Remember the earlier discussions pointing out that the fuel distribution was more even in fuel-injected engines because it was injected at the intake port of each cylinder? It was also noted that the carburetor did not allow this good distribution, and an engine so equipped can be leaned by ear or feel, since the leanest cylinder would start complaining first as the mixture control was moved out and the rough running engine tells you to richen it forward just a tad. Some pilots are afraid that this roughness means detonation and so hesitate to lean. If leaning is done at the manufacturer's recommended top cruise power setting or below, no detonation can occur. Leaning in climb or other high-power settings *can* cause detonation. Peak EGT operations are limited to 75 percent rated power or below in some direct drive, normally aspirated (nonsupercharged) engines.

Best economy mixture—For practical purposes, the best economy for some engines starts at the peak temperature. Expect a slight loss of horsepower and a loss of 2–3 knots at cruise if you use this. Other engines may use a temperature drop of 125°F on the rich side of peak.

Best power mixture—This is sometimes referred to as *maximum power range*, which is in the range of a temperature drop of 100°F–150°F from the peak *on the rich side*. (Remember that the temperature will drop from the peak when the mixture is either leaned or richened.) This provides a safe mixture for higher than cruise power settings (except for takeoff). A rule of thumb compromise between best economy and best power mixtures has been a mixture setting of 50°F on the rich side of the peak. The *Pilot's Operating Handbook* for a particular airplane is the final word on this as well as for other operations.

ELECTRICAL SYSTEM

As a pilot, the electrical system may be a mystery to you (that is, how the electrons move through it), but you should know how to check it in the preflight and know what procedures to use in case of problems. Note the electrical system in Figure 3-C of this book (Figure 3-25, *SPFM*). Maybe it doesn't make sense with all the symbols, but at least you can tell what components of the airplane are electrically powered by looking at the circuit breakers. Maybe you didn't know that the oil temperature gauge depended on electrical power for indication (the oil *pressure* gauge does not). The oil pressure switch seen at the left of the electrical system diagram energizes the flight recorder when the engine starts, and oil pressure is then available.

Note that the ignition switch is in the electrical system, not because the magnetos are battery powered, but because the spring-loaded starter position is part of that switch.

■ The Alternator

The airplane's alternator is like that of your automobile. It is engine-driven by gears or a belt, and it has more than enough capacity to keep the battery charged when working properly. If an overvoltage occurs, the system will automatically turn off the alternator and you are warned by a red light or other indication. Check with your instructor concerning procedures in event of overloading and alternator loss. Procedures will differ among airplane types.

The alternator has replaced the generator in airplanes and cars because it develops electrical power at lower engine rpm and is more efficient in the idle power range. (While it's working at lower rpm or down to idle, it still may not be keeping up with the electrical requirements, so run the engine up a little if in doubt.) The older generators required 1200 rpm or more even to "cut in," and the battery could be discharged when the situation called for low rpm and large electrical requirements (such as taxiing at night with taxi and navigation lights and radios on). Figure 4-K shows components of the electrical system for a light trainer. This system is protected by circuit breakers (which can be *reset* in the event of an electrical overload) except for the clock, flight hour recorder, and external power plug, which are protected by fuses that are replaced if an overload burns them out. In other words, the circuit breakers and fuses are deliberately established "weaker" spots so that if an electrical overload in the system occurs, the circuit breaker will "pop" or an inexpensive fuse will burn out rather than damaging such components as radios or other expensive electrically operated items. Of course, you should have all unnecessary electrical items off for starting, particularly radios that could be damaged by surges of transient voltages during the start.

AMMETER. The ammeter indicates the current flow in amperes from the alternator through the battery to the system. If the ammeter shows a discharge, it means that either the alternator is not keeping up with the load being placed on the system or it's out of action and the battery is being discharged at the rate shown (amperes). For instance, if the battery in your airplane is rated at 32 amp-hours, it means that the

Fig. 4-K. Electrical components: (1) alternator, (2) belt drive of alternator, (3) battery box (the battery is inside), (4) fuses for the clock and flight hour recorder and external power receptacle. (See item 4, Fig. 4-H.)

battery when fully charged without alternator input should produce an electric current flow of 16 amps for 2 hours, or 8 amps for 4 hours, etc. However, at high usage the battery loses power at a higher rate; if 32 amps were being used with a 32 amp-hour battery, it might last only 30 minutes or less rather than an hour as indicated by the earlier arithmetic. If you have an alternator overvoltage problem and have to pull it from the system (turn that ALT half of the switch off), you'd lengthen the battery power availability by turning off unnecessary electrical components. For instance, landing and taxi lights are usually the biggest users of current. The cigar lighter takes a great deal of current, and you shouldn't be smoking in the airplane anyway; it's bad for the vacuum-driven gyro instruments (attitude indicator and heading indicator) as will be shown shortly.

VACUUM SYSTEM

Older airplanes used a venturi as shown by Figure 3-15, *SPFM*, but the drawback with that system is that the airplane had to be moving for some time before the suction got the instruments up to speed. Now, even the smaller trainers have an engine-driven vacuum pump to operate the gyro instruments. As noted in Chapter 3, the usual procedure is to have the attitude and heading indicators run by the vacuum system and the turn and slip or turn coordinator electrically driven. Figure 4-L shows a vacuum system installation for a light trainer.

The vacuum pump is at the rear of the engine (at the accessory section) and pulls air from the cockpit

Fig. 4-L. Vacuum system schematic. The overboard vent line shown here can be seen in Figure 4-K behind and above the oil filler cap; it's that aluminum tube with two 90° bends. If you look closely, you can see that the vacuum pump, which is behind the oil filler, is a black drum with a light metallic band around it. You also might look just above item 8 in Figure 4-I to see the pump and overboard vent line. (The pump is almost hidden by part of the engine mount.)

area through the gyro instruments and discharges it into the engine compartment.

Note in Figure 4-L that a suction gauge is a part of the system, and for this airplane the normal range is 4.6–5.4 inches of mercury. These figures indicate the drop in pressure in the system as compared to atmospheric pressure and give the suction available to the instruments.

The air filter is located on the aft side of the firewall and, as just noted, takes air from the cockpit area. This is a good reason for not smoking in the airplane, since tars and other contaminants will clog the filter and cut down the accuracy and dependability of the gyro instruments.

The more you know about the systems, the better able you are to avoid or correct problems in flight. Most systems are based on simple principles and are presented here from a pilot's standpoint. The bibliography contains references for further reading.

Okay, answer the following questions on this chapter, and after finding out those you missed (if any), read Chapter 4, *SPFM* and this section again.

401. The four strokes of an Otto-cycle airplane engine are

1—thrust, rotary, power, and exhaust.
2—intake, power, thrust, and exhaust.
3—intake, compression, power, and exhaust.
4—intake, thrust, compression, and power.

402. Which of the following would most likely result in a sudden increase in oil consumption in the engine of an airplane? (There are no outside leaks in evidence.)

1—Eroded spark plug electrodes.
2—Worn or broken piston rings.
3—A poorly adjusted carburetor.
4—A coagulated frammis.

403. A horizontally opposed six-cylinder, direct drive, nonturbocharged engine with fuel injection has a bore of 5 inches and a stroke of 4 inches. Its designation by the manufacturer would be

1—GO-470.
2—IO-470.
3—IO-540.
4—TIO-470.

404. The addition of carburetor heat

1—leans the mixture.
2—has no effect on the mixture.
3—richens the mixture.
4—causes oil pressure fluctuations.

405. An advantage in the fuel injection system over the carburetor is that it

1—has better fuel distribution to the cylinders.
2—does not require an alternate air system.
3—can be used best with fixed-pitch propellers.
4—has a simpler oil system.

406. As an all-around procedure you should

1—deliberately run a tank dry to use all the fuel only if it is a fuel injection system.
2—expect a delay of 1–2 seconds in power after the selector is switched from an empty to a usable tank with the fuel injection system.
3—deliberately run a tank dry only at altitudes above 1500 feet MSL.
4—never deliberately run a tank dry.

407. During the pretakeoff check after checking the mags, you pull the carburetor heat ON at 1800 rpm (or the manufacturer's recommended number). There is no change of rpm (plus or minus) when you pull it ON or for 30 seconds thereafter. This is a sign that

1—carburetor ice was present before the heat was applied.
2—there was no carburetor ice present before the heat was applied.
3—the carburetor is not getting heat from the system.
4—you did not leave the heat on long enough to get an effect.

408. Smoking in an airplane

1—is useful in finding out the wind direction by blowing the smoke out a window.
2—may cause you to be thrown overboard by a non-smoker.
3—can cause clogging of the vacuum system air filter.
4—can clog the carburetor heat.

Questions 409–417 are based on Figure 4-M.

409. Item A is the

1—carburetor air filter.
2—oil cooler.
3—alternator.
4—carburetor heat muff.

410. If item B is ruptured, you would

1—expect a rapidly rising oil temperature.
2—lose use of the carburetor heat.
3—have ignition problems on the vacuum pump.
4—lose tire pressure.

411. Item C is the

1—magneto overflow simplex routing system (MOSRS).
2—air line to the nosewheel, used for filling the tire in flight.
3—carburetor heat hose.
4—oil breather line.

412. Item D is a component of which system?

1—Oil.
2—Fuel.
3—Electrical.
4—Ignition.

413. Item G is important in the event of

1—low oil pressure.
2—electrical overload.
3—carburetor ice.
4—alternator failure.

414. Item H is

1—a magneto.
2—the alternator.
3—the carburetor.
4—the oil reservoir.

415. Item I is

1—an intake manifold.
2—a fuel line.
3—an oil line.
4—an exhaust manifold.

Fig. 4-M. Engine and system components for questions 409–417.

416. If item J was severed, the result would be

1—a drop in oil pressure.
2—an ignition problem.
3—a fuel leak.
4—an alternator failure.

417. Items E and F are respectively part of which systems?

1—Oil and fuel.
2—Electrical and fuel.
3—Oil and electrical.
4—Oil and brake.

5

STARTING THE AIRPLANE

The *Pilot's Operating Handbook* for your airplane is the final authority (that's been said before in these books), and you'll use the starting procedure described there. The procedure given in *SPFM* is a general one to cover some points for discussion.

501. After starting your airplane's engine on a cold morning, you taxi out and make your pretakeoff check. After the mag and carburetor heat check you reduce the power to idle and find that even though the engine is warmed up it lopes and runs very rough, nearly quitting but not quite. A likely problem is that the

1—fuel selector valve has been in the OFF position since before starting.
2—cabin heat is ON.
3—primer is not in and locked.
4—electric fuel pump is not ON.

502. The "best" fuel-to-air ratio is approximately

1—1-15.
2—15-1.
3—1-7.
4—20-1.

503. The following is a general analysis of steps that might be taken in a situation when starting. Your *Pilot's Operating Handbook* is the final answer (again) but find the most likely procedure for the conditions cited.

The situation—It's a very hot day and the trainer you are going to use has just come down from a flight. After a thorough preflight check you get fastened in. After using your usual procedures you holler CLEAR and hit the starter; the propeller turns over and over with no indication that the engine wants to start. This is probably because

1—the mixture is not rich enough.
2—the engine is loaded (flooded).
3—the carburetor heat is not ON.
4—the engine has cooled too rapidly.

504. You start the engine and check the oil pressure gauge. The needle doesn't move right away, but you figure that since it's summer you can expect it to come to normal operation within

1—42 hours and 26 minutes.
2—5 seconds.
3—30 minutes.
4—30 seconds.

505. You hit the starter of your trainer, and as the propeller turns over (the engine hasn't started well yet), you note that spectators are staring wide-eyed at the bottom area of the cowling. Your *initial* best move is to

1—open the window and state firmly that it is impolite to stare.
2—pump the throttle to help assure that plenty of fuel is getting to the carburetor.
3—keep the engine turning over and turn off the mixture and fuel.
4—stop the starting procedure until they stop staring.

506. You have your private certicate and are taking a friend for a first ride. You find that the battery is dead. It's late and there is no one else at the airport, but jumper cables are available. Also, you have been checked out to hand-crank the airplane. Your next move would be to

1—carefully show the friend how to hold the brakes and turn the ignition switch ON while you hand-crank the airplane.
2—show the friend how to hold the brakes and use the starter while you set up jumper cables from your car.
3—stay in the airplane to start it, and the friend can work the jumper cables (revving up the car and then removing the cables after the start).
4—cancel the flight until the airplane's electrical system is back to normal.

6
TAXIING

Probably the most common error of students (and all other pilots too) is that of taxiing too fast. You've been driving cars and are used to fast rates of ground travel, but the airplane just isn't intended to be operated that way. Review Chapter 6, *SPFM*.

As stated several times before, the answers and discussions in this book and *SPFM* are general and aren't intended to replace the *Pilot's Operating Handbook* procedures or those recommended by your instructor for *your* operating conditions. If these discussions and questions make you want to find out more, so much the better.

MORE NOTES ON BRAKES

The brakes in smaller airplanes are an independent hydraulic system; that is, they have their own reservoir, separate from a main hydraulic system that might actuate the landing gear and flaps. On some airplanes the brakes are the *only* hydraulic system on board.

Hydraulics for brakes, flaps, or landing gear work because liquid, unlike gas, is incompressible. Any force transmitted at one end goes directly to the other end of the system. (Purists will argue that liquids are compressible, but compared to air, not much.) If the lines had been filled with air, there would be little action at the far end because the air would allow itself to be compressed before passing on some of the forces. An analogy might be pushing against the back of a toy wagon with an iron bar (liquid) and a rubber hose (air). The iron bar will send your force directly and get the wagon rolling, but the rubber hose may bend and flex before transmitting part of your force to get the same (or lesser) result.

You may run into the problem of air in the brake lines in the airplane. The air is compressible, so as you press the pedal(s) there is no immediate response to pedal pressure because the air compresses rather than sending a direct message as the liquid brake fluid would do. A small amount of air in the system would mean a relatively small amount of "sponginess" of the pedals, but if the pedals start feeling this way, you'd better check with the mechanic who will "bleed" the system of air and check for loose connections or tighten up the system to stop the further encroachment of air. More about this later.

One type of light-airplane brake system consists of a master cylinder for each brake pedal, with its own reservoir of hydraulic fluid. Additional components consist of a mechanical linkage from each pedal to its cylinder, with required fluid lines to a brake assembly on each main wheel. In other words, each wheel has its own separate brake system.

Airplanes with a brake handle (no toe brakes) have a single master cylinder that transfers pressure to both main wheels at the same time.

Other systems may have a separate reservoir in the engine compartment, and the fluid level should be checked during each preflight inspection (if you can get to it).

During the preflight check you should look at the brake lines and at the surface under each main wheel to check for signs of brake fluid leaks. The wheel covers (speed fairings) on some airplanes make it difficult to check the condition of the brake disks and cylinders. Incidentally, if your airplane is such that the disks and brake can be seen—and touched—don't put your hand on the disk if the airplane has just come in from a flight. A painful burn could result because the disks will remain hot for a while.

The parking brake is essentially a valve that locks pressure in the wheel cylinders. You'll press on the pedals and then set the parking brake, which (it says here) will hold the pressure exerted until released.

The parking brake generally should not be

trusted. The pressure may bleed off, and the brakes would no longer hold. More than one pilot has set the parking brake for the engine run-up and looked up from a checklist to find that the airplane was moving rapidly toward some expensive object.

If the parking brake is set in the morning, rising temperatures during the day can cause fluid expansion and destroy seals in the system. Chocks or tie-downs are more dependable for an airplane that is to be left sitting for more than a few minutes.

■ Brake Problems

Probably one of the most common problems you'll run into is "soft brakes" or air in the system. The pedal or pedals may go easily to the limit with little or no brake effectiveness. If you unexpectedly encounter such a problem (you've taxied into the ramp too fast and suddenly realize that a very expensive mistake is about to be made), *pump* the brake pedals. This will build up temporary pressure for braking (Fig. 6-A). It's a good idea to press the brakes—and release them—before coming in to land, so that you'll know whether the pedals feel normal. If they are soft, you might plan on pumping the brakes during roll-out or consider that you may not have *any* braking effectiveness and should make a short-field approach or fly to another airport with longer runways.

If on roll-out you discover that one brake of your tricycle-gear airplane isn't working, press the other brake gently and use rudder pedal pressure on the failed brake side to help keep the airplane straight.

People have opened doors on the roll-out after brake failure; the air drag of the door(s) can definitely help slow a smaller airplane.

Another problem is that of "hard" brakes. The brake pedals feel like they are solid and not hinged, and braking effectiveness is very low. You should get a mechanic on this also, as soon as practicable.

Dragging brakes (you can hear them sometimes) can cause tire wear on touchdown, brake heating problems, and longer takeoff runs. You can sometimes see the effects of a brake dragging by looking at a

Fig. 6-A.

main wheel (high-wing airplane) as the airplane is taxied on a smooth surface; one landing gear shakes while the nondragging side moves smoothly.

Older airplanes have mechanical brakes in which a cable is used instead of the hydraulic line. When the pedal (usually a heel brake) was pressed, the cable moved the brake pad against the disk. A disadvantage of this type of system was that one of the cables would wear and break, usually at an "inopportune time." (See Fig. 6-8, *SPFM* to check their use.) Press the brake pedals *before* starting the engine and check their effectiveness just as the airplane starts to move for taxi.

You aren't expected to be a mechanic, and these problem descriptions are presented so you'll know that people in maintenance should be consulted and you can give them an idea of what to look for, thus saving time (and money).

601. Look at Figure 6-B. The runways are 5-23 and 14-32. If you are landing on Runway 5 using a standard traffic pattern in a very light or calm wind, your approximate magnetic heading while on base would be

1—320°.
2—230°.
3—050°.
4—140°.

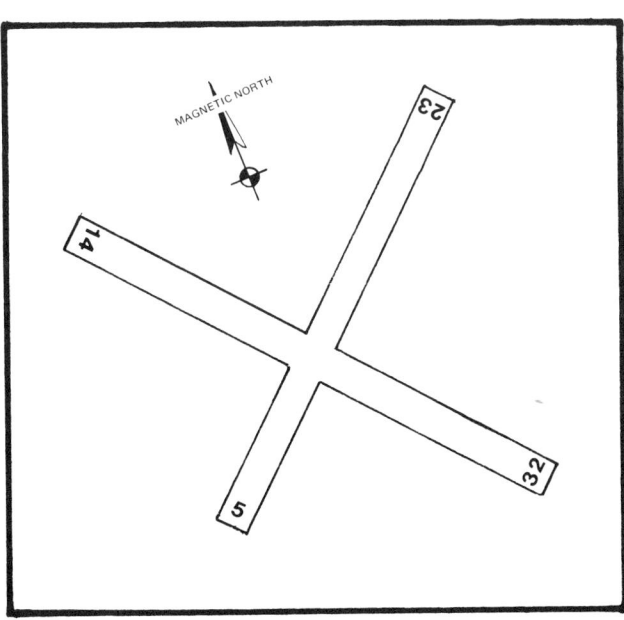

Fig. 6-B.

602. Taxiway markings are

1—white dashed lines.
2—yellow solid lines.
3—yellow dashed lines.
4—white solid lines.

603. Hold lines are a combination of two solid and two dashed lines crossing the taxiway before it intercepts a runway. The taxi guidance line extends through the hold lines and onto the runway. This means that

1—you do not have to slow up before taxiing onto the runway at uncontrolled airports.
2—you only need to recognize hold lines at controlled airports because ground control will give or refuse clearance to cross them.
3—hold lines should be recognized at all airports. You'll need ATC clearance to cross them at controlled airports; at uncontrolled airports you should always hold and check for traffic before going onto the runway.
4—the taxi line has precedence over the hold lines at all airports.

604. A soft or spongy brake is usually the result of having air in the system. To get braking action you should do which of the following?

1—Pump the brake pedals.
2—Hold the pressure but do not pump.
3—Pull the parking brake handle outward.
4—Stay completely off the brake.

605. You are taxiing a tricycle-gear airplane with a strong wind from the right rear. The control positions should be as follows:

1—Control wheel forward and turned right, rudder as necessary to keep the airplane straight.
2—Control wheel forward and turned left, rudder as necessary to keep the airplane straight.
3—Control wheel aft and turned left, full left rudder.
4—Control wheel forward and turned left, full right rudder.

7

PRETAKEOFF OR COCKPIT CHECK

The use of a checklist cannot be overemphasized. The human memory isn't good enough to cover all the points to be checked before takeoff, even for a so-called noncomplex airplane. Review Chapter 7, *SPFM* before answering the following questions.

701. You are checking the magnetos at the run-up spot and inadvertently turn the switch to OFF. The best move for you before turning it back on is to

1—pull the carburetor heat ON.
2—close the throttle.
3—pull the mixture to idle cutoff.
4—switch tanks.

702. You have just completed the run-up. Just before starting to taxi into the takeoff position, you realize that the fuel gauge shows the tank you ran up on is *very* low in fuel while the other is nearly three-quarters full. You recall that this was the case when you visually checked the tanks, but you forgot to put the selector on the fullest tank. You should

1—switch tanks and continue the takeoff.
2—keep the airplane on the tank you did the run-up on and go ahead and take off.
3—switch tanks and run the engine up to at least 1500 rpm for a minute or more, or redo the mag and carburetor heat check.
4—do none of the above.

703. You are solo and just after lifting off (with the runway gone behind) it sounds as if the engine is banging itself to destruction. The airplane is performing as usual (rpm, pressures, and temperatures are okay). The best move in this case is to

1—maintain control of the airplane as you continue to climb.
2—land straight ahead immediately.
3—turn back to the airport without delay.
4—start dumping ballast overboard.

704. Which of the following combinations would most likely cause loss of power and/or a rough-running engine during the pretakeoff check?

1—Airport at a high elevation, high outside air temperature, mixture full rich, and carburetor heat ON.
2—Airport at sea level, low outside air temperature, mixture full rich, and carburetor heat ON.
3—Airport at a high elevation, high outside air temperature, mixture leaned, and carburetor heat OFF.
4—Airport at sea level, high outside air temperature, mixture full rich, and carburetor heat OFF.

705. You are a private pilot and plan to fly a trainer into a 2000-foot farm strip. You check the *Pilot's Operating Handbook* and see that the airplane can land or take off with about 500 feet to spare under the existing conditions. At the end of the pretakeoff check you close the throttle and the engine idles at 800 instead of the recommended 600 rpm. You should

1—continue the flight, glad that the engine is not likely to idle too slow and quit.
2—taxi back and get a mechanic to reset the idle to the recommended value before flying.
3—continue the flight but expect a steeper approach and shorter landing roll because the extra windmilling effects will create drag.
4—be sure to notify an instructor or mechanic about the higher idle value after you get back to the home airport.

PART TWO PRESOLO

8 EFFECTS OF CONTROLS

801. A pilot cannot extend the nosewheel on his airplane. The main gear can be gotten down and locked, but the nosewheel won't come down. He wants to keep the nose up to as slow a speed as possible in the landing roll so that damage will be minimized. The airplane has elevators with standard trim tabs, and the pilot could, in addition to the usual procedures as outlined in the *Pilot's Operating Handbook* for such a situation, trim the airplane during the landing roll to a position of nose

1—down.
2—up.
3—right.
4—back.

802. During the preflight check of your airplane you note that the simple mechanical trim tab on the elevator is full "down" as far as the elevator is concerned. You know that if you take off with it in this position the following might occur:

1—The nose will be very heavy during the takeoff run and climbout.
2—The nose could rise abruptly after lift-off, creating a stall hazard.
3—The down position of the tab will offset any up elevator you use so that a neutral effect would result.
4—The tab will automatically align itself with the relative wind, having no effect on control.

803. When considering how the elevators affect the airplane's pitching action, you should think of it as follows:

1—Wheel back, nose moves up.
2—Wheel forward, nose moves down.
3—Wheel back, nose moves toward you.
4—Wheel back, nose moves away from you.

804. The ailerons are the roll controls, and when the stick or wheel is moved (turned) left the airplane will roll

1—left, around the vertical (Z) axis.
2—right, around the longitudinal (X) axis.
3—left, around the lateral (Y) axis.
4—left, around the longitudinal (X) axis.

805. Your airplane has a bendable tab on the left aileron. (It's not controllable from the cockpit.) The airplane, even when the wing tanks are equal in fuel, continually wants to roll to the right. After landing, to correct this problem, you would bend the tab

1—up.
2—left.
3—down.
4—either up or down, it wouldn't matter in this case.

806. In straight and level flight you notice that the airplane's nose wants to yaw to the right and you have to hold left rudder for straight flight. To correct for this, the rudder tab should be adjusted or bent to the

1—left.
2—right.
3—neutral position.
4—down position.

807. The rudder controls movement around the

1—longitudinal (X) axis.
2—longitudinal pitch point.
3—vertical (Z) axis.
4—lateral (Y) axis.

9

THE FOUR FUNDAMENTALS

901. Refer to Figure 9-A for this question. An airplane stalls at 72 knots with gear and flaps up. In a 40° banked, level, balanced turn the stall speed (in knots) under the same configuration will be approximately

1—144.
2—102.
3—97.
4—83.

902. *Given:* Airplane weight = 2000 pounds. Brake horsepower available for climb at this particular altitude = 200 HP. Propeller efficiency at best rate of climb speed = 75 percent. Required for level flight at best rate of climb speed = 100 thrust horsepower (THP).

What is the approximate rate of climb (feet per minute)?

1—1650.
2—825.
3—660.
4—1980.

903. Pick the best statement for what is happening to the forces acting on the airplane during a steady-state climb.

1—Lift is less than weight.
2—Thrust is greater than drag.
3—Weight is acting rearward and downward to the flight path.
4—All the above statements are correct.

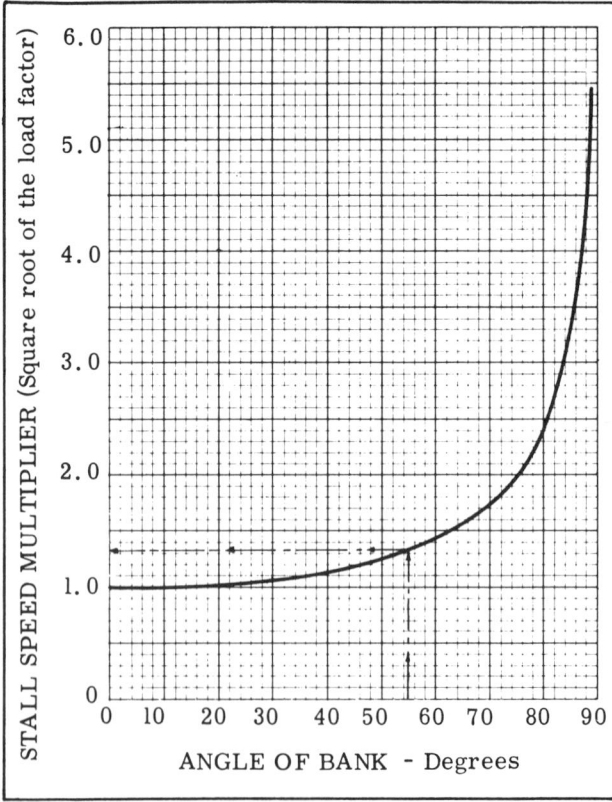

Fig. 9-A. Stall speed versus angle of bank. As an example, if the airplane is maintaining altitude in a 55° bank, the load factor produced will cause the stall speed to increase by a ratio of 1.32. Assuming the airplane stalls at 60 knots in level flight, its stall speed in a 55° bank will be 1.32 × 60 = 79 knots.

904. To establish a glide from cruising flight, you would use carburetor heat as recommended by the manufacturer and close the throttle,

1—lower the nose, and maintain that pitch attitude
2—while raising the nose.
3—hold the nose level, then lower it to the glide pitch attitude.
4—hold the nose level, then ease it up slightly above the horizon.

905. *Given:* Airplane weight = 2000 pounds. Brake horsepower being used = 80 HP. Propeller efficiency at the descent speed = 50 percent. Thrust horsepower required for level flight at the chosen airspeed = 100 THP.

Which of the following statements is correct? (Remember that rate of *descent* is proportional to *deficit* THP.)

1—The airplane is climbing at approximately 990 fpm.
2—The airplane is descending at a rate of approximately 660 fpm.
3—The airplane is descending at approximately 990 fpm.
4—The airplane is climbing at a rate of approximately 660 fpm.

906. An airplane that stalls at 70 knots in wings-level flight will—in a constant-altitude, 60° banked, balanced turn—stall at approximately

1—99 knots.
2—99 mph.
3—80 knots.
4—70 knots.

907. To enter a normal climb from cruising flight, the best procedure is to

1—open the throttle to climb power, ease the nose up to the climb attitude, and use the right rudder as needed to maintain a straight climb.
2—ease the nose up to the proper climb attitude, open the throttle to climb power, and use right rudder as needed to maintain a straight climb.
3—ease the nose up to the proper climb position and add left rudder.
4—apply right rudder, add climb power, and ease the nose up to the proper climb attitude.

908. Refer to Figure 9-B and choose the best descriptive statement.

1—Airplane A is climbing.
2—Airplane B is flying level at approximately cruising airspeed.
3—Both A and B are flying level.
4—There is not enough information given to indicate the airplanes' actions.

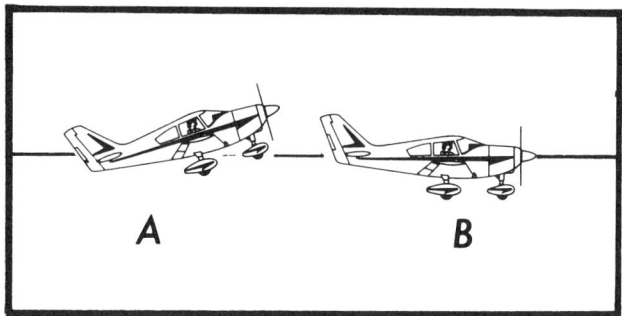

Fig. 9-B.

909. A jet fighter flying at 600 knots is in a 60° banked, coordinated, constant-altitude turn. A light trainer flying at 100 knots is also in a 60° banked, coordinated, constant-altitude turn. Which of the following statements is true concerning the two airplanes?

1—The jet fighter will be pulling 6 times the g force pulled by the light trainer.
2—The light trainer will be pulling one-twelfth the g force pulled by the jet fighter.
3—The two airplanes will have the same radius of turn.
4—The occupants of both airplanes will have 2 g's imposed upon them.

10

ELEMENTARY PRECISION MANEUVERS

1001. You are starting the second turn of a 60° banked 720° power turn (using full power) and notice that the nose is dropping slightly and an altitude loss has started. The proper procedure to stop the altitude loss is to
1—increase back pressure then shallow the bank to bring the nose up.
2—shallow the bank and add back pressure as needed to bring the nose up to the proper attitude.
3—maintain a constant bank, using back pressure as needed to bring the nose to the proper position.
4—use top rudder and back pressure to bring the nose up, since in the steep bank the rudder acts as an elevator.

1002. Which of the following are common errors made by student pilots doing 720° power turns?

A. Poor wind drift correction.
B. Back pressure added too soon at the beginning of the turn.
C. Not releasing the added back pressure as the airplane is rolled out.
D. "Losing" the checkpoint.
  1—ABCD.
  2—ABD.
  3—ABC.
  4—BCD.

1003. You are headed due east in a trainer that cruises at 100 knots true airspeed. A jet is also on a heading of due east at the same altitude at 500 knots true airspeed. The wind at both your altitudes is from the south at 40 knots. At the end of 1 hour of flight you know that with respect to the original course line

1—your airplane will be 40 NM north of the line, while the jet will be 8 NM north of it.
2—both airplanes will be 40 NM south.
3—both airplanes will be 40 NM north.
4—your airplane will not be affected as much by the wind because of its lower true airspeed.

Look at Figure 10-A and answer questions 1004 and 1005.

1004. At which point of the rectangular course will the bank be steepest as the turn is started?

1—8.
2—7.
3—3.
4—6.

1005. At which point in Figure 10-A will the shallowest bank be required?

1—3.
2—6.
3—8.
4—7.

Chapter 10. Elementary Precision Maneuvers 31

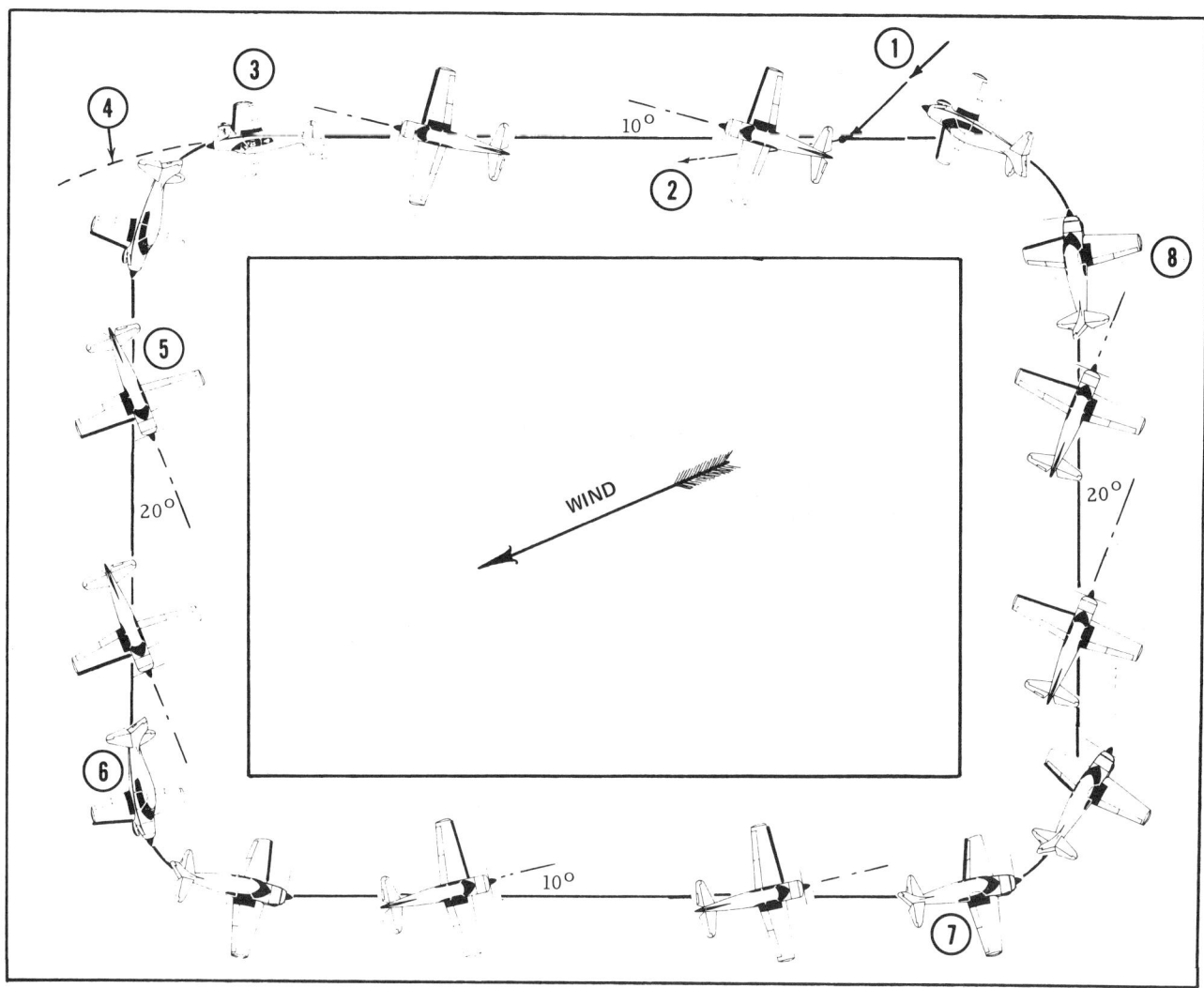

Fig. 10-A.

11
Elementary Forced Landings

1101. Which one of the following moves would *not* be done following an engine failure while you are doing a rectangular course?

1—Using the starter.
2—Applying full carburetor heat.
3—Switching tanks.
4—Establishing a normal glide.

1102. As you are practicing S-turns across a road, you have been gradually required to open the throttle more to maintain power. Now the engine is running rough and acts as if it might fade out any minute. You would go through the full cockpit check, but which of the following should you do first?

1—Switch fuel tanks.
2—Electric boost pump ON (if equipped).
3—Apply full carburetor heat.
4—Get out the *Pilot's Operating Handbook* and see what it recommends.

1103. Which of the following statements is correct concerning an actual forced landing?

1—It is mandatory that the airplane be landed into the wind.
2—Terrain or obstructions may require that a landing be made upslope and downwind.
3—A field of mature wheat is better for a landing than a pasture of freshly cut wheat or barley.
4—If a freshly plowed field is chosen it's best to land across the furrows.

12

STALLS AND SLOW FLIGHT

1201. To recover from a stall, the pilot must

1—increase the angle of incidence.
2—increase the lift angle.
3—increase the angle of attack.
4—decrease the angle of attack.

1202. Choose the correct statement concerning stalls. An airplane will stall

1—at a higher angle of attack when at a higher weight for any given flap setting.
2—at a lower angle of attack when at a higher weight.
3—at the same angle of attack for a particular flap setting, regardless of weight.
4—at twice the normal listed airspeed if the max certificated weight is doubled.

1203. Just as the break occurs in a takeoff and departure stall from a right bank, you would expect the ball in the turn and slip or turn coordinator to be

1—to the left of center.
2—to the right of center.
3—centered.
4—moving from full left to full right.

1204. In an approach to landing stall (power at idle and landing flaps used) you would expect that (compared to the clean airplane) at the break

1—the nose attitude will be lower and the stall angle of attack will be less.
2—the nose attitude will be lower and the stall angle of attack will be greater.
3—the nose attitude will be higher and the stall angle will be less.
4—the nose attitude will be higher and the stall angle of attack will be greater.

1205. Assuming that weight, bank, and other factors are the same for a particular airplane, which of the following combinations would most likely result in the *lowest* calibrated (or indicated) airspeed at the stall?

1—Full flaps, power at idle.
2—Full flaps, full power.
3—No flaps, full power.
4—No flaps, power at idle.

1206. Assuming that weight, bank, and other factors are the same for a particular airplane, which of the following combinations would most likely result in the *highest* calibrated (or indicated) airspeed at the stall?

1—Full flaps, power at idle.
2—Full flaps, full power.
3—No flaps, full power.
4—No flaps, power at idle.

1207. An airplane is flying straight and level, using *full* power and maintaining a constant altitude. To climb, the pilot would

1—move the stick or wheel back.
2—move the stick or wheel forward.
3—use up-elevator or up-stabilator trim.
4—not know which way to move the stick or wheel or how to trim, based on the above information.

1208. Which of the following aircraft categories is always placarded against spins?

1—Utility.
2—Acrobatic.
3—Normal.
4—Commercial.

Assume that the instruments shown for questions 1209 and 1210 are on the pilot's side of a side-by-side trainer.

1209. The instruments in Figure 12-A show the probable indications of an airplane in a

1—spiral.
2—spin.
3—normal gliding turn.
4—720° power turn.

Fig. 12-A.

1210. The pilot's instruments in Figure 12-B show the probable indications of an airplane in a

Fig. 12-B.

1—spiral.
2—spin.
3—720° power turn.
4—normal gliding turn.

1211. You are practicing power-off stalls (full flaps) and overcontrol, thus getting into an accidental spin. The *general* best recovery method is to

1—apply full rudder opposite to the rotation, followed by brisk forward motion of the wheel or stick; keep ailerons neutral; up the flaps as soon as possible after recovery is started and keep the power at idle.
2—apply rudder and aileron opposite to rotation, followed by brisk forward motion of the wheel or stick; add full power, leaving the flaps down until the pullout is complete.
3—retract the flaps; use full rudder against the rotation while applying ailerons with the spin; keep the throttle closed.
4—apply rudder with the rotation; keep ailerons neutral; keep the power at idle and retract the flaps.

13
TAKEOFFS AND LANDINGS

1301. Which of the following statements is correct concerning the takeoff roll in a tricycle-gear airplane? (Assume that the wind is directly down the runway.)

1—As the nosewheel is eased off, added right rudder is required.
2—To avoid overcorrecting to the right, the pilot should be prepared to relax pressure from the right rudder as the nosewheel is raised.
3—It's best to use forward pressure on the control wheel or stick in the run so that the nosewheel steering will be more effective.
4—Keep the nosewheel well on the ground until the airplane flies itself off, so there will be no danger of a postlift-off stall.

1302. The best normal landing is made

1—by starting the rotation at about 1 foot above the surface.
2—by holding the airplane just off the ground as long as possible.
3—on Sunday afternoon when there are thousands of admirers lining the airport fence.
4—when trying to impress that good-looking person of the opposite sex who's riding with you.

1303. If you are consistently landing the airplane one wing low (even when not correcting for a crosswind), it's possible that you

1—are holding right rudder to correct for "torque."
2—do not have the correct pitch attitude at the touchdown during the landing.
3—have not retarded the power to idle.
4—are turning the control wheel or moving the stick sideways as you move it back in the latter stages of the landing.

1304. *One* of the purposes of flaps on landing is to

1—decrease the drag.
2—provide a steeper descent angle without an increase in approach airspeed.
3—allow a shallower approach angle at a higher airspeed.
4—allow the tricycle-gear airplane to touch down with all three wheels at once.

1305. You are on final approach and realize that you are too low. You should

1—ease the nose up to climb attitude to stretch the glide, keeping the power at idle to avoid getting too fast.
2—keep the nose down at glide attitude, adding full power to make the runway.
3—add power as necessary to make the runway, maintaining the approach airspeed with the elevators.
4—ease the nose up to climb attitude and apply climb power until over the end of the runway.

1306. When executing a go-around, the order of actions should be:

1—Carburetor heat OFF, full power, flaps immediately full UP.
2—Full power, carburetor heat OFF, flaps UP in increments.
3—Full power, flaps immediately full UP.
4—Flaps UP, carburetor heat OFF, power to cruise.

1307. In shooting landings with your flight instructor, you are continually leveling off too high and tend to drop the airplane in. A factor that could be contributing to this is that

1—you are looking at the surface too far ahead of the airplane.
2—you are trying to look straight ahead over the nose during the landing process.
3—a gust catches the airplane at exactly the same spot every time.
4—you are looking at the surface too close to the airplane.

1308. Your airplane has a calibrated stall speed (power off, gear down, and landing flaps extended) of 50 knots and is limited to a crosswind component of 0.2 V_{so}. The maximum crosswind component allowed for this airplane would be

1—10 knots.
2—12 knots.
3—25 knots.
4—20 knots.

1309. You are just about to touch down on Runway 33, and the wind is moderate from 270° (magnetic). As the airplane continues to slow just above the runway, you would be applying the controls as follows:

1—More up-elevator, more left aileron, less right rudder.
2—More up-elevator, more right aileron, more left rudder.
3—More up-elevator, more left aileron, more right rudder.
4—Less up-elevator, more left aileron, more right rudder.

1310. Under which of the following conditions would wake turbulence be most concentrated?

1—A heavy airplane, full flaps extended, flying at an airspeed near the top of the white arc on the airspeed indicator.
2—A heavy airplane, full flaps extended, flying at an airspeed near the bottom of the yellow arc.
3—A heavy airplane, clean, flying at an airspeed near the top of the yellow arc.
4—A heavy airplane, clean, flying at an airspeed near the bottom of the green arc.

PART THREE: POSTSOLO MANEUVERS

14

ADVANCED STALLS

1401. You are on your first solo cross-country, and as you turn on final at the first stop (using a normal, or standard, traffic pattern), you feel that you are tending to slide to the right side of your seat. To cause this, you are probably holding

1—slight left rudder, full left aileron, and added back pressure.
2—left rudder, right aileron, and added back pressure.
3—right rudder, full left aileron, and the same amount of back pressure as earlier in the approach.
4—slight right rudder, full left aileron, and added back pressure.

1402. In the condition cited in question 1401 the airplane, if stalled with you tending to slide to the right side of the seat, would most likely

1—roll to the left.
2—pitch up straight ahead.
3—roll to the right.
4—pitch down with no tendency to roll.

1403. The best all-around recovery procedure as a roll to the left starts in a cross-control (skidding) stall is to

1—neutralize the ailerons, use right rudder, and relax the back pressure.
2—apply full ailerons against the roll and use full right rudder and forward wheel or stick.
3—apply left aileron and hold the wheel or stick fully back.
4—neutralize the ailerons and hold the nose up with the elevators while using right rudder.

1404. The best bank angle for setting up a practice accelerated stall is

1—0°.
2—15°.
3—90°.
4—45°.

1405. A normal category airplane has a 1-g calibrated stall speed of 70 knots at a certain weight. If it is stalled at that same weight at 105 knots calibrated airspeed (CAS),

1—the positive limit load factor will be exceeded.
2—a load factor of 2.25 g's will result, and the positive limit load factor will not be exceeded.
3—a load factor of 1.5 g's will result, and the positive limit load factor will be exceeded.
4—a load factor of 2.25 g's will result, and the positive limit load factor will be exceeded.

1406. A clean airplane has a 1-g stall speed of 60 knots (CAS) at a certain weight. The pilot, who is not instrument qualified, uses poor judgment, flies into clouds, and loses all visual references. A very high-speed spiral results; the airplane suddenly breaks out of the bottom of the overcast at 500 feet, and the pilot abruptly hauls back on the control wheel, stalling the airplane at 240 knots (CAS). In theory, the airplane will pull

1—9 g's.
2—12 g's.
3—16 g's.
4—4 g's.

1407. Accelerated stalls prove that stalls

1—are the result of a too high airspeed.
2—are the result of a too low airspeed.
3—are the result of carrying too little power.
4—result from exceeding the critical angle of attack.

1408. The airplane's elevators (or stabilator) control

1—rate of climb and positive and negative g's.
2—the angle of attack (airspeed) and positive and negative g's.
3—movement around the longitudinal (X) axis.
4—altitude only.

1409. The positive and negative limit load factors for a utility category airplane are

1—+4.4 and −1.52 g's.
2—+3.8 and −1.76 g's.
3—+4.4 and −1.76 g's.
4—+4.4 and −3.8 g's.

1410. Back in the questions on Chapter 9, *SPFM* the problem of taking off with a nose-up trim setting was covered but Chapter 14, *SPFM* goes into more detail as to how to cope with it. Which of the following items is the most critical in the event of a full nose-up trim setting on takeoff in the average trainer?

1—Surprise.
2—Elevator or stabilator control forces.
3—A forward center of gravity position.
4—Runway length.

15

EMERGENCY FLYING BY REFERENCE TO INSTRUMENTS

1501. Which of the following maneuvers would be part of a realistic hooded training syllabus for actual emergency flying by reference to instruments?

A. Recovery from the start of a power-on spiral.
B. Turns of 60° bank for 360° or more.
C. Shallow climbing turns to a predetermined altitude.
D. Accelerated stalls.
E. Shallow descending turns at reduced power to a predetermined altitude.
F. Straight and level flight.
  1—ABCD.
  2—ACDF.
  3—ACEF.
  4—CDEF.

1502. Which of the following instrument indications would be found in a power-on spiral?

A. Turn and slip or turn coordinator shows a measurable rate of turn.
B. Airspeed is low and decreasing.
C. Airspeed is high and increasing.
D. Altimeter indicates a rapid loss of altitude.
E. Altimeter indicates a constant altitude.
F. Increasing rpm (fixed-pitch propeller).
  1—ACDF.
  2—ABDF.
  3—ABEF.
  4—ACEF.

1503. Pick the steps in the recovery from a power-on spiral in an airplane with a fixed-pitch propeller and select the *proper order*.

A. Level the wings with coordinated controls.
B. Use forward pressure on the stick or wheel.
C. Use back pressure on the stick or wheel.
D. Retard the throttle.
E. Stop the altimeter with the elevators (stabilator).
F. Use full rudder against the bank, keeping the ailerons neutral.
  1—ACDF.
  2—EBDA.
  3—BAEC.
  4—DACE.

Questions 1504 and 1505 are based on Figure 15-A. Don't check the answers until you have completed both questions.

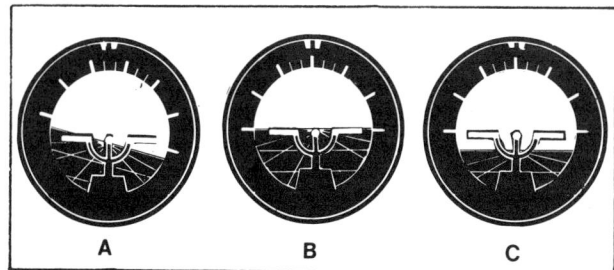

Fig. 15-A.

1504. Choose the correct statement.

1—Instrument A indicates a balanced constant-altitude turn to the left.
2—Instrument A indicates a bank to the right.
3—Instrument B indicates that the airplane is flying straight and level.
4—Instrument A indicates an approximate 15° bank to the left.

1505. Choose the correct statement.

1—Instrument B indicates that the airplane is flying straight and level.
2—Instrument C indicates a climb.
3—Instrument C indicates a nose-high attitude.
4—Instrument B indicates a nose-level attitude descent.

1506. In a recovery from an approach to a climbing stall using the emergency panel, the most important (and first) step is to

1—lower the nose.
2—level the wings by reference to the turn and slip indicator or turn coordinator.
3—reduce the power.
4—apply full power.

1507. After getting into actual instrument conditions, you recover from a power-on spiral at an altitude of 3300 feet and a heading of 135°. You need to climb to 4500 feet and turn to a heading of 270° to get back to a safe situation. The rate of climb is 900 fpm, and you will use a standard-rate turn. The desired direction of turn and times required to complete the heading and altitude requirements will be:

1—Left; 45 seconds to turn and 30 seconds to climb.
2—Right; 45 seconds to turn and 1 minute 20 seconds to climb.
3—Left; 30 seconds to turn and 1 minute 20 seconds to climb.
4—Left; 45 seconds to turn and 1 minute 20 seconds to climb.

Refer to Figure 15-B for questions 1508 and 1509.

1508. The airplane shown in Figure 15-B is making several constant, *shallow-banked* left turns in the southern United States. At point A, the magnetic compass will be

1—approximately correct.
2—leading by 30° or more.
3—lagging by 30° or more.
4—indicating 90° from the heading at point B.

1509. At point D, the magnetic compass at 30° north latitude will be indicating approximately

1—030°.
2—330°.
3—N.
4—150°.

1510. In a shallow climbing turn to a predetermined altitude at 100 knots indicated airspeed, you discover that the turn coordinator is not working. Using the attitude indicator during the climb, you would keep the bank to a maximum of

1—30°.
2—45°.
3—15°.
4—25°.

1511. Refer to the fictitious airspeed indicator in Figure 15-C for an answer to this question. If you were trapped on top of an overcast and had to decide on a safe airspeed for a descent (using the proper power to set up approximately 500 fpm), you'd establish approximately

1—150 knots.
2—110 knots.
3—50 knots.
4—85 knots.

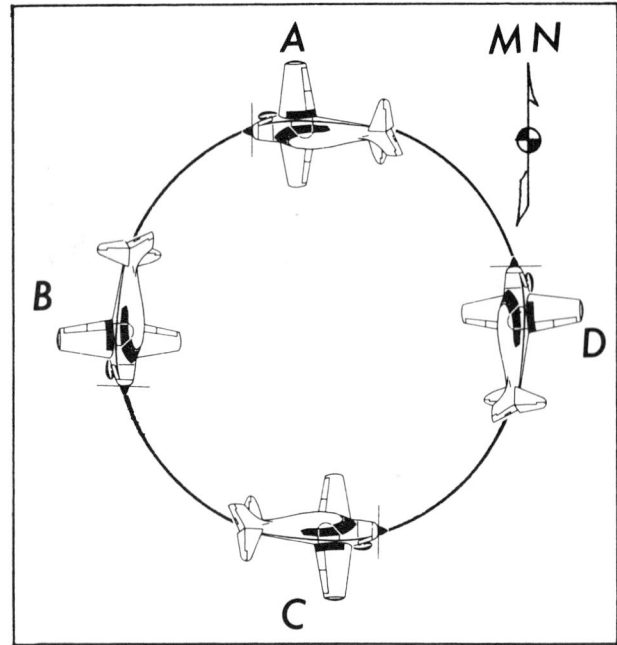

Fig. 15-B.

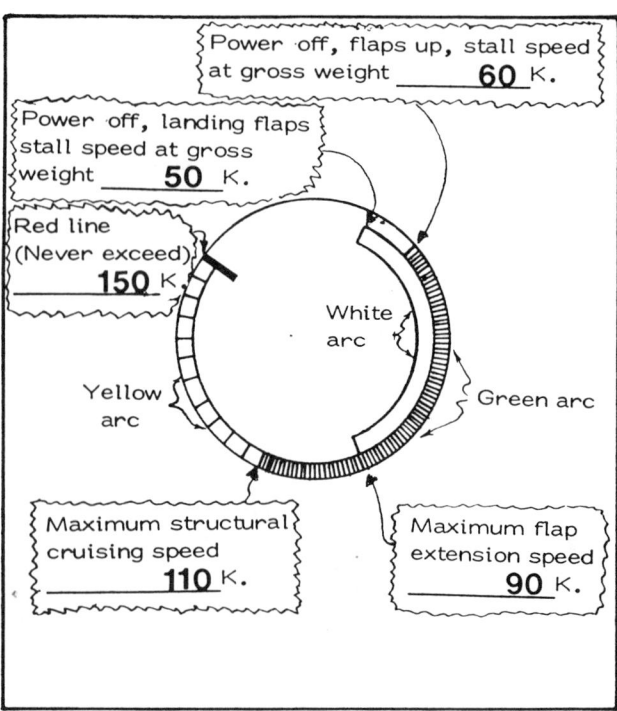

Fig. 15-C.

1512. You are on top of an overcast that stretches hundreds of miles in all directions and have no direction (bank) indicator other than the magnetic compass. (How do you let yourself get into these fixes?) You would have the best chance of a successful descent on a heading of

1—East or West.
2—North, because the compass leads the turn.
3—South, because the compass leads the turn.
4—North, because the compass lags the turn.

16

POSTSOLO PRECISION MANEUVERS

For questions 1601–1603 use Figure 16-A, which shows turns around a point. The airplane is flying around the circle in the direction indicated by the arrows.

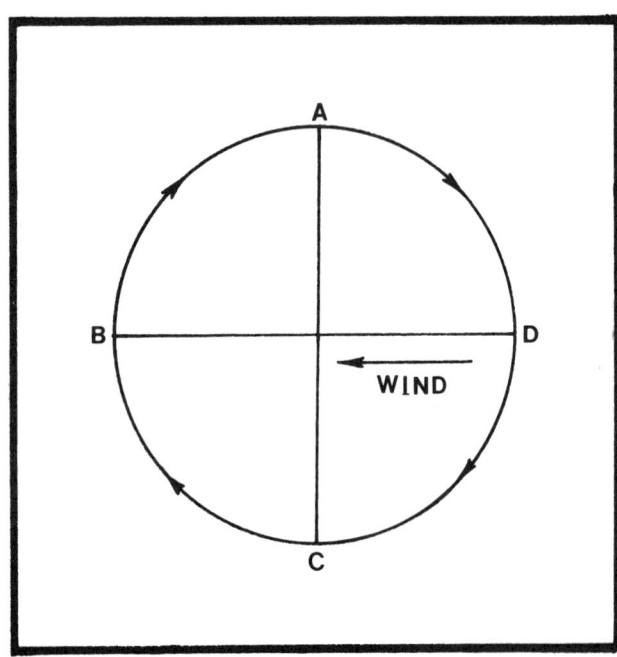

Fig. 16-A.

1601. The steepest bank will be required at

1—A.
2—B.
3—D.
4—C.

1602. The shallowest bank will be required at

1—C.
2—A.
3—B.
4—D.

1603. There will be banks of similar steepness at

1—B and D.
2—B and C.
3—A and C.
4—A and D.

1604. The best method of picking pylons for the around-pylon eights is to

1—fly downwind, looking well ahead.
2—fly upwind, checking both sides of the projected flight path.
3—fly crosswind, looking to the downwind side.
4—fly crosswind, looking to the upwind side.

1605. When doing eights across a road, you would pick a road that is

1—at 90° to the wind.
2—parallel to the wind.
3—hard surfaced.
4—at a 45° angle to the wind.

17

SPECIAL TAKEOFF AND LANDING PROCEDURES

As a student pilot, if you have to make an "unplanned" off-airport solo landing, you should *always* contact your flight instructor before attempting to fly the airplane out. He or she will most likely want to fly it out or oversee the dismantling in preparation for trucking it home.

The *Pilot's Operating Handbook* figures are normally based on a dry, level, paved runway, sometimes with a fudge factor thrown in for a dry grass surface. (How high is the grass?) You also know from mowing the lawn that wet grass can cause more drag than dry grass. And maybe obstacles would mean an uphill takeoff; this normally isn't included in the *POH* because, while the runways at certificated airports are held to certain maximum slopes, "your" off-airport site could have any kind. Too many *experienced* pilots take off from an area that was "eyeballed" for length rather than pacing it off. A big factor, too, is that everybody assumes that the average pace is 3 feet. Unless you are a 7-foot basketball player you'd better count on 2.5 feet per step; the pilot who steps off a field could be 15–20 percent wrong—on the bad side.

If it's hot, you may have to off-load fuel, baggage, or even people and wait until early morning to get the best performance.

If you and the airplane are down without damage in a farmer's field, you might consider that there have been fatal accidents caused by pushing too hard to take off again. Okay, now for the questions you've been waiting for:

1701. An airplane at sea level (and 15°C) requires a ground roll of 760 feet and 1360 feet total distance to clear a 50-foot obstacle (no wind). In making a short-field takeoff in that airplane at sea level (15°C), you stop and line up to barely clear that obstacle exactly 1360 feet away and then notice that you could have gotten about another 36 feet of run if you'd started at the very end of the takeoff area. You decide that

1—the added usable distance of 36 feet is insignificant when compared to the 1360 feet required to clear the obstacle.
2—if the added distance is used, it will mean a difference of 36 feet of height when the original point is reached.
3—the airplane will be approximately 12 feet higher at the obstacle if the extra 36 feet is used.
4—the airplane will be approximately 3 feet higher at the obstacle if the extra 36 feet is used.

1702. The airplane in question 1701, at a density altitude of 6000 feet, requires a ground roll of 1300 feet and a *total* distance of 2500 feet to clear a 50-foot obstacle. By moving the airplane's tail back to a fence and getting 48 feet more takeoff run, you would get to the *original* 2500-foot point with an added height of approximately

1—6 feet.
2—2 feet.
3—12 feet.
4—24 feet.

1703. You're making a short-field approach. On final before you start breaking the glide, you note that a reference spot (the point of intended touchdown) on the runway is apparently moving toward you. This means that

1—the airplane will be too high to land on the spot.
2—the airplane will land well short of the spot.

3—the approach is right on for a touchdown exactly on the spot.

4—the airplane will leave a large airplane-shaped hole in the runway unless power is added.

1704. Which one of the following statements would correctly apply in making a short-field approach and landing?

1—The pattern should be tighter, with the downwind leg closer to the runway than normal.
2—The angle of approach is controlled by the elevators or stabilator.
3—To get the most effective braking, the control wheel or stick should be held full back.
4—Pulling the landing gear up after touchdown shortens the landing roll but means that more power is required to taxi.

1705. Which one of the following statements would correctly apply to a soft-field takeoff?

1—Keep the airplane rolling as you turn onto the takeoff area.
2—Make sure the elevators or stabilator are kept neutral throughout the takeoff roll so that the airplane can fly itself off.
3—Avoid using flaps since they will add to the drag condition.
4—Line up with the takeoff area, stop, hold the brakes and apply full power, then release the brakes for maximum takeoff performance.

1706. Which of the following combinations of barometric pressure and temperature for an airplane sitting at sea level would give the *lowest* air density (or highest density-altitude)?

1—Altimeter setting 29.92 and temperature 74°F.
2—Altimeter setting 30.42 and temperature 74°F.
3—Altimeter setting 30.42 and temperature 89°F.
4—Altimeter setting 29.42 and temperature 44°F.

1707. For a given barometric pressure, which of the following conditions would result in the *worst* takeoff performance of an airplane?

1—Low temperature and high humidity.
2—High temperature and high humidity.
3—High temperature and low humidity.
4—Low temperature and low humidity.

Questions 1708–1710 are based on the Take-off Distance Chart shown in Figure 17-A.

TAKEOFF DISTANCE
SHORT FIELD

CONDITIONS:
Flaps Up
Full Throttle Prior to Brake Release
Paved, Level, Dry Runway
Zero Wind

NOTES:
1. Short field technique as specified in Section 4.
2. Prior to takeoff from fields above 5000 feet elevation, the mixture should be leaned to give maximum RPM in a full throttle, static runup.
3. Decrease distances 10% for each 9 knots headwind. For operation with tailwinds up to 10 knots, increase distances by 10% for each 2 knots.
4. Where distance value has been deleted, climb performance after lift-off is less than 150 fpm at takeoff speed.
5. For operation on a dry, grass runway, increase distances by 15% of the "ground roll" figure.

WEIGHT LBS	TAKEOFF SPEED KIAS		PRESS ALT FT	0°C		10°C		20°C		30°C		40°C	
	LIFT OFF	AT 50 FT		GRND ROLL	TOTAL TO CLEAR 50 FT OBS	GRND ROLL	TOTAL TO CLEAR 50 FT OBS	GRND ROLL	TOTAL TO CLEAR 50 FT OBS	GRND ROLL	TOTAL TO CLEAR 50 FT OBS	GRND ROLL	TOTAL TO CLEAR 50 FT OBS
1600	53	60	S.L.	655	1245	710	1335	765	1435	820	1540	880	1650
			1000	720	1365	775	1465	835	1575	900	1690	970	1815
			2000	790	1500	855	1615	920	1735	990	1865	1065	2005
			3000	870	1650	935	1780	1010	1915	1090	2065	1170	2225
			4000	955	1820	1030	1965	1115	2125	1200	2290	1290	2475
			5000	1050	2015	1140	2185	1230	2360	1325	2555	1430	2770
			6000	1160	2245	1255	2435	1360	2640	1465	2870	1580	3120
			7000	1285	2510	1390	2730	1505	2970	1625	3240	---	---
			8000	1420	2820	1540	3080	1670	3370	---	---	---	---

Fig. 17-A.

1708. At a pressure altitude of 5000 feet and a temperature of 10°C (wind calm) and taking off from a paved, level, dry runway, the airplane would require a ground roll and total distance to clear a 50-foot obstacle respectively of

1—1050 and 2015 feet.
2—1230 and 2185 feet.
3—1140 and 2185 feet.
4—1050 and 2185 feet.

1709. At a pressure altitude of 4000 feet and a temperature of 15°C (wind calm) and taking off from a paved, level, dry runway, the airplane would require a ground roll and total distance (rounded off) to clear a 50-foot obstacle of

1—1030 and 1965 feet.
2—1075 and 2045 feet.
3—1115 and 2125 feet.
4—1075 and 1965 feet.

1710. With a 9-knot headwind you would expect the distances under the other conditions cited in question 1709 to be

1—1075 and 2045 feet.
2—927 and 1770 feet.
3—1075 and 1965 feet.
4—968 and 1841 feet.

Look at the Landing Chart (short-field techniques) in Figure 17-B for answers to questions 1711 and 1712.

1711. Compute the landing ground roll and total distance to clear a 50-foot obstacle at a pressure altitude of 2000 feet and 30°C (no wind) on a level, dry grass runway. The distances are

1—732 and 1392 feet.
2—490 and 1140 feet.
3—277 and 640 feet.
4—505 and 1165 feet.

1712. What are the landing ground roll and distance over a 50-foot obstacle at 4500 feet pressure altitude and 15°C on a paved, level, dry runway with a headwind of 14 knots?

1—525 and 1195 feet.
2—446 and 1016 feet.
3—515 and 1180 feet.
4—535 and 1210 feet.

LANDING DISTANCE

SHORT FIELD

CONDITIONS:
Flaps 40°
Power Off
Maximum Braking
Paved, Level, Dry Runway
Zero Wind

NOTES:
1. Short field technique as specified in Section 4.
2. Decrease distances 10% for each 9 knots headwind. For operation with tailwinds up to 10 knots, increase distances by 10% for each 2 knots.
3. For operation on a dry, grass runway, increase distances by 45% of the "ground roll" figure.

WEIGHT LBS	SPEED AT 50 FT KIAS	PRESS ALT FT	0°C		10°C		20°C		30°C		40°C	
			GRND ROLL	TOTAL TO CLEAR 50 FT OBS	GRND ROLL	TOTAL TO CLEAR 50 FT OBS	GRND ROLL	TOTAL TO CLEAR 50 FT OBS	GRND ROLL	TOTAL TO CLEAR 50 FT OBS	GRND ROLL	TOTAL TO CLEAR 50 FT OBS
1600	52	S.L.	425	1045	440	1065	455	1090	470	1110	485	1135
		1000	440	1065	455	1090	470	1110	485	1135	505	1165
		2000	455	1090	470	1115	490	1140	505	1165	520	1185
		3000	470	1115	490	1140	505	1165	525	1195	540	1215
		4000	490	1140	505	1165	525	1195	545	1225	560	1245
		5000	510	1170	525	1195	545	1225	565	1255	585	1285
		6000	530	1200	545	1225	565	1255	585	1285	605	1315
		7000	550	1230	570	1260	590	1290	610	1320	630	1350
		8000	570	1260	590	1290	610	1320	630	1350	655	1385

Fig. 17-B.

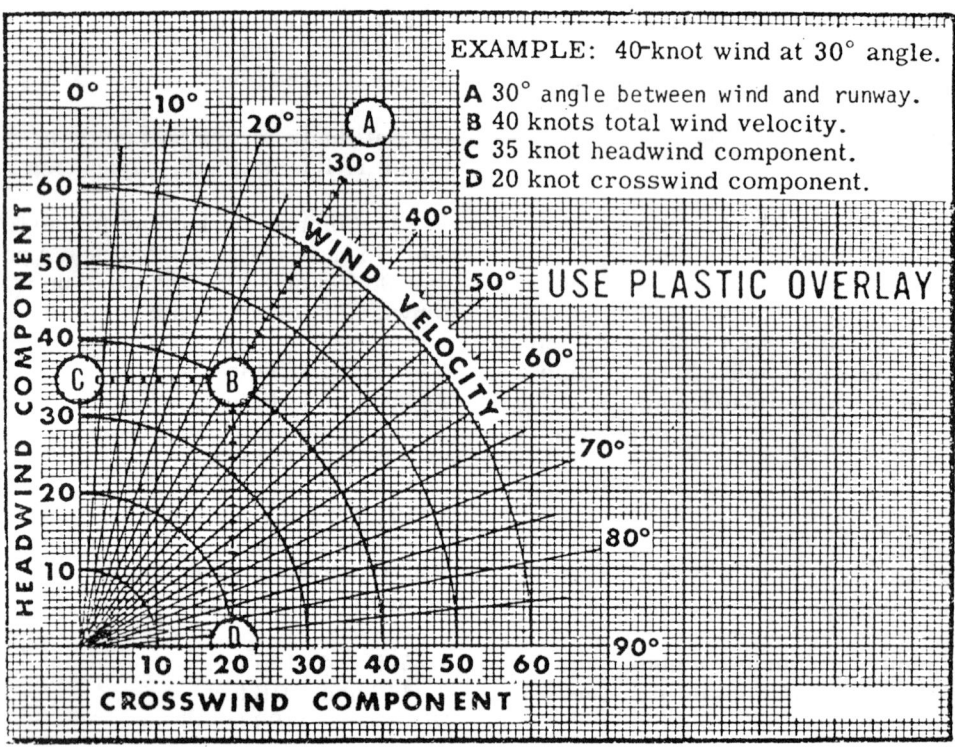

Fig. 17-C.

1713. The V_{so} airspeed (calibrated) for your airplane is 50 knots. The major demonstrated crosswind component allowed for the airplane is 0.2 V_{so}, or 10 knots. Assume that you are landing on Runway 34 (actual magnetic bearing 344°) and the wind is from 010° magnetic at 20 knots. Using the Wind Component Chart in Figure 17-C, you find that the *headwind* and *crosswind* components will be approximately

1—35 and 20 knots.
2—22 and 8 knots.
3—19 and 5 knots.
4—18 and 9 knots.

18
HIGH-ALTITUDE
EMERGENCIES

1801. Pick the one correct statement concerning the ability to tell surface wind directions from the air.

1—The darkest sides of the trees are on the upwind side.
2—If all other methods fail, sticking your hand out the window is one method of finding wind direction.
3—The undisturbed area of a pond or lake is on the upwind side of that body.
4—None of the above answers apply.

1802. The Key Position is

1—where you keep the Key.
2—at the same point at which you close the throttle for a 180° power-off approach but at a slightly higher altitude.
3—at the same point at which you close the throttle for a 180° power-off approach but at a slightly lower altitude.
4—at a point slightly farther out from the landing area than for a 180° power-off approach.

Check the Glide Performance Chart in Figure 18-A for question 1803.

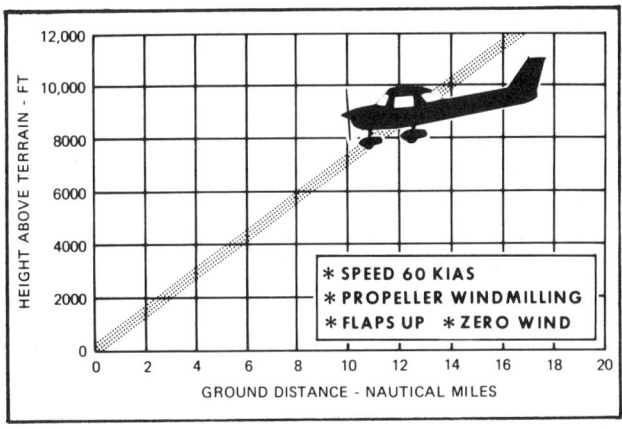

Fig. 18-A.

1803. From an altitude of 7000 feet above the ground, the airplane can cover a ground distance of approximately

1—8 nautical miles.
2—12 nautical miles.
3—10 nautical miles.
4—5 nautical miles.

PART FOUR: CROSS-COUNTRY AND NIGHT FLYING

19

THE NAVIGATION IDEA

When you decided to learn to fly, the primary purpose was to be able to use the airplane for business and/or pleasure and take advantage of the ability of the airplane to fly directly (and fast) to a particular spot. This and the following chapters are aimed at getting you out of the traffic pattern.

You'll find that navigation is challenging and enjoyable, but to do the job you'll have to know how to use the basic tools. Maybe the chart, plotter, and computer seem a little complicated at first and arithmetic and you aren't good friends, but it all boils down to your wanting to fly from L to M and the just-mentioned tools are merely *aids* to that end.

Read Chapter 19, *SPFM* before working on the following questions. Any subject areas you have trouble with should be reviewed in Chapter 19 and those questions redone. Pick the nearest answer to that gotten on *your* computer, since there was a slight variation between computers used to check the answers here.

THE BASICS

1901. The primary method of navigation for the student pilot is

1—dead reckoning.
2—pilotage.
3—celestial.
4—radio navigation.

1902. The earth is divided by meridians and parallels. Meridians extend

1—from the geographic north pole to the geographic south pole.
2—in lines parallel to the equator.

3—from the Magnetic North Pole to the Magnetic South Pole.
4—along the equator.

1903. Each degree between parallels (measured along a meridian) is equal to 60 minutes. Each minute of latitude is equal to

1—1 hour of time.
2—1 statute mile.
3—1 nautical mile.
4—1 minute of longitude.

1904. Each 15° of longitude change is equal to approximately

1—1 hour of time.
2—Coordinated Universal (Zulu) Time plus 1 hour.
3—15 nautical miles.
4—60 minutes of latitude.

1905. At a particular geographic position, the magnetic angle between the True North Pole and the Magnetic North Pole is known as the

1—isotherm.
2—variation.
3—deviation.
4—agonic line.

USING THE PLOTTER

1906. Directions on a map are measured clockwise from geographic north. Direction of northwest would mostly closely be

1—215° magnetic.

2—135° true.
3—135° magnetic.
4—315° true.

1907. Plotters are primarily used in navigation to find

1—variation and compass heading.
2—deviation and distances.
3—magnetic heading and latitude.
4—true courses and distances.

Use the chart in the back of this book for questions 1908 and 1909.

1908. The true course from Murfreesboro Airport (35°53′N, 86°23′W) to Bomar (Shelbyville) Airport (35°34′N, 86°27′W) is approximately

1—010°.
2—190°.
3—350°.
4—280°.

1909. The true course from Warren County Airport (35°42′N, 85°50′W) to Bomar Airport is approximately

1—075°.
2—255°.
3—285°.
4—165°.

USING THE COMPUTER

■ True Airspeed

If, in working with the computer, you aren't sure of the relationships of pressure and temperature on the airplane's performance (or other factors of flight), pick a pressure altitude and temperature and get an answer, then change the pressure or temperature to see the effects.

1910. What happens to true airspeed (TAS) at a constant calibrated airspeed (CAS) and pressure altitude when the temperature changes? The TAS will

1—increase with an increase in temperature.
2—decrease with an increase in temperature.
3—increase with a decrease in temperature.
4—remain the same, regardless of temperature changes.

1911. What is the TAS when the CAS is 100 knots at a pressure altitude of 5000 feet with outside air temperature of +10°C?

1—92 knots.
2—100 knots.
3—105 knots.
4—109 knots.

1912. Assuming a constant CAS, what happens to the TAS when you go to a higher pressure altitude with the temperature changing at the standard adiabatic lapse rate?

1—TAS remains the same.
2—TAS decreases with altitude.
3—TAS increases with altitude.
4—It is impossible to compute because of lack of data.

■ True and Density-Altitudes

1913. What is the true altitude when the pressure altitude is 6000 feet at a temperature of +20°C?

1—6000 feet.
2—5500 feet.
3—7950 feet.
4—6350 feet.

1914. Under which conditions will your true altitude be less than your pressure altitude?

1—When you have a temperature that is lower than standard temperature.
2—When you have a temperature that is higher than the standard temperature.
3—When you are flying at pressure altitudes above 10,000 feet.
4—None of the above conditions apply.

1915. Density-altitude will increase with

1—a decrease in indicated pressure.
2—a decrease in temperature.
3—an increase in the density of the air.
4—a decrease in relative humidity.

■ Some Practical Problems

1916. Using the information given in Figure 19-A, find the compass heading for a trip from A to B.

1—090°.
2—076°.
3—074°.
4—072°.

50 PART FOUR CROSS-COUNTRY AND NIGHT FLYING

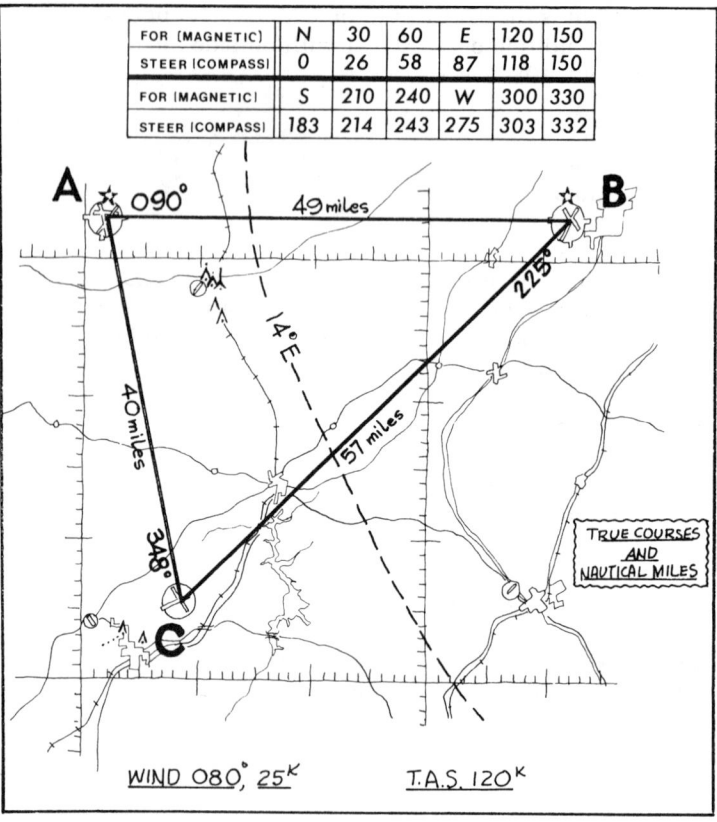

Fig. 19-A.

1917. What is the magnetic course from B to C?

1—225°.
2—218°.
3—211°.
4—239°.

1918. What is the total time required to go from A to B to C to A?

1—1 hour and 7 minutes.
2—1 hour and 16 minutes.
3—1 hour.
4—1 hour and 10 minutes.

1919. After you have leveled off at your altitude on a cross-country, you noted the time of 1405 EST (1905Z) as you crossed your first checkpoint. The time is 1416 EST (1916Z) over your second checkpoint 20 nautical miles away. What is your actual groundspeed?

1—109 knots.
2—113 mph.
3—109 mph.
4—105 knots.

1920. If your airplane fuel tanks hold a total of 50 gallons of gasoline, 48 usable, how long could you fly when burning 7.5 gph?

1—6 hours 24 minutes.
2—6 hours 40 minutes.
3—5 hours 55 minutes.
4—6 hours 10 minutes.

1921. The distance between two points was given as 63 nautical miles. Your airspeed reads in miles per hour. Since you will need to convert so the measurements will make sense, you elect to change nautical to *statute* miles, which turns out to be a distance of

1—55 statute miles.
2—70 statute miles.
3—68 statute miles.
4—73 statute miles.

1922. The temperature given over Automatic Terminal Information Service was −23°F. To use the performance charts (and also the true altitude, true airspeed windows on the computer), you need to

1—change this particular temperature to a Celsius reading of −30°.
2—use the temperature given, as it is already in Celsius.
3—change this temperature to a Fahrenheit reading of −9°.
4—use the conversion of statute to nautical and convert this to 20.

■ Computer Exercises

Fill in the blanks; the correct answers are given at the end of the answers and explanations for this chapter in the back of the book. Your answer may vary slightly because of computer differences.

Exercise A: Computation of True Airspeed

Pressure Altitude	Free Air Temperature	Calibrated Airspeed (knots)	True Airspeed (knots)
3,000 feet	0°C	140	_____
8,000 feet	−5°C	160	_____
12,000 feet	−10°C	190	_____
5,000 feet	+30°C	140	_____

Exercise B: Time-Speed-Distance Problems

Time (hours:minutes)	Groundspeed (knots)	Distance (NM)
_____	104	643
3:32	_____	563
0:45	_____	125
4:17	133	_____

Chapter 19. The Navigation Idea

Exercise C: Fuel Consumption Problems (to nearest 0.1 gallon)

Time (hours:minutes)	Rate (gph)	Usable Fuel (gallons)
————	7.5	58
4:25	11.5	————
1:20	————	12.5
3:45	18.5	————

Exercise D: True Altitude

Free Air Temperature	Pressure Altitude	True Altitude
+15°C	6,000 feet	————
−10°C	10,000 feet	————

Exercise E: Wind Vectors—Use knots and nautical miles for all speeds and distances. (Note that some of the wind directions and speeds aren't "standard," but these are exercises.)

Wind Direction	Wind-speed	True Course	True Airspeed	True Heading	Ground-speed
(from) 350°	30	075°	140	————	————
115°	28	240°	155	————	————
100°	32	310°	140	————	————
170°	26	080°	160	————	————

Exercise F: Wind Vectors (continued)

Wind Direction	Wind-speed	Vari-ation	True Course	True Airspeed	True Heading	Ground-speed	Magnetic Heading
078°	30	3E	190°	175	————	————	————
110°	38	8E	028°	200	————	————	————
060°	35	10W	130°	180	————	————	————
045°	25	1E	292°	165	————	————	————

Exercise G: Wind Vectors Corrected to Compass Heading

Wind Direction	Wind-speed	Vari-ation	True Course	Devi-ation	True Air-speed	True Heading	Ground-speed	Compass Heading
220°	20	2E	340°	+1	————	————	169	————
150°	25	0	183°	+3	————	————	113	————
230°	10	7W	005°	−2	————	————	161	————
070°	20	12W	112°	+2	————	————	110	————

Exercise H: Conversion Problems

Statute Miles	Nautical Miles
160	————
————	240
8	————

Celsius	Fahrenheit
+32°	————
−20°	————

20

THE CHART AND
OTHER PRINTED AIDS

It's strongly suggested for best learning that you review both Chapters 20 and 21 of *SPFM* and this book before taking the sample tests for either chapter. The two are closely tied in subject matter and are complementary.

THE SECTIONAL CHART

Communications and navigation equipment may fail, but rivers, highways, and railroads don't change places that fast; so, as *SPFM* says, the sectional chart is the student pilot's best friend. On the other hand, road projects or industrial plants that were started and completed since the issuance of a particular sectional nearly six months ago could cause a little confusion, since the chart doesn't show them. Usually a newly completed road project still has raw earth around it, and this tells the story. The point is, however, to check ground references against each other; just because *that* town has a railroad running through it doesn't mean that it's the one you're looking for. Check the road system coming into the town. (Is that drive-in movie on the right highway for Jonesville?)

In Chapter 19 of this book a look was taken at how to locate an airport when its latitude and longitude are known. Consider a practical situation. Suppose later, as a charter pilot in a midwestern state, you're told that the customer wants to go to Abernathy Airport at Pulaski, Tennessee, where he's looking at a possible plant site. If you don't know the airport, you can spend much time trying to locate it. (Is it near Memphis in western Tennessee or by Bristol nearly 400 nautical miles east?)

The *Airport/Facility Directory* (to be covered in detail later) gives a clue immediately. Figure 20-A is the data for Abernathy Field. It notes that the airport

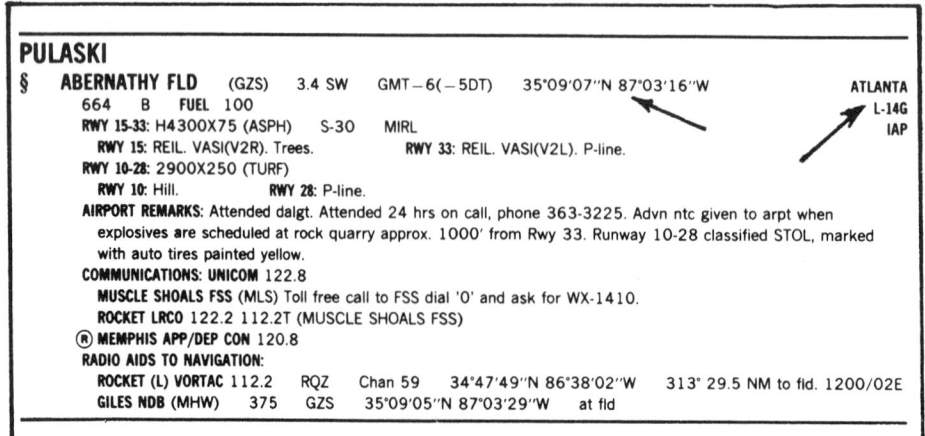

Fig. 20-A. Airport information for Abernathy Field as given in the *A/FD*.

52

is on the Atlanta sectional chart as well as on the Low-Altitude (IFR) Enroute Chart 14 (panel G), and it has an Instrument Approach Procedures Chart (IAP). You want to find it on the sectional chart, however, and you see that the airport is located at 35°09′07″N and 87°03′16″W (arrows).

As you fumble with *any* sectional chart, the odds are that you will look at the wrong side first. These are the same Fates that decide that a piece of bread and jelly will always land jelly-side down when dropped. Hints are given on the legend as to which way to unfold it (NORTH, SOUTH), but unfortunately, who reads directions?

Looking at the left margin of the chart, you see that the latitude runs from 32° to 34°N. (*Not* that side.) The other side runs from about 34°12′N to about 36°12′N. Abernathy Field (35°09′07″) should be somewhere there. Look up the left margin and find 35°N, move over to 87°W, and the rest is completed as outlined in Chapter 19.

Note that the geographic position given in the *Airport/Facility Directory* is to the nearest second (″) of latitude and longitude. For practical purposes on the sectional chart, checking to the nearest minute (′) is fine. Later, when you're flying that supersonic transport over the pole(s), the finer navigation equipment may give your position to the nearest second or much closer.

If *you* were making up a pilot's written test, you might put in a question like, "The coordinates (latitude and longitude) of Abernathy Airport are...." You'd then give four (close) choices, which is a backward look at the problem, but written tests have been known to do this and quite often. (See the questions in this chapter.) Sometimes it's easier to make up questions than to answer them.

You don't always have to look at the extreme top and left border of the sectional chart, but note that the primary latitude and longitude values are given in the upper left corner of that quadrant. Sectional charts are getting crowded and you may have to look awhile to find them. Figure 20-B shows the relative position of the numbers and how they look on the chart.

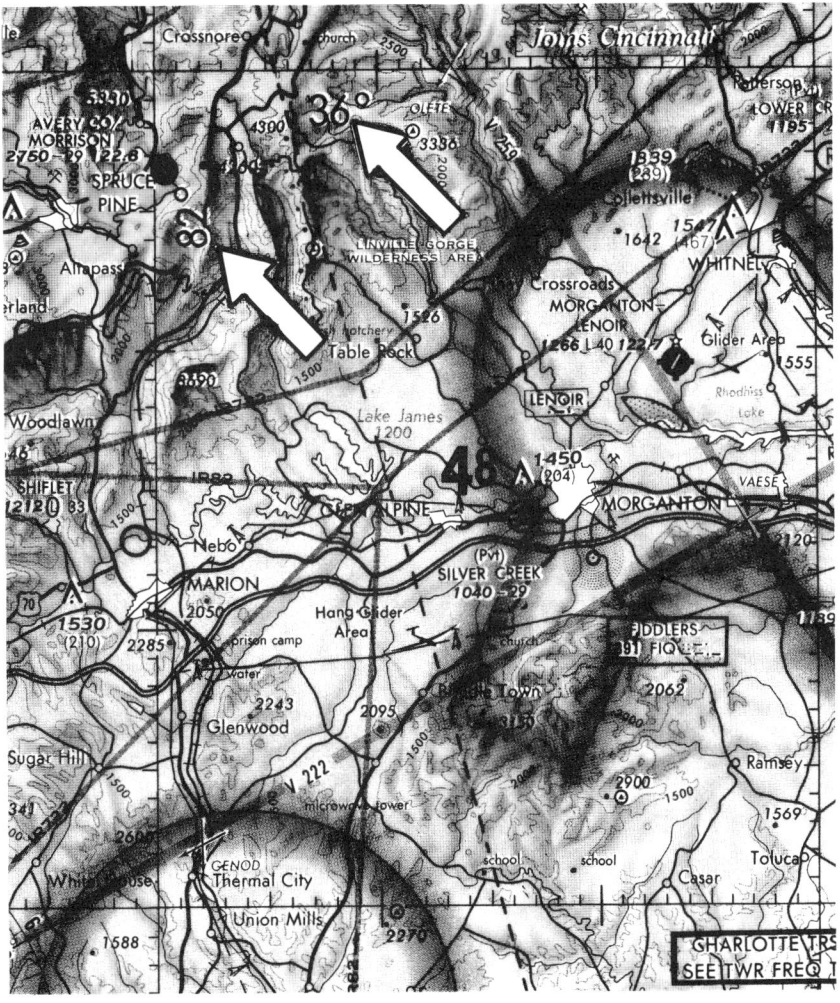

Fig. 20-B. Finding primary latitude and longitude numbers (36°N and 82°W).

Some Topography Notes

The sectional chart has different colors for the various elevations of terrain. There was a problem in the area of the Sewanee–Franklin County Airport (Tennessee) some years ago because of the chart color breakdown. That airport is on the top and near the western edge of the Cumberland Plateau, and the terrain a couple of miles north and west is approximately 900 feet lower. The elevation of the Tullahoma Soesbe-Martin Airport (35°22′47″N, 86°15′23″W) is 1081 feet, and the Sewanee Airport elevation is 1950 feet. Since both airports fall between the 1000- to 2000-foot elevation values, the chart color for the areas is the same green shade. A transient pilot flying to Chattanooga through the area from the relatively flat terrain of Nashville, after a quick look at the older sectional charts, might decide that the terrain between Tullahoma and Sewanee airports was level and of approximately the same elevation because of the "common" color of the areas. Even looking at the two airport elevations might lead the pilot to believe that the rise of terrain was gradual over the 20 nautical miles from Tullahoma to Sewanee.

The western edge of the Cumberland Plateau rises nearly 1000 feet in 3000 feet of horizontal distance, and this proved to be a fatal slope for several pilots "flying VFR" from the level and lower country to the west and northwest in low ceilings and visibilities in earlier years. Scud running (trying to stay VFR underneath low clouds) can result in fatal consequences in strange, or even so-called familiar, terrain.

Figure 20-C compares terrain in the vicinity of Sewanee on the sectional chart and a Tennessee Valley

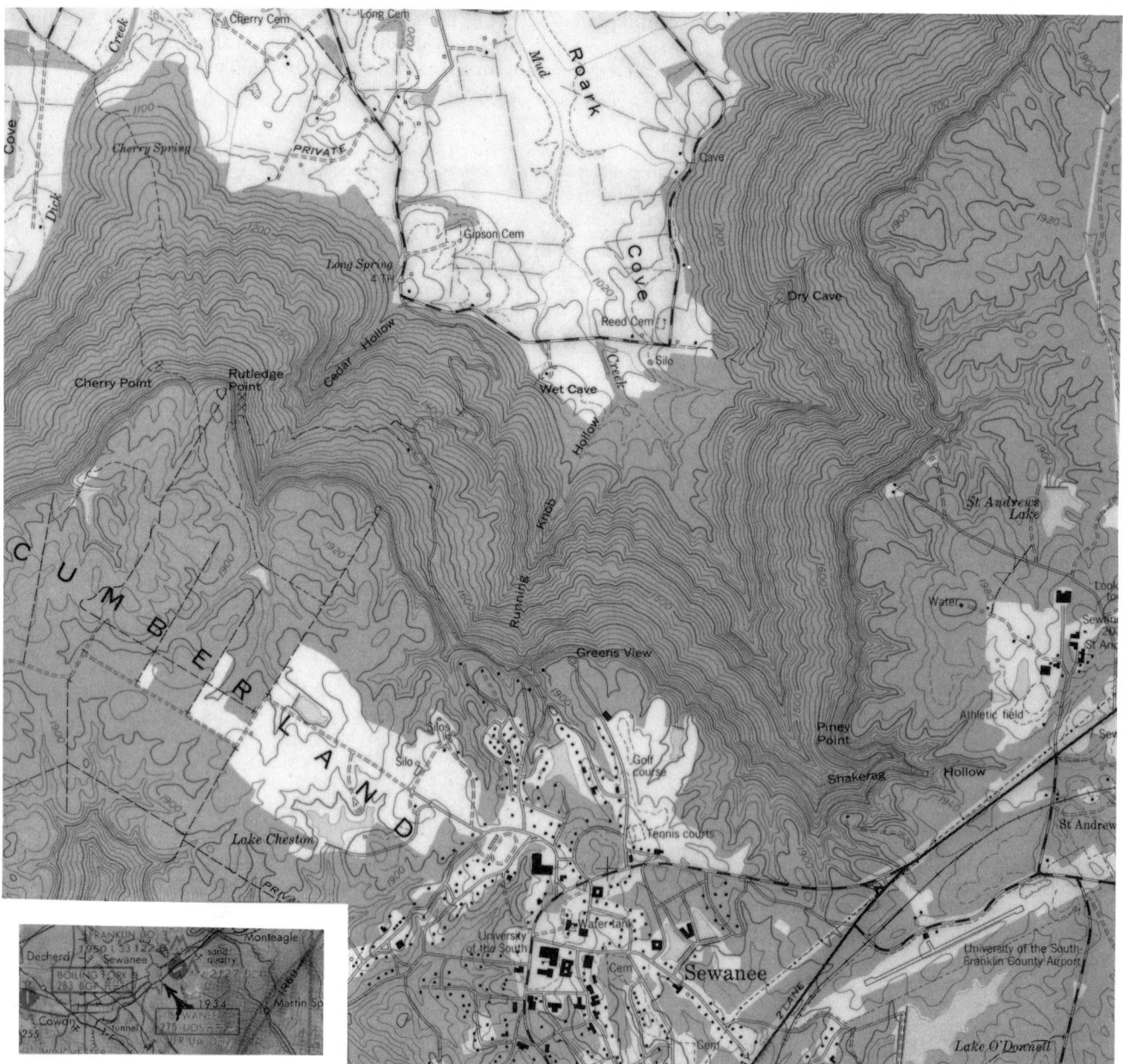

Fig. 20-C. A comparison of terrain as depicted on the sectional chart (1 inch = 7 nautical miles) and a topographic map (1 inch = 2000 feet). Both have been reduced slightly here.

Authority topographic chart. The arrow points out the area on the sectional chart segment.

You are not going to get topographical maps of your cross-country routes, since (1) you couldn't afford to and (2) the airplane couldn't carry them. But you should look carefully at the terrain clues provided by the sectional chart.

Because of the number of accidents caused by pilots flying into the Cumberland Plateau in earlier years in bad weather, the sectional chart of the area, and other areas in the United States like it, includes a hashed line and a warning about *rapidly rising terrain* (Fig. 20-D). The original warning was *caution—escarpment*, but it may have been felt that there might be some confusion so the warning was changed.

■ **Sectional Chart Legend**

Carefully study the legend of the foldout sectional chart in the back of this book (or the back of *SPFM*). You won't be able to memorize all the data, but by looking it over now you'll be able to remember more easily and to pick out needed information in flight.

For instance, on a cross-country flight you are going to need services for your airplane. Which of the two airports symbolized in Figure 20-E would be more likely to have fuel and to be tended during normal working hours?

Your first assumption is that the hard-surfaced airport (B) would be more likely to have fuel and other services than the nonhard-surfaced runway type (A), and in real life this is likely to be true, but not here. The four "cogs" sticking out indicate services available. If an airport with hard-surfaced runways has services, the "cogs" will be shown on the symbol.

Fig. 20-E. Symbols for two types of airports.

Take some time to look over the sectional chart. Check symbols on the chart to compare them with the legend. You'll remember items as you use them more, but you'll still run into fairly rare symbols that need to be checked.

As noted in Chapter 19, *SPFM*, if you've forgotten your protractor or ruler, distances in nautical miles may be found by laying the marked distance (north and south) along a *meridian*. Measuring distance along a parallel would only be accurate at the equator. The sectional chart here shows that the "grids" at the latitudes covered are rectangular rather than square as *far as distance is concerned*. At the equator (only) the grids would be square.

AIRPORT/FACILITY DIRECTORY

The appendix of this book contains the legend for the *Airport/Facility Directory* (*A/FD*). Spend about 20 minutes looking through it so that you have a good idea of the symbols and abbreviations for use in writ-

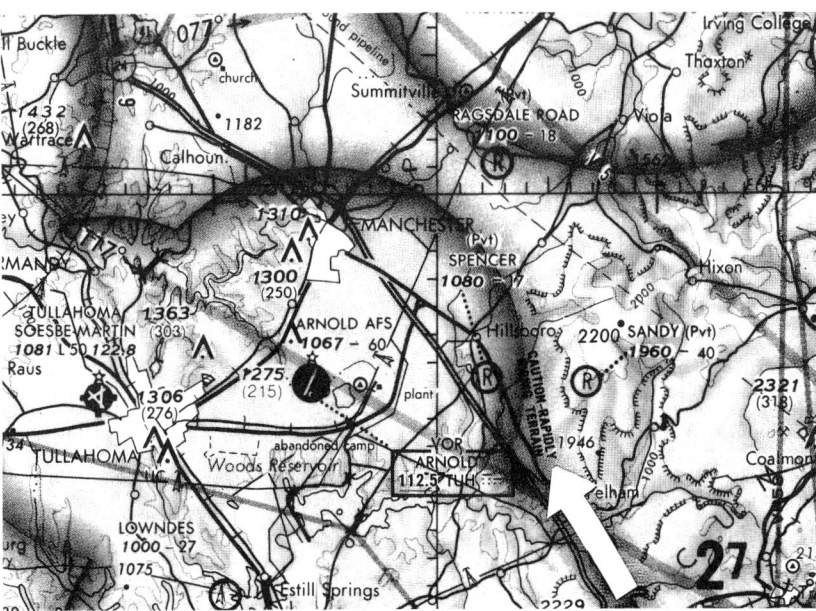

Fig. 20-D. An extension of the escarpment just north of Sewanee. Check the chart in the back of the book for an overall look at the area. Note the warning (arrow).

56 PART FOUR CROSS-COUNTRY AND NIGHT FLYING

ten tests or, more importantly, later when you're planning an actual cross-country.

Figure 20-F is a sample of actual data from an *A/FD*, and some of the questions in this chapter will be based on the information there.

Continuing with the contents of the *A/FD*, after the airport and facility information, heliports and seaplane bases are listed by state and city alphabetically, followed by "Notices." Figure 20-G is sample material that can be found in the "Special Notices" section.

Other data is supplied in the following order: Flight Service Stations and Combined Station/Towers

---

§ **ANDALUSIA-OPP** (79J) 4.3 E GMT−6(−5DT) 31°18'31"N 86°23'37"W **NEW ORLEANS**
   330 B S4 **FUEL** 100LL H-4G, L-18F
   RWY 11-29: H5000X100 (ASPH) S-30 MIRL IAP
      RWY 11: VASI(V4L)—GA 3.0°TCH 26'. Trees.   **RWY 29:** VASI(V4L)—GA 3.0°TCH 27.2'. Trees.
   AIRPORT REMARKS: Attended 1400-2300Z‡. Later hours available on request. ACTIVATE MIRL Rwy 11-29 and VASI
      Rwy 11-29—122.8.
   COMMUNICATIONS: CTAF/UNICOM 122.8
      DOTHAN FSS (DHN) Toll free call dial 1-800-842-7511. NOTAM FILE DHN.
   ® **CAIRNS APP/DEP CON** 133.45
      RADIO AIDS TO NAVIGATION: NOTAM FILE DHN.
         CRESTVIEW (H) VORTAC 115.9 CEW Chan 106 30°49'34"N 86°40'45"W 024°32.4 NM to fld. 254/03E.
            NOTAM FILE CEW.
         (T)**VORW** 110.2 UIA 31°18'34"N 86°23'32"W at fld. VOR unusable 020°–050°. (VOR unmonitored)
         JUDD NDB (MHW) 264 JUY 31°18'15"N 86°23'27"W at fld.

§ **ANNISTON-CALHOUN CO** (ANB) 5.2 SW GMT−6(−5DT) 33°35'17"N 85°51'29"W **ATLANTA**
   611 B S4 **FUEL** 100LL, JET A OX 2 CFR Index A H-4G, L-14H
   RWY 05-23: H7001X150 (ASPH-GRVD) S-30, D-60 HIRL .34% up NE IAP
      RWY 05: VASI(V2L)—GA 3.0°TCH 52'. Trees. Rgt tfc.
      RWY 23: VASI(V2L)—GA 3.75°TCH 25'. Building.
   AIRPORT REMARKS: Attended 1300-0200Z‡. For service and fuel after 0200Z‡ call (205) 237-9586, service fee
      0200-1300Z‡. CAUTION-Large numbers of black birds on and in the vicinity of arpt dawn-dusk from Nov-Apr.
      CLOSED to unscheduled air carrier opr with more than 30 passenger seats except with prior approval call arpt
      manager 205-831-3831. Control Zone effective continuously.
   COMMUNICATIONS: CTAF 123.6   **UNICOM** 123.0
      ANNISTON FSS (ANB) on arpt. 123.6, 122.3, 122.2, 108.8T (205) 831-2303. NOTAM FILE ANB.
   ® **BIRMINGHAM APP/DEP CON** 124.95
      RADIO AIDS TO NAVIGATION: NOTAM FILE ANB. VHF/DF ctc Anniston FSS
         TALLADEGA (L) VORTAC 108.8 TDG Chan 25 33°34'30"N 86°02'34"W 082°9.4 NM to fld. 530/02E.
         NDB (MH) 278 ANB 33°35'25"N 85°51'04"W at fld. (out of svc indefinitely)
         ILS 111.5 I-ANB Rwy 05 localizer only

GLENS FALLS 43°20'30"N 73°36'44"W. NOTAM FILE GFL. **NEW YORK**
   (L) **VORTAC** 110.2 GFL Chan 39 at Warren Co. 320/14W. L-25C, 26F
      DME unusable 305°-315° beyond 35 NM below 7000' 315°-350° beyond 30 NM below 8000'
      VOR Portion unusable 175°-200° byd 20 NM blo 2500'.
   FSS (GFL) on Warren Co. 123.6 122.4 122.2 122.1R 518-793-2593.
   RCO 122.1R 110.2T (POUGHKEEPSIE FSS)

WASHINGTON

§ **DULLES INTL** (IAD) 20 W GMT−5(−4DT) 38°56'39"N 77°27'26"W **WASHINGTON**
   313 B S4 **FUEL** 100, JET A OX 1, 2, 3 LRA CFR Index E H3C, L-22G, 24G, 27D, 28E, A
   RWY 01L-19R: H11501X150 (CONC-GRVD) S-200, D-250, DT-450 HIRL CL IAP
      RWY 01L: MALSR. Building.   **RWY 19R:** SSALR. TDZ.
   RWY 01R-19L: H11500X150 (CONC-GRVD) S-200, D-250, DT-450 HIRL CL
      RWY 01R: ALSF2. TDZ. Building.   **RWY 19L:** MALSR.
   RWY 12-30: H10001X150 (CONC-GRVD) S-200, D-250, DT-450 HIRL
      RWY 12: MALSR. VASI(V4L)—GA 3.0°TCH 50'.
      RWY 30: REIL. VASI(V6L)—Upper GA 3.0°TCH 84', Lower GA 2.5°TCH 44'.
   RWY 11L-29R: H3080X75 (CONC) S-200, D-250, DT-450 Rwy designated on taxiway for day VFR use by prop. acft
      12,500 lbs or less.
   AIRPORT REMARKS: Attended continuously. Birds frequently on or in vicinity of arpt. Landing fee. 165' AGL crane lgtd
      and marked, located 2000' east Rwy 01R until March 1986. Acft using Jet ramp must clear for ground control.
      Itinerant acft 12,500 lbs or less contact FBO on UNICOM prior to landing. 4 NW of Chantilly, Va. Private pilot
      certificate required. See FAR 159.53. B747 opers shall be parked on N side of jet apron only. Acft shall not park on
      ramp position 23. B747 shall not taxi on T-1 or R-2. B747 acft may deviate from the standard clockwise flow of
      traffic on jet apron prior permission required from Dulles tower. Acft may request 180° turns into ramp position from
      twr. Acft 180° turns out of ramp positions prohibited. Flight Notification Service (ADCUS) available.
   WEATHER DATA SOURCES: LLWAS.
   COMMUNICATIONS: ATIS 134.85 (703-471-7127)   **UNICOM** 122.95
      WASHINGTON FSS (DCA) LC 557-2853 NOTAM FILE IAD
   ® **APP/DEP CON** 126.1 (007°-097°) 120.45 (098°-225°) 126.65 (226°-007°) 125.05 (W of 007° and 20 NM
      N-AML)
      TOWER 120.1   **GND CON** 121.9   **CLNC DEL** 127.35   **PRE TAXI CLNC** 127.35
      STAGE III SVC ctcAPP CON
   RADIO AIDS TO NAVIGATION: NOTAM FILE IAD.
      ARMEL (L) VORTAC 113.5 AML Chan 82 38°56'05"N 77°28'01"W at fld. 297/08W
      TILLE NDB (LOM) 346 IA 38°50'50"N 77°26'17"W 010° 4.6 NM to fld.
      ILS 111.3 I-DLX Rwy 19R
          111.3 I-OSZ Rwy 01L
          110.1 I-SGC Rwy 19L
          110.1 I-IAD Rwy 01R LOM TILLE NDB
          109.3 I-AJU Rwy 12
      ASR

Fig. 20-F. Sample airport and facility data from the *A/FD*. To be used with questions in this chapter.

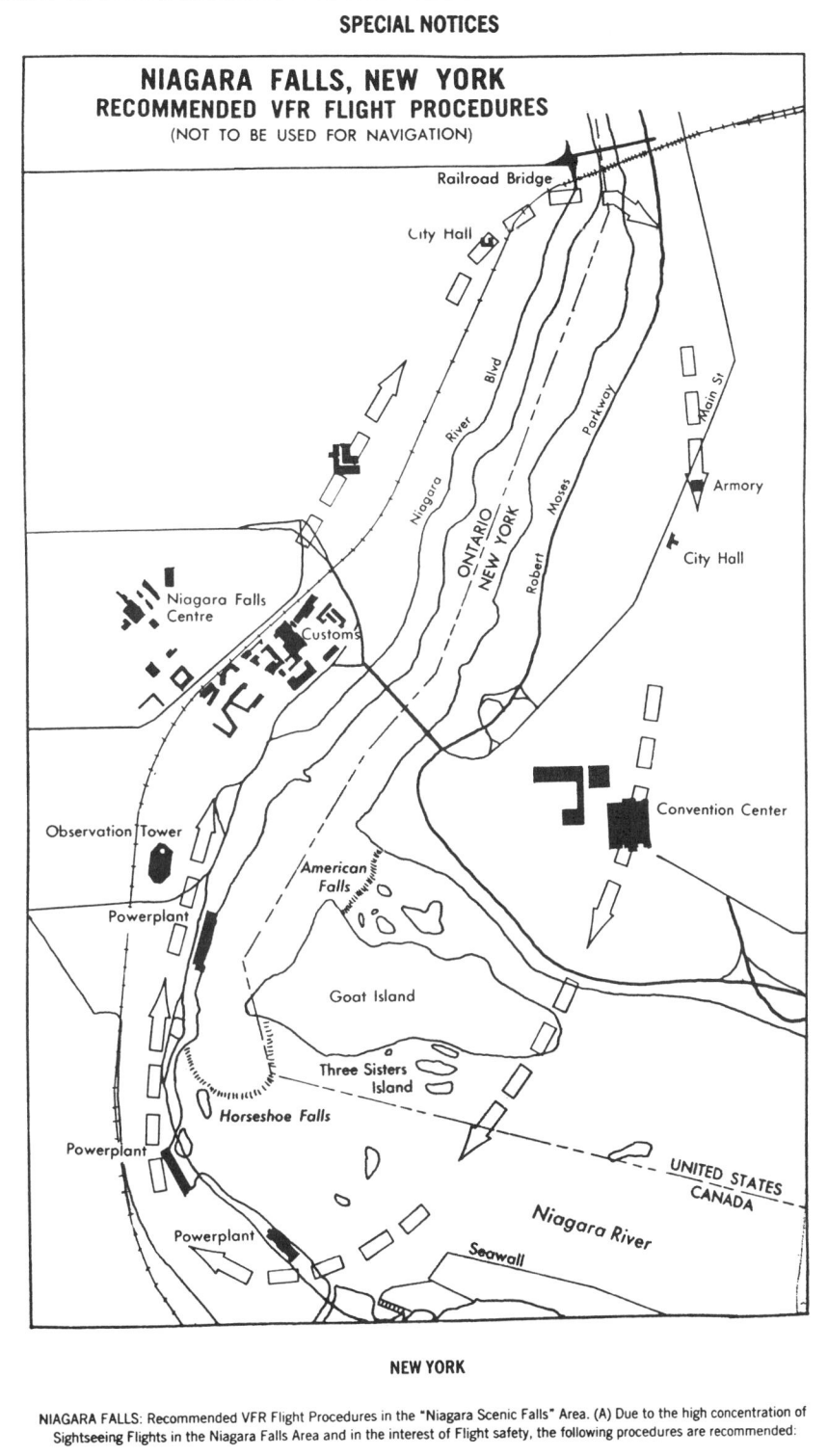

Fig. 20-G. A sample item from the Special Notices section of the *A/FD*. This one concerns VFR scenic flights in the Niagara Falls area.

and National Weather Service telephone numbers (Fig. 20-H); Air Route Traffic Control Centers (Fig. 20-I); General Aviation District Offices and Flight Standards District Offices (Fig. 20-J).

A listing of Preferred IFR Routes is carried in the *A/FD*, and these are designed to simplify IFR filing and to minimize route changing during flight. There is also a listing of Tower Enroute Control routes (IFR). Neither is included here, as these aren't for your use yet.

In Chapter 21 the VHF Omnirange (VOR) and methods of checking the VOR receiver will be covered;

FAA AND NWS TELEPHONE NUMBERS

Flight Service Station (FSS) numbers provide direct contact with an FAA pilot weather briefer.

Pilots Automatic Telephone Weather Answering Service (PATWAS) provides a recorded summary of weather conditions over a limited area in the vicinity of the associated facility.

Telephone Information Briefing Service (TIBS) provides continuous recordings of meteroligical and/or aeronautical information including area and/or route briefings, airspace procedures and special announcements. A touch-tone telephone is required to fully utilize this service.

Transcribed Weather Broadcast telephone numbers (TEL-TWEB) provide access to the transcribed weather broadcast on selected navigational facilities.

National Weather Service (WS) numbers will connect you with a national weather service pilot briefer.

Interim Voice Response System (IVRS), available in some metropolitan areas as listed at the end of this section provides selected weather products via computer voice-generated system on touch-tone telephones.

Further information can be found in the Airman's Information Manual, Chapter 6.

Numerous additional telephone numbers are listed under COMMUNICATIONS in the A/FD tabulation. If you wish to call an FSS, but do not have access to a directory listing, call the toll-free number, 1-800-555-1212.

FAST FILE FLIGHT PLAN SYSTEM

Some flight service stations have inaugurated this system for pilots who already have obtained a weather briefing and desire only to file a flight plan. Pilots may call the discrete telephone numbers listed and file flight plans in accordance with recorded taped instructions. IFR flight plans will be extracted and entered in the appropriate ARTCC computer. VFR flight plans will be retained at the FSS for activation by the pilot. This equipment is designed to automatically disconnect after 8 seconds of no transmission, so pilots are instructed to speak at a normal speech rate without lengthy pauses between flight plan elements. Pilots are urged to file flight plans into this system at least 30 minutes in advance of proposed departure.

★ PATWAS or TIBS
■ TWEB
◆ Restricted Number for Aviation Weather Information
§§ Fast File (Flight Plan Filing Only)

Location and Identifier		Area Code	Telephone
TENNESSEE			
Chattanooga	WS	(615)	892-6302 ◆
Crossville CSV (Mem)	FSS	(615)	484-9541
Dyersburg DYR	FSS	(901)	285-4842
INWATS (TN Statewide)			1-800-345-7944
			(1200-0400Z‡ Others hrs. Jackson)
Jackson MKL (McKellar)	FSS	(901)	422-1522
INWATS (WEST TN)			1-800-WX-BRIEF
Knoxville TYS (McGhee Tyson)	FSS	(615)	970-3066
Alcoa-Maryville		(615)	970-3066
Morristown		(615)	581-2420
INWATS (TN statewide)		(800)	362-9800
Nashville BNA	FSS	(615)	360-3619
INWATS (TN Statewide)			1-800-WX-BRIEF
Local Area		(615)	360-2344 ★
Tri City TRI (Bristol)	FSS	(615)	323-6204
			(1100-0300Z‡)

Fig. 20-H. Flight Service Stations and National Weather Service numbers (*A/FD*). Chapter 22 covers weather services available.

Figure 20-K shows a sample of the type of information you would use in running such a check. You may want to take another look at this illustration after reading the material in Chapter 21 of this book and *SPFM*.

Figures 20-L and 20-M are samples of Parachute Jumping Areas and an Aeronautical Chart Bulletin.

Enroute Flight Advisory Service (EFAS) information is shown on a map of the states covered by a particular *A/FD* (Fig. 20-N).

AIR ROUTE TRAFFIC CONTROL CENTERS

® **MEMPHIS CENTER** - 134.25 124.35 120.85 119.3   H-3-4, L-6-8-14-17-21
   Brinkley - 126.85
   Columbus - 135.3 127.1 124.25   (KZME)
   Fayetteville - 132.55
   Graham - 132.35 125.85
   Greenville - 135.7 132.5 123.75
   Harrison - 126.1
   Huntsville - 120.8
   Jackson - 132.1
   McKellar - 134.65 126.45
   Nashville - 133.6 126.75 125.4
   South Fulton - 135.5 128.05
   Tupelo - 135.9 134.4 128.5
   Walnut Ridge - 133.0

Fig. 20-I. Memphis Air Route Traffic Control Center frequencies as shown in the *A/FD*. Each center is broken down into sectors, each with an assigned frequency. IFR traffic is switched to each sector's frequency as it moves into it enroute. You'll be using this material after you get the instrument rating.

GADOs AND FSDOs

**GENERAL AVIATION DISTRICT OFFICES (GADO) AND
FLIGHT STANDARDS DISTRICT OFFICES (FSDO)**

The following is a list of GADOs and FSDOs in the area of coverage of this Directory. (FSDOs also perform the same functions as GADOs. All locations listed are GADOs unless specifically identified as FSDOs.) Address letters to Chief, General Aviation District Office or Chief, Flight Standards District Office—Federal Aviation Administration.

Flight Standards personnel in these offices are responsible for serving the aviation industry and the general public on all matters relating to the certification and operation of general aviation aircraft.

TENNESSEE

Flight Standards District Office
International Airport General Aviation Bldg.
Room 137
2488 Winchester Road
Memphis, Tennessee 38130
Telephone: 901-345-0600

Flight Standards District Office
Nashville Metropolitan Airport
322 Knapp Blvd., Room 101
Nashville, Tennessee 37217
Telephone: 615-251-5661

Fig. 20-J. GADO and FSDO telephone numbers for FAA offices in Tennessee (*A/FD*). Other southeastern states would also be included in the full listing.

VOR RECEIVER CHECK
VOR RECEIVER CHECK POINTS
AND
VOR TEST FACILITIES (VOT)

The use of VOR airborne and ground check points is explained in Airman's Information Manual. Basic Flight Information and ATC Procedures.

NOTE: Under columns headed "Type of Check Point" & "Type of VOT Facility" G stands for ground. A/ stands for airborne followed by figures (2300 or (1000-3000) indicating the altitudes above mean sea level at which the check should be conducted. Facilities are listed in alphabetical order, in the state where the check points or VOTs are located.

TENNESSEE

VOR RECEIVER CHECK POINTS

Facility Name (Arpt Name)	Freq/Ident	Type Check Pt. Gnd. AB/ALT	Azimuth from Fac. Mag	Dist. from Fac. N.M.	Check Point Description
Chattanooga (Lovell Field)	115.8/CHA	G	338	5.1	On cntrin S twy 175' NE of cntrin rwy 32.
Dyersburg Muni	116.8/DYR	G	250	4.2	At intersection of ramp and center twy.
Hinch Mountain (Crossville Memorial)	117.6/HCH	A/2900	333	11	Over metal hangar.
Holston Mountain (Tri-City)	114.6/HMV	G	284	13.7	On ramp S of terminal building.
Jacks Creek (Franklin Wilkins)	109.4/JKS	A/1800	320	7.5	Over 785' rdo twr.
Jacks Creek (McKellar Field)	109.4/JKS	A/1500	268	27	Over rotg beacon.
McKellar	112.0/MKL	G	254	0.5	At intersection of S twy and ramp.

VOR TEST FACILITIES (VOT)

Facility Name (Airport Name)	Freq.	Type VOT Facility	Remarks
Knoxville (McGhee-Tyson)	112.0	G	
Memphis Intl	111.0	G	
Nashville Metro	111.0	G	

Fig. 20-K. VHF Omnirange (VOR) checkpoints and test facilities for Tennessee (*A/FD*). Chapter 21 of this book and *SPFM* explain how the VOR works and cover the accuracy requirements for checking the airplane's VOR receiver(s).

PARACHUTE JUMPING AREAS

The following tabulation lists all reported parachute jumping sites in the area of coverage of this directory. Unless otherwise indicated, all activities are conducted during daylight hours and under VFR conditions. The busiest periods of activity are normally on weekends and holidays, but jumps can be expected at anytime during the week at the locations listed. Jumps within restricted airspace are not listed.

All times are local and altitudes MSL unless otherwise specified.

Refer to Federal Aviation Regulations, Part 105 for required procedures relating to parachute jumping.

Organizations desiring listing of their jumping activities in this publication should contact the nearest FAA facility (FSS, tower, or ARTCC).

Qualified parachute jumping sites will be depicted on sectional charts.

Note: (c) in this publication indicates that the parachute jump area is charted.

To qualify for charting, a jump area must meet the following criteria:
   (1) Been in operation for at least 1 year.
   (2) Operate year round (at least on weekends).
   (3) Log 4,000 or more jumps each year.

In addition, jump sites can be nominated by FAA Regions if special circumstances require charting.

LOCATION	DISTANCE AND RADIAL FROM NEAREST VOR/VORTAC	MAXIMUM ALTITUDE	REMARKS
TENNESSEE			
Chattanooga	13 NM; 087° Chattanooga	10,000	Continuous
Clarksville, Outlaw Fld	Over Clarksville	12,500 AGL	2 NM radius. Daily SR-SS, occasional ngts.
Cookeville, Putnam County Arpt	32 NM; 214° Livingston	12,500	Weekends SR-SS.
Fort Campbell, Son Drop Zone	4.1 NM; 302° Clarksville	12,500	Daily.
(c) Jonesboro, Decker Farm Arpt	22 NM; 233° Holston Mt.	14,000	5 NM radius. Daily SR-SS occasional ngts.
(c) Lafayette	43 NM; 050° Nashville	12,500 AGL	Weekends SR-SS 10 NM radius
Livingston Arpt	13 NM; 212° Livingston	12,500	Weekends
Springfield Muni Arpt	27 NM; 336° Nashville	12,500	Weekends and holidays SR-SS

Fig. 20-L. Parachute jumping areas (*A/FD*). Later in this book a cross-country flight will be discussed and part of the route will pass about 12 NM south of the Cookeville–Putnam County Airport. Parachute jumping will be done there from 12,500 feet MSL to the *surface* (naturally) from sunrise to sunset on weekends.

AERONAUTICAL CHART BULLETIN

The purpose of this Bulletin is to provide a tabulation of the major changes in aeronautical information that have occurred since the last publication date of each Sectional Aeronautical Chart and Terminal Area Chart listed. The general policy is to include only those changes to controlled airspace and special use airspace that present a hazardous condition or impose a restriction on the pilot; major changes to airports and radio navigational facilities, thereby providing the VFR pilot with the essential data necessary to update and maintain his chart current. When the Aeronautical Chart is republished, the corrective tabulation will be removed from this Bulletin. Inasmuch as this Bulletin provides major changes only; pilots should consult the airport listing in this directory for all new information. Users of U.S. World Aeronautical Charts (WAC) and U.S. Gulf Coast VFR Aeronautical Charts should make appropriate revisions to their charts from this Bulletin. NOTE: New data which have been added to this issue are shown below the rule line under the appropriate chart.

Military Training Routes (MTRs) are shown on Sectional Aeronautical Charts and VFR Terminal Area Charts. Only the route centerline, direction of flight and the route designator are shown — route widths and altitudes are not shown. Since these routes are subject to change every 56 days and the charts are reissued every 6 months, routes with a change in the alignment of the charted route centerline will be listed in this Aeronautical Chart Bulletin below. You are advised to contact the nearest FSS for route dimensions and current status for those routes effecting your flight.

ATLANTA SECTIONAL
26th Edition, April 16, 19____

Revise FORT STEWART B MOA BEGINNING AT 31-51-30N 081-41-45W TO 31-51-00N 081-41-45W TO 31-51-00N 082-00-00W TO 32-05-00N 081-57-00W TO 32-11-00N 081-46-00W TO 32-10-00N 081-39-00W TO 32-06-30N 081-35-00W TO 32-07-00N 081-43-30W TO 32-07-28N 081-47-17W TO 32-05-24N 081-50-03W TO 32-02-59N 081-51-26W TO 32-02-21N 081-50-42W TO 31-59-45N 081-51-06W TO 31-57-00N 081-53-15W TO 31-55-30N 081-53-00W TO 31-55-00N 081-53-00W THENCE TO POINT OF BEGINNING. REST OF DATA UNCHANGED.

Add obst. 920' MSL (500' AGL) UC 34°07'10"N, 81°03'16"W. Add obst. 1750' MSL (755' AGL) UC 35°27'11"N, 86°08'20"W. Add obst. 1649' MSL (869' AGL) UC 34°32'55"N, 82°33'33"W. Add obst. 990' MSL (500' AGL) UC 34°08'50"N, 81°02'55"W. Add obst. 1160' MSL (420' AGL) UC 34°31'52"N, 82°36'50"W.

Revise Merdian 1 East MOA; BEGINNING AT 33-25-00N 088-00-00W TO 33-18-30N 087-49-20W TO 33-11-00N 087-48-30W TO 33-07-30N 087-53-30W TO 33-03-35N 087-59-10W TO 32-51-12N 088-17-11W THENCE VIA A 45 DME ARC CLOCKWISE OF THE TUSCALOOSA VORTAC TO 33-23-48N 088-25-04W THENCE TO POINT OF BEGINNING.

Fig. 20-M. Aeronautical chart bulletin (*A/FD*). The data is there, but it's wondered what student or private pilot would actually revise and mark in, for instance, the Fort Stewart MOA boundaries. But at least you've been warned about changes and the obstruction notice could be vital information for a transient pilot who plans to be passing through that area.

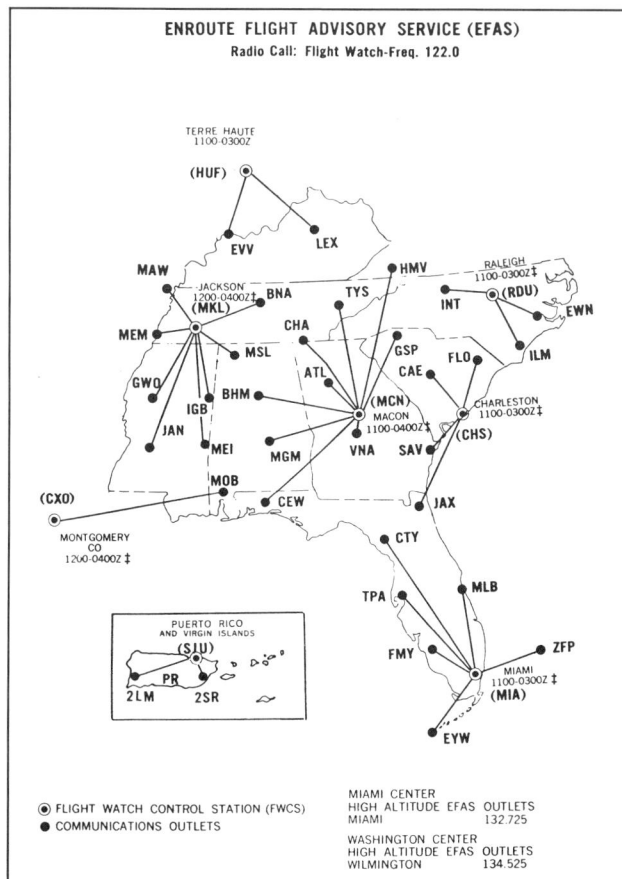

Fig. 20-N. Enroute Flight Advisory Service locations in the southeastern United States. More details about this are in Chapter 21 and 22.

AIRMAN'S INFORMATION MANUAL—BASIC
FLIGHT INFORMATION AND
ATC PROCEDURES

The *Airman's Information Manual—Basic Flight Information and ATC Procedures* (hereafter referred to as *AIM*, for obvious reasons) contains, as implied, basic flight information and air traffic control (ATC) procedures for use in the United States. Material in this publication has fundamental information that doesn't change as rapidly as other data. It is issued every 16 weeks and has such material as health and medical facts, factors affecting flight safety, a pilot-controller glossary of terms used in the ATC system, and information on safety as well as accident and hazard reporting.

Figure 20-O shows the full Table of Contents of *AIM* to give an idea of the coverage, but detail will be covered here only for certain information of more interest to the student and private VFR pilot (page references have been deleted). The main point is for you to see what is available for further information in *AIM*. Your flight school should have a copy available for your use.

Review the various types of airspace limits so that you can tie them together as the need arises. Figures 20-P, 20-Q, 20-R, and 20-S from *AIM* may help you see the way things are laid out. (Also see Fig. 21-14, *SPFM*.)

Fig. 20-O. A general look at the Table of Contents of *AIM*. By the time you read this there may have been some deletions or additions to the subject matter.

Chapter 1. NAVIGATION AIDS

Section 1. AIR NAVIGATION RADIO AIDS

1. GENERAL
2. NONDIRECTIONAL RADIO BEACON (NDB)
3. VHF OMNI-DIRECTIONAL RANGE (VOR)
4. VOR RECEIVER CHECK
5. TACTICAL AIR NAVIGATION (TACAN)
6. VHF OMNI-DIRECTIONAL RANGE/TACTICAL AIR NAVIGATION (VORTAC)
7. DISTANCE MEASURING EQUIPMENT (DME)

8-9. RESERVED

10. CLASS OF NAVAIDS
11. MARKER BEACON
12. INSTRUMENT LANDING SYSTEM (ILS)
13. SIMPLIFIED DIRECTIONAL FACILITY (SDF)
14. INTERIM STANDARD MICROWAVE LANDING SYSTEM (ISMLS)
15. MAINTENANCE OF FAA NAVAIDS
16. NAVAIDS WITH VOICE

17-18. RESERVED

19. USER REPORTS ON NAVAID PERFORMANCE
20. LORAN
21. OMEGA AND OMEGA/VLF NAVIGATION SYSTEMS
22. VHF DIRECTION FINDER

23-29. RESERVED

Section 2. RADAR SERVICES AND PROCEDURES

30. RADAR
31. AIR TRAFFIC CONTROL RADAR BEACON SYSTEM (ATCRBS)
32. SURVEILLANCE RADAR
33. PRECISION APPROACH RADAR (PAR)

34-39. RESERVED

Chapter 2. AERONAUTICAL LIGHTING AND AIRPORT MARKING AIDS

Section 1. AIRPORT LIGHTING AIDS

40. APPROACH LIGHT SYSTEMS (ALS)
41. VISUAL APPROACH SLOPE INDICATOR (VASI)
42. OTHER VISUAL APPROACH SLOPE SYSTEMS
43. RUNWAY END IDENTIFIER LIGHTS (REIL)
44. RUNWAY EDGE LIGHT SYSTEMS
45. IN-RUNWAY LIGHTING
46. CONTROL OF LIGHTING SYSTEMS
47. PILOT CONTROL OF AIRPORT LIGHTING
48. AIRPORT ROTATING BEACON
49. RESERVED

Section 2. AIR NAVIGATION AND OBSTRUCTION LIGHTING

50. AERONAUTICAL LIGHT BEACONS
51. AUXILIARY LIGHTS
52. OBSTRUCTION LIGHTS

53-59. RESERVED

Section 3. AIRPORT MARKING AIDS

60. AIRPORT MARKING AIDS
61. AIRCRAFT ARRESTING DEVICES

62-69. RESERVED

Chapter 3. AIRSPACE

Section 1. GENERAL

70. GENERAL
71. GENERAL DIMENSIONS OF AIRSPACE SEGMENTS

72-79. RESERVED

Section 2. UNCONTROLLED AIRSPACE

80. GENERAL
81. VFR REQUIREMENTS
82. IFR REQUIREMENTS
83. MINIMUM VFR VISIBILITY AND DISTANCE FROM CLOUDS
84. ALTITUDES AND FLIGHT LEVELS

85-89. RESERVED

Section 3. CONTROLLED AIRSPACE

90. GENERAL
91. CONTINENTAL CONTROL AREA
92. CONTROL AREAS
93. POSITIVE CONTROL AREA
94. TRANSITION AREAS
95. CONTROL ZONES
96. TERMINAL CONTROL AREA
97. TERMINAL CONTROL AREA (TCA) OPERATIONS
98. IFR ALTITUDES AND FLIGHT LEVELS
99. VFR REQUIREMENTS

100-109. RESERVED

Section 4. SPECIAL USE AIRSPACE

110. GENERAL
111. PROHIBITED AREA
112. RESTRICTED AREA
113. WARNING AREA
114. MILITARY OPERATIONS AREAS (MOA)
115. ALERT AREA
116. CONTROLLED FIRING AREAS
117. PARACHUTE JUMP AIRCRAFT OPERATIONS

118-129. RESERVED

Section 5. OTHER AIRSPACE AREAS

130. AIRPORT TRAFFIC AREAS
131. AIRPORT ADVISORY AREA
132. MILITARY TRAINING ROUTES (MTR)
133. TEMPORARY FLIGHT RESTRICTIONS

134-149. RESERVED

Chapter 4. AIR TRAFFIC CONTROL

Section 1. SERVICES AVAILABLE TO PILOTS

150. AIR ROUTE TRAFFIC CONTROL CENTERS
151. CONTROL TOWERS
152. FLIGHT SERVICE STATIONS
153. RECORDING AND MONITORING
154. COMMUNICATIONS RELEASE OF IFR AIRCRAFT LANDING AT AN AIRPORT NOT SERVED BY AN OPERATING TOWER
155. PILOT VISITS TO AIR TRAFFIC FACILITIES
156. VFR ADVISORY SERVICE
157. AIRPORT ADVISORY PRACTICES AT NONTOWER AIRPORTS
158. AERONAUTICAL ADVISORY STATIONS (UNICOM)
159. RESERVED
160. AERONAUTICAL MULTICOM SERVICE
161. AUTOMATIC TERMINAL INFORMATION SERVICE (ATIS)
162. RADAR TRAFFIC INFORMATION SERVICE
163. SAFETY ADVISORY
164. RADAR ASSISTANCE TO VFR AIRCRAFT
165. TERMINAL RADAR PROGRAMS FOR VFR AIRCRAFT

166-169. RESERVED

170. TRANSPONDER OPERATION
171. HAZARDOUS AREA REPORTING SERVICE

172-189. RESERVED

Section 2. RADIO COMMUNICATIONS PHRASEOLOGY AND TECHNIQUES

190. GENERAL
191. RADIO TECHNIQUE
192. CONTACT PROCEDURES
193. AIRCRAFT CALL SIGNS
194. DESCRIPTION OF INTERCHANGE OR LEASED AIRCRAFT
195. GROUND STATION CALL SIGNS
196. PHONETIC ALPHABET

197-199. RESERVED

200. FIGURES
201. ALTITUDES AND FLIGHT LEVELS
202. DIRECTIONS
203. SPEEDS
204. TIME
205. COMMUNICATIONS WITH TOWER WHEN AIRCRAFT TRANSMITTER/RECEIVER OR BOTH ARE INOPERATIVE
206. COMMUNICATIONS FOR VFR FLIGHTS

207-219. RESERVED

Section 3. AIRPORT OPERATIONS

220. GENERAL
221. TOWER CONTROLLED AIRPORTS
222. UNCONTROLLED AIRPORTS
223. TRAFFIC PATTERNS
224. UNEXPECTED MANEUVERS IN THE AIRPORT TRAFFIC PATTERN
225. WIND DIRECTION AND VELOCITY
226. USE OF RUNWAYS
227. LOW-LEVEL WIND SHEAR ALERT SYSTEM
228. BRAKING ACTION REPORTS
229. RESERVED
230. INTERSECTION TAKEOFFS

Chapter 20. The Chart and Other Printed Aids

231. SIMULTANEOUS OPERATIONS ON INTERSECTING RUNWAYS
232. LOW APPROACH
233. TRAFFIC CONTROL LIGHT SIGNALS
234. AIRPORT ROTATING BEACON
235. COMMUNICATIONS
236. GATE HOLDING DUE TO DEPARTURE DELAYS
237. VFR FLIGHTS IN TERMINAL AREAS
238–239. RESERVED
240. FUEL ADVISORY DEPARTURE (FAD) PROCEDURES
241. TAXIING
242. TAXI DURING LOW VISIBILITY
243. EXITING THE RUNWAY AFTER LANDING
244. PRACTICE INSTRUMENT APPROACHES
245. OPTION APPROACH
246. USE OF AIRCRAFT LIGHTS
247. HAND SIGNALS
248–259. RESERVED

Section 4. ATC CLEARANCE/SEPARATIONS

260. CLEARANCE
261. CLEARANCE PREFIX
262. CLEARANCE ITEMS
263. AMENDED CLEARANCES
264. SPECIAL VFR CLEARANCES
265. PILOT RESPONSIBILITY UPON CLEARANCE ISSUANCE
266. IFR CLEARANCE WITH VFR RESTRICTIONS
267–269. RESERVED
270. ADHERENCE TO CLEARANCE
271. IFR SEPARATION STANDARDS
272. SPEED ADJUSTMENTS
273. RUNWAY SEPARATION
274. VISUAL SEPARATION
275. USE OF VISUAL CLEARING PROCEDURES
276–289. RESERVED

Section 5. PREFLIGHT

290. PREFLIGHT PREPARATION
291. FOLLOW IFR PROCEDURES EVEN WHEN OPERATING VFR
292. VFR AT NIGHT
293. AIRCRAFT CHECKLISTS
294. NOTICE TO AIRMEN (NOTAM) SYSTEM
295. FLIGHT PLAN—VFR FLIGHTS
296. FLIGHT PLAN—DEFENSE VFR (DVFR) FLIGHTS
297. COMPOSITE FLIGHT PLAN (VFR-IFR FLIGHTS)
298. FLIGHT PLAN—IFR FLIGHTS
299. FLIGHTS OUTSIDE THE UNITED STATES AND U.S. TERRITORIES
300. CHANGE IN FLIGHT PLAN
301. CHANGE IN PROPOSED DEPARTURE TIME
302. CLOSING VFR/DVFR FLIGHT PLANS
303. CANCELLING IFR FLIGHT PLAN
304. GENERAL INSTRUCTIONS FOR THE FAA FLIGHT PLAN FORM
305–319. RESERVED

Section 6. DEPARTURE PROCEDURES

320. PRE-TAXI CLEARANCE PROCEDURES
321. TAXI CLEARANCE
322. ABBREVIATED IFR DEPARTURE CLEARANCE (CLEARED...AS FILED) PROCEDURES
323. CLEARANCE VOID TIMES
324. DEPARTURE CONTROL
325. INSTRUMENT DEPARTURES
326–339. RESERVED

Section 7. EN ROUTE PROCEDURES

340. ARTCC COMMUNICATIONS
341. POSITION REPORTING
342. ADDITIONAL REPORTS
343. AIRWAYS AND ROUTE SYSTEMS
344. AIRWAY OR ROUTE COURSE CHANGES
345. CHANGEOVER POINTS (COP's)
346. OPERATION IN RESTRICTED AIRSPACE
347. HOLDING
348–359. RESERVED

Section 8. ARRIVAL PROCEDURES

360. STANDARD TERMINAL ARRIVAL (STARS)
361. LOCAL FLOW TRAFFIC MANAGEMENT PROGRAM
362. APPROACH CONTROL
363. ADVANCE INFORMATION ON INSTRUMENT APPROACH
364. INSTRUMENT APPROACH PROCEDURE CHARTS
365. APPROACH CLEARANCE
366–369. RESERVED

370. INSTRUMENT APPROACH PROCEDURES
371. PROCEDURE TURN
372. TIMED APPROACHES FROM A HOLDING FIX
373. RADAR APPROACHES
374. RADAR MONITORING OF INSTRUMENT APPROACHES
375. SIMULTANEOUS ILS APPROACHES
376. PARALLEL APPROACHES
377–379. RESERVED
380. SIDE-STEP MANEUVER
381. WEATHER MINIMUMS
382. MISSED APPROACH
383. VISUAL APPROACH
384. CONTACT APPROACH
385. LANDING PRIORITY
386–399. RESERVED

Section 9. PILOT/CONTROLLER ROLES AND RESPONSIBILITIES

400. GENERAL
401. AIR TRAFFIC CLEARANCE
402. CONTACT APPROACH
403. INSTRUMENT APPROACH
404. MISSED APPROACH
405. RADAR VECTORS
406. SAFETY ADVISORY
407. SEE AND AVOID
408. SPEED ADJUSTMENTS
409. TRAFFIC ADVISORIES (Traffic Information)
410. VISUAL APPROACH
411. VISUAL SEPARATION
412. INSTRUMENT DEPARTURES
413. MINIMUM FUEL ADVISORY
414–429. RESERVED

Section 10. NATIONAL SECURITY AND INTERCEPTION PROCEDURES

430. NATIONAL SECURITY
431. INTERCEPTION PROCEDURES
432. INTERCEPTION SIGNALS
433. ADIZ BOUNDARIES AND DESIGNATED MOUNTAINOUS AREAS
434–439. RESERVED

Chapter 5. EMERGENCY PROCEDURES

Section 1. GENERAL

440. PILOT RESPONSIBILITIES AND AUTHORITY
441. EMERGENCY CONDITION-REQUEST ASSISTANCE IMMEDIATELY
442–449. RESERVED

Section 2. EMERGENCY SERVICES AVILABLE TO PILOTS

450. RADAR SERVICE FOR VFR AIRCRAFT IN DIFFICULTY
451. TRANSPONDER EMERGENCY OPERATION
452. DIRECTION FINDING INSTRUMENT APPROACH PROCEDURE
453. INTERCEPT AND ESCORT
454. EMERGENCY LOCATOR TRANSMITTERS
455. FAA SPONSORED EXPLOSIVES DETECTION (DOG/HANDLER TEAM) LOCATIONS
456. SEARCH AND RESCUE
457–459. RESERVED

Section 3. DISTRESS AND URGENCY PROCEDURES

460. DISTRESS AND URGENCY COMMUNICATIONS
461. OBTAINING EMERGENCY ASSISTANCE
462. DITCHING PROCEDURES
463. SPECIAL EMERGENCY (AIR PIRACY)
464. FUEL DUMPING
465–469. RESERVED

Section 4. TWO-WAY RADIO COMMUNICATIONS FAILURE

470. TWO-WAY RADIO COMMUNICATIONS FAILURE
471. TRANSPONDER OPERATION DURING TWO-WAY COMMUNICATIONS FAILURE
472. REESTABLISHING RADIO CONTACT
473–499. RESERVED

Chapter 6. SAFETY OF FLIGHT

Section 1. METEOROLOGY

500. GENERAL
501. IN-FLIGHT WEATHER ADVISORIES
502. PREFLIGHT BRIEFING SERVICE
503. PILOTS AUTOMATIC TELEPHONE WEATHER ANSWERING SERVICE (PATWAS)
504. FLIGHT SERVICE STATION PREFLIGHT BRIEFING
505. EN ROUTE FLIGHT ADVISORY SERVICE (EFAS)
506. TRANSCRIBED WEATHER BROADCASTS (TWEB)
507. SCHEDULED WEATHER BROADCASTS (SWB)
508–509. RESERVED

510. WEATHER RADAR SERVICES
511. ATC IN-FLIGHT WEATHER AVOIDANCE ASSISTANCE
512. RUNWAY VISUAL RANGE (RVR)
513. REPORTING OF CLOUD HEIGHTS
514. REPORTING PREVAILING VISIBILITY
515. ESTIMATING INTENSITY OF PRECIPITATION
516. ESTIMATING INTENSITY OF DRIZZLE
517. ESTIMATING INTENSITY OF SNOW
518–519. RESERVED
520. PILOT WEATHER REPORTS (PIREP's)
521. PIREPS RELATING TO AIRFRAME ICING
522. PIREPS RELATING TO TURBULENCE
523. WIND SHEAR PIREPS
524. CLEAR AIR TURBULENCE (CAT) PIREPS
525. THUNDERSTORMS
526. THUNDERSTORM FLYING
527. KEY TO AVIATION WEATHER OBSERVATIONS AND FORECASTS
528–529. RESERVED

Section 2. ALTIMETER SETTING PROCEDURES
530. GENERAL
531. PROCEDURES
532. ALTIMETER ERRORS
533–539. RESERVED

Section 3. WAKE TURBULENCE
540. GENERAL
541. VORTEX GENERATION
542. VORTEX STRENGTH
543. VORTEX BEHAVIOR
544. OPERATIONS PROBLEM AREAS
545. VORTEX AVOIDANCE PROCEDURES
546–549. RESERVED
550. HELICOPTERS
551. PILOT RESPONSIBILITY
552. AIR TRAFFIC WAKE TURBULENCE SEPARATIONS
553–559. RESERVED

Section 4. BIRD HAZARD AND MIGRATORY PATTERNS
560. BIRD HAZARDS
561. MIGRATORY PATTERNS
562. REPORTING BIRD STRIKES OR INCIDENTS
563. WILDLIFE REFUGE AREAS
564. NOISE-SENSITIVE AREAS
565–569. RESERVED

Section 5. POTENTIAL FLIGHT HAZARDS
570. ACCIDENT CAUSE FACTORS
571. VFR IN CONGESTED AREAS
572. AVOID FLIGHT BENEATH UNMANNED BALLOONS
573. MOUNTAIN FLYING
574–579. RESERVED

Section 6. SAFETY, ACCIDENT AND HAZARD REPORTS
580. AVIATION SAFETY REPORTING PROGRAM
581. AIRCRAFT ACCIDENT AND INCIDENT REPORTING
582. NEAR MIDAIR COLLISION REPORTING
583–599. RESERVED

Chapter 7. MEDICAL FACTS FOR PILOTS
Section 1. FITNESS FOR FLIGHT
600. FITNESS FOR FLIGHT
601. EFFECTS OF ALTITUDE
602. HYPERVENTILATION IN FLIGHT
603. CARBON MONOXIDE POISONING IN FLIGHT
604. ILLUSIONS IN FLIGHT
605. VISION IN FLIGHT
606–619. RESERVED

Chapter 8. AERONAUTICAL CHARTS AND RELATED PUBLICATIONS
Section 1. TYPES OF CHARTS AVAILABLE
620. GENERAL
621. OBTAINING AERONAUTICAL CHARTS
622. TYPES OF CHARTS AVAILABLE
623. GENERAL DESCRIPTION OF EACH CHART SERIES
624. RELATED PUBLICATIONS
625. AUXILIARY CHARTS
626–999. RESERVED

SUPPLEMENT
PILOT CONTROLLER GLOSSARY

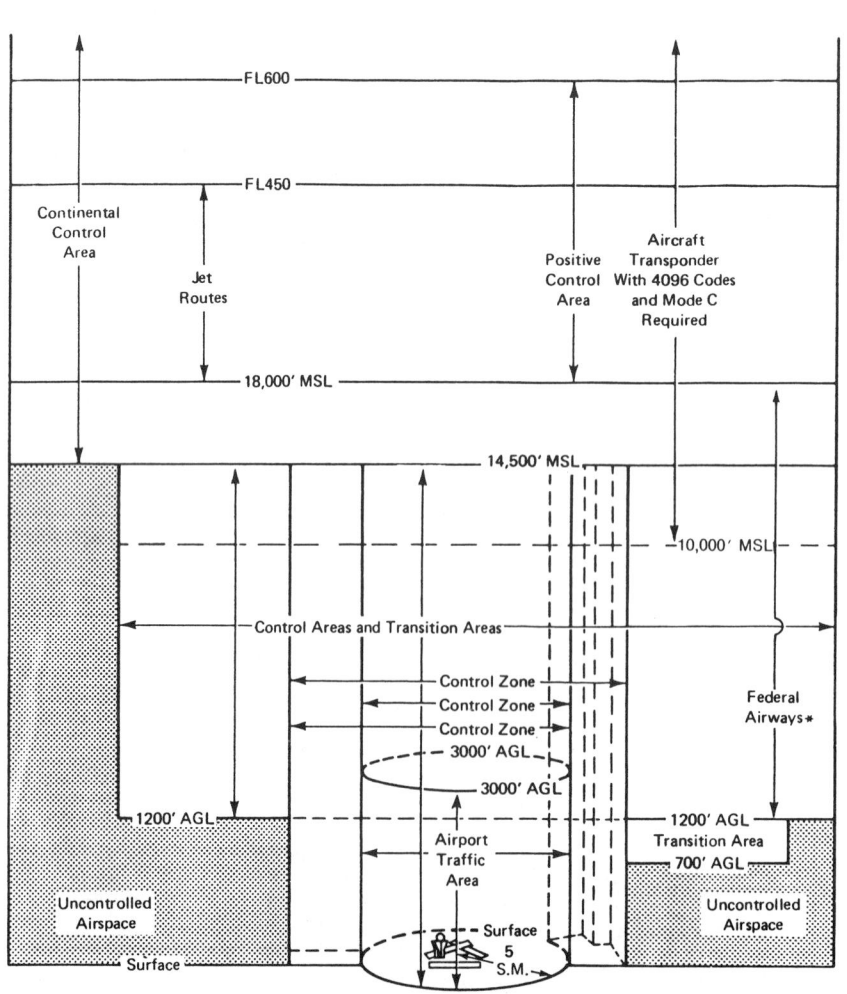

Fig. 20-P. Airspace boundaries (*AIM*).

Chapter 20. The Chart and Other Printed Aids   65

CONTROLLED AIRSPACE

90. GENERAL

Controlled airspace consists of those areas designated as Continental Control Area, Control Area, Control Zones, Terminal Control Areas and Transition Areas, within which some or all aircraft may be subject to ATC. Safety, users' needs, and volume of flight operations are some of the factors considered in the designation of controlled airspace. When so designated, the airspace is supported by ground to air communications, navigation aids, and air traffic services.

91. CONTINENTAL CONTROL AREA

The Continental Control Area consists of the airspace of the 48 contiguous States, the District of Columbia and Alaska, excluding the Alaska peninsula west of longitude 160 degrees 00 minutes 00 seconds W, at and above 14,500 feet MSL, but does not include:

   a. The airspace less than 1,500 feet above the surface of the earth; or

   b. Prohibited and Restricted areas, other than the Restricted areas listed in FAR 71 Subpart D.

92. CONTROL AREAS

Control areas consist of the airspace designated as Colored Federal airways, VOR Federal airways, Additional Control Areas, and Control Area Extensions, but do not include the Continental Control Area. Unless otherwise designated, control areas also include the airspace between a segment of a main VOR airway and its associated alternate segments. The vertical extent of the various categories of airspace contained in control area is defined in FAR 71.

93. POSITIVE CONTROL AREA

Positive control a ea is airspace so designated as positive control area in FAR 71.193. This area includes specified airspace within the conterminous U.S. from 18,000 feet to and including FL 600, excluding Santa Barbara Island, Farallon Island, and that portion south of latitude 25 degrees 04 minutes north. In Alaska, it includes the airspace over the State of Alaska from 18,000 feet to and including FL 600, but not including the airspace less than 1,500 feet above the surface of the earth and the Alaskan Peninsula west of longitude 160 degrees 00 minutes west. Rules for operating in positive control area are found in FAR 91.97 and FAR 91.24.

94. TRANSITION AREAS

   a. Transition areas are designated to contain IFR operations in controlled airspace during portions of the terminal operation and while transitioning between the terminal and en route environments.

   b. Transition areas are controlled airspace extending upward from 700 feet or more above the surface when designated in conjunction with an airport for which an instrument approach procedure has been prescribed; or from 1,200 feet or more above the surface when designated in conjunction with airway route structures or segments. Unless specified otherwise, transition areas terminate at the base of overlying controlled airspace.

95. CONTROL ZONES

   a. Control zones are controlled airspace which extend upward from the surface and terminate at the base of the continental control area. Control zones that do not underlie the continental control area have no upper limit. A control zone may include one or more airports and is normally a circular area within a radius of 5 statute miles and any extensions necessary to include instrument departure and arrival paths.

   b. Control zones are depicted on charts (for example, on the sectional charts the control zone is outlined by a broken blue line). If a control zone is effective only during certain hours of the day (a part-time control zone) this fact will also be noted on the charts.

Fig. 20-Q. Controlled airspace (*AIM*).

MINIMUM VFR VISIBILITY AND DISTANCE FROM CLOUDS

ALTITUDE	UNCONTROLLED AIRSPACE		CONTROLLED AIRSPACE	
	Flight Visibility	Distance From Clouds	** Flight Visibility	** Distance From Clouds
1200' or less above the surface, regardless of MSL Altitude	*1 statute mile	Clear of clouds	3 statute miles	500' below 1000' above 2000' horizontal
More than 1200' above the surface, but less than 10,000' MSL	1 statute mile	500' below 1000' above 2000' horizontal	3 statute miles	500' below 1000' above 2000' horizontal
More than 1200' above the surface and at or above 10,000' MSL	5 statute miles	1000' below 1000' above 1 statute mile horizontal	5 statute miles	1000' below 1000' above 1 statute mile horizontal

* Helicopters may operate with less than 1 mile visibility, outside controlled airspace at 1200 feet or less above the surface, provided they are operated at a speed that allows the pilot adequate opportunity to see any air traffic or obstructions in time to avoid collisions.

** In addition, when operating within a control zone beneath a ceiling, the ceiling must not be less than 1000'. If the pilot intends to land or takeoff or enter a traffic pattern within a control zone, the ground visibility must be at least 3 miles at that airport. If ground visibility is not reported at the airport, 3 miles flight visibility is required. (FAR 91.105)

ALTITUDES AND FLIGHT LEVELS

CONTROLLED AND UNCONTROLLED AIRSPACE VFR ALTITUDES AND FLIGHT LEVELS			
If your magnetic course (ground track) is	More than 3000' above the surface but below 18,000' MSL fly	Above 18,000' MSL to FL 290 (except within Positive Control Area, FAR 71.193) fly	Above FL 290 (except within Positive Control Area, FAR 71.193) fly 4000' intervals
0° to 179°	Odd thousands, MSL, plus 500' (3500, 5500, 7500, etc)	Odd Flight Levels plus 500' (FL 195, 215, 235, etc)	Beginning at FL 300 (FL 300, 340, 380, etc)
180° to 359°	Even thousands, MSL, plus 500' (4500, 6500, 8500, etc)	Even Flight Levels plus 500' (FL 185, FL 205, 225, etc)	Beginning at FL 320 (FL 320, 360, 400, etc)
UNCONTROLLED AIRSPACE – IFR ALTITUDES AND FLIGHT LEVELS			
If your magnetic course (ground track) is	Below 18,000' MSL, fly	At or above 18,000' MSL but below FL 290, fly	At or above FL 290, fly 4000' intervals
0° to 179°	Odd thousands, MSL, (3000, 5000, 7000, etc)	Odd Flight Levels, FL 190, 210, 230, etc)	Beginning at FL 290, (FL 290, 330, 370, etc)
180° to 359°	Even thousands, MSL, (2000, 4000, 6000, etc)	Even Flight Levels (FL 180, 200, 220, etc)	Beginning at FL 310, (FL 310, 350, 390, etc)

Fig. 20-R. VFR visibilities and cloud clearance and VFR altitudes (*AIM*).

SPECIAL USE AIRSPACE

110. GENERAL

Special use airspace consists of that airspace wherein activities must be confined because of their nature, or wherein limitations are imposed upon aircraft operations that are not a part of those activities, or both. Except for Controlled Firing Areas, special use airspace areas are depicted on aeronautical charts.

111. PROHIBITED AREA

Prohibited Areas contain airspace of defined dimensions identified by an area on the surface of the earth within which the flight of aircraft is prohibited. Such areas are established for security or other reasons associated with the national welfare. These areas are published in the Federal Register and are depicted on aeronautical charts.

112. RESTRICTED AREA

Restricted Areas contain airspace identified by an area on the surface of the earth within which the flight of aircraft, while not wholly prohibited, is subject to restrictions. Activities within these areas must be confined because of their nature or limitations imposed upon aircraft operations that are not a part of those activities or both. Restricted areas denote the existence of unusual, often invisible, hazards to aircraft such as artillery firing, aerial gunnery, or guided missiles. Penetration of Restricted Areas without authorization from the using or controlling agency may be extremely hazardous to the aircraft and its occupants. Restricted Areas are published in the Federal Register and constitute FAR 73. (See PARA. 346 – OPERATION IN RESTRICTED AIRSPACE.)

113. WARNING AREA

Warning Areas are airspace which may contain hazards to nonparticipating aircraft in international airspace. Warning Areas are established beyond the 3 mile limit. Though the activities conducted within Warning Areas may be as hazardous as those in Restricted Areas, Warning Areas cannot be legally designated as Restricted Areas because they are over international waters. Penetration of Warning Areas during periods of activity may be hazardous to the aircraft and its occupants. Official descriptions of Warning Areas may be obtained on request to the FAA, Washington, D.C.

114. MILITARY OPERATIONS AREAS (MOA)

a. MOAs consist of airspace of defined vertical and lateral limits established for the purpose of separating certain military training activities from IFR traffic. Whenever a MOA is being used, nonparticipating IFR traffic may be cleared through a MOA if IFR separation can be provided by ATC. Otherwise, ATC will reroute or restrict nonparticipating IFR traffic.

b. Some training activities may necessitate acrobatic maneuvers, and the United States Air Force (USAF) is exempted from the regulation prohibiting acrobatic flight on airways within MOAs.

c. Pilots operating under VFR should exercise extreme caution while flying within a MOA when military activity is being conducted. Information regarding activity in MOAs may be obtained from any FSS within 100 miles of the area.

d. These areas are depicted on Sectional, VFR Terminal and Low Altitude En Route Charts.

115. ALERT AREA

Alert Areas are depicted on aeronautical charts to inform nonparticipating pilots of areas that may contain a high volume of pilot training or an unusual type of aerial activity. Pilots should be particularly alert when flying in these areas. All activity within an Alert Area shall be conducted in accordance with FARs, without waiver, and pilots of participating aircraft as well as pilots transiting the area shall be equally responsible for collision avoidance. Information concerning these areas may be obtained upon request to the FAA, Washington, D.C.

Fig. 20-S. Special-use airspace. On the sectional chart the areas more restrictive in nature use blue outlines or color coding (TCAs, restricted areas, airport traffic areas). Magenta denotes less restrictive requirements (MOAs, TRSAs). An exception to this rule is the ARSA (see Chapter 29), a more stricted area bounded by magenta hashed lines on the sectional chart. This coloration was done to avoid confusion when TCAs (blue outlines) and ARSAs are in close proximity in areas of high-density traffic (*AIM*).

NOTICES TO AIRMEN—CLASS TWO

Current *Notices to Airmen* (NOTAMS) (Fig. 20-T) are considered essential to the safety of flight and contain supplemental data affecting other operational publications listed here. It also includes current Flight Data Center (FDC) NOTAMS, which are regulatory in nature, issued to establish restrictions to flight or to amend charts or published Instrument Approach Procedures. This publication is issued every 14 days and is available through subscription from the Superintendent of Documents. Class one NOTAMS are transmitted by telecommunications and include NOTAM-D (Distance) and NOTAM-L (Local, or nice-to-know information).

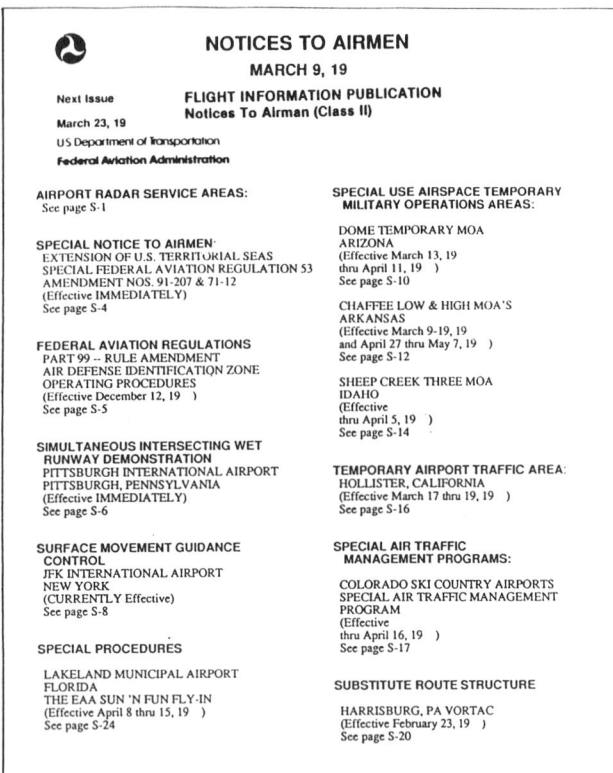

Fig. 20-T. Sample cover for *Notices to Airmen (Class II)*.

SUMMARY

The material in this chapter is an expanded version of Chapter 20, *SPFM*. Take the following test and review any questions missed. Since many of the questions are "open book" it's possible to misread the data (this can happen on the FAA written exam also).

Certain material in the various publications discussed here should be covered before proceeding with the book. Other information in this chapter should be reexamined after it is mentioned in the following chapters. The idea has been to present the publications in total at first rather than covering them only piecemeal in later chapters as the need arose. Basically, this chapter is to help you remember in which publication particular information is found and how to read it.

Now for the questions.

Questions 2001 through 2005 are based on the sectional chart segment and legend in the back of this book.

2001. You are given the latitude and longitude of an airstrip to which you are to secretly fly arms for a pocket of Rebels who are not yet aware that the War Between the States (or Civil War) ended in 1865. Since you are flying a short takeoff and landing plane, you know that you can land in nearly any field with the cargo but need to pin down the location. The numbers given are 35°45′N, 86°02′W. From this you know that the nearest town or village is

1—Centertown.
2—Sheybogan.
3—Bradyville.
4—Spencer.

2002. To call for airport information at Putnam County Airport (36°12′N, 85°29′W), you would transmit on

1—122.8 MHz and listen on 326 kHz.
2—326 kHz and listen on 326 MHz.
3—326 kHz and listen on 122.8 MHz.
4—122.7 MHz and listen on 122.7 MHz.

2003. Which radio beacon (NDB) in the Nashville area has voice transmission capability?

1—Opery.
2—Sewart.
3—Lascassas.
4—None of the above.

2004. It's a weekend and the weather is clear with unrestricted visibility. In taking a cross-country in a Cessna 152, on which of the following routes between airports would you *expect* to find an aircraft with right-of-way over your airplane?

1—Tullahoma (35°23′N, 86°15′W) to Ellington (35°30′N, 86°48′W).
2—Ellington (35°30′N, 86°48′W) to Murfreesboro (35°53′N, 86°23′W).
3—Warren County (35°42′N, 85°50′W) to Crossville (35°57′N, 85°05′W).
4—Sewanee-Franklin County (35°12′N, 85°54′W) to Murfreesboro (35°53′N, 86°23′W).

2005. Which of the following airports is at the lowest elevation?

1—Fayetteville (35°04′, 86°34′W).
2—Ellington (35°30′, 86°48′W).
3—Warren County (35°42′, 85°50′W).
4—Bomar (35°34′, 86°27′W).

Refer to Figure 20-F and the Appendix (*A/FD*) for questions 2006 through 2010.

2006. To communicate with Glens Falls radio, you could

1—transmit on 110.2 MHz and receive on 122.1 MHz.
2—transmit and receive on 122.1 MHz.
3—transmit on 122.2 MHz and receive on 122.1 MHz.
4—transmit on 122.1 MHz and receive on 110.2 MHz.

2007. Which of the following statements is correct?

1—The Talladega VORTAC is at an elevation of 530 feet, and the magnetic variation at the site is 2°E.
2—Anniston-Calhoun County Airport has pilot-controlled lighting.
3—The Anniston-Opp Airport has more services available than Anniston-Calhoun County Airport.
4—Your heading on base to Runway 5 at Anniston-Calhoun County Airport in light wind conditions would be approximately 140° magnetic.

2008. Assume that you are a private pilot flying into Dulles International Airport, 25 miles out, and approaching on a magnetic course of 080°. After listening to the Automatic Terminal Information Service (ATIS), you would contact Dulles approach control on

1—126.1 MHz.
2—122.95 MHz.
3—120.45 MHz.
4—126.65 MHz.

2009. Which one of the following statements is correct?

1—Talladega VORTAC is located 9.4 NM east-northeast of the Anniston-Calhoun County Airport.
2—The Glens Falls VORTAC is inaccurate between the 305 and 315 radials beyond 35 NM below 7000 feet.
3—Weather and operational matter may be received by listening to the Judd nondirectional beacon (NDB) at Andalusia-Opp Airport.
4—Andalusia-Opp Airport has right traffic for some runways.

2010. The threshold crossing height (TCH) of the Glide Angle of the VASI (Visual Approach Slope Indicator) for Runway 11 at Andalusia-Opp Airport is

1—26 feet.
2—27.2 feet.
3—3.0 feet for general aviation (GA) aircraft.
4—100 feet.

2011. Refer to Figure 20-F. Which of the following statements about the airport and facilities at Dulles International Airport is true?

1—Runway 12-30 is concentrated and graveled.
2—Runway 12-30 is 1000 feet long and 150 feet wide.
3—Runway 01L is concrete and grooved.
4—Only minor servicing is available.

2012. Refer to Figure 20-H. Which of the following facilities has Pilot's Automatic Weather Answering Service (PATWAS) or Telephone Information Briefing Service (TIBS)?

1—Nashville (BNA).
2—Jackson (MKL).
3—Chattanooga.
4—Knoxville.

2013. Refer to Figure 20-K. A VOR receiver may be checked at Hinch Mountain VOR

1—on the ground.
2—at 2900 feet mean sea level (MSL) at a point 333°, 11 nautical miles from the station.
3—at 2900 feet above ground over the VOR.
4—at 2900 feet MSL at a point 153°, 11 nautical miles away from the station.

2014. The Continental Control Area extends from

1—14,500 feet MSL upward, or 1500 feet AGL, whichever is higher.
2—14,500 feet above ground level (AGL) upward.
3—18,000 feet MSL to 60,000 feet (or flight level 600).
4—12,500 feet MSL upward, or 1500 feet AGL, whichever is higher.

2015. Review Figure 20-R. You are flying an airplane in VFR conditions at an altitude of 11,500 feet MSL at an absolute altitude of 700 feet in uncontrolled airspace. Regulations require that flight visibility and distance from clouds be respectively

1—5 statute miles and 1000 feet below, 1000 feet above, and 1 statute mile horizontal.
2—3 statute miles, 500 feet below, 1000 feet above, and 2000 feet horizontal.
3—1 statute mile and clear of clouds.
4—5 statute miles, 1000 feet above, 500 feet below, and 2000 feet horizontal.

2016. Refer to Figure 20-R. On a cross-country VFR flight, flying at 5000 feet over the terrain, your magnetic heading is 194°, and you're holding a right-wind correction of 20°. You should fly an altitude (MSL) of

1—odd thousands.
2—odd thousands plus 500 feet.
3—even thousands.
4—even thousands plus 500 feet.

2017. Airspaces established more than 3 miles out to sea are designated as

1—alert areas.
2—restricted areas.
3—prohibited areas.
4—warning areas.

21
USING THE RADIO

In addition to reviewing and asking questions on Chapter 21, *SPFM*, some material on Distance Measuring Equipment and Area Navigation, plus added tips on communications, are included here. Read this material and Chapter 21, *SPFM* before answering the questions at the end of this chapter.

RADIO NAVIGATION AIDS

■ Automatic Direction Finder

The Automatic Direction Finder (ADF) receives frequencies in the low to medium frequency range from FAA Nondirectional Beacons (NDBs) between 190 and 535 kHz to commercial broadcast stations between 540 and 1600 kHz. Remember it is an *automatic direction finder*; its indicator, or "needle," points toward the station in relation to the nose of the aircraft and displays an angle called the "relative bearing"; this angle is measured clockwise from the nose of the aircraft. An NDB relative bearing of 90° (090) will cause the needle to point to the right wing. The ADF is used with the magnetic compass and heading indicator. Figure 21-A shows four airplanes with the same relative bearing, although all four are in different locations. Combining the relative bearing with the magnetic heading of the aircraft results in getting the magnetic bearing, or the magnetic course, to the station at that "point in time." (If it is over 360°, subtract 360° to find the magnetic bearing.)

If you continually keep the aircraft pointed so that the ADF pointer shows a relative bearing of 000° or 360°, you will eventually get to the station (homing), but a crosswind will cause the path of the airplane to be curved (Fig. 21-3, *SPFM*). If there's a crosswind, you should "track," setting up a wind correction angle to maintain a straight course over the ground to the station.

You can find your bearing from a radio beacon, as can be done from a VOR. Use magnetic bearings FROM a station (think of these bearings as radials). The magnetic bearing FROM the station is the reciprocal of the bearing TO the station. (If the magnetic bearing TO a station was 090°, the magnetic bearing

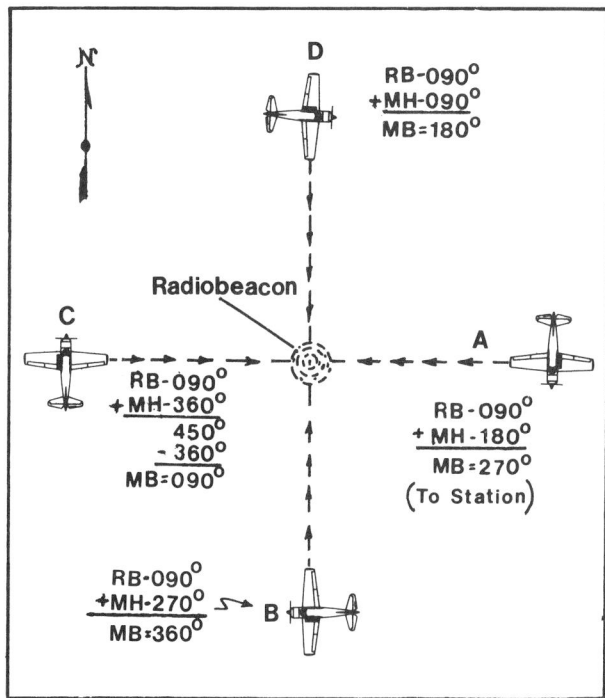

Fig. 21-A. Example of four airplanes all with the same relative bearing (RB) of 90° to the same radio beacon. Each has a different magnetic heading (MH), so the magnetic bearing to the station (MB) is different also. The method of calculating the magnetic bearing is shown for each case.

FROM the station would be 270°—a seemingly obvious but sometimes confused point.)

The normal procedure for tuning the ADF is to set the selector on REC or ANT (Receive or Antenna), which gives the best audio reception, then dial or select the proper frequency. (Double-check the station identification.) Once the identified signal is received, switch to the ADF function. (See Fig. 21-1, *SPFM*.)

The ADF has some disadvantages. The needle will tend to point to thunderstorm activity, making it unreliable in the vicinity of the storms unless you're interested in flying to one. (Don't.) It also may give unreliable indications when crossing shorelines at small angles or in mountainous areas. One advantage of ADF navigation is that you can pick up strong signals a considerable distance away. Also, transmission of low to medium frequencies is not limited to line of sight as with a VOR.

■ VHF Omnirange

The operating principles, characteristics, and use of VHF Omnirange (VOR) are described in Chapter 21, *SPFM*. The following material supplements that discussion and emphasizes use of the VOR in selected navigational problems.

ANOTHER LOOK AT VOR COMPONENTS. The aircraft VOR equipment consists of (1) a VHF receiver, which can be tuned to stations in the frequency range from 108.00 to 117.95 MHz; (2) a device for selecting magnetic bearings (radials) extending from VOR stations, usually called the Omni Bearing Selector (OBS), calibrated from 0 to 359; (3) a Course Deviation Indicator (CDI), a needle (or in some all-electronic systems, a "light bar"), which moves left or right; and (4) a TO-FROM indicator. With this equipment you can fly directly TO or FROM the VOR station or determine the magnetic bearing TO or FROM a station located to one side of the course.

AIRCRAFT POSITION AND VOR INDICATIONS. For a single position of the aircraft, several CDI and TO-FROM indications are possible, all depending on the way you have set the OBS. To show how the VOR indicators work in practice, a diagram of the area around a VOR station is shown in Figure 21-B. As shown in the drawing, selecting a radial with the OBS automatically divides the area around the VOR into quadrants.

If the template as shown by (A) in Figure 21-B was printed on clear plastic, you could set the center of it over a VOR station on a chart, turn the large arrow to the chosen OBS setting, and see the instrument indications in the four quadrants. As an example, in (B) in

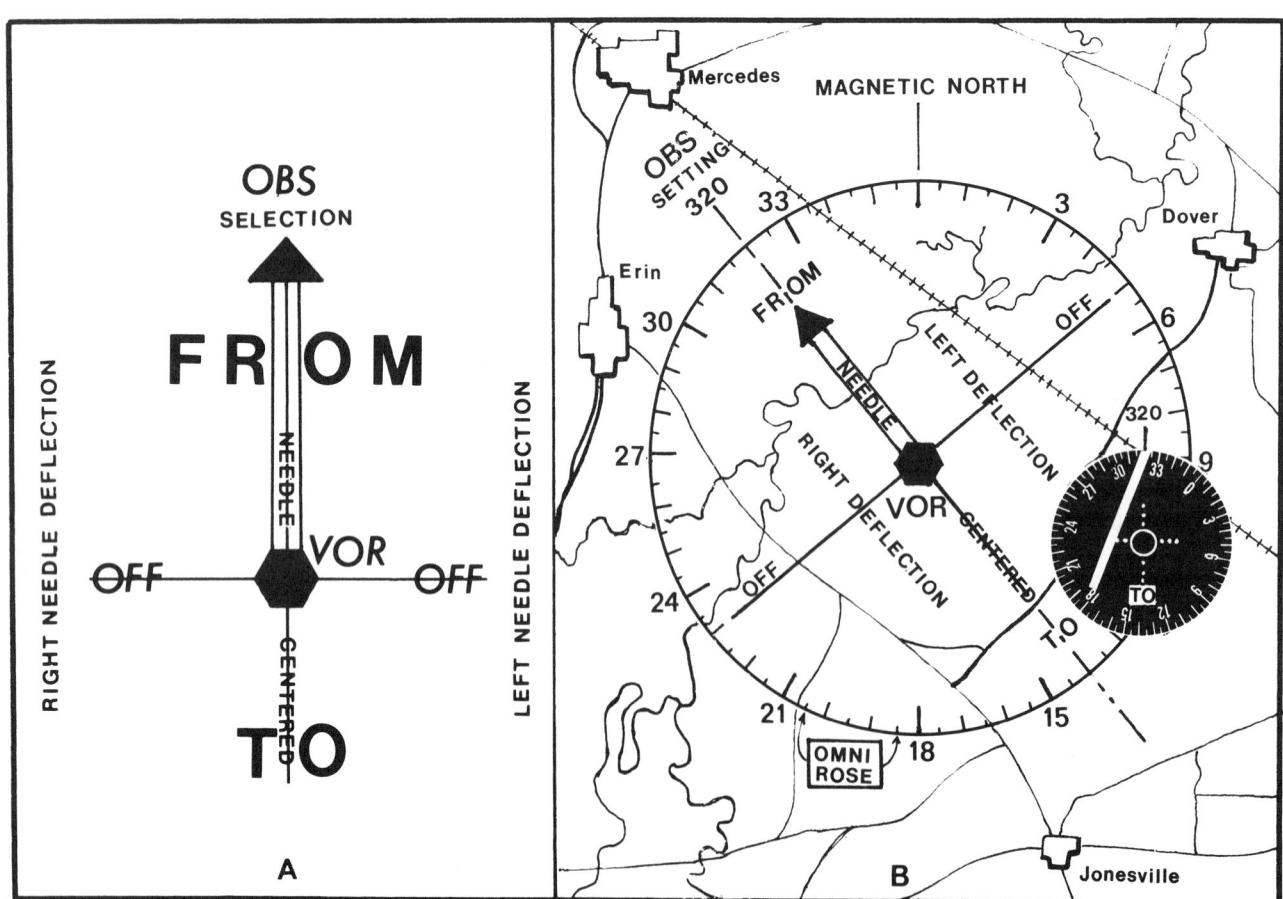

Fig. 21-B. Diagram showing the VOR indications for an aircraft in the four quadrants around the VOR station defined by the setting of the OBS. The use is described in the text.

Figure 21-B you've selected an OBS setting of 320 and placed the center of the template over the VOR station, lining up the large arrow on 320. The VOR instrument (CDI and TO-FROM) located in the quadrant as shown would have a left needle deflection and a TO indication.

An airplane flying over the town of Erin (with the same OBS setting of 320) would have a right needle deflection and a FROM indication *regardless of the heading it was flying.* (More about this later.) An airplane flying on the west edge of Dover would have a full *left* needle deflection and the TO-FROM panel would indicate OFF.

Over the west edge of Mercedes with the OBS setting as shown, the instrument would have a centered needle and a FROM indication. If the pilot of that airplane over west Mercedes wanted to fly to the VOR, she would be smart to set the OBS on 140 so that the needle indicates properly. Suppose, however, after turning on the course to the VOR, the OBS setting was left at 320. As the pilot progresses, a strong wind from the east drifts the airplane over Erin. The needle has a right deflection (and the FROM indication is ignored). Before, when the OBS was set properly, as pilot you always corrected *into* the needle and so do it here, but something isn't working. At this rate there is no hope of getting to the VOR, and the airplane sinks slowly over the western horizon as you keep trying to find that elusive "line" to the VOR.

One confusing aspect of VOR navigation to the newcomer is that the equipment will show the CDI needle deflection and TO-FROM indication of the quadrant you are in, regardless of the heading of the airplane. Figure 21-C(A) shows how the information in Figure 21-B can be used when the OBS is set to 270 on eight airplanes in the vicinity of a VOR station. Airplanes 1, 2, 3, and 8 will show a FROM indication. Airplanes 1, 6, 7, and 8 will have a left-needle indication, while 2, 3, 4, and 5 will show a right-needle indication on the CDI. Got that? (Turn those airplanes in your mind to the selected OBS setting and it will seem clearer.)

In Figure 21-C(B) the setting of the OBS has been changed to 180. Airplanes 2, 3, 4, and 5 will show a FROM indication, and the others will indicate TO. Airplanes 1, 2, 3, and 8 will deflect the CDI needle to the left, and 4, 5, 6, and 7 to the right. Talk about crowded skies!

As shown in Figure 21-B, if an aircraft is on the selected radial (or diametrically opposite), the CDI needle is centered. Another aspect of VOR navigation that should be recognized is that if the course is not directly over the VOR site but to one side, the TO-FROM indicator will switch to OFF as the aircraft crosses either radial perpendicular to the radial selected on the OBS. For example, in Figure 21-C(A) the 270 radial is selected; if airplane 7 continues to fly its present heading, it will receive the OFF indication as it passes the 360 (i.e., 000) radial; if airplane 3 continues as shown, it will receive the OFF when it crosses the 180 radial.

To test your skill in using the VOR, do the exercise in Figure 21-D. Using Figure 21-B to help you picture the indications in the four areas around a VOR, *draw*

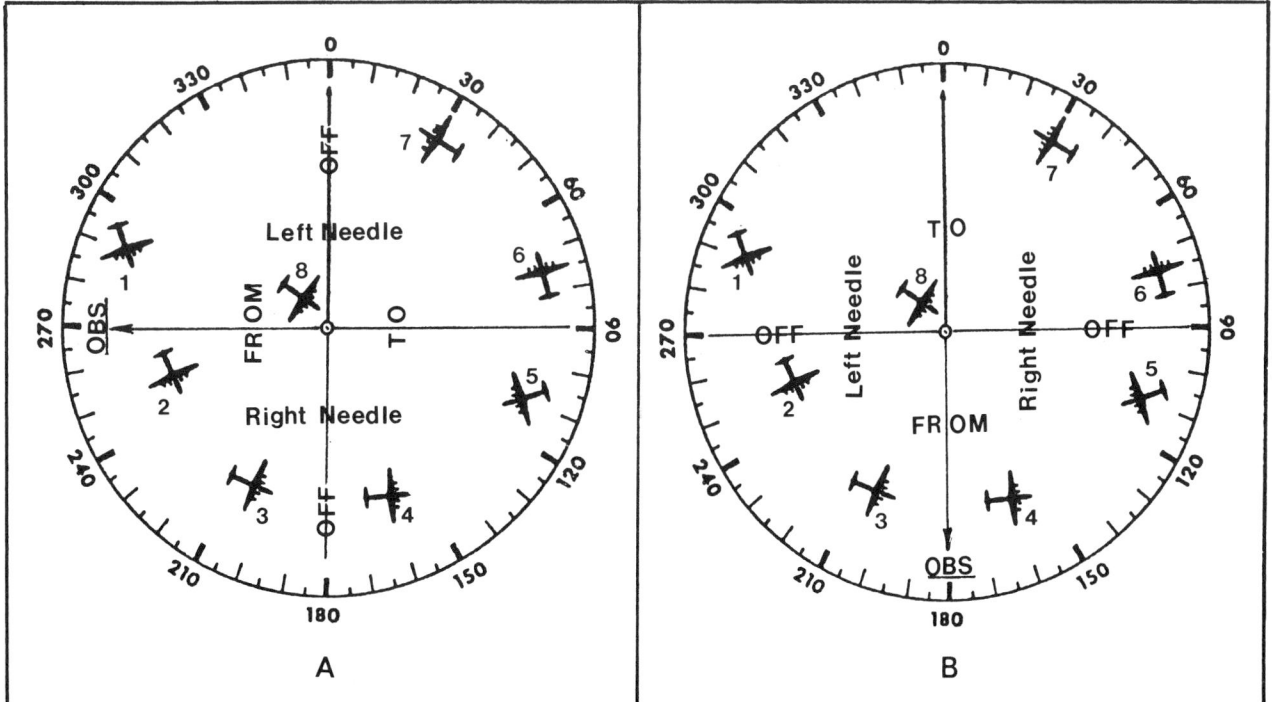

Fig. 21-C. Examples of VOR indications for eight aircraft: (A) OBS set to 270°, (B) OBS set to 180°.

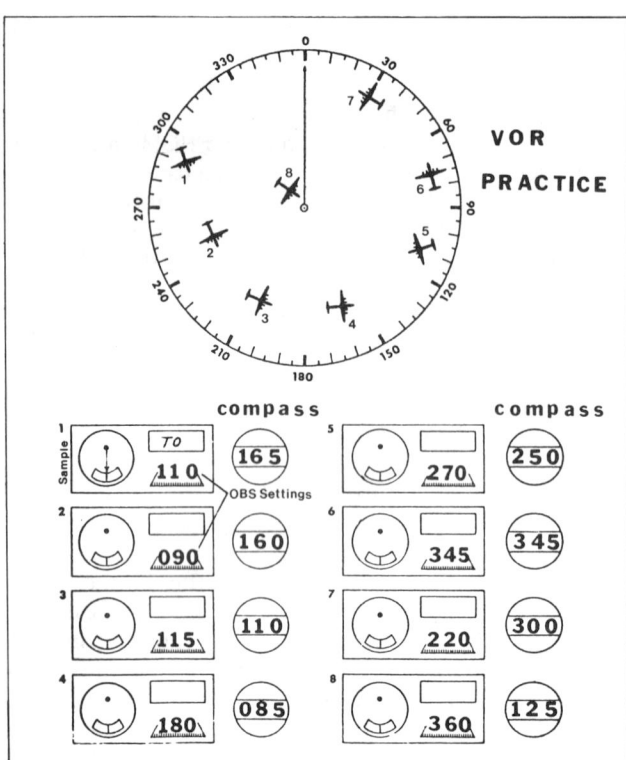

Fig. 21-D. Exercise in VOR interpretations. For each of the eight airplanes the magnetic compass heading is shown beside a box representing the VOR indicators. The radial selected and the OBS are shown in the lower right of the VOR box. Write TO or FROM in the empty box above the OBS selection and draw the correct postion for the CDI needle on the indicator at the left. Complete the exercise in pencil and then check Figure 21-E for the answers.

the CDI needle and TO-FROM indications you would expect for the cases shown. Answers will be found in Figure 21-E.

VOR ACCURACY CHECK. Of the several methods used for checking the accuracy of the airplane's VOR receiver, a VOR Test (VOT) facility is probably the best. The VOT can *only* be used on the ground at the airport where it is located. By turning the OBS first to 360 and adjusting the OBS to center the CDI needle, the reading on the OBS should be within plus or minus 4° of 360 (000) and a FROM indication. The reading on the OBS should be within plus or minus 4° of 180°, with a TO indication. If the needle centers with the OBS reading *more* than plus or minus 4°, you should have your VOR receiver checked. These limits are those required for IFR operations, and if you follow these specifications, you'll have a more accurate cross-country flight. Several airports also have specified locations at the airport to check VORs. These "VOR receiver checkpoints" can be found in the *A/FD*. (See Fig. 20-K.) VOT frequencies can also be found in that publication. The VOR accuracy using these places should be the same as a VOT, that is, a plus or minus 4° of the specified OBS reading. Other VORs have checks to be

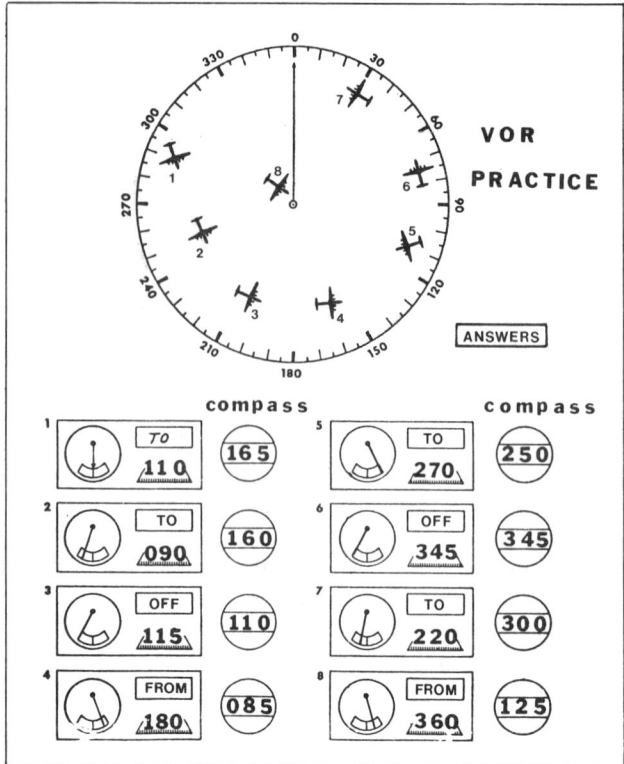

Fig. 21-E. Answers to exercise of Figure 21-D.

used in the air, that is, flying over certain ground references at specified altitudes and manually centering the OBS needle. These readings should be accurate to plus or minus 6° of the specified radial.

If the airplane has a dual system VOR (two units independent of each other except for the antenna), you can tune both systems to the same ground facility and note the indicated bearings to that station. The maximum permissible variation between the two bearings is 4°.

■ Transponders

The electronic transponder is discussed in *SPFM* and in *AIM*. It is a component of the Air Traffic Control (ATC) system that helps ATC to locate and identify aircraft. The unit in the aircraft sends a coded pulse reply when interrogated by an ATC radar facility, and this allows the aircraft to be identified and its position to be displayed on the radar scope (Mode A). If the aircraft also is equipped with an encoding altimeter, the transponder can be switched to report altitude in 100-foot increments (Mode C) in addition to the position information.

TRANSPONDER CODES. When flying VFR, only code 1200 or the emergency codes discussed later should be used, unless advised by ATC. When operating VFR, the pilot is authorized to use code 1200, Mode A, or Mode A/C to indicate position, regardless of altitude.

However, when operating above 10,000 feet MSL, in controlled airspace, the transponder must be set to Mode A/C, unless prior authorization has been obtained from ATC.

In addition to the standard VFR code, there are two *emergency* codes important for VFR pilots to know. Code 7700 means "MAYDAY" and sets off an alarm at most ATC ground radar facilities to attract attention to your situation. The other code, 7600, shows radio failure. If you experience radio failure and need to let the ATC controllers know of your predicament, *AIM* suggests that you select transponder code 7700 for one minute and then 7600 for 15 minutes. If your flight is longer than 16 minutes, then repeat the two codes as many times as feasible. When ATC assigns you a particular transponder code to squawk, do *not* use that code when you are out of that controller's radar coverage. For example, if approach control directed you to "SQUAWK 0315" when approaching the airport to land and if you failed to change from that code when you took off later in the day, it could cause problems for other aircraft.

TERMS. Some common terms used by controllers and their meanings are listed:

1. SQUAWK (4-digit code)—Operate the transponder on the specified code in Mode A/C if available; otherwise use Mode A.
2. IDENT—Operate the IDENT switch of the transponder (*only* when directed by ATC).
3. SQUAWK and IDENT—Set the transponder to the specified code and then operate the IDENT switch.
4. SQUAWK STANDBY—Switch the transponder to the STANDBY position.
5. SQUAWK VFR—set the transponder to code 1200 in Mode A/C if available; otherwise, use Mode A.

■ **Distance Measuring Equipment**

While it's unlikely that your trainer has Distance Measuring Equipment (DME), you'll get a chance to use it later, so a brief look should be taken. Ground facilities of this type are VOR/DME, VORTAC, ILS/DME, and LOC/DME stations. The DME system operates at microwave frequencies and so can give only line-of-sight reception. The microwave frequencies used are paired with VHF navigation frequencies, so the dials of DME are typically calibrated for the same frequency range of 108.00–117.95 MHz that is used for VHF navigation radios. A VORTAC station that provides VOR navigation on a frequency of 117.40 MHz and distance information on the paired microwave frequency can yield both navigation and distance information by tuning both the VOR and DME receivers to 117.40 MHz.

SLANT RANGE. The DME readout displays distance to the pilot as direct nautical miles between the airplane and the ground station, sometimes called the "slant range." As illustrated in Figure 21-F, the difference between the slant range and the distance over the ground may be large near the DME ground station and at high altitude. At long distances from the station there is little error in assuming that the slant range is the same as the ground distance. Some of the more elaborate (and expensive) DMEs include a microcomputer that converts slant range to accurate ground distance.

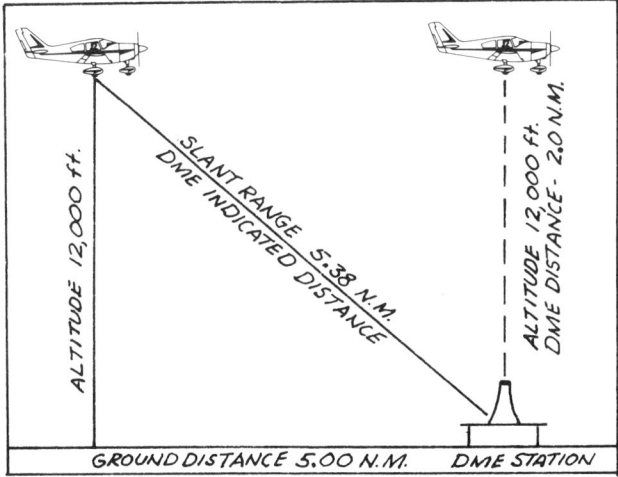

Fig. 21-F. Relationship between slant range and true ground distance. Aircraft A, at an altitude of 12,000 feet and 5 NM true ground distance from the station, reads 5.38 NM on the DME, a distance error of almost 8 percent. Directly over the station at an altitude of 12,000 feet, aircraft B shows a DME distance of 2 NM, but the true ground distance is 0. Farther from the station DME readings become more accurate: at 14 NM from the station and 12,000 feet altitude, the slant range error is less than 1 percent. This figure shows that the DME can give a very accurate indication of passing a VORTAC when using VOR navigation. The DME distance will decrease as the station is approached until it indicates the height of the airplane above the VORTAC, then will increase as the airplane flies outbound from the station. (1 NM = 6080 feet, but 12,000 feet was used instead of 12,160, which would have been the exact 2-mile height.)

GROUNDSPEED. Most DMEs can also compute groundspeed in knots and the time to fly to the station at that groundspeed. The distance to the station indicated by the DME does not depend on the aircraft heading. However, the groundspeed reading is only accurate, for the less complex equipment, when you are flying *directly* to or from that station.

It is important to note that the DME receiver can only operate with the special ground equipment that adds the distance capability. A VOR station alone does not have this special ability. This point is explained in more detail in *SPFM*.

Area Navigation

Area navigation (RNAV) is becoming more common as the price of the equipment becomes reasonable. It uses an on-board microcomputer, along with information from a VOR receiver and DME, to move a "phantom" VOR station anywhere the pilot chooses as long as the aircraft is within operating range of a ground station. There are several types of area navigation computers that may be used to navigate between "waypoints." The general procedure to follow is to dial into the computer a preselected radial from a VORTAC (or VOR/DME) station and set the exact DME distance in nautical miles you wish the waypoint to be located from the VORTAC. With this information in the computer and the "RNAV" mode selected, the waypoint becomes a phantom VOR station and you use the VOR receiver just as if it was a VOR located at the waypoint. Similarly, later model DME displays indicate distance to the waypoint. About the only difference you will note is that there is no zone of confusion and no change in the sensitivity of the CDI needle as you approach the waypoint.

The principal advantage in the use of RNAV is in shortening distances enroute, since it allows a pilot to fly directly from point to point in a straight line rather than from one VOR station to another, which may produce a saw-toothed route. Figure 21-G shows this advantage and illustrates how VORTAC radials and distances are used to create waypoints.

COMMUNICATIONS

In using communications equipment, there are certain procedures to follow that can make the process easier. For instance, most microphones used in light airplanes need to be held very close to the mouth while you talk at a natural volume. (Most student pilots hold the mike too far away.) Before transmitting, listen to be sure that no one else is talking. If you talk at the same time as someone else, neither can be heard, and the resulting squeal gets all listeners' attention. Also, the procedures used to talk to Flight Service Stations (FSSs) and ATC are different.

Tower Talk

ATC personnel (that is, tower or local controller, ground controller, approach and departure controllers) are "plugged in" to the system, waiting for you to make the first call. Use a standard procedure, such as stating:

1. *Whom* you are calling (because you may have the wrong facility—you may be talking to ground control when you really need to call tower).
2. *Who* you are (type of airplane and number, such as Viking 1234 Romeo).

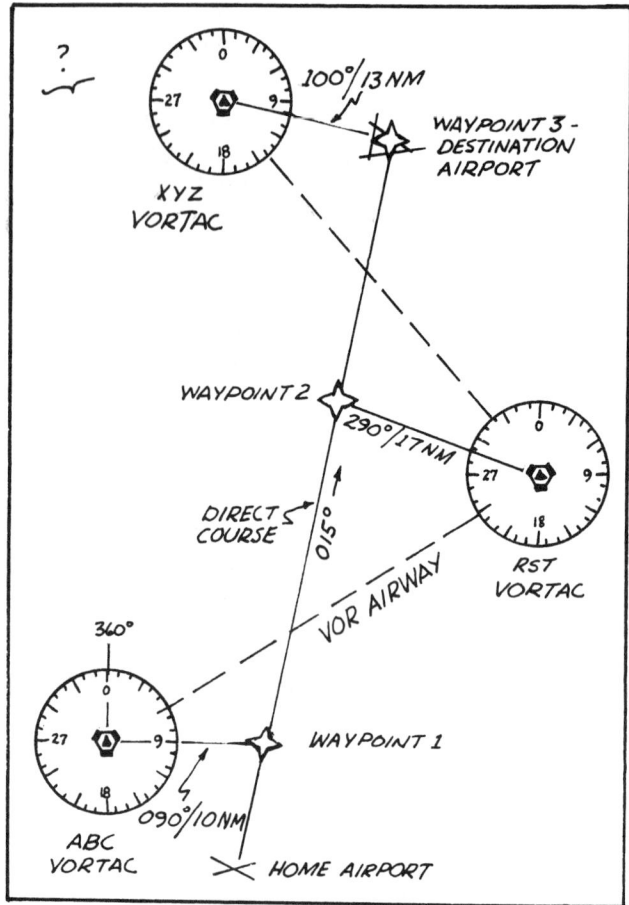

Fig. 21-G. Navigation between two airports using RNAV to define a direct magnetic course of 015°. After takeoff from the home airport, the pilot can fly directly to waypoint 1, then to waypoint 2, and finally to waypoint 3, which has been located at the destination airport. Note that the distance along the VOR airway would be much greater.

3. *Where* you are so they can locate you (such as "10 miles south of the airport").
4. *What* you want with them (ready for takeoff or landing).

To the tower, you might say, "NASHVILLE TOWER, CHEROKEE 33521, 2 LEFT, READY FOR TAKEOFF." If you say *all* this in the first transmission, most controllers will appreciate it, since it saves time. With the radio frequencies getting more and more crowded, if you say "NASHVILLE TOWER, CHEROKEE 33521, OVER" and then waited for a reply before saying what you wanted, you might not get the controller's attention again for a long time. One thing to remember is to use your full call sign, all the numbers and letters after the N, in the first transmission. After ATC shortens it to the last three characters, you may also.

The first few times it might be helpful beforehand to write what you plan to say, as few words as possible, until the procedure is familiar. If you are calling an approach controller, it will also help if you include, in addition to the four items above, your altitude, the letter of the current Automatic Terminal Information Service (ATIS) broadcast, and whether you are squawking a transponder code. For example, "SPRINGFIELD APPROACH CONTROL. CHEROKEE 33521, TWO ZERO MILES SOUTHWEST AT THREE THOUSAND, SQUAWKING ONE TWO ZERO ZERO, WITH ECHO. LANDING SPRINGFIELD."

The ECHO in the last paragraph means that you have information Echo, or the fifth information release that day. As *SPFM* indicates, a change in the information (such as a wind shift or other factors) would mean a new broadcast released as information Foxtrot and so on through the phonetic alphabet. Figure 21-H is the phonetic alphabet as taken from *AIM*.

PHONETIC ALPHABET

A	●▬	Alfa	(AL-FAH)
B	▬●●●	Bravo	(BRAH-VOH)
C	▬●▬●	Charlie	(CHAR-LEE) or (SHAR LEE)
D	▬●●	Delta	(DELL-TAH)
E	●	Echo	(ECK-OH)
F	●●▬●	Foxtrot	(FOKS-TROT)
G	▬▬●	Golf	(GOLF)
H	●●●●	Hotel	(HOH-TEL)
I	●●	India	(IN-DEE-AH)
J	●▬▬▬	Juliett	(JEW-LEE-ETT)
K	▬●▬	Kilo	(KEY-LOH)
L	●▬●●	Lima	(LEE-MAH)
M	▬▬	Mike	(MIKE)
N	▬●	November	(NO-VEM-BER)
O	▬▬▬	Oscar	(OSS-CAH)
P	●▬▬●	Papa	(PAH-PAH)
Q	▬▬●▬	Quebec	(KEH-BECK)
R	●▬●	Romeo	(ROW-ME-OH)
S	●●●	Sierra	(SEE-AIR-RAH)
T	▬	Tango	(TANG-GO)
U	●●▬	Uniform	(YOU-NEE-FORM) or (OO-NEE-FORM)
V	●●●▬	Victor	(VIK-TAH)
W	●▬▬	Whiskey	(WISS-KEY)
X	▬●●▬	Xray	(ECKS-RAY)
Y	▬●▬▬	Yankee	(YANG-KEY)
Z	▬▬●●	Zulu	(ZOO-LOO)
1	●▬▬▬▬	One	(WUN)
2	●●▬▬▬	Two	(TOO)
3	●●●▬▬	Three	(TREE)
4	●●●●▬	Four	(FOW-ER)
5	●●●●●	Five	(FIFE)
6	▬●●●●	Six	(SIX)
7	▬▬●●●	Seven	(SEV-EN)
8	▬▬▬●●	Eight	(AIT)
9	▬▬▬▬●	Nine	(NINE-ER)
0	▬▬▬▬▬	Zero	(ZEE-RO)

Fig. 21-H. The phonetic alphabet.

If you have a lengthy request, you might say "MOBILE APPROACH, CESSNA 3644 JULIETT" and wait for a reply. Even though two transmissions are needed instead of one, if the request is unusual or long, it's best to make sure the controller is listening before taking over the frequency for a long transmission.

When departing an airport in a Terminal Radar Service Area (TRSA) and you want to use the service, you also need to let ATC know where you are going, as well as the altitude to be flown. If you don't want radar services in this area, say "NEGATIVE STAGE THREE," or they will assume you'll be participating.

When departing or approaching a larger airport, there is a certain sequence of frequencies to be used (if that facility has them). When leaving a tie-down area, (1) ATIS (listen only), (2) clearance delivery, (3) ground control, (4) tower, and (5) departure will be the frequencies used, in that order. When approaching to land, the order will be (1) ATIS, (2) approach, (3) tower, and (4) ground control (after the tower tells you to do so). One of the most important things to remember is that if you are in any doubt, ask for clarification. If you don't understand, tell them to "SAY AGAIN." *DON'T* just do what you *think* the controller meant. Also, if you tell them you are a student pilot, they can go beyond their usual ATC procedures to give you a hand.

If you are operating at an airport with an ATC tower, you should visit that facility. Most ATC people are glad to have pilots stop by, particularly if you explain that you are a student pilot and need to learn more about their procedures. It's best to call and ask when a visit would be convenient.

■ Flight Service Stations

Flight Service Stations have a different function and working arrangement, so the procedure in talking to them is different from that of ATC facilities. As indicated in *SPFM*, the FSS specialists have many jobs, so they aren't just sitting plugged in to the communications console. They take weather data, answer telephones, compile flight data, file flight plans, and check navigational facilities besides talking over the radio to in-flight aircraft. So when calling an FSS, you should say "MEMPHIS RADIO, SUNDOWNER 35416 on 122.2" and wait for an answer before going ahead with your message. (The FSS specialist may be across from the console, taking a flight plan over the telephone.) It's important to specify the frequency on which you are receiving because some FSSs will monitor as many as 11 communications and 4 or more VORs. If you don't give them your receiving frequency, they have to call on all the frequencies they monitor, which may block calls at other FSSs. Check your volume; many times, FSSs will answer calls when pilots don't have the volume turned up loud enough to hear them.

Okay, an FSS also takes flight plans. When you file a VFR flight plan, it must be activated by you after takeoff. So when things are under control, call and tell them to activate your flight plan as of the time of takeoff. (If you are flying in an isolated area, tell them that you'll be off at a certain time and *ask* them to open your flight plan for you automatically. (If for some reason you don't leave when planned, it's your responsibility to call back and cancel. Otherwise, the plan will be activated.) Once you activate a flight plan, it is your responsibility to close it.

Some facilities have Transcribed Weather Broadcasts, and these TWEBs give weather continually. The

78 PART FOUR — CROSS-COUNTRY AND NIGHT FLYING

transcribed broadcasts provide continuous weather and aeronautical information over L/MF or VOR facilities.

Another communication useful on cross-country flights, as noted in Chapter 22 of *SPFM*, is the Enroute Flight Advisory Service, part of the FSS system, commonly called Flight Watch, which gives information such as current weather, radar reports, and pilot reports for your specific route of flight. For this service, transmit and receive on 122.0 MHz.

Also, as noted in *SPFM*, at certain airports not served by a control tower, FSSs also provide Airport Advisory Service on 123.6 MHz (transmit and receive). The frequency to use can be found on current sectional charts and in the *Airport/Facility Directory*, as indicated in Chapter 20.

UNICOMS AND MULTICOMS. Review the sections on these facilities in *SPFM*, noting the procedures and frequencies used, before tackling the questions.

2101. To tune an ADF receiver properly, you should

1—tune or dial the frequency on the ANT or REC setting, listen to the identification signal, and then turn to the ADF mode and read the relative bearing.
2—turn up the volume control and listen to the AM radio stations, since they are good entertainment on a long flight.
3—have the frequencies listed on your flight plan for easy identification.
4—set in the frequency and read the relative bearing.

2102. Of the following frequencies, which pair could you receive on your ADF?

1—121.5 MHz, 121.7 MHz.
2—110.3 MHz, 116.4 MHz.
3—125.05 MHz, 123.6 MHz.
4—281 kHz, 890 kHz.

2103. The term "homing" to a station with ADF means

1—to maintain a straight ground track toward the station, correcting for wind drift.
2—keeping the relative bearing on zero, regardless of the wind.
3—flying around the station, with a wind correction angle set in.
4—keeping the needle pointed to 180°.

2104. With the instrument readings in Figure 21-I, what would be your magnetic course to fly to the station?

1—060°.
2—090°.
3—150°.
4—030°.

2105. With a relative bearing reading 290°, what should you do to turn to a nondirectional beacon?

1—Turn to a heading of 290°.
2—Turn 290° plus 90° to get the bearing to the station.
3—Turn to the left 70°.
4—You would not be able to turn to the station with the information given.

2106. If your magnetic heading is 150° and the relative bearing on the ADF is 120°, you are located

1—northwest of the station.
2—southeast of the station.
3—east of the station.
4—west of the station.

2107. ADFs may not be reliable, even when properly tuned, if

1—thunderstorms are in the area.
2—you are flying at small angles to a shoreline.
3—the flight is over mountainous terrain.
4—any of the above conditions exist.

2108. Of the following frequencies, which pair could you receive on your airplane's VOR equipment?

1—121.5 MHz, 121.7 MHz.
2—122.0 MHz, 122.2 MHz.
3—110.3 MHz, 116.4 MHz.
4—281 kHz, 890 kHz.

2109. If the OBS was set on 315 and you were on a heading of 315°, to correct for deviations from course, you would

1—fly away from the needle indication.
2—fly toward the needle to get a centered needle indication.
3—turn the airplane 180° to get a more accurate reading.
4—keep flying on that heading, and it will take you to the station.

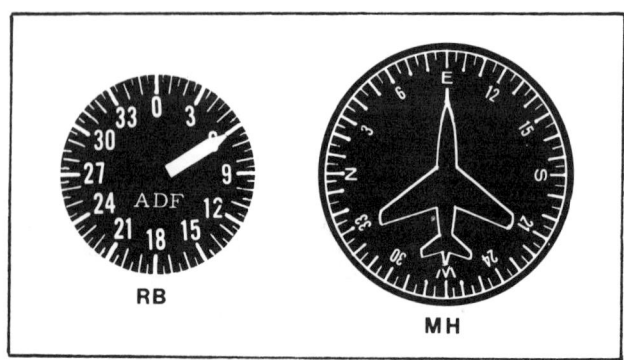

Fig. 21-I.

2110. When tracking in-bound to the VOR station, you should fly toward the needle to center it if

1—the OBS setting and the airplane's magnetic heading are within 90° of each other.
2—you have a FROM reading on your VOR receiver.
3—you have a TO reading on your VOR receiver, regardless of your magnetic heading.
4—you listen in for the identification signal and are not able to receive the Morse or voice code identifier.

2111. The advantage of VOR navigation is

1—static-free signals, which can be very helpful in areas where there are few prominent checkpoints.
2—the ability to receive signals, even when the station is over the horizon or behind mountains.
3—being able to spot thunderstorms, since the needle will swing toward the lightning.
4—being able to use these signals to home to the station, always keeping the needle pointed toward the nose of the aircraft.

2112. What is meant when ATC says you are on the 045 radial?

1—You are on a 225° heading to fly from the station.
2—You are on a 045° bearing to the station.
3—You are located to the southwest of the station.
4—You are located to the northeast of the station.

2113. In Figure 21-J the airplanes are tuned to the XYZ VORTAC and have selected the 270 radial. With the VOR receivers set up in this manner,

1—airplanes C and D show a left indication, although their headings are different; airplanes A and F show a right indication, although their headings are different.
2—the needles are centered with a FROM reading for airplanes B and E.
3—the VOR indication will show a needle pointing to the side of the instrument toward the station until you get to the radial, then it centers and points to the side of the instrument away from the station when you pass that radial.
4—all the above statements are correct.

2114. You are tracking North TO your destination VOR. You tune in the other VOR receiver to a VOR station that is off to your left and set that OBS to 090, FROM. The needle is showing a left deflection, so you know that

1—you are past the 090 radial.
2—you have not passed the 090 radial.
3—you should have turned the OBS to a TO indication for a better line from the other VOR.
4—you do not have enough information to confirm your position.

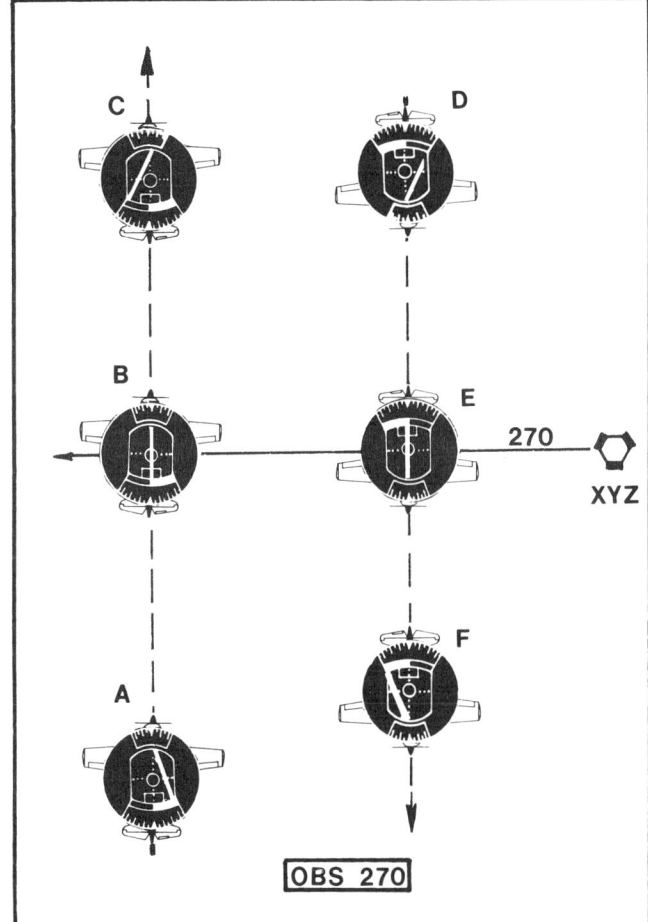

Fig. 21-J.

2115. If you have just become lost but have an hour of fuel remaining, which of the following procedures would be best (see Fig. 21-K)?

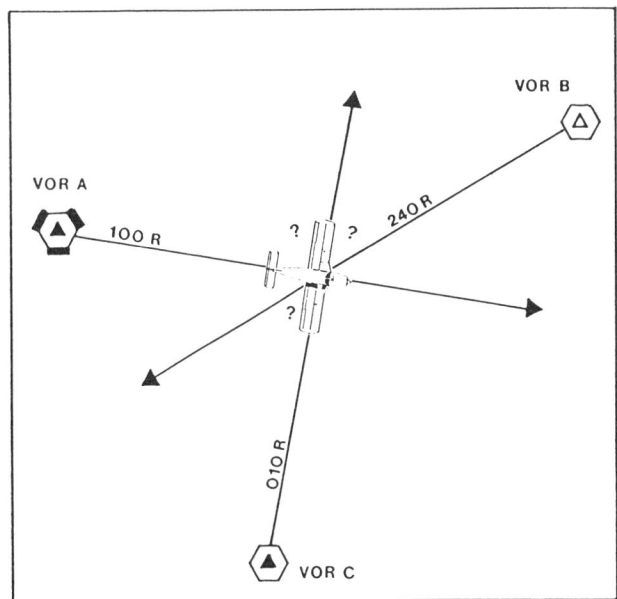

Fig. 21-K.

1—Tune in all three stations and center the needles of the OBS with a FROM reading. Note the OBS reading and draw a line from each station outward on that magnetic course.
2—Tune in all three stations and center the needles of the OBS. When the needle centers with a TO reading, note the OBS reading and draw a line from each station outward on that magnetic course.
3—Call "Mayday, Mayday, Mayday" on 122.8 MHz to see if radar can find you.
4—Land in the nearest pasture immediately and ask the farmer where you are.

2116. If the VOR receiver is properly calibrated, then tuning in a VOT should indicate

1—TO with the OBS set on 360.
2—TO with the OBS set on 180.
3—FROM with the OBS set on 180.
4—FROM with the OBS set on 270.

2117. You can communicate with FSSs having voice facilities on VORs by

1—transmitting on 122.1 MHz and listening on the VOR frequency.
2—transmitting on the VOR frequency and listening on 122.1 MHz.
3—listening and transmitting on 122.1 MHz.
4—transmitting on the VOR frequency and listening to the FSS discrete frequency.

2118. Which of these statements on transponders and their operation is correct?

1—Use code 1200 with Mode C only.
2—Turn to 7777 to declare an emergency.
3—For communications failure (an emergency situation), use 7700 for 1 minute then code 7600 for 15 minutes.
4—Use STANDBY when entering a traffic area.

2119. One of the advantages that can be gained by using RNAV is that of

1—shortening the distances to be flown.
2—being able to use stations that are out of "line of sight."
3—being able to disregard the TO-FROM indicator.
4—showing the exact distance to the VOR station that is being used.

2120. The DME gives distance information as

1—slant distance in nautical miles.
2—actual distance over the ground.
3—statute miles, as for the visibility in weather reports.
4—distance above the ground.

2121. After a tower facility tells you to contact ground on "point niner," you know that you should contact ground control on

1—199.9 MHz.
2—123.9 MHz.
3—122.9 MHz.
4—121.9 MHz.

2122. When approaching a large controlled airport, the sequence of frequencies used would most likely be

1—ATIS, ground control, tower, approach control.
2—ATIS, approach control, tower, clearance delivery, ground.
3—ATIS, approach control, tower, ground.
4—ATIS, departure, ground control, tower, approach control.

2123. Automatic Terminal Information Service (ATIS) concerns

1—essential but routine information, which may include the latest weather, sequence report, altimeter setting, runways in use, and any *Notices to Airmen* that are important to that airport.
2—only information that the pilot needs to navigate the taxiways.
3—permission to taxi to the active runway.
4—information for all airports in that terminal area.

2124. Flight Watch can be contacted by transmitting on

1—122.1 MHz and listening over the nearest VOR station.
2—122.0 MHz.
3—122.8 MHz.
4—121.9 MHz.

2125. You should call Flight Watch when you

1—want to know the current sequence report and forecast for your destination airport, which is over 500 miles away.
2—need to extend the time for your flight as filed in your flight plan.
3—would like to know what the latest weather radar shows with regard to thunderstorms in your local area.
4—wish to cancel your flight plan.

2126. After listening to the ATIS broadcast prior to taxiing, you should call ground control and inform them that you have

1—the numbers.
2—airport information (using the appropriate letter designator), such as "Delta."
3—received your clearance.
4—all the frequencies needed for takeoff.

Chapter 21. Using the Radio   81

2127. The proper Unicom frequency

1—can be found on the sectional charts along with the airport data.
2—will always be 122.8 MHz.
3—will be 122.95 MHz.
4—can only be found in the *Airport/Facility Directory* information for that particular airport.

2128. As a student pilot calling an FSS for a weather briefing by telephone to get the best information, or the "big picture," you need to tell them

1—that you are a student and need the sequence reports for (the destination airport).
2—you would like the forecasts for (your destination).
3—you want only certain items required for your trip, then be specific about destination.
4—that you are a student pilot and want a weather briefing for a trip to (your destination), giving time of departure, route, and approximate flying time to that point.

2129. If you are unable to raise an FSS after several calls, you should

1—go over to the nearest Air Traffic Control Center frequency and tell them you could not get the FSS.
2—give up, since it isn't important to talk to the FSS enroute.
3—call on another frequency listed for that facility.
4—assume the FSS got the message you gave them but was too busy to answer.

2130. You would communicate with an FSS that provides airport advisories on

1—122.2 MHz and listen on the closest VOR.
2—their discrete frequency.
3—123.6 MHz.
4—122.8 MHz.

2131. The correct procedure for any *initial* call to an FSS would be

1—TALLAHASSEE RADIO, VIKING ONE, TWO, ONE, SEVEN, NINE. PLEASE ACTIVATE MY FLIGHT PLAN TO MIAMI.
2—LONDON RADIO, CHEROKEE ONE, FIVE, THREE, SIX, NINER, ON 123.6.
3—KEY WEST FSS, CESSNA THREE, SIX, FOUR, FOUR, MIKE.
4—CROSSVILLE FLIGHT SERVICE STATION, SUNDOWNER ONE, TWO, FOUR, SIX, NINE. WAITING FOR TAKEOFF CLEARANCE.

2132. Which of the following frequencies is *not* a Unicom frequency?

1—122.8 MHz.
2—123.0 MHz.
3—122.7 MHz.
4—121.5 MHz.

2133. The Visual Approach Slope Indicator (VASI) provides a visual light path within the approach zone. The proper indication for an "on-glide-path" approach with a two-bar system is

1—white light over white.
2—red light over red.
3—red light over white.
4—white light over red.

2134. After landing at a controlled airport, you find that your communications equipment has failed. You need to get back to the home field for repairs and arrange with the tower by phone to use light signals to get on your way. While taxiing out you receive a flashing red light signal. This means that you

1—are to return to the starting point at the airport.
2—must taxi clear of the landing area now in use (runway).
3—must stop and hold position where you are.
4—must give way to other aircraft and continue circling.

22

WEATHER INFORMATION

This chapter is intended to review information on the weather as presented in Chapter 22, *SPFM*.

It is suggested that you make the books *Aviation Weather* (AC 00-6A) and *Aviation Weather Services* (AC 00-45C) a part of your library for references to more detailed weather theory and government services available to the pilot. They are inexpensive and may be ordered through the United States Government Printing Office.

After reading Chapter 22, *SPFM* try to answer the following questions without reference to any text, then grade yourself by using the answers provided at the end of this book. Explanations are also given so that you can understand why your particular response might be incorrect. When you have completed this procedure, review areas of weakness before taking the test in Chapter 27.

2201. Standard *sea level pressure* may be expressed in inches of mercury (Hg), millibars (mb), pounds per square inch (psi) or pounds per square foot (psf). The correct figures for the appropriate measure are:

	Inches Hg	Millibars	psi	psf
1—	29.92	760.0	24.0	2116
2—	760.0	1013.2	14.7	2992
3—	29.92	1013.2	14.7	2116
4—	29.92	760.0	1013.2	996

2202. In the Northern Hemisphere the *usual* characteristics associated with a high-pressure area are

1—good weather and counterclockwise circulation.
2—poor weather and counterclockwise circulation.
3—good weather and clockwise circulation.
4—poor weather and clockwise circulation.

2203. The cold front can be described by the following factors. The most correct answer is:

	Depiction Code	Speed of Movement When Compared to Warm Front	Width of Weather	Clouds
1—	▲▲▲▲	Faster	Narrow	Stratus
2—	▲⌒▲⌒	Slower	Wide	Cumulus
3—	⌒⌒⌒	Faster	Wide	Cumulus
4—	▲▲▲	Faster	Narrow	Cumulus

2204. The rotation of the earth is one cause for the deflection of winds; in the Northern Hemisphere the winds are deflected to the right. This phenomenon is called

1—torque.
2—Coriolis force.
3—Bernoulli force.
4—P-factor.

2205. The characteristics of rapid clearing, lowering temperatures, strong gusty winds on the surface, and a wind shift are usually associated with

1—troughs.
2—fast-moving cold fronts.
3—slow-moving cold fronts.
4—slow-moving warm fronts.

2206. The warm front may be described by its graphics code, width of weather area, speed in comparison to a cold front, typical clouds, and general weather phenomena. Select the correct combination that best describes a warm front:

	Graphics Code	Width of Weather	Speed	Clouds	Weather
1—	⌒⌒⌒⌒	Wide	Slow	Cumulus	Good visibility
2—	▲▲▲▲	Narrow	Fast	Cumulus	Low ceilings
3—	▲▲▲	Narrow	Slow	Stratus	Low ceilings
4—	⌒⌒⌒⌒	Wide	Slow	Stratus	Low ceilings

Chapter 22.   Weather Information   83

2207. The weather associated with a stationary front usually includes

	Duration	Width	Intensity	Clouds
1—	Long-term	Wide	Intense	Cumulus
2—	Long-term	Narrow	Intense	Stratus
3—	Short-term	Narrow	Low intensity	Cumulus
4—	Long-term	Wide	Low intensity	Stratus

2208. Clouds consist of four general families. These are

1—high, middle, low, and convective.
2—stratus, alto, cirrus, and nimbo.
3—high, middle, low, and clouds of vertical development.
4—fog, stratus, alto, and cirrus.

2209. Clouds are composed of minute ice crystals or water droplets and are the result of moist air being cooled to the point of condensation. The higher clouds are almost totally composed of

1—water droplets.
2—fine ice crystals.
3—large hail.
4—supercooled moisture.

2210. Clouds are formed by moist air being cooled to the point of condensation. The normal lapse rate per 1000 feet of altitude is

1—1°F.
2—2°F.
3—2°C.
4—3.5°C.

2211. In comparing typical cold and warm fronts, the warm air is usually

1—above the cold air.
2—below the cold air.
3—below the freezing level.
4—mixing very well in both fronts.

2212. Isobars are lines that join points of

1—unequal pressure.
2—equal pressure.
3—diverse circulation.
4—increasing pressure changes.

2213. Stratus clouds are normally considered to be

1—composed of ice crystals and often hail.
2—vertically developing.
3—layered.
4—made up of festoons.

2214. Hail is normally associated with what particular cloud?

1—Cirrocumulus.
2—Nimbostratus.
3—Stratocumulus.
4—Cumulonimbus.

2215. Hazards to flight associated with thunderstorms are worse during the

1—peristatic genesis.
2—mature stage.
3—initial wind development.
4—dissipating stage.

2216. The cumulus stage of a thunderstorm is evidenced by

1—an increasing vertical development.
2—decreasing turbulence and rain.
3—the anvil head.
4—squall lines.

2217. Squall lines are

1—lines of equal pressure.
2—lines of equal variation of pressure.
3—lines of nimbostratus clouds.
4—lines of cumulonimbus clouds.

2218. This ice resembles that found in ice cubes and is formed by large droplets. It is called

1—frost.
2—rime ice.
3—hoar ice.
4—clear ice.

2219. Read the following five definitions. Then match them to the appropriate type of fog name.

1—Warm moist air moving from the Gulf of Mexico onto the cooler North American continent causes this fog.
2—Usually occurs during the early morning hours, with clear sky, very little wind, and a narrow dew-point temperature spread.
3—Moist air is moved up a mountain and is cooled as the air progresses upward.
4—Occurs when water vapor sublimates directly into ice crystals because of very cold temperature.
5—Usually occurs when moisture falls into cool air, as during a recent rain.

Fog Type	Definition Number
Advection	_____
Precipitation	_____
Ice	_____
Upslope	_____
Radiation	_____

2220. As a pilot flies the airplane to higher altitudes, a decrease in the air pressure is encountered. Continuing to climb to higher altitudes without operating oxygen equipment or pressurization would lead to

1—hyperventilation—an excess of carbon dioxide.
2—decompression—an excess of oxygen.
3—hypoxia—a deficiency of oxygen.
4—Euphoria—a mid-European country.

2221. Flying from a high-pressure area to a low-pressure area, your altimeter (without resetting) will read

1—high.
2—low.
3—accurately.
4—pressure altitude only.

2222. When you work the computer and performance problems, you will need to know the meaning of the term, "standard day." You should know that this term includes a pressure of 29.92 inches of mercury and a temperature of

1—59°C at sea level.
2—15°C at flight altitude.
3—59°F at 10,000 feet pressure altitude.
4—15°C at sea level.

2223. The two common temperature scales used in flying are °C (Celsius) and °F (Fahrenheit). Some flight computers have a direct conversion scale, but suppose you dropped your computer and couldn't get to it? To convert the temperature from Fahrenheit to Celsius you would

1—subract 32 from the °F reading and multiply by 5/9.
2—subtract 32 from the °F reading and multiply by 9/5.
3—add 32 to the °F reading and multiply by 9/5.
4—add 32 to °F reading and multiply by 5/9.

2224. When an altimeter is set at the local pressure, that instrument registers the

1—pressure altitude.
2—density altitude.
3—true altitude.
4—indicated altitude.

2225. The vertical action of air resulting from surface heating by the sun is referred to as

1—advection.
2—convection.
3—Coriolis force.
4—general circulation.

2226. The wind flowing over the surface is slowed by the resultant friction. On a smooth terrain the friction is less than that resulting from a rough or mountainous terrain. As the wind speed decreases, the Coriolis force will

1—increase.
2—decrease.
3—remain the same.
4—increase geometrically.

2227. Adjacent air currents of different directions and/or velocities will create friction, resulting in turbulence being produced. The result is commonly called

1—wind shear.
2—wind pressure.
3—sea breezes.
4—katabatic winds.

2228. Frost on the airplane's wings is a hazard for takeoff because

1—the added weight may cause the airplane to use excess runway for lift-off.
2—the roughness of the frost surface may cause separation and loss of lift, precluding a safe takeoff.
3—the added drag of the rough surface will keep the airplane from accelerating properly.
4—cold wing surfaces do not produce as much lift as warm surfaces.

2229. The term that expresses the percentage and degree of air saturation, or the ratio of the actual water vapor present to the water vapor that *could* be present under the given circumstances, is

1—dewpoint.
2—wet lapse rate.
3—relative temperature.
4—relative humidity.

2230. The term for the temperature to which air must be cooled to become saturated by the water vapor in that air is

1—dewpoint.
2—water vapor density.
3—dry lapse rate.
4—relative humidity.

2231. The phenomenon described as precipitation from a cloud, which evaporates and does not reach the ground, is called

1—rain.
2—drizzle.
3—dew.
4—virga.

Chapter 22. Weather Information 85

2232. Drizzle, rain, ice pellets, snow, hail, and ice crystals are referred to as

1—cooling processes.
2—precipitation.
3—supercooled water.
4—results of the sublimation process.

2233. You are flying VFR from Sewanee, Tennessee, to Blacksburg, Virginia. As you approach Knoxville, Tennessee, you start getting a bumpy ride and see cumulus clouds developing over the Great Smoky Mountains. You could determine that you are encountering

1—stable air.
2—katabatic air.
3—unstable air.
4—advection.

Decode the following hourly report: DYR RS 1657 E10 BKN 20 OVC 7 097/63/58/2420G25/981 PK WND 2326/35. Use this information to answer questions 2234 through 2238.

2234. The "RS 1657" in the sequence means

1—report service at 1657 CST.
2—record special report at 1657Z.
3—rain and snow at 1657Z.
4—rain and snow at 1657 CST.

2235. The portion of the weather sequence that reads "E10 BKN 20 OVC" means that Dyersburg has a

1—measured ceiling 1000 feet above MSL (broken) with an overcast at 2000 feet.
2—estimated ceiling 1000 feet MSL and a broken 2000 feet overcast.
3—estimated ceiling 1000 feet MSL and broken 2000 feet MSL overcast.
4—estimated ceiling (broken clouds) 1000 feet above the surface with an overcast at 2000 feet above the surface.

2236. The portion of the weather sequence for DYR that reads "7 097/63/58" indicates the

1—visibility is 7 nautical miles and the pressure corrected to sea level is 1009.7 mb, with a temperature of 63°F and a 58°F dewpoint.
2—visibility is 7 statute miles, the pressure corrected to sea level is 1009.7 mb, the temperature is 63°F, and the dewpoint is 58°F.
3—visibility is 7 nautical miles and the altimeter setting is 30.97, with a temperature of 63°C and a 58°C dewpoint.
4—visibility is 7 statute miles, pressure corrected to sea level is 90.97 mb, the temperature is 63°C with a 58°C dewpoint.

2237. The portion of the DYR sequence that reads "/2420G25/981" means that

1—wind is from 240° true at 20 knots, gusting to 25 knots; altimeter setting is 29.81 inches of mercury.
2—wind is from 240° magnetic at 20 knots, gusting to 25 knots; altimeter setting is 29.81 inches of mercury.
3—wind is from 242° true at 05 knots, gusting to 25 knots; altimeter setting is 29.81 inches of mercury.
4—wind is from 240° true at 20 mph, gusting to 25 mph; altimeter setting is 29.81 mb.

2238. The portion of the DYR sequence that reads "PK WND 2326/35" means that the

1—peak wind was from 230° at 26 knots at 35 minutes past the last hour.
2—peak wind occurred at 2326 CST at 35 mph.
3—peak wind occurred at 2326 GMT at 35 mph.
4—peak wind occurred at 2326 EST at 35 knots.

2239. In the terminal forecast, the wind is not mentioned if it is expected to be less than

1—10 mph.
2—8 mph.
3—10 knots.
4—6 knots.

2240. Reading a particular terminal forecast, you note that the visibility figure has been deleted. You know by this that the visibility is forecast to be greater than

1—6 nautical miles.
2—10 nautical miles.
3—10 statute miles.
4—6 statute miles.

2241. In the last part of a terminal forecast, you find the abbreviation "VFR." You should expect conditions to be *at least*

1—ceiling of 1000 feet MSL, visibility of 3 nautical miles.
2—ceiling of 3000 feet, visibility of 5 statute miles.
3—ceiling of 1000 feet, visibility of 5 nautical miles.
4—ceiling of 3000 feet MSL, visibility of 5 nautical miles.

2242. As you read a terminal forecast, you encounter the abbreviation "MVFR." You could expect weather conditions of:

	Ceilings	Visibility
1—	1000-3000 feet	3-5 nautical miles
2—	3000-5000 feet	1-3 statute miles
3—	500-1000 feet	1-5 statute miles
4—	1000-3000 feet	3-5 statute miles

2243. The area forecasts are normally valid for a specific number of hours. These are _____ hours with an outlook for an additional _____ hours.

1—18 and 12.
2—12 and 12.
3—12 and 6.
4—18 and 6.

2244. In the discussion and study of AIRMETS you should be aware of items included that are particularly applicable to AIRMETS. Pick the items that apply:

A. Moderate icing.
B. Tornadoes.
C. Sustained winds of 30 knots or more at the surface.
D. Moderate turbulence.
E. Lines of thunderstorms.
F. Embedded thunderstorms.
 1—ABCD.
 2—BCDF.
 3—ACD.
 4—ACE.

2245. SIGMETS and CONVECTIVE SIGMETS are advisories that concern significant weather that could be potentially hazardous to all aircraft in flight. Pick out items that will be contained in various SIGMETS:

A. Moderate icing.
B. Severe icing.
C. Moderate turbulence.
D. Tornadoes.
E. Hail ¾ inch in diameter or larger.
F. Severe and extreme turbulence.
G. Dust storms, sandstorms, or volcanic ash lowering visibilities to less than 3 miles.
 1—BDEFG.
 2—ACDFG.
 3—ADEFG.
 4—ACFG.

2246. The pilot report (PIREP) is one of the most valuable bits of information a pilot can give or receive. These are observation reports of what is going on *now*. You could normally find PIREPS as additions to the hourly sequence reports. You could best identify them on printed reports by the letters

1—FT.
2—UA.
3—PR.
4—FD.

2247. The airplane's altimeter accuracy is affected not only by atmospheric pressure changes but also by variations from standard of the temperature of the air surrounding the airplane. Which of the following statements is true concerning this factor?

1—If the temperature is higher than standard, the altimeter will read inaccurately high.
2—A lower than standard temperature will cause the altimeter to read inaccurately low.
3—A lower than standard temperature will cause the altimeter to read inaccurately high.
4—The error is greatest at sea level and decreases with altitude.

Questions 2248 through 2252 are based on Figure 22-A.

2248. Which of the following statements is correct concerning the 1000 CST hourly reports?

1—Nashville (BNA) has a ceiling of 4000 feet.
2—Huntsville (HSV) has a ceiling of 800 feet overcast.
3—Huntsville (HSV) has a visibility of 11 statute miles in light drizzle and fog.
4—The wind at Nashville (BNA) is from 020° at 4 knots.

2249. Choose the correct statement concerning the 1000 CST reports.
1—Chattanooga (CHA) has had a significant weather change in one or more of the reporting elements.
2—The "999" at the end of the Chattanooga (CHA) and Huntsville (HSV) reports means that the wind is calm.
3—Nashville (BNA) has a visibility of 1½ miles.
4—The Huntsville (HSV) air traffic control tower (ATCT) is in operation from 1200 to 0500 CST.

2250. Choose the correct statement concerning the 1000 CST reports.

1—McKellar Field (MKL) has a rigid ceiling.
2—The pilot of a Beech 90 reports light to moderate turbulence at 1605Z to Crossville (CSV).
3—At Nashville (BNA) the rain began at 2 minutes past the last hour and the drizzle (L) is variable to rain (R) at 60 minutes past the last hour.
4—The altimeter setting at Memphis (MEM) is 31.11 inches of mercury.

2251. Choose the correct statement concerning the 1100 CST reports.

1—The altimeter setting at Memphis (MEM) is 29.07 inches of mercury.
2—After the scheduled observation, Nashville (BNA) had a drop of 100 feet in ceiling and one-half mile in visibility.

```
1000 CST

        BNA SA 1553 M4 OVC 1/2 L-F 164/41/38/0204/001/R02LVR60 CIG RGD
        BNA UA
        UA /OV BNA23024Ø 1500 FL 180 /TP MU2 /SK OVC 40 E200 OVC
        /RM BTWN LYRS

        CSV SA 1554 E5 OVC 2L-F 150/40/39/1805/995
        CSV UA
        /OV CHA 300025 1605 FL 180 /TP BE90 /TB LGT-MDT
        !CSV 09/019 HDI NDB OTS

        CHA RS 1550 M5 OVC 3/4R-F 159/41/38/3604/999
        !CHA 10/008 CHA ILS UNMON 04-1100 DAILY

        HSV SA 1551 M4 BKN 8 OVC 11/2L-F 157/42/40/0703/999
        !HSV 11/007 HSV ATCT 12-0500 DAILY

        MEM SA 1553 M7 OVC 21/2F 179/39/37/0111/005

        MKL SA 1556 E6 OVC 4F 170/40/38/3610/003 CIG RGD


1100 CST

        BNA SA 1653 M5 OVC 1F 157/41/38/3405/999/R02LVR60+ CIG RGD LE30
        BNA SP 1712 M4 OVC 1/2F 3306/999/R02LVR60 CIG RGD

        CSV SA 1655 E5 OVC 2L-F 138/41/40/1904/992
        !CSV 09/019 HDI NDB OTS

        CHA RS 1651 M7 OVC 3/4R-F 149/41/39/0804/996

        HSV SA 1653 E7 OVC 11/2L-F 147/43/40/0503/996

        MEM SA 1656 M9 OVC 21/2F 182/40/37/0208/007

        MKL SA 1657 E7 OVC 4F 170/40/38/3608/003
```

Fig. 22-A. Actual hourly weather reports, NOTAMS, and Pilot Reports for six stations at 1000 CST and 1100 CST on the fourteenth of the month.

3—The barometric pressure at CSV (Crossville) is reported as 99.2 mb.

4—The wind is calm at Nashville (BNA) (999).

2252. Which one of the following statements is correct concerning the hourly reports at 1000 CST and 1100 CST?

1—The Crossville (CSV) ceiling and visibility have improved.

2—The Chattanooga (CHA) ceiling and visibility have deteriorated.

3—The Huntsville (HSV) ceiling has dropped at 1100 CST.

4—The regular 1100 CST report indicates that at Nashville (BNA) the drizzle ended at 30 minutes past the last hour.

Questions 2253–2255 are based on Figure 22-B.

```
BNA 132222 C30 BKN. 04Z C25 OVC 5H. 07Z C20 OVC CHC 4R-F. 11Z C12
   OVC 2R-F. 16Z IFR CIG R F..
MKL 132222 C50 OVC. 00Z 20 SCT C35 OVC SCT OCNL BKN. 07Z C12 OVC
   CHC 4R-. 10Z C8 OVC 3R-F. 16Z IFR CIG R F..
HSV 132222 C15 OVC 5H 1212. 04Z C10 OVC 4FH CHC 2L-F. 08Z CS OVC
   2L-F. 10Z C5 OVC 2R-F. 16Z IFR CIG R F..
MEM 13222 20 SCT C38 OVC. 23Z 13 SCT C20 OVC SCT OCNL BKN. 06Z
   C13 OVC CHC 5R-. 10Z C8 OVC 3R-F. 16Z IFR CIG R..
MSL 132222 C15 OVC 5H 1010. 02Z C10 OVC 4FH CHC 3L-F. 06Z C8 OVC
   3L-F. 10Z C5 OVC 1R-F. 16Z IFR CIG R F..
CSV 132222 C50 BKN. 03Z C30 OVC 5H. 06Z C20 OVC CHC 3R-F. 09Z C9 OVC
   2R-F. 16Z IFR CIG R F..
CHA 132222 C30 BKN. 01Z 13 SCT C20 BKN CHC R-. 05Z C13 BKN 4R-F.
   10Z C7 OVC 2R-F. 16Z IFR CIG R F..
```

Fig. 22-B. Actual terminal forecast for seven stations from 2200Z on the thirteenth to 2200Z on the fourteenth of the month.

2253. The forecast weather for Huntsville (HSV) indicates that starting at 0400 CST the weather will be

1—ceiling 1000 overcast; 4 miles visibility in fog and haze, with a chance of visibility of 2 miles in light drizzle and fog.
2—ceiling 800 overcast; 2 miles visibility in light drizzle and fog.
3—ceiling 500 overcast; 2 miles visibility in light rain and fog, with a wind of less than 6 knots.
4—ceiling 500 overcast; 2 miles visibility, with a wind of 10 knots or more.

2254. For which of the following stations is the worst weather forecast for 0600 CST?

1—Huntsville (HSV).
2—Crossville (CSV).
3—McKellar (MKL).
4—Nashville (BNA).

2255. Based on the 1100 CST hourly report for Chattanooga (CHA) (also see Fig. 22-A), the terminal forecast for that period is

1—correct because the actual weather reported is IFR (or worse).
2—incorrect because the actual weather reported is MVFR.
3—correct because the actual weather reported is MVFR.
4—incorrect because a ceiling of 700 feet does not constitute IFR conditions.

Questions 2256-2258 refer to Figure 22-C, an Area Forecast issued by Boston.

2256. Under the heading "hazards" (BOS*H*), thunderstorms imply that

1—AIRMETS are still in effect.
2—there will be moderate to severe turbulence.
3—there will be light to moderate icing.
4—low-level wind shear is possible.

2257. In the "turbulence" section (BOS*T*), certain parts of the forecast area are forecast to have

1—occasional moderate turbulence below 1000 feet.
2—turbulent conditions continuing beyond 2200Z.
3—continual moderate to severe turbulence below 10,000 feet.
4—light to moderate updrafts over rough terrain.

2258. Under the "significant clouds and wx" (weather) portion of the forecast (BOS*C*), which area will have the lowest cloud layers during the forecast period?

1—Northern New York State.
2—Northern New England.
3—Coastal waters.
4—Southern New England.

Refer to Figure 22-D for question 2259.

2259. The AIRMET indicates that

1—there will be occasional ceilings and visibilities below 10,000 feet and 3 miles.
2—there will be occasional ceilings and visibilities below 1000 feet and 3 miles in stratus, fog, and precipitation.

```
10000 120945
BOSH FA 120945
HAZARDS VALID UNTIL 122200
ME NH VT MA RI CT NY LO NJ PA OH LE WV MD DC DE VA AND CSTL WTRS
.
FLT PRCTNS...TURBC...ME NH VT LO NY PA LE OH WV VA MD
.
TSTMS IMPLY SVR OR GTR TURBC SVR ICING AND LLWS.
NON MSL HGTS NOTED BY AGL OR CIG
.
THIS FA ISSUANCE INCORPORATES THE FOLLOWING AIRMETS STILL IN
EFFECT...NONE.
....

BOSS FA 120945
SYNOPSIS VALID UNTIL 130400
.
HIGH PRES CNTR MID ATLC CST WILL CONT DRFTG EWD THRU 04Z. SFC
LOW CNTRL PLNS WITH CDFNT
ICG AND FRZLVL VALID UNTIL 122200
.
NO SGFNT ICG XPCD.
.
FRZLVL...030 SLK-PVD SLPG TO 060 FDY-SBY AND TO NR 080 SWRN VA.
....

BOST FA 120945
TURBC VALID UNTIL 122200
.
ME NH VT LO NY PA LE OH WV VA MD
FROM CAR TO BGR TO ALB TO CLT TO MEM TO ACT TO LBB TO MSP TO SSM
TO CAR
OCNL MDT TURBC BLO 100 IN MDT TO STG LOW LVL WNDS WITH MDT TO
STG UDDFS OVER RUF TRRN. CONDS CONTG BYD 22Z. SEE MIA CHI AND
DFW FAS FOR DETAILS IN THOSE AREAS.
....
BOSC FA 120945
SGFNT CLDS AND WX VALID UNTIL 122200...OTLK 122200-130400Z.
.
NRN NEW ENG
40-60 SCT-BKN 120. OTLK...VFR.
.
SRN NEW ENG
CLR. 16Z SCT CI. OTLK...VFR.
.
LO NY PA NJ
NRN NY...30-50 SCT-BKN LYRD TO 120. OTLK...VFR.
BKN LYRD TO 200.
OTLK...VFR.
E OF A BWI-RDI LINE...CLR 3-5F WITH LCL VSBYS BLO 3F. 16Z SCT-
BKN CI. OTLK...VFR.
.
CSTL WTRS
20-30 SCT-BKN LYRD TO 120 ERN PTN TIL ARND 16Z OTRW CLR. 19Z SCT
-BKN CI. OTLK...VFR.
....
```

Fig. 22-C. An actual area forecast.

```
CHI WA 141110
AIRMET WHISKEY 1 141110-141710
KY
FM 30N DYR TO 80SE FAM TO 30SW EVV TO CVG TO 20SE YRK TO 40ENE BRG
TO 40SE LOZ
OCNL CIGS AND VSBYS BLO 010 AND 3 IN ST FOG AND PCPN. CONDS CONTG
BYD 1710Z.
```

Fig. 22-D. An AIRMET for an area centered in Kentucky.

3—there will be occasional ceilings and visibilities below 1000 feet and 3 miles in the towns of St. Fog and Participation.
4—there will be occasional ceilings and visibilities below 100 feet and 3 miles.

Refer to Figure 22-E for questions 2260-2262.

2260. The wind at 3000 feet at Nashville (BNA) is

1—missing from the report (9900).
2—from 090° true at 9 knots.
3—light and variable.
4—from 240° true at 19 knots.

2261. The wind at 34,000 feet at Knoxville (TYS) is

1—from 075° true at 2 knots, with a temperature of −51°C.
2—from 250° true at 102 knots, with a temperature of −51°C.
3—from 250° true at 102 knots, with a temperature of +51°F.
4—from 075° true at 102 knots, with a temperature of −51°C.

2262. The wind at 6000 feet at Memphis (MEM) is

1—from 030° true at 9 knots, with a temperature of +2°C.

2—from 300° true at 90 knots, with a temperature of +1°C.
3—from 300° true at 9 knots, with a temperature of +1°F.
4—from 300° true at 9 knots, with a temperature of +1°C.

2263. The best reference for finding the location of fronts and pressure systems is the latest

1—Surface Analysis Chart.
2—Radar Summary Chart.
3—Terminal Forecast.
4—Hourly Weather Report.

Refer to Figure 22-F for questions 2264-2267.

2264. The front depicted as running from the Low at Mobile through eastern North Carolina

1—is stationary.
2—is a warm front moving slowly southeast.
3—is a warm front moving northwest.
4—has a rapid change in pressure along its length.

2265. The lowest pressure of the Lows depicted on the chart is at the

1—Low north of Minnesota and Wisconsin.
2—Low north of Montana.

```
DATA BASED ON 140000Z
VALID 141200Z     FOR USE 0900-1800Z.   TEMPS NEG ABV 24000
  FT   3000     6000     9000    12000    18000    24000    30000    34000    39000

  BNA  9900    2412+01  2419-03  2526-08  2543-19  2462-30   248643   249651   740558
  MEM  3507    3009+01  2812-03  2616-09  2532-20  2453-30   248044   249151   740459
  TYS  1714    2121+02  2328-02  2334-07  2449-19  2567-30   259043   750251   751058
  LOU  9900    2107-01  2414-06  2522-10  2540-21  2560-32   258545   259352   259859
  BEM  2011    2315+05  2424+00  2434-05  2453-17  2458-28   248941   249949   740558
```

Fig. 22-E. Winds aloft forecast. All heights are MSL.

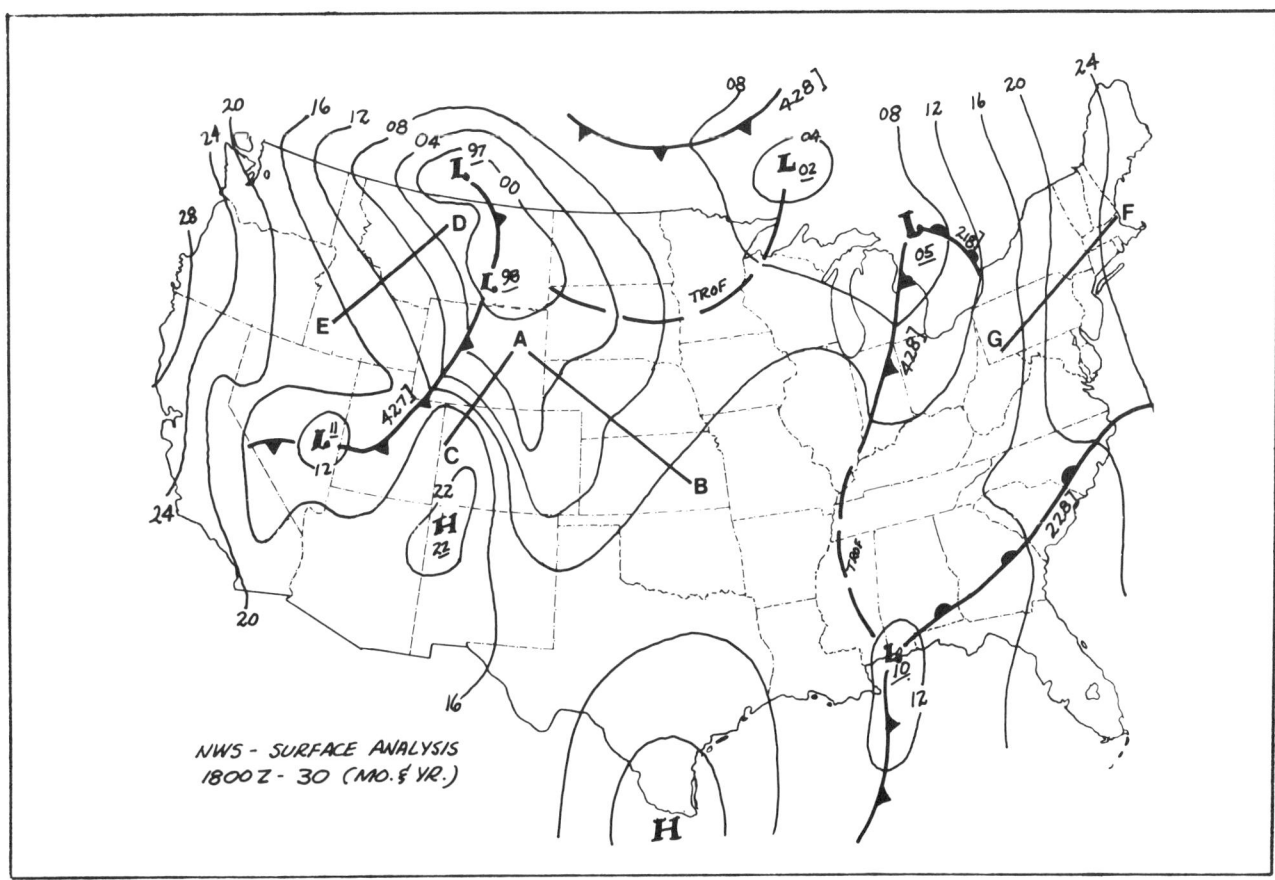

Fig. 22-F. A Surface Analysis Chart. (*SPFM*)

3—Low near Mobile, Alabama.
4—Low just northeast of Michigan.

2266. On which of the following trips would you expect to get the *fastest* rate of change of pressure enroute?

1—D to E.
2—A to B.
3—F to G.
4—A to C.

2267. On which of the following trips would you expect to get the slowest rate of change of pressure enroute?

1—F to G.
2—A to B.
3—A to C.
4—D to E.

Refer to Figure 22-G, a Weather Depiction Chart, for questions 2268–2270.

2268. You would expect to find weather conditions of ceilings less than 1000 feet and/or visibility less than 3 miles at the following stations.

1—Harrisburg (HAR), Asheville (AVL), and Indianapolis (IND).
2—St. Louis (STL), Indianapolis (IND), and Des Moines (DSM).
3—Asheville (AVL), St. Louis (STL), and Indianapolis (IND).
4—Phoenix (PHX), Seattle (SEA), and Asheville (AVL).

2269. Which of the following stations have weather conditions of ceilings between 1000 and 3000 feet and/or visibility of 3–5 miles inclusive?

1—Des Moines (DSM), Nashville (BNA), and Harrisburg (HAR).
2—St. Louis (STL), Nashville (BNA), and Seattle (SEA).
3—Indianapolis (IND), Des Moines (DSM), and Nashville (BNA).
4—Phoenix (PHX), Corpus Christi (CRP), and Harrisburg (HAR).

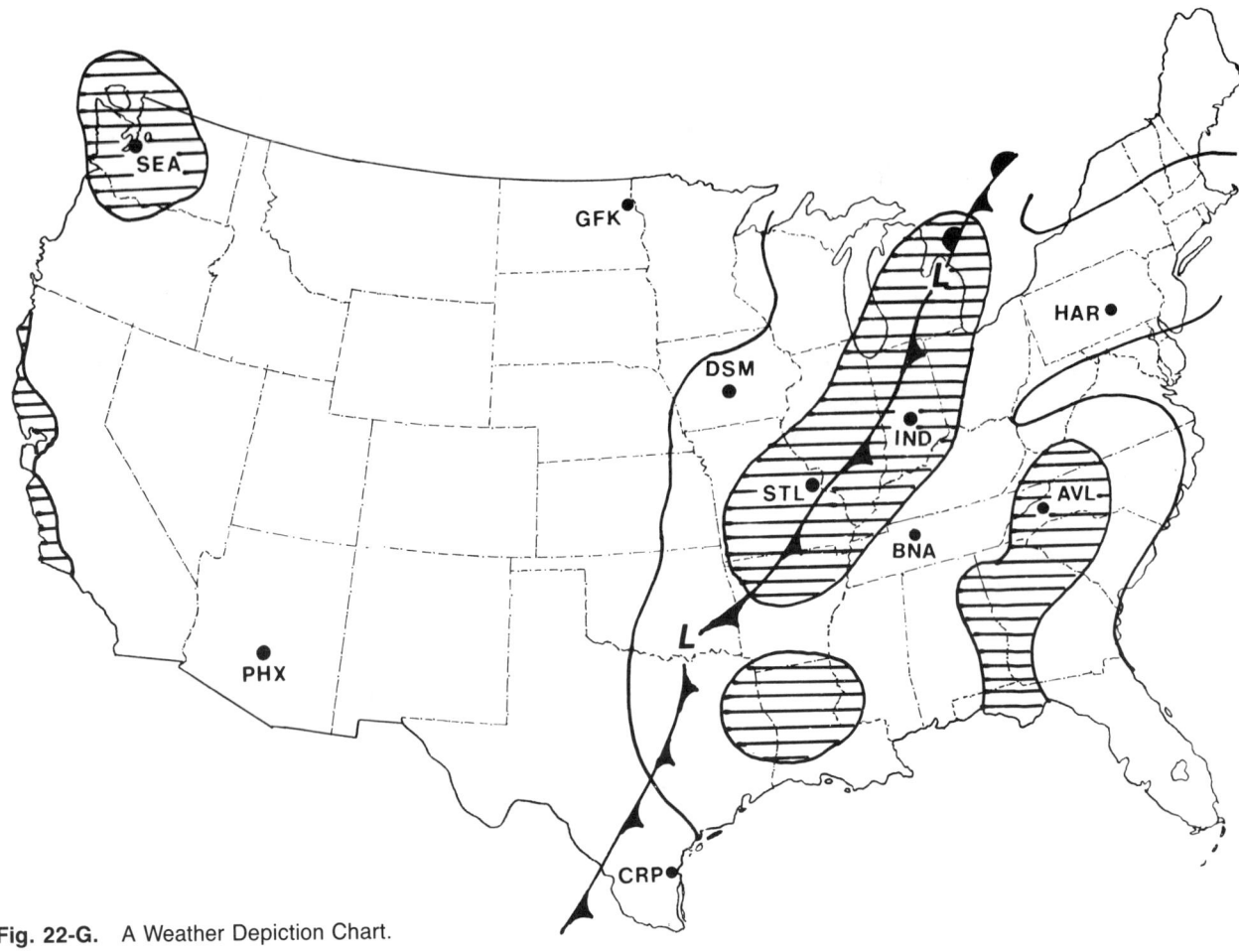

Fig. 22-G. A Weather Depiction Chart.

2270. Which of the following stations have ceilings greater than 3000 feet, or unlimited, and visibility greater than 5 miles.

1—Phoenix (PHX), Asheville (AVL), and Corpus Christi (CRP).
2—Grand Forks (GFK), Corpus Christi (CRP), or Nashville (BNA).
3—Seattle (SEA), Grand Forks (GFK), and Harrisburg (HAR).
4—Grand Forks (GFK), Phoenix (PHX), and Corpus Christi (CRP).

23

THE CROSS-COUNTRY: KNOWING YOUR AIRPLANE

Review Chapter 23, *SPFM* before answering the questions here.

2301. According to FAR 91, which of the following statements is correct?

1—The *registration certificate* must be displayed so that it is legible to passengers or crew.
2—The *airworthiness certificate* must be displayed so that it is legible to passengers and crew.
3—The *aircraft and engine logbooks* must be in the aircraft any time it is being operated.
4—The *aircraft radio station license* is required only for voice communications (transmitting) equipment.

2302. Your airplane weighs 2000 pounds, and in a sharp pull-up you are able to produce 6000 pounds of lift. The load factor being imposed is

1—3 g's.
2—9 g's.
3—1 g.
4—6 g's.

2303. The airplane's maneuvering speed, V_A,

1—decreases with a weight increase.
2—decreases with a weight decrease.
3—remains constant as marked on the airspeed indicator.
4—always remains in the yellow arc of the airspeed indicator.

Read the answer to question 2303 before going on to the next question.

2304. A *normal* category airplane stalls at 55 knots at its maximum certificated weight. The maximum maneuvering speed listed (rounded off) is

1—55 knots.
2—120 knots.
3—107 knots.
4—97 knots.

2305. A 4000-pound airplane has a maneuvering speed of 140 knots at that weight. The maneuvering speed at a weight of 3200 pounds should be approximately

1—140 knots.
2—70 knots.
3—107 knots.
4—126 knots.

2306. Find the "center of gravity" of the system shown in Figure 23-A. The center of gravity is located at

1—17 inches.
2—20 inches.
3—30 inches.
4—14 inches.

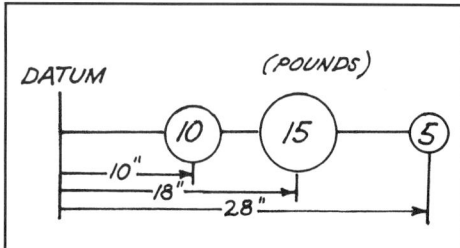

Fig. 23-A. A simple system of weights and moments.

2307. Check Figure 23-B. You and a competitor are going to have a race from point to point in four-place airplanes of the same model. The race requirements are that the airplanes must start at the gross weight of 3000 pounds. Assume that both must use the same power. Flying solo, you both will have to add ballast to bring the weight up to 3000 pounds. Your competitor elects to load so that the center of gravity (CG) is near the aft boundary of the Weight and Balance Envelope but is safe (A). You load your airplane so that the CG is near its forward allowable limit for that weight (B). Which of the following statements are correct?

A. Airplane B will cruise faster at the forward CG.
B. Airplane A will cruise faster at the aft CG.
C. Airplane B will be more stable in rough air.
D. Airplane A will be more stable in rough air.
E. Airplane A will have the higher stall speed.
F. Airplane B will have the higher stall speed.
  1—ACD.
  2—BCF.
  3—ADF.
  4—ACDE.

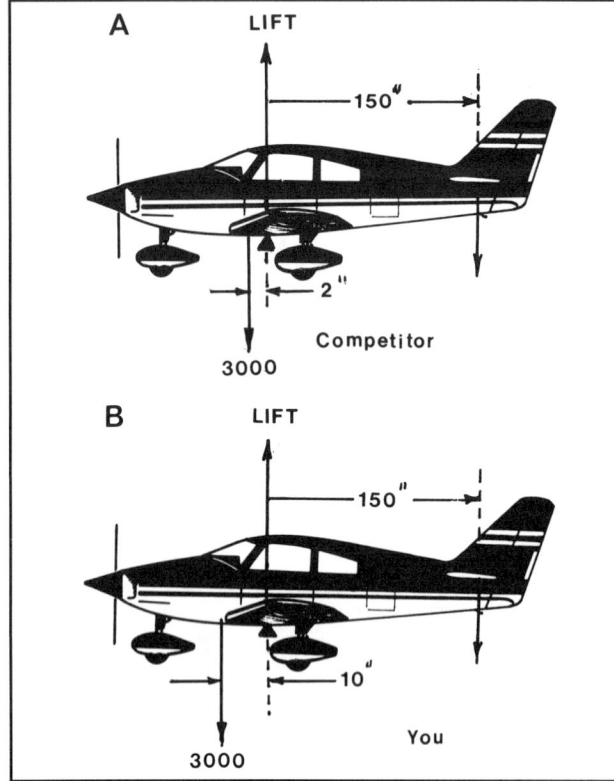

Fig. 23-B. A comparison of the effects of CG positions on tail-down forces and on cruise.

2308. The airplane shown in Figure 23-C has just rolled off the assembly line, and your job is to find the basic empty weight. For this example, the airplane has full oil, unusable fuel, hydraulic fluid, and optional equipment. (The airplane may be weighed without oil or unusable fuel and their values are computed *after* the weighing process, but not in this case.) The scales under the nosewheel and each main wheel register the weight value in pounds, as shown. Anyway, your job is to find the basic empty-weight moment and also the CG. Round off the inches to the nearest tenth. The basic empty-weight moment (pound-inches) and CG (inches aft of datum) are

1—149,800 and 84.1.
2—81,400 and 149.8.
3—88,400 and 84.1.
4—149,800 and 81.4.

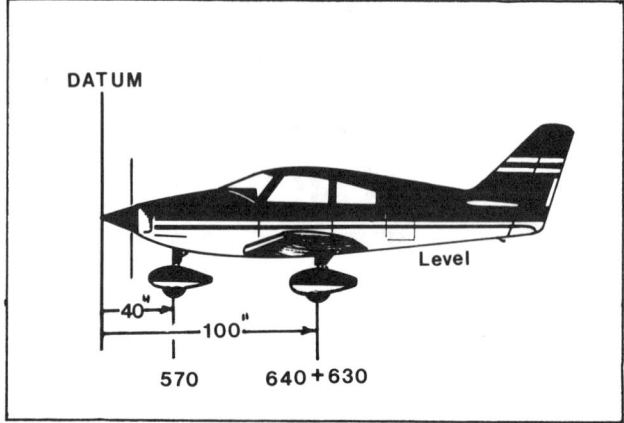

Fig. 23-C. Finding the empty weight CG. The airplane is placed on three scales in a level position and the weights noted. The nosewheel point indicates a value of 570 pounds; the two main wheels total 1270 pounds.

2309. The maximum weight of the four-place airplane just discussed is 3000 pounds, the baggage compartment (behind the back seat) is limited to 120 pounds, and the airplane has a total of 60 gallons of usable fuel. With four persons weighing a total of 732 pounds and 80 pounds of baggage, the airplane could carry a usable fuel load of

1—348 gallons.
2—58 gallons.
3—46 gallons.
4—51 gallons.

2310. Two of you are going to fly cross-country in a two-place airplane with a basic empty weight of 1120 pounds and empty-weight moment of 37,200 pound-inches. Using the information given below and Figure 23-D, find the CG position and confirm that the airplane is or is not safe to fly.

Pilot = 170 pounds
Copilot = 120 pounds
Baggage in area 1 = 90 pounds (including swim suits and snorkeling gear)
Fuel = 15 gallons in standard tanks

Chapter 23.   The Cross-Country: Knowing Your Airplane   95

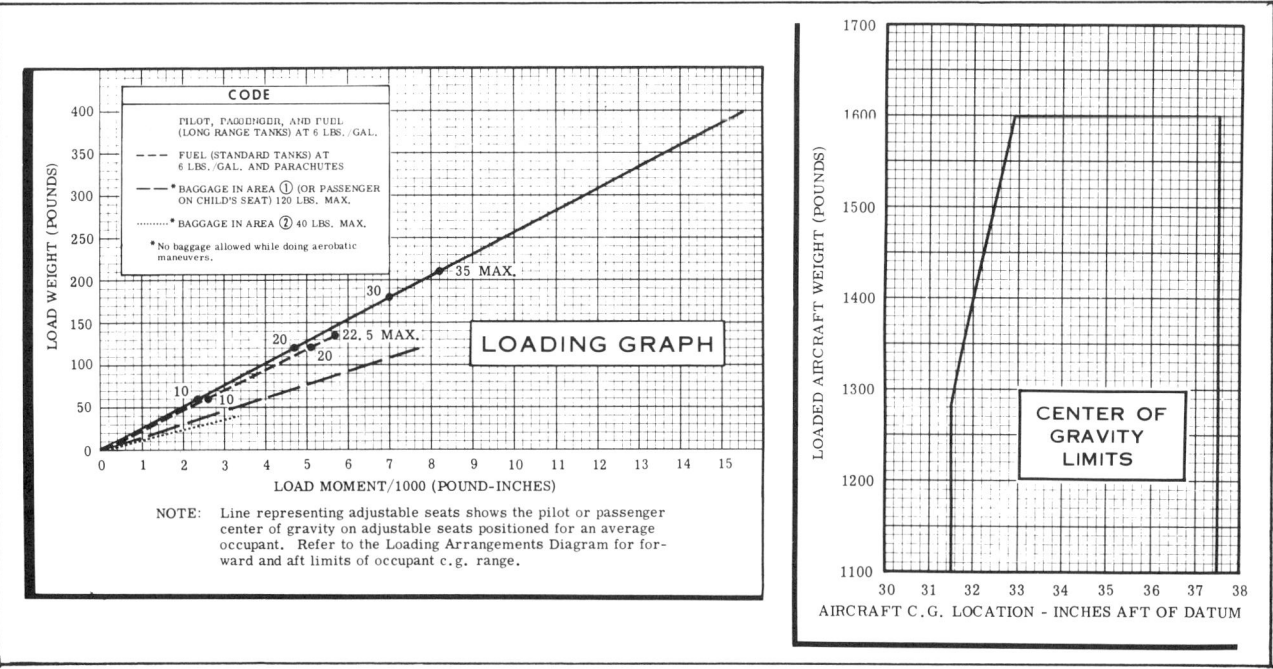

Fig. 23-D. Loading Graph and Center of Gravity Envelope for question 2310.

The weight of the airplane (pounds) and CG location (inches aft of datum to the nearest tenth) are respectively

1—1490 pounds and 34.1 inches.
2—1490 pounds and 36.5 inches.
3—1590 pounds and 36.5 inches.
4—1590 pounds and 35.0 inches.

2311. The airplane in Figure 23-E is flying straight and level in balanced, unaccelerated flight and weighs 2000 pounds. Find the (1) tail-down force, (2) lift being produced, and (3) average pressure on the horizontal tail (pounds per square foot) resulting from the forces and moments shown. (The area of the horizontal tail is 30 square feet.)

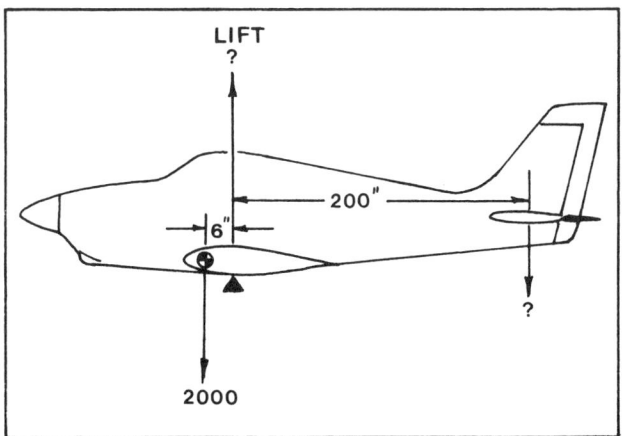

Fig. 23-E. An airplane flying straight and level in balanced, unaccelerated flight.

1—(1) 60 pounds, (2) 2060 pounds, and (3) 2 pounds per square foot.
2—(1) 120 pounds, (2) 2120 pounds, and (3) 4 pounds per square foot.
3—(1) 60 pounds, (2) 1940 pounds, and (3) 2 pounds per square foot.
4—(1) 60 pounds, (2) 2120 pounds, and (3) 4 pounds per square foot.

2312. Choose the correct statement concerning ground effect:

1—Ground effect results from air being compressed between the wing and the surface.
2—The airplane tends to pitch up while in ground effect.
3—The airplane is more stable (pitch) in ground effect.
4—Induced drag rises sharply when the airplane is in ground effect.

2313. The *Pilot's Operating Handbook* of your airplane recommends use of minimum grade fuel 100/130. In checking the fuel during preflight, you discover that someone has filled the tanks with fuel that is dyed green. Your best move is to

1—continue the preflight check and make your flight.
2—drain all the fuel and replace it with red-dyed fuel.
3—drain all the fuel and replace it with 100/130.
4—fly, but carry less-than-normal power under all conditions so as to avoid detonation.

2314. Your airplane uses Aviation 100 oil in the summer and on warmer days. As the weather gets cooler and temperatures drop to 40°F and below, you would likely switch to which of the following oil viscosities?

1—Aviation 120.
2—SAE 60.
3—SAE 80.
4—Aviation 80.

2315. Refer to the Time, Fuel, and Distance to Climb Chart (Fig. 23-F). You are taking off from an airport at a pressure altitude of 1500 feet and will climb to 7500 feet pressure altitude on a cross-country (temperatures standard). Under the no-wind conditions cited, you would expect to have used the following flying time, fuel (in the climb only), and in-flight distance to reach that altitude:

1—13 minutes, 1.8 gallons, and 14.5 NM.
2—13 minutes, 2.6 gallons, and 17.5 NM.
3—17.5 minutes, 1.8 gallons, and 13 NM.
4—18 minutes, 2.4 gallons, and 19 NM.

2316. Your airplane is equipped with a fixed-pitch propeller and requires 2400 rpm at sea level density-altitude to produce 65 percent power. When cruising at 6000 feet density-altitude, 65 percent power would require approximately what rpm setting?

1—1400.
2—2550.
3—2250.
4—2000.

2317. An engine properly leaned in cruise at 65 percent at sea level uses, for instance, 7.2 gallons per hour. At 6000 feet, in cruise and properly leaned, at 65 percent, the engine will use

1—approximately 20 percent more fuel.
2—the same amount of fuel.
3—approximately 20 percent less fuel.
4—approximately 30 percent less fuel.

2318. You are descending in very dry air to an airport with an elevation of 200 feet after a 2-hour cruising flight at 8500 feet MSL. (You know the air is very dry because the Transcribed Weather Broadcast just indicated a 20°F spread between temperature (62°F) and dewpoint (42°F) at the airport.) As you start to enter the traffic pattern at 1200 feet MSL, the engine gets very rough and temporarily quits. Which of the following would be the most likely cause of the problem?

1—The battery is dying, causing a loss of power to the spark plugs.
2—Carburetor ice.
3—Mixture too rich.
4—Mixture too lean.

Use the Cruise Performance Chart in Figure 23-G for questions 2319 and 2320.

2319. You are cruising at 5000 feet pressure altitude with an outside temperature of +5°C, carrying 2650 rpm. Leaned, the example airplane will have a fuel consumption (gallons per hour) of

1—5.3.
2—5.5.
3—4.5.
4—5.1.

2320. At 6000 feet pressure altitude, with a temperature of +13°C and carrying 2450 rpm, the fuel consumption (gallons per hour) will be

1—4.5.
2—4.0.
3—4.3.
4—3.9.

Refer to Figures 23-G and 23-H for question 2321.

TIME, FUEL, AND DISTANCE TO CLIMB
MAXIMUM RATE OF CLIMB

CONDITIONS:
Flaps Up
Full Throttle
Standard Temperature

NOTES:
1. Add 0.8 of a gallon of fuel for engine start, taxi and takeoff allowance.
2. Increase time, fuel and distance by 10% for each 8°C above standard temperature.
3. Distances shown are based on zero wind.

WEIGHT LBS	PRESSURE ALTITUDE FT	TEMP °C	CLIMB SPEED KIAS	RATE OF CLIMB FPM	FROM SEA LEVEL		
					TIME MIN	FUEL USED GALLONS	DISTANCE NM
1600	S.L.	15	68	670	0	0	0
	1000	13	68	630	2	0.2	2
	2000	11	67	590	3	0.5	4
	3000	9	66	550	5	0.7	6
	4000	7	65	510	7	1.0	8
	5000	5	65	470	9	1.3	10
	6000	3	64	425	11	1.6	13
	7000	1	64	385	14	1.9	16
	8000	-1	63	345	17	2.3	19
	9000	-3	63	305	20	2.7	23
	10,000	-5	62	265	23	3.2	27
	11,000	-7	62	220	27	3.7	32
	12,000	-9	61	180	33	4.3	38

Fig. 23-F. Time, Fuel, and Distance to Climb Chart.

CRUISE PERFORMANCE

CONDITIONS:
1600 Pounds
Recommended Lean Mixture

PRESSURE ALTITUDE	RPM	20°C BELOW STANDARD TEMP			STANDARD TEMPERATURE			20°C ABOVE STANDARD TEMP		
		% BHP	KTAS	GPH	% BHP	KTAS	GPH	% BHP	KTAS	GPH
2000	2650	---	---	---	78	103	5.9	72	102	5.4
	2600	80	102	6.0	73	101	5.5	68	100	5.1
	2500	70	97	5.3	65	96	4.9	60	95	4.6
	2400	62	92	4.7	57	91	4.3	53	91	4.1
	2300	54	87	4.1	50	87	3.9	47	86	3.7
	2200	47	83	3.7	44	82	3.5	42	81	3.3
4000	2700	---	---	---	78	105	5.8	72	104	5.4
	2600	75	101	5.6	69	100	5.2	64	99	4.8
	2500	66	96	5.0	61	95	4.6	57	95	4.3
	2400	58	91	4.4	54	91	4.1	50	90	3.9
	2300	51	87	3.9	48	86	3.7	45	85	3.5
	2200	45	82	3.5	42	81	3.3	40	80	3.2
6000	2750	---	---	---	77	107	5.8	71	105	5.3
	2700	79	105	5.9	73	104	5.4	67	103	5.1
	2600	70	100	5.2	64	99	4.8	60	98	4.5
	2500	62	95	4.7	57	95	4.3	53	94	4.1
	2400	54	91	4.2	51	90	3.9	48	89	3.7
	2300	48	86	3.7	45	85	3.5	42	84	3.4
8000	2700	74	104	5.5	68	103	5.1	63	102	4.8
	2600	65	99	4.9	60	99	4.6	57	98	4.3
	2500	58	95	4.4	54	94	4.1	51	93	3.9
	2400	52	90	4.0	48	89	3.7	45	88	3.5
	2300	46	85	3.6	43	84	3.4	40	82	3.2
10000	2700	69	103	5.2	64	102	4.8	59	102	4.5
	2600	61	99	4.6	57	98	4.3	53	97	4.1
	2500	55	94	4.2	51	93	3.9	48	92	3.7
	2400	49	89	3.8	45	88	3.6	43	87	3.4
12000	2650	61	100	4.6	57	99	4.3	53	98	4.1
	2600	58	98	4.4	54	97	4.1	50	96	3.9
	2500	52	93	4.0	48	92	3.7	45	91	3.5
	2400	46	89	3.6	43	87	3.4	41	84	3.3

Fig. 23-G. Cruise Performance Chart.

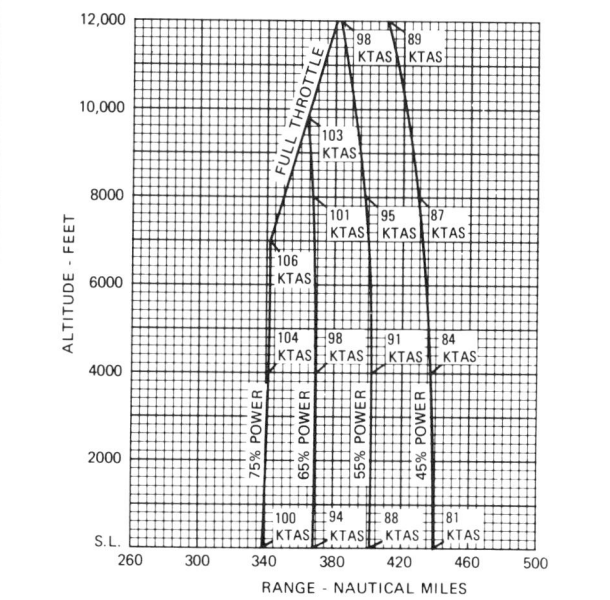

Fig. 23-H. Range Profile Chart. The problem is to find the range of the airplane based on the cruise performance. Assume that the airplane takes off and cruises at 4000 feet with allowance for start, taxi, takeoff, and climb, with the reserve as indicated here.

97

2321. At 4000 feet pressure altitude (standard temperature) and 2550 rpm, you would expect to have a range (NM) (with a 45-minute reserve) of approximately

1—340.
2—370.
3—437.
4—402.

2322. Which one of the following statements concerning fuel management is correct?

1—It's best to switch to a different tank just before takeoff so that a newer fuel source is available.
2—Switch to a different fuel tank during the climbout immediately after takeoff to see that the other tank is operational.
3—Take off only on the fuel tank that was used during the engine run-up or that has been run at least a minute at fairly high power settings (1500 rpm or above).
4—Use fuel on one tank during and after takeoff and in cruise until it is depleted, then switch to the other tank to assure maximum utilization of the fuel available.

Check Figure 23-I for the answer to questions 2323 and 2324.

2323. Which of the following statements concerning fuel systems is correct?

1—A venting system is only necessary for the gravity fuel system shown.
2—In system A, fuel going to the primer bypasses the fuel strainer.
3—System A allows the pilot to select tanks separately.
4—System B has an electric standby fuel pump.

2324. Assume that your front-seat passenger is a pilot (and a King Kong type) and wants to help you by pulling the carburetor heat while you are out in the area getting ready to make an idle descent, say, from 5000 feet above the ground. He, instead, pulls the mixture control *all* the way out of the panel, and now the engine is at idle cutoff but is windmilling. The throttle is still at the cruise setting as you look at the mixture control (and cable) in his lap. You are over bad terrain and at the current "power" setting won't *quite* make it back to the area of good fields or the airport. Looking carefully at fuel system A, you can see that there is a source of fuel available to the engine or intake manifolds in addition to the usual route. This is the

1—engine-driven fuel pump.
2—auxiliary fuel pump.
3—hand-operated primer.
4—carburetor.

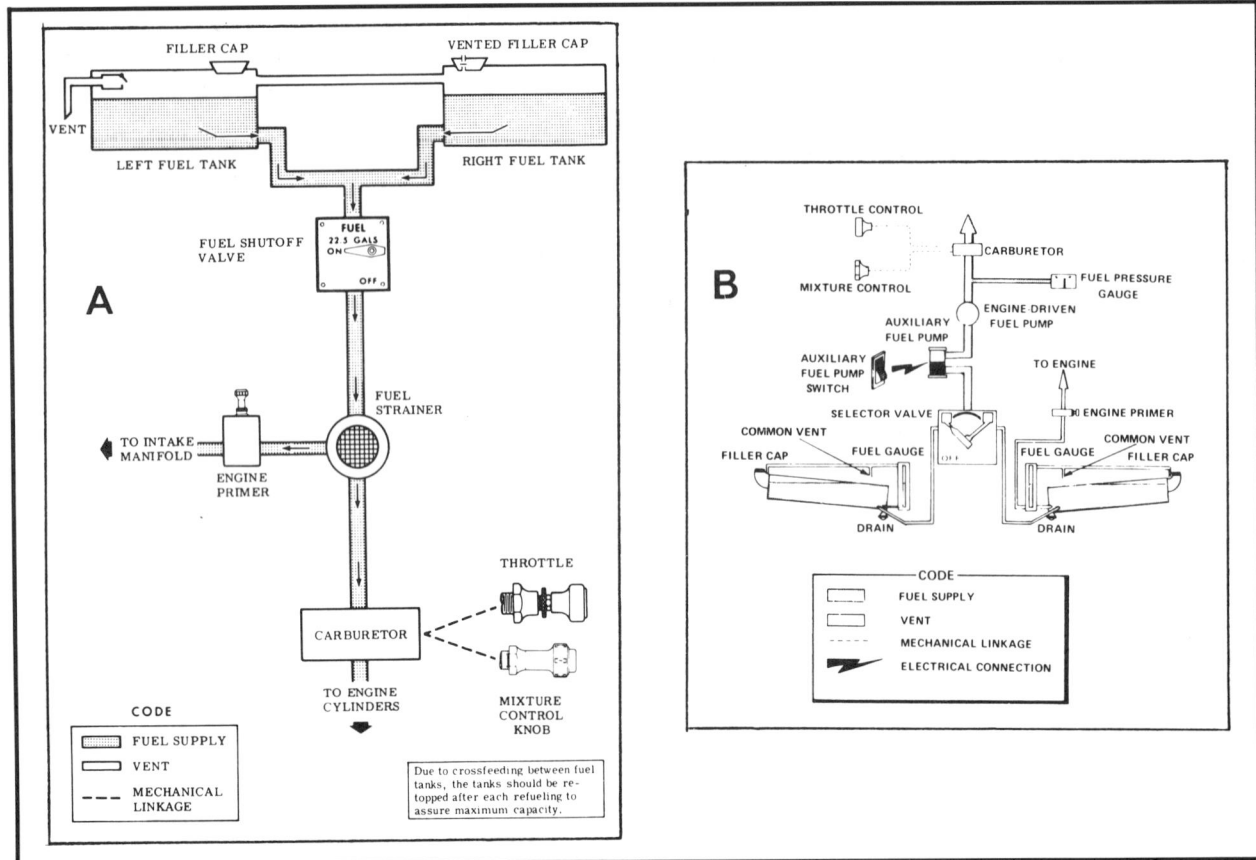

Fig. 23-1. (A) A high-wing gravity-fed fuel system and (B) a low-wing fuel system (*SPFM*).

NOTES ON CONSTANT-SPEED PROPELLER OPERATION
(NONTURBOCHARGED ENGINES)

A study has shown that the vast majority of flight schools use only smaller trainers with fixed-gear and fixed-pitch propellers for their students and that most pilots are introduced to constant-speed propellers well after receiving the private certificate. However, a brief discussion should be given here so that if you get a chance to fly an airplane so equipped you will have some background.

An analogy might be that the propeller pitch control is the "gear shift" and the throttle is the "foot pedal" of an automobile.

The prop control is moved forward for low pitch (high rpm) for takeoff and other high-power requirements and would be the equivalent of first or low gear. The engine would be revving up, developing higher horsepower. When the control is moved aft, the rpm decreases (the pitch or angle of attack *increases*) and less horsepower is being developed; also, the propeller is more efficient at cruise airspeeds at lower rpm. The constant-speed propeller acts as if you were automatically changing fixed-pitch props as needed.

Since, within the constant-speed operating range, the propeller automatically maintains the rpm set by the pilot, checking the mags in that range would mask any drop. (The propeller would automatically flatten pitch to maintain constant rpm, even with the slight power loss of running on one mag.) In the pretakeoff check the mags are normally checked below 2000 rpm so that the prop reacts to the rpm drop like the fixed-pitch trainer you've been flying.

Taking a typical flight, after checking the mags, you would "exercise" the prop by moving the control rearward and then forward a couple of times. This is done to ensure that it's responding properly and to recirculate the oil in the prop dome in systems using engine oil as a method of changing pitch.

Before the takeoff you'd make sure that the prop control was in the full-forward (high rpm) position and the mixture was full rich (or leaned as necessary for density altitude effects—see Chapter 5, *SPFM*), then, after checking that the area was clear, you would open the throttle fully.

Sometime during the climbout you would, as the manufacturer requires, throttle back to a specific manifold pressure setting, *then* ease the prop control back to get recommended climb rpm (usually leaving the mixture rich until a particular density altitude is reached).

After reaching the chosen altitude, climb power would be left on until cruise speed is reached, then the procedure for reducing power would be to (1) ease the throttle back to the cruise setting, (2) move the prop control back to reduce the rpm to the cruise setting, and (3) lean the mixture.

Note that this is the safe way to do it. The throttle is moved back first because a lot of fuel/air mixture pressure (manifold pressure) and low rpm could cause a rise in pressure in the cylinders to such a point that damage could occur. (Figure what would happen if you were in fourth gear in a very powerful car and jammed on the gas to try to burn rubber.) The mixture is leaned *last* as a safety procedure when power is reduced.

If you suddenly had to climb, you would reverse the procedure just discussed to avoid detonation and damage. To *increase power*: (1) mixture—rich, (2) prop rpm—increase, and (3) throttle—open. To *decrease power*: (1) throttle—back, (2) prop control—back, and (3) mixture—lean (as desired).

For further reading on the subject you might check Kershner, *Advanced Pilot's Flight Manual*, Chapter 12, and *Flight Instructor's Manual*, Chapter 17.

Now look at questions 2325 and 2326:

2325. When adding full power in an airplane with a constant-speed propeller, the order of control usage would be

1—throttle forward, mixture rich, propeller control forward.
2—mixture rich, throttle forward, propeller control forward.
3—throttle forward, propeller control forward, mixture rich.
4—mixture rich, propeller control forward, throttle forward.

2326. When reducing power with a constant-speed propeller, which of the following procedures should be used?

1—Throttle back, reduce rpm, and set (lean) the mixture.
2—Reduce rpm, throttle back, and set (lean) the mixture.
3—Lean the mixture, reduce rpm, and throttle back.
4—Richen the mixture, reduce rpm, and throttle back.

24

NAVIGATION PLANNING

All of the questions in this chapter are based on planning a triangular route from Sewanee-Franklin County Airport, to Crossville Memorial Airport, to Nashville Metro Airport, and return to Sewanee. Figure 24-A has the information for the three airports as given in the *Airport/Facility Directory,* and references will have to be made to the legend of that publication, the sectional chart in the back of this book, and other figures as indicated.

As background for making your judgments on planning a solo cross-country flight, assume that you are a student pilot with 12 hours solo flight time. You've made a couple of short solo cross-countries (the last trip was to Maury County Airport and to Huntsville Jetport as covered in *SPFM*) but have never flown *this* route before. You're flying a two-place trainer and using the information as given in Figure 24-B.

You may do part of your planning well in advance of the flight by laying out course lines and checking the *Airport/Facility Directory*. However, checking the weather two weeks in advance would be an exercise in futility, as would be looking at NOTAMS too far ahead. (Some critical information might be dropped or added, so you'd get NOTAMS and weather a short time before the flight.)

Another point: a late check of weather may show that the trip should be postponed or canceled. Sometimes there is a lot of pressure, conscious or unconscious, to go anyway after you've put a lot of work into getting ready, but more about that later.

As *SPFM* indicates, carefully look along and near the course lines to check for outstanding checkpoints and possible hazards to flight. If your course is close to the edge of the chart, take the adjacent chart too.

Each leg will be covered by asking questions about the route and facilities. All distances and speeds will be to the nearest nautical mile and knot unless otherwise noted.

LEG 1—SEWANEE TO CROSSVILLE

2401. The magnetic course from Sewanee-Franklin County Airport to Crossville Memorial Airport is

1—042°.
2—047°.
3—220°.
4—052°.

2402. As you are passing west and north of the town of Monteagle, you'll cross

1—directly over the town of Pelham.
2—directly over Martin Springs.
3—directly over the town of Tracy City.
4—U.S. Interstate 24 and U.S. 41.

2403. At a distance of 12 NM on course you can look directly off to the right of your course and see

1—Tracy City.
2—Coalmont.
3—Laager.
4—Altamont.

2404. If at 17 miles enroute you had a very rough-running engine or an electrical fire, you would turn toward which *closest landing area?*

1—Marion County-Brown Field.
2—Sewanee-Franklin County Airport.
3—Warren County at McMinnville Airport.
4—Sandy (private) Airstrip.

2405. Choose the correct statements concerning checkpoints or references on the portion of the route

```
                              TENNESSEE
SEWANEE
      FRANKLIN CO    (UOS)   .9 E   UTC-6(-5DT)   35°12'14"N 85°53'55"W          ATLANTA
      1950   B    FUEL 100LL, MOGAS                                              L-14H
         RWY 06-24: H3300X50 (ASPH)   S-20   LIRL.
            RWY 06: SAVASI(S2L)—GA 3.5°TCH 28'. Trees.     RWY 24: VASI(V2L). Trees.
         AIRPORT REMARKS: Attended 1500-0600Z‡. Sporadic crosswinds and turbulence. Deer on and in vicinity of rwy.
         COMMUNICATIONS: CTAF/UNICOM 122.8
            NASHVILLE FSS (BNA) TF 1-800-WX-BRIEF. NOTAM FILE BNA.
         RADIO AIDS TO NAVIGATION: NOTAM FILE BNA.
            SHELBYVILLE (L) VOR/DME 109.0   SYI   Chan 27   35°33'43"N 86°26'21"W   130°34.1 NM to fld. 810/01W.
            SEWANEE NDB (MHW) 275   UOS   35°12'15"N 85°53'45"W   at fld. (VFR only).

   §  CROSSVILLE MEM    (CSV)   2.6 W   UTC-6(-5DT)   35°57'04"N 85°05'06"W       ATLANTA
      1881   B   S4   FUEL 100LL, JET A                                           H-4H, L-14H, 21D
         RWY 08-26: H5418X100 (ASPH)   S-33,  D-62   HIRL   0.3% up W.            IAP
            RWY 08: VASI(V4R)—GA 3.0°TCH 49.7'. Trees.    RWY 26: REIL. Trees.
         AIRPORT REMARKS: Attended 1400Z‡-dark.
         COMMUNICATIONS: CTAF 123.6
            CROSSVILLE FSS (CSV) on arpt. 123.6 122.5 122.2 LC 484-9541 (1200-0400Z‡). NOTAM FILE CSV.
            NASHVILLE FSS (BNA) TF 1-800-WX-BRIEF (0400-1200Z‡).
            RCO 122.5 122.2 (NASHVILLE FSS)
         ® ATLANTA CENTER APP/DEP CON 133.6
         RADIO AIDS TO NAVIGATION: NOTAM FILE CSV. VHF/DF ctc NASHVILLE FSS.
            HINCH MOUNTAIN (L) VORTAC 117.6   HCH   Chan 123   35°46'51"N 84°58'43"W   336°11.4 NM to fld.
               3040/02W.
            ILS 109.1 I-CSV Rwy 26 BC unusable.

   §  NASHVILLE METROPOLITAN   (BNA)   5.2 SE   UTC-6(-5DT)   36°07'37"N 86°40'52"W    ST. LOUIS
      599   B   S4   FUEL 100LL, JET A   OX 2   LRA   ARFF Index C                H-4H, 4F, L-14H, 21D
         RWY 13-31: H8500X150 (ASPH-GRVD)   S-129, D-151, DT-229   HIRL            IAP
            RWY 13: REIL. SAVASI(V6L)—Upper GA 3.25°TCH 113.6'. Lower GA 2.75°TCH 43.5'. Trees.
            RWY 31: REIL. MALSR. Fence.
         RWY 02L-20R: H7702X150 (CONC-GRVD)   S-100, D-175, DT-360   HIRL, CL   0.6% up S
            RWY 02L: ALSF1. TDZ.     RWY 20R: ODALS. VASI(V4L)—GA 3.0°TCH 56'. Tree.
         RWY 02R-20L: H5186X150 (ASPH-CONC-GRVD)   S-60, D-84, DT-128   MIRL
            RWY 02R: SAVASI(S2L)—GA 3.0°TCH 38'. Thld dsplcd 881'. Road.
            RWY 20L: REIL. VASI(V4L)—GA 3.0°TCH 40'. Ground.
         AIRPORT REMARKS: Attended continuously. Fee charged to Coml users only. Acft conducting visual apch to Rwy 20R,
            20L, or 13 avoid Cornelia Fort Airpark (5 mi NW of Nashville) below 2000' MSL. Rwy 02R-20L length of dsplcd thld
            not grvd. Flight Notification Service (ADCUS) available.
         WEATHER DATA SOURCES: LLWAS.
         COMMUNICATIONS: ATIS 120.0   UNICOM 122.95
            NASHVILLE FSS (BNA) on arpt 122.55 122.2 121.R. LC 360-3619. TF 1-800-WX-BRIEF. NOTAM FILE BNA.
         ® APP CON 124.0 (019°-199°) 120.6 (200°-018°)
         ® DEP CON 124.0 118.4 (019°-199°) 120.6 119.35 (200°-018°)
            TOWER 118.6    GND CON 121.9   CLNC DEL 126.05
            ARSA   ctc APP CON
         RADIO AIDS TO NAVIGATION: NOTAM FILE BNA.
            (H) VORTAC 114.1   BNA   Chan 88   36°07'10"N 86°40'57"W   at fld. 620/01W.
            DOBBS NDB (HW/LOM) 304   BN   36°02'18"N 86°43'02"W   019°5.0 NM to fld.
            OPERY NDB (MHW/LOM) 344   VI   36°12'13"N 86°39'07"W   199°4.1 NM to fld.
            ILS/DME 109.9 I-BNA Chan 36 Rwy 02L LOM DOBBS NDB
            ILS 109.7 I-PNO Rwy 31
            ILS 111.3 I-VIY Rwy 20R LOM OPERY NDB
            ASR
```

Fig. 24-A. Information on Sewanee, Crossville, and Nashville Metro airports as given in the *Airport/Facility Directory*.

that is between 10-25 NM from Sewanee. (An "escarpment" is a long cliff or steep slope separating two comparatively level or more gently sloping surfaces and resulting from erosion or faulting.)

A. Coalmont has a lake about 2 miles southeast of town.
B. Beersheba Springs is on the top edge of the escarpment.
C. Tarlton is in a valley just below the escarpment.
D. Altamont has three roads coming from it.
E. Altamont has a water tank.
F. Beersheba Springs is in a valley just below the escarpment.
G. You will fly over a cove or sunken part of the Cumberland Plateau as you pass southeast of Beersheba Springs.

1—BCEG.
2—ABCE.
3—BDFG.
4—DEFG.

TIME, FUEL, AND DISTANCE TO CLIMB

MAXIMUM RATE OF CLIMB

CONDITIONS:
Flaps Up
Full Throttle
Standard Temperature

NOTES:
1. Add 0.8 of a gallon of fuel for engine start, taxi and takeoff allowance.
2. Increase time, fuel and distance by 10% for each 8°C above standard temperature.
3. Distances shown are based on zero wind.

WEIGHT LBS	PRESSURE ALTITUDE FT	TEMP °C	CLIMB SPEED KIAS	RATE OF CLIMB FPM	FROM SEA LEVEL		
					TIME MIN	FUEL USED GALLONS	DISTANCE NM
1600	S.L.	15	68	670	0	0	0
	1000	13	68	630	2	0.2	2
	2000	11	67	590	3	0.5	4
	3000	9	66	550	5	0.7	6
	4000	7	65	510	7	1.0	8
	5000	5	65	470	9	1.3	10
	6000	3	64	425	11	1.6	13
	7000	1	64	385	14	1.9	16
	8000	-1	63	345	17	2.3	19
	9000	-3	63	305	20	2.7	23
	10,000	-5	62	265	23	3.2	27
	11,000	-7	62	220	27	3.7	32
	12,000	-9	61	180	33	4.3	38

CRUISE PERFORMANCE

CONDITIONS:
1600 Pounds
Recommended Lean Mixture

PRESSURE ALTITUDE	RPM	20°C BELOW STANDARD TEMP			STANDARD TEMPERATURE			20°C ABOVE STANDARD TEMP		
		% BHP	KTAS	GPH	% BHP	KTAS	GPH	% BHP	KTAS	GPH
2000	2650	- - -	- - -	- - -	78	103	5.9	72	102	5.4
	2600	80	102	6.0	73	101	5.5	68	100	5.1
	2500	70	97	5.3	65	96	4.9	60	95	4.6
	2400	62	92	4.7	57	91	4.3	53	91	4.1
	2300	54	87	4.1	50	87	3.9	47	86	3.7
	2200	47	83	3.7	44	82	3.5	42	81	3.3
4000	2700	- - -	- - -	- - -	78	105	5.8	72	104	5.4
	2600	75	101	5.6	69	100	5.2	64	99	4.8
	2500	66	96	5.0	61	95	4.6	57	95	4.3
	2400	58	91	4.4	54	91	4.1	50	90	3.9
	2300	51	87	3.9	48	86	3.7	45	85	3.5
	2200	45	82	3.5	42	81	3.3	40	80	3.2
6000	2750	- - -	- - -	- - -	77	107	5.8	71	105	5.3
	2700	79	105	5.9	73	104	5.4	67	103	5.1
	2600	70	100	5.2	64	99	4.8	60	98	4.5
	2500	62	95	4.7	57	95	4.3	53	94	4.1
	2400	54	91	4.2	51	90	3.9	48	89	3.7
	2300	48	86	3.7	45	85	3.5	42	84	3.4
8000	2700	74	104	5.5	68	103	5.1	63	102	4.8
	2600	65	99	4.9	60	99	4.6	57	98	4.3
	2500	58	95	4.4	54	94	4.1	51	93	3.9
	2400	52	90	4.0	48	89	3.7	45	88	3.5
	2300	46	85	3.6	43	84	3.4	40	82	3.2
10000	2700	69	103	5.2	64	102	4.8	59	102	4.5
	2600	61	99	4.6	57	98	4.3	53	97	4.1
	2500	55	94	4.2	51	93	3.9	48	92	3.7
	2400	49	89	3.8	45	88	3.6	43	87	3.4
12000	2650	61	100	4.6	57	99	4.3	53	98	4.1
	2600	58	98	4.4	54	97	4.1	50	96	3.9
	2500	52	93	4.0	48	92	3.7	45	91	3.5
	2400	46	89	3.6	43	87	3.4	41	84	3.3

FOR (MAGNETIC)	N	30	60	E	120	150
STEER (COMPASS)	0	26	58	87	118	150
FOR (MAGNETIC)	S	210	240	W	300	330
STEER (COMPASS)	183	214	243	275	303	332

Fig. 24-B. Performance and compass deviation information for the questions in this chapter. Assume that IAS = CAS in the climb.

2406. How far along the course from Sewanee to Crossville are you when the Warren County Airport is exactly 90° off the course line?

1—17 NM.
2—24 NM.
3—20 statute miles.
4—30 NM.

2407. On course, you see that a transmission line crosses a secondary road at an enroute distance of approximately

1—38 NM.
2—29 statute miles.
3—32 NM.
4—29 NM.

2408. At 38 NM on course you should be

1—abeam of a dam.
2—passing over a 2100-foot (MSL) tower.
3—crossing an airway.
4—crossing a road and power line.

You've looked over the route to Crossville and now need to plan times, fuel, and other navigation factors for that leg.

You will be flying at 5500 feet from Sewanee-Franklin County Airport (assume a 2000-foot elevation at Sewanee) to Crossville, cruising at 64 percent power. Assume for practice purposes that the weather for a 500-mile radius is clear with 15 miles visibility. (More about weather judgment later.) Average altitude of the climb to 5500 feet is 4000 feet MSL. Winds aloft are: Nashville 3000—1912, 6000—2616, 9000—2730.

You will take off from Sewanee on Runway 6 and climb on course. Use the preceding wind data and Figures 24-A and 24-B to answer questions 2409 through 2412. Average wind for the climb: 210° at 13 knots; assume standard temperatures. (Make a work sheet for this.)

2409. While enroute to Crossville, when you get to the cruising altitude of 5500 feet MSL, you should be at a distance from the Franklin County Airport of approximately

1—7 NM.
2—5 statute miles.
3—10 NM.
4—3 NM.

2410. Use the wind given at 6000 feet and assume a standard temperature at 5500 feet. The compass heading on the cruise portion of the trip to Crossville at 64 percent power setting is

1—038°.
2—040°.
3—042°.
4—032°.

2411. Assume that the letdown portion of the trip maintains the same groundspeed. If your climb from Sewanee had started at 1128 CST, you'd expect to be over Crossville Airport (above the traffic pattern) at approximately

1—1154 CST.
2—1209 CST.
3—1202 CST.
4—1216 CST.

2412. The total fuel used for that leg, assuming that 64 percent power is used both for the cruise and letdown portions and discounting any used in circling or approach at Crossville, should be approximately
1—3.7 gallons.
2—4.7 gallons.
3—4.0 gallons.
4—3.2 gallons.

2413. The elevation of the Crossville Memorial Airport is

1—5418 feet.
2—1881 feet.
3—100 feet.
4—3040 feet.

2414. Assume that you set up a rate of descent of 500 feet per minute so as to be over Crossville Airport at 3500 feet MSL. If you started the climb from Sewanee Airport at 1128 CST, you should start the descent at approximately

1—1206 CST.
2—1158 CST.
3—1212 CST.
4—1150 CST.

2415. For Airport Advisory Service from the FSS at Crossville (the Common Traffic Advisory Frequency) you would communicate (transmit and receive) on

1—122.1 MHz.
2—Unicom 122.8 MHz.
3—121.5 MHz.
4—123.6 MHz.

2416. Before leaving the ground at Sewanee, you could get the weather and file a flight plan for the trip with the Crossville FSS by calling

1—1-484-9541.
2—(615) 555-6787.
3—on 123.6 MHz.
4—on 122.8 MHz.

2417. In planning the triangular flight from Sewanee to Crossville to Nashville Metro and return, you find that the total distance to be flown is

1—204 statute miles.
2—204 NM.
3—224 NM.
4—224 statute miles.

LEG 2—CROSSVILLE TO NASHVILLE

2418. The true course from Crossville Memorial Airport to Nashville Metro is

1—282°.
2—288°.
3—294°.
4—278°.

2419. The *compass course* from Crossville Memorial to Nashville Metro (using Fig. 24-B) is

1—278°.
2—274°.
3—284°.
4—288°.

Assume that you will be cruising at 4500 feet MSL from Crossville (assume a 2000-foot elevation at CSV)

to Nashville Metro and will be climbing on course. Cruise power at 4500 feet will be 2450 rpm. Assume a standard temperature at that altitude. Refer to Figure 24-B.

2420. For the *climb portion* of this leg assume for this question that the average wind is from 190° true at 12 knots and 3000 feet MSL is the median altitude. The compass heading during the climb will be

1—278°.
2—268°.
3—263°.
4—274°.

2421. Based on your climb calculations and assuming you take off and immediately climb on course, you should level off approximately abeam

1—Pleasant Hill.
2—Smithville.
3—Bon Air.
4—Sparta.

2422. On the level cruise portion of the trip your compass heading will be

1—283°.
2—271°.
3—277°.
4—266°.

Note: Interpolate the wind between 3000 and 6000.

2423. Which of the following statements concerning the flight from Crossville Airport is correct?

1—Shortly after passing DeRossett you will fly toward rapidly rising terrain.
2—You will cross a power transmission line at about 10 NM out from Crossville Airport.
3—You will see the 1°W isogonic line in the vicinity of the Hurricane radio beacon.
4—You should pass about 1 mile south of the Sparta–White County Airport.

2424. When approaching Nashville Metro Airport from Crossville, you would use the following order of communications. Make sure also that the frequencies (MHz) in the parentheses are correct.

1—ATIS (120.0), approach control (120.6), tower (118.6), ground control (121.9).
2—Approach control (120.6), tower (118.6), ground control (120.6).
3—ATIS (120.0), tower (118.6), approach control (124.0), ground control (121.9).
4—ATIS (120.0), approach control (124.0), tower (118.6), ground control (121.9).

2425. Checking the facilities at Nashville Metro Airport (BNA), which of the following statements is correct?

1—The surface of Runway 13-31 consists of asphalt and has been graveled.
2—You will be expected to pay a landing fee.
3—You would contact Nashville approach control 25 NM out, which in your case would be about 2 NM southwest of Watertown.
4—You would contact Nashville approach control 25 NM out, which in your case would be about 1 NM north of the village of Norene.

2426. Assume for this question that the trainer you are flying on this solo cross-country has single main wheels and weighs 110,000 pounds. (Okay, so the airplane is about 108,000 pounds overweight, but you were *told* to leave that luggage at home.) You may legally and safely land on

1—Runway 02R-20L.
2—Runway 13-31.
3—Runway 02L-20R.
4—none of the above listed runways.

2427. After landing at Nashville (assume now that the trainer is back to a normal weight), while you are rolling down the runway, the tower says, "(Your number) turn right next taxiway, ground on point nine." You should

1—contact Nashville ground control on 121.9 MHz after clearing the active runway.
2—immediately switch to 121.9 MHz and contact Nashville ground control.
3—immediately switch to 122.9 MHz and contact Nashville ground control.
4—contact Nashville ground control on 122.9 MHz after clearing the active runway.

2428. After spending 45 minutes longer on the ground at Nashville than planned, you are in the FBO office about to walk out to the airplane. Which of the statements below is correct?

1—You plan that after starting you would contact ground control on 121.9 MHz for taxi instructions and then listen to ATIS for further details on active runway and wind.
2—If you filed a VFR flight plan for the entire trip, you should call the Nashville FSS on the telephone and revise your ETA to Sewanee before leaving.
3—You need not listen to ATIS because it does not apply to airplanes leaving the airport; it is set up for inbound traffic information only.
4—ATIS may be received on 114.1 MHz, the VOR frequency.

Chapter 24. Navigation Planning 105

LEG 3—NASHVILLE TO SEWANEE

Refer to Figure 24-B and the sectional chart at the back of this book for questions 2429-2434.

2429. Assume a no-wind condition for the climbout from Nashville Metro to Sewanee. Use 500 feet as the Nashville elevation. The temperatures at all altitudes are 8°C above normal. The climb to 5500 feet would require (rounded off to the nearest mile, 0.1 gallon, and full minute and including fuel for start, taxi, and takeoff) approximately

1—9 minutes, 1.4 gallons, and 11 NM.
2—9 minutes, 1.9 gallons, and 9 NM.
3—10 minutes, 1.4 gallons, and 14 NM.
4—10 minutes, 2.3 gallons, and 12 NM.

2430. Given: use the wind at 6000 feet for this problem (260° at 16 knots); standard temperature at 5500 feet; and power at 5500 feet = 2600 rpm. The compass heading (see Fig. 24-B again) for the leg from Nashville Metro to Sewanee-Franklin County Airport is

1—153°.
2—137°.
3—145°.
4—161°.

2431. Using the wind and other data as given for question 2430, you find that the groundspeed after cruise is established is

1—99 knots.
2—94 knots.
3—105 knots.
4—109 knots.

2432. You are on course from Nashville to Sewanee (compass heading at this time is 151°), tune in the Warren County Airport radio beacon (209 RNC), and note a relative bearing of 288°. This indicates that the town below is

1—Murfreesboro.
2—Beechgrove.
3—Calhoun.
4—Manchester.

2433. At 1434 CST you are over the junction of Interstate 24 and a four-lane road into Murfreesboro (about 20 NM on your route). At 1451 CST you are directly abeam of the drive-in theatre northwest of Manchester. Your groundspeed is

1—106 knots.
2—101 knots.
3—95 knots.
4—89 knots.

2434. Assume for this question that you would be descending from 7500 (repeat, *7500*) feet at 500 fpm at cruise true airspeed (99 knots) to cross the Sewanee-Franklin County Airport at 3500 feet MSL. With an average wind during the descent of 260° at 16 knots, you should start an on-course descent when

1—crossing the road and power line 5 NM northwest of the Sewanee-Franklin County Airport.
2—just passing the end of the east end of Woods Reservoir.
3—crossing the road between Manchester and Tullahoma.
4—directly abeam of the Arnold Air Force Base field.

Use Figure 24-B and the following information to answer questions 2435 and 2436.

A. No-wind conditions.
B. Cruise altitude from Sewanee to Crossville—5500 feet, Crossville to Nashville—4500 feet, and Nashville to Sewanee—5500 feet.
C. Usable fuel—22 gallons.
D. Power carried at cruise 64 percent (4.8 gph, leaned at 4500 or 5500 feet).
E. One-hour reserve at 64 percent must be retained.
F. The letdown is made at the same power consumption and true airspeed (groundspeed).
G. Assume that 0.4 gallon is used for approach, landing, and taxi in at each stop.
H. Assume Sewanee elevation 2000 feet, Crossville 2000 feet, and Nashville 500 feet.
I. Standard temperatures.

2435. Based on the above information the total fuel required to make the flight safely is

1—14.3 gallons.
2—19.9 gallons.
3—20.3 gallons.
4—15.5 gallons.

2436. Assuming an allowance of 30 minutes on the ground at Crossville and Nashville, the total estimated no-wind time to make the trip would require *approximately*

1—3 hours and 11 minutes.
2—3 hours and 41 minutes.
3—2 hours and 51 minutes.
4—2 hours and 11 minutes.

ANALYZING THE WEATHER, GO OR NO-GO

When the time comes to make the trip, the weather normally becomes the deciding factor unless you discover at the last minute that one of the airports has been closed or your airplane has problems. Figure 24-C gives a summary of the preflight briefing.

SUMMARY—
The Preflight Briefing

In person or by phone from either a FSS or the NWS.

Your preflight weather briefing should include:

- Synopsis and area weather
- Adverse weather, including SIGMETs, convective SIGMETs, and AIRMETs
- Current reported weather
- En route weather forecast
- Destination weather forecast
- Winds and temperatures aloft forecast
- PIREPs, including "top" reports, icing, and turbulence
- Temperature/dew point spread (4°F or less = fog potential)
- Better weather area
- Alternate airport weather forecast
- NOTAMs (not available from NWS)

Don't forget — first give the briefer the flight information he needs to compile a good briefing, then *listen* to the briefer.

Use your flight planner form to record the weather information provided, *then* ask questions if you don't understand or if you *need* more information.

Fig. 24-C. The preflight weather briefing, a summary. (*How to Obtain a Good Weather Briefing* by the *FAA, GAMA,* and *Ohio State University*)

As indicated earlier in the chapter you have 12 hours solo, have not flown this route before, and will be flying it alone.

Look carefully at the weather given here.

You plan to leave Sewanee at about 1130 CST and get back at about 1500 CST, so at about 1110 CST you call and check the current weather with the Crossville FSS and note earlier weather reports as well as terminal and other forecasts.

■ Hourly Reports

0900 CST
(Crossville) CSV SA 1454 35 SCT 45 SCT 4H
          131/65/47/1605/992
(Nashville) BNA SA 1453 35 SCT 50 SCT 3H
          131/63/48/1708/992
        MKL SA 1455 35 SCT 50 OVC 4H
          089/61/51/1805/980
        (MKL is McKellar Field, Jackson, Tennessee, about 87 NM WSW of Nashville Metro Airport.)
(Chattanooga) CHA SA 1451 CLR 12
          135/67/44/1505/993
        (Chattanooga Lovell Field is 35 NM ESE of Sewanee-Franklin County Airport.)

1000 CST
CSV SA 1554 35 SCT M45 BKN 3H
    121/65/52/1708/989
BNA SA 1553 M35 BKN 50 OVC 3H
    111/66/54/1605/986
MKL SA 1555 M35 OVC 4H 088/61/56/1803/976
CHA SA 1551 M50 SCT 5HK 121/69/55/1506/989

1100 CST
CSV SA 1654 M30 BKN 40 OVC 3H
    101/65/58/1605/983
BNA SA 1653 M30 BKN 40 OVC 3HK
    091/66/61/1604/980
MKL RS 1655 M20 OVC 2½L-F
    073/60/59/1904/970/PRESFR
CHA SA 1651 M50 BKN 5HK 121/69/601506/989

■ Terminal Forecast

The terminal forecasts are released at 1440Z on the fourteenth.

CSV 141515 50 SCT 18Z 40 SCT 21Z C40 BKN 00Z
    C30 BKN 4L-F 09Z IFR CIG R F . .
BNA 141515 50 SCT 5H.18Z C40 BKN 4H. 21Z C30
    OVC 3H. 00Z C30 OVC 2R-F 09Z IFR CIG R F . .
MKL 141515 C50 BKN 4H 18Z C30 BKN 3R-F. 21Z
    C30 OVC 2R F 09Z IFR CIG R F . .
CHA 141515 50 SCT 18Z 50 BKN 21Z 40 BKN 5H 00Z
    35 OVC 3R-F . . 09Z IFR CIG R-F . .

■ Winds Aloft Forecast

(Valid for the period of the flight.)

	3000 ft	6000	9000
BNA	1912	2616 + 10	2730 + 5

Use this material to answer questions 2437–2440.

2437. Which one of the following statements is correct?

1—Nashville's actual weather, for the three hours reported, shows a greater improvement than forecast.
2—McKellar weather reports and forecasts are of little or no value for planning the trip, since it is well west of Nashville.
3—Crossville weather has shown a slow deterioration since the 0900 CST report.
4—Chattanooga will be IFR after 0900 CST on the fifteenth of the month.

2438. By checking the weather reports for the four stations from 0900, 1000, 1100 CST, you can see that in addition to ceiling and visibility variations, a valuable clue to the trend is given here by

1—decreasing of temperature/dewpoint spreads.
2—definite wind direction and velocity changes.
3—the rising barometric pressure reported by the stations.
4—moderate rain occurring at MKL at 1000 CST.

2439. The forecast for BNA from 1200 CST to 1500 CST is that it will have a ceiling 4000 broken and visibility 4 miles in haze. Based on the 0900–1100 hourly reports and checking the trend, which of the following ceiling and visibility values will BNA most likely have at 1200 CST?

1—Measured 3500 feet broken, 5000 overcast, visibility 4 miles in haze.
2—Measured 2500 feet broken, 3000 feet overcast, visibility 3 miles in haze.
3—Clouds scattered at 3500 feet and at 4500 feet, visibility 5 miles in haze.
4—Measured 300 overcast, visibility 1 mile in rain and fog.

2440. Based on the weather information just given and your experience, you would make the following decision concerning the round robin cross-country to Crossville and Nashville and return. (Departure time scheduled for around 1130 CST.) See Figure 24-D.

1—Leave as scheduled but keep a close eye on the weather as you fly.
2—Leave 2 hours later.
3—Fly to Crossville and make your decision to fly the rest of the trip from there.
4—Cancel the flight until further notice.

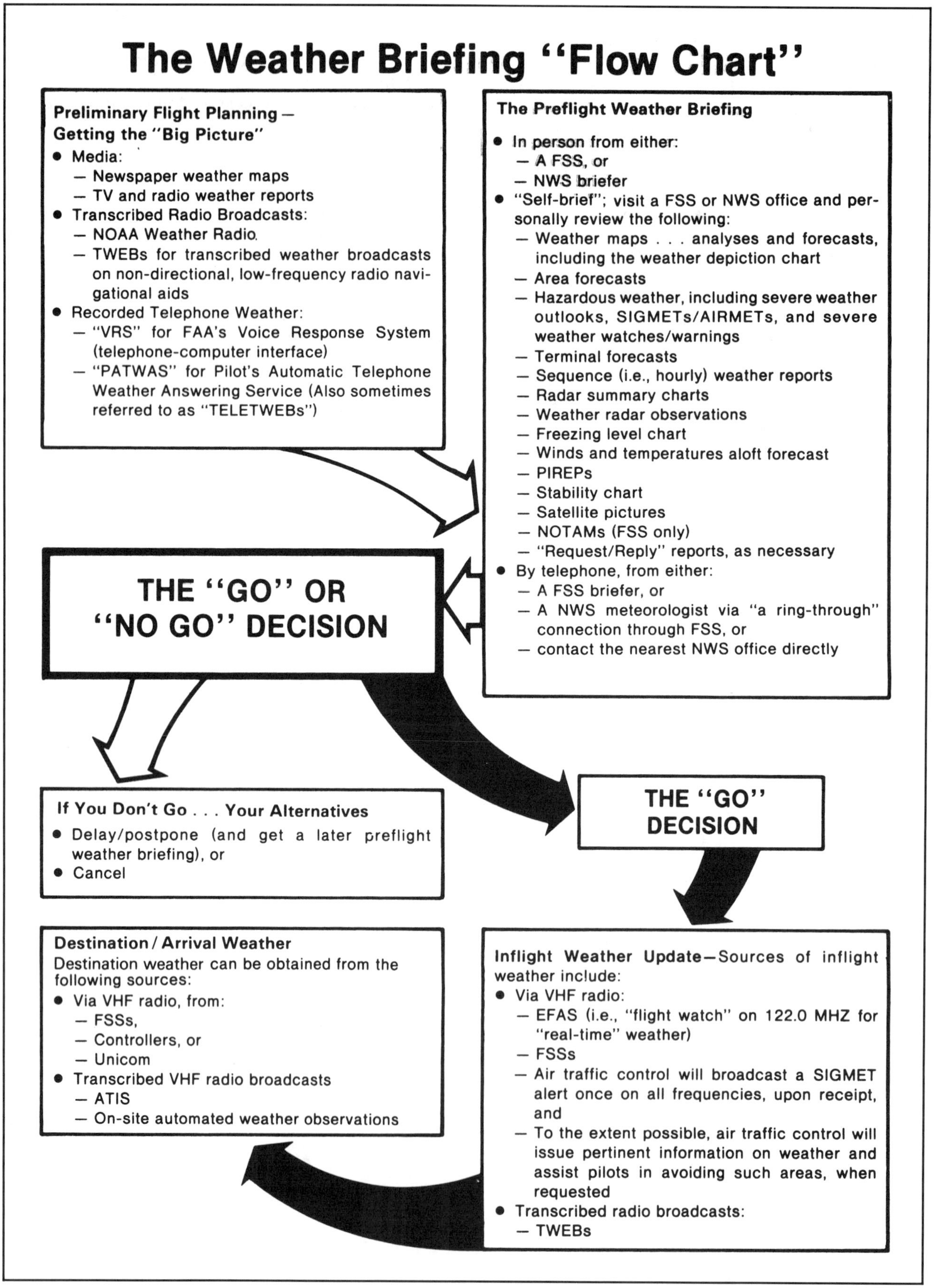

The Weather Briefing "Flow Chart"

Preliminary Flight Planning — Getting the "Big Picture"
- Media:
  - Newspaper weather maps
  - TV and radio weather reports
- Transcribed Radio Broadcasts:
  - NOAA Weather Radio
  - TWEBs for transcribed weather broadcasts on non-directional, low-frequency radio navigational aids
- Recorded Telephone Weather:
  - "VRS" for FAA's Voice Response System (telephone-computer interface)
  - "PATWAS" for Pilot's Automatic Telephone Weather Answering Service (Also sometimes referred to as "TELETWEBs")

The Preflight Weather Briefing
- In person from either:
  - A FSS, or
  - NWS briefer
- "Self-brief"; visit a FSS or NWS office and personally review the following:
  - Weather maps . . . analyses and forecasts, including the weather depiction chart
  - Area forecasts
  - Hazardous weather, including severe weather outlooks, SIGMETs/AIRMETs, and severe weather watches/warnings
  - Terminal forecasts
  - Sequence (i.e., hourly) weather reports
  - Radar summary charts
  - Weather radar observations
  - Freezing level chart
  - Winds and temperatures aloft forecast
  - PIREPs
  - Stability chart
  - Satellite pictures
  - NOTAMs (FSS only)
  - "Request/Reply" reports, as necessary
- By telephone, from either:
  - A FSS briefer, or
  - A NWS meteorologist via "a ring-through" connection through FSS, or
  - contact the nearest NWS office directly

THE "GO" OR "NO GO" DECISION

If You Don't Go . . . Your Alternatives
- Delay/postpone (and get a later preflight weather briefing), or
- Cancel

THE "GO" DECISION

Destination/Arrival Weather
Destination weather can be obtained from the following sources:
- Via VHF radio, from:
  - FSSs,
  - Controllers, or
  - Unicom
- Transcribed VHF radio broadcasts
  - ATIS
  - On-site automated weather observations

Inflight Weather Update — Sources of inflight weather include:
- Via VHF radio:
  - EFAS (i.e., "flight watch" on 122.0 MHZ for "real-time" weather)
  - FSSs
  - Air traffic control will broadcast a SIGMET alert once on all frequencies, upon receipt, and
  - To the extent possible, air traffic control will issue pertinent information on weather and assist pilots in avoiding such areas, when requested
- Transcribed radio broadcasts:
  - TWEBs

Fig. 24-D. The Weather Briefing "Flow Chart." (*How to Obtain a Good Weather Briefing* by the *FAA, GAMA,* and *Ohio State University*)

25
FLYING THE CROSS-COUNTRY

The questions below are based on Chapter 25, *SPFM* and, as in that chapter, assume that after the planning is complete you're now ready to face the actual flying of the cross-country.

ENROUTE CONSIDERATIONS

2501. You should set the heading indicator with the magnetic compass

1—before departure and once on one of the three legs.
2—at least once during each leg or every 15 minutes during the flight, whichever is more often.
3—before each takeoff and immediately before each landing.
4—if the difference between the indications of the two instruments is more than 30°.

2502. You may get an estimate of the wind at your altitude by

1—sticking your hand out the window.
2—checking cloud shadow movement on the ground if scattered or broken clouds are near your altitude.
3—watching smoke, waves on lakes, or clothes on clotheslines.
4—checking the airspeed indicator.

2503. As you circle the destination airport, you see a runway marked as shown in Figure 25-A. You may

1—taxi on this area but not take off or land there.
2—taxi and take off on this area but not land there.
3—use this at your discretion with reasonable caution.
4—not use this area for taxiing, taking off, or landing.

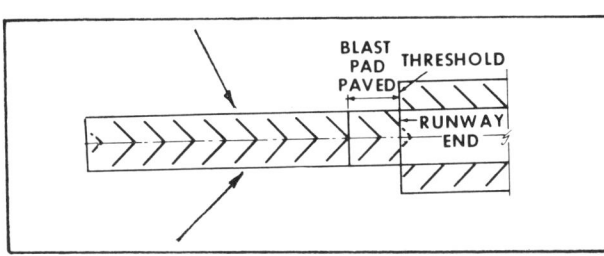

Fig. 25-A.

2504. Shown in Figure 25-B are the displaced thresholds for a basic runway (top) and a precision/nonprecision runway. You may

1—use the area behind the displaced threshold for taxiing, takeoffs, and landing roll-out.

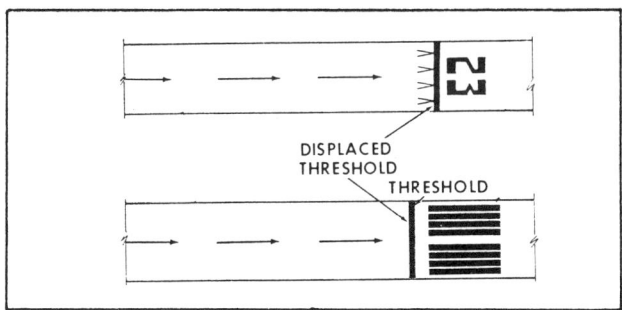

Fig. 25-B.

109

2—touch down before the displaced threshold but not use it for takeoffs.
3—use the area behind the displaced threshold for taxi only.
4—not use the area behind the displaced threshold for any aircraft traffic.

2505. When flying cross-country, you fly over an airport with an "X" painted where the number should be. The runway marking indicates that

1—the runway is called Runway X.
2—the runway is closed.
3—aircraft should touch down at that point (X marks the spot).
4—the runway is only used for VFR operations.

2506. Pilots are encouraged to turn on their landing lights (day or night) to help being seen by other aircraft. According to AIM, you should turn the landing lights on

1—when on final approach to landing.
2—when operating within 10 miles of any airport.
3—when on the downwind leg.
4—after contacting the tower.

2507. You've landed at your destination airport and are taxiing in for service. The line attendant picks you up and starts directing your airplane into the parking area. As you approach, his left hand is pointing to the right main wheel and his right hand is beckoning you forward. You should

1—come to a complete stop, shut down the engine, get out, and check that the right tire is not flat.
2—start a left turn.
3—start a right turn.
4—taxi straight ahead.

2508. Assume that you've been flying out of a grass strip all your flying career and when taxiing out at a "foreign" airport on the cross-country you notice yellow striped lines across the taxiway as shown in Figure 25-C. The stripes mean that

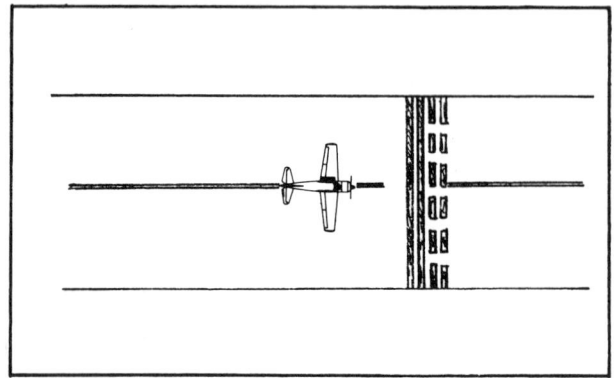

Fig. 25-C.

1—you are to hold short of this line until cleared by the tower or you have checked for takeoff or landing traffic at a noncontrolled airport.
2—it is a displaced threshold and not important for airplanes taxiing.
3—this part of the runway is an overrun area used for IFR traffic only.
4—this denotes a certain fixed distance from the end of the runway.

PROBLEMS AND EMERGENCIES

2509. You notice that while this leg of the flight had been working very well, you haven't seen a checkpoint in several minutes. Generally the best action is to

1—take a 30° change in heading in what you consider the proper direction to rejoin the course.
2—circle while looking for an outstanding landmark that might be on the chart.
3—maintain the heading that has been working so far, continuing to look for the next checkpoint.
4—make a 180° turn to go back to pick up an earlier known checkpoint.

2510. After flying on, looking for checkpoints on the Crossville to Nashville leg, you decide that the situation is more serious than first thought. The fuel gauge is closer to EMPTY than it should be, and you need to get to the nearest airport. Assume for this question that you are able to get completely accurate bearings on your VOR receiver (which is not usually the case, as noted in SPFM).

Use the sectional chart in the back of this book.
You tune in 117.6 MHz on the VOR receiver, and when the needle centers on FROM the OBS indicates 280 (Hinch Mountain VOR, 11 NM southeast of the Crossville Airport). When you tune in 109.0 MHz, the FROM indication (needle centered) gives an OBS indication of 040 (Shelbyville VOR). The true course to the nearest airport is approximately

1—147°.
2—258°.
3—318°.
4—074°.

2511. The "Six Cs" procedure to be used when lost is

1—Confess, Climb, Communicate, Comply, Conserve, and Cool, keeping of.
2—Confess, Collate, Certify, Compensate, Confuse, and Connive.
3—Climb, Comfort, Collect, Cancel, Compose, and Connect.
4—Communicate, Construct, Contrive, Convert, Create, and Correspond.

Chapter 25. Flying the Cross-Country 111

2512. Which of the following is a true statement?

1—The radius of turn for a given angle of bank is proportional to the airspeed.
2—The radius of turn for a given angle of bank is proportional to the square of the airspeed.
3—If after making an off-airport landing the airplane has plenty of fuel remaining and the weather has cleared, you should use your short-field takeoff training to get back to the home airport as soon as possible.
4—It's considered poor technique to follow a road to get to an alternate airport; a course line should be drawn and a heading computed.

2513. If you are approaching an airport and there is a thunderstorm in the near area, be prepared

1—for snow and snow showers.
2—for fog forming rapidly.
3—to land straight in.
4—for strong and shifting winds.

2514. If on a cross-country you noted that the oil pressure had dropped to 0, you would

1—land immediately.
2—watch the oil temperature gauge as you turn toward better terrain and/or an airport.
3—continue enroute, since it's more than likely that the gauge itself has failed.
4—use full carburetor heat.

2515. It's summer and you have just flown into a very heavy rain shower. In addition to the visibility problem, the engine is losing power badly. Which of the following is most likely to help get power back in this situation?

1—Applying carburetor heat or alternate air.
2—Switching tanks.
3—Richening the mixture.
4—Turning the master (electrical) switch OFF.

26

INTRODUCTION TO NIGHT FLYING

The night flying requirement for the private certificate should be considered a minimum and is something to fall back on if you get caught away from an airport after dark. Like the instrument training (Chapter 15, *SPFM*) it is to be used as an aid to safety, not as an excuse to push into that particular situation. You will probably get more night dual and the flight instructor may solo you in the local area at night and send you out on short cross-countries, depending on how far you both want to go in the training.

Sure, you'll run into Zilch's Law (Fig. 26-1, *SPFM*), and it can be particularly startling if over bad terrain at night you swallow or yawn, losing your hearing for a split second. (The engine quit!) But you'll find that the engine is fine, even if it takes a couple of minutes for your nerves to get back to normal.

This book and *SPFM* are not intended to do more than introduce you to night flying. To lay out all the airport lighting facilities, for instance, would require memorization of material that would be better checked in *AIM*.

You should have had at least 3 hours of dual hood work before flying at night on your own, because you could inadvertently fly into clouds or lose sight of the ground light references. Also, when you are flying over a sparsely populated area with few lights, you may lose control of the airplane if you depend on outside references only. Pilots who are catapulted off of carriers on hazy nights find that the horizon may be nonexistent, and a quick transition to instruments is vital as they find themselves in "instant IFR flight" only 60 or 70 feet above the water. *Landing* on a carrier at night requires a little attention too.

Answer the following questions.

CONES AND RODS

2601. A deer hunter can get away with wearing a bright orange jacket and hat without scaring the animals

1—because deer eyes have only cones.
2—only if the rest of the outfit doesn't clash with the orange.
3—only if hunting at night.
4—because deer eyes primarily have rods and cannot distinguish colors.

2602. Which of the following statements is correct?

1—The fovea is the central area of the eye containing the top visual acuity cells.
2—The rods are the night cells surrounding the fovea and do not furnish as much detail as the cones.
3—To best pick out an object at night, don't look directly at it but slightly to the side.
4—All the above statements are correct.

2603. Which of the following statements is correct?

1—A blind spot is present only in night vision.
2—It normally takes about 30 minutes for your vision to come near to full night adaptation.
3—Use of alcohol, tobacco, and oxygen are all detrimental to night vision.
4—If flying over a brightly lighted city, keep the instrument lights as low as possible.

Chapter 26. Introduction to Night Flying 113

AIRPLANE AND AIRPORT LIGHTING

2604. This question applies to land-aircraft position light requirements in the 48 states portion of the United States. Unless the aircraft has *lighted position lights,* you may not operate an aircraft, park, move an aircraft in, or be in dangerous proximity to a night flight operations area unless that area is clearly illuminated or is marked by obstruction lights during a period from

1—sunset to sunrise.
2—one hour after sunset to one hour before sunrise.
3—one hour before sunset to one hour after sunrise.
4—midnight to 0600 local time.

2605. During one of your night flights you observe the white anticollision light of another aircraft at the two o'clock position. The light remains on the horizon in the same relative position to you and is appearing brighter as time passes. The other aircraft

1—will pass behind your airplane to the right.
2—will move ahead of your airplane to the left.
3—poses a collision threat.
4—will pass well below your airplane.

2606. Which of the following items is correct concerning the flashing of airport rotating beacons?

1—Civilian airports—green-white-white-green.
2—Military airports—green-white-white-green.
3—Civilian airports—white-green-green-white.
4—Military airports—green-white-green.

■ Notes on Approach Lights

The Instrument Approach Light Systems (ALS) are used to make the transition from the electronic approach aids to visual flight and landing.

The Visual Approach Slope Indicator (VASI) was discussed in Chapter 21, *SPFM.* Runway End Identifier Lights (REILs) are installed at many airports to provide rapid and positive identication of the approach end of a particular runway. The system consists of a pair of synchronized (bright, white) flashing lights, one of which is located on each side of the runway threshold. They are used in identification of runways with problems from surrounding lights, those lacking contrast with the surrounding terrain, or during reduced visibility. These lights are distracting for some pilots; also, people living near the end of some runways have been known to "adjust" them with a hammer.

Runway Edge Light Systems (RELS) are classified according to the intensity or brightness they are capable of producing and are listed as *high* (high-intensity runway lights) (HIRL), *medium* (MIRL), and *low* (LIRL). These lights are white except on instrument runways where aviation yellow is used for the last 2000 feet or half the runway length, whichever is less.

Selected airports provide the pilot airborne or ground control of lights by keying the microphone a certain number of times. The lights may stay on for a period of 15 minutes (see Fig. 26-A).

Suggested use is to always initially key the mike 7 times; this assures that all controlled lights are turned on to the maximum available intensity. If desired, adjustment can then be made, where the capability is provided, to a lower intensity (or the REIL turned off) by keying 5 and/or 3 times. Even though the runway lights are on when arriving over an airport of intended landing, always key mike as directed in order to assure a full 15 minutes lighting duration. Approved lighting systems may be activated by keying the mike (within 5 seconds) as indicated below:

RADIO CONTROL SYSTEM

Key Mike	Function
7 times within 5 seconds	Highest intensity available
5 times within 5 seconds	Medium or lower intensity (Lower REIL or REIL-Off)
3 times within 5 seconds	Lowest intensity available (Lower REIL or REIL-Off)

For all public use airports with FAA standard systems the Airport/Facility Directory contains the types of lighting, runway and the frequency that is used to activate the system. Airports with IAPs include data on the approach chart identifying the light system, the runway on which they are installed, and the frequency that is used to activate the system.

**AIRMAN'S INFORMATION MANUAL (AIM)
BASIC FLIGHT INFORMATION AND ATC PROCEDURES**

Fig. 26-A.

Other lighting abbreviations you may see as you prepare to fly into a precision approach runway are TDZL (Touchdown Zone Lighting) and RCLS (Runway Centerline Lighting System).

The Appendix (*Airport/Facility Directory* legend) lists the abbreviations and explanations of runway lighting.

2607. Dangerous obstructions near airports may be marked during nighttime operations by

1—red lights.
2—blue lights.
3—amber lights.
4—green lights.

2608. An industrial chimney extends 400 feet above the terrain. It will be marked by

1—steady green lights at every 50 feet of elevation.
2—flashing green lights at every 50 feet of elevation.
3—steady aviation white lighting.
4—high-intensity, flashing white lights.

2609. If at an airport in a control zone the rotating beacon is on in the daytime hours,

1—the airport is using right traffic patterns for all runways in use.
2—weather conditions are less than VFR minimums (1000 foot ceiling and 3 miles visibility).
3—the weather conditions are marginal IFR.
4—a normal condition exists because airports with control towers are required to have the rotating beacon on continuously.

TIPS FOR NIGHT FLYING

2610. Before starting an airplane at night with no line attendant available, the following procedure would be a good operating practice to avoid striking someone with the propeller:

1—Turn the landing lights on.
2—Turn the cockpit lights up full.
3—Turn the strobe lights on.
4—Turn the position lights on.

2611. Which of the following should be turned *off* when the airplane reaches the run-up area?

1—Strobes, landing/taxi lights, and position lights.
2—Landing/taxi lights and cockpit lights.
3—Landing/taxi lights and strobes.
4—Cockpit lights and position lights.

2612. At night, assuming that you have no transmitter, you would acknowledge tower instructions by

1—blinking the position or landing lights.
2—turning up the cockpit lighting.
3—turning all lights off for 30 seconds or more.
4—moving the ailerons.

2613. Which of the following general statements concerning night flying is correct?

1—It's best to get the airplane airborne as soon as possible in a night takeoff.
2—The traffic pattern at night should be slightly wider and more leisurely than in the daytime.
3—For a better-judged approach, landing lights should be turned on halfway along the downwind leg.
4—It's best to make power-off approaches at night.

PART FIVE: THE WRITTEN AND FLIGHT TESTS

27

THE WRITTEN TEST

PULLING IT ALL TOGETHER

At this point you should have taken the tests for Chapters 2 through 26 and the sample test in Chapter 27, *SPFM*. An attempt is made in those earlier chapters to select problem-causing questions from actual ground school sessions.

This chapter has questions representative of the *FAA Private Pilot Question Book*, so when you take that test you'll see some familiar items. The questions in this chapter are considered to be the final review in preparation for the written test; the questions in Chapters 28 and 29 are to be used in preparation for the oral and practical parts of the Flight Test.

Following are some publications that will be useful in studying for the written tests.

The FAA issues *Advisory Circulars* to inform the aviation public in a systematic way of nonregulatory material of interest. Many of the study materials in this guide are issued as *Advisory Circulars*. Before ordering any FAA publication, it is advisable to obtain a copy of AC 00-2 (latest revision), which is the *Advisory Circular Checklist* and includes the most current prices on the FAA publications that are cost items, information regarding their availability, and instructions for ordering them from the Superintendent of Documents. All free advisory circulars are also listed in the *Advisory Circular Checklist*. To obtain a free copy of AC 00-2, send the request to U.S. Department of Transportation, Publications Section M-443.1, Washington, DC 20590.

Pilot's Handbook of Aeronautical Knowledge (AC 61-23B) contains authoritative information used in training pilots and on most subject areas in which an applicant may be tested. It is suggested that this publication be read thoroughly.

Plane Sense (AC 20-5F) acquaints the prospective airplane owner with certain fundamentals of owning and operating an airplane. It is free upon request.

Flight Training Handbook (AC 61-21A) deals with certain basic flight information such as load factor principles, weight and balance, and related aerodynamic aspects of flight as well as principles of safe flight. Thus it serves as a text for student pilots and for pilots improving their qualications or preparing for additional ratings.

Aviation Weather (AC 00-6A) contains information on weather phenomena for pilots and other flight operations personnel whose interest in meteorology is primarily in its application to flying.

Aviation Weather Services (AC 00-45B) supplements AC 00-6A, *Aviation Weather*, in that it explains the weather service in general and the use and interpretation of reports, forecasts, weather maps, and prognostic charts in detail. It is an excellent source of study for pilot certification examinations.

Pilot's Weight and Balance Handbook (AC 91-23A) provides an easily understood text on aircraft weight and balance. It progresses from an explanation of fundamentals to the application of weight and balance principles.

Wake Turbulence (AC 90-23D) presents information on the subject of wake turbulence and suggests techniques that may help pilots avoid the hazards of wing-tip vortex turbulence. It is free upon request.

Medical Handbook for Pilots (AC 67-2) is an aviation medicine handbook written in pilots' language, which provides guidance on when and when not to fly. It emphasizes the fact that a good pilot must be physically fit, psychologically sound, and well trained.

The FAA publishes the *Federal Aviation Regulations* (FARs) to make readily available to the aviation community the regulatory requirements placed upon them. These regulations are sold as individual parts by the Superintendent of Documents. The more frequently amended parts are sold on subscription service (that is, subscribers will receive changes automatically as issued), while the less active ones are sold on a single-sale basis. Changes to single-sale parts will be sold separately as issued. Information concerning these changes will be furnished by the FAA through its *Status of Federal Aviation Regulations,* latest revision). The status list is free upon request.

A check or money order made payable to the Superintendent of Documents should be included with each order. Submit orders for single sales and subscription parts on different order forms. No COD orders are accepted. All FAR parts should be ordered from the Superintendent of Documents, U.S. Government Printing Office, Washington, DC 20402.

The suggested parts for study are Part 1, Definitions and Abbreviations; Part 61, Certification: Pilots and Flight Instructors; Part 71, Designation of Federal Airways, Controlled Airspace, and Reporting Points; and Part 91, General Operating and Flight Rules.

National Transportation Safety Board (Part 830) deals with procedures required in the notification and reporting of accidents and lost or overdue aircraft within the United States, its territories, and possessions. It is free upon request from the National Transportation Safety Board, Publications Branch, Washington, DC 20594.

■ Parts of the Examination

QUESTION SELECTION SHEET. When you take the written test, you'll be given a Question Selection Sheet. You would put the answer for question 1014 in one of the four spaces provided for item 1 and mark the proper space in item 2 for question 1032, and so on, as shown in Figure 27-A. You'd use only the first 50 items on the answer sheet (Airman Written Test Application, Fig. 27-B) on the actual FAA test.

The Question Selection Sheet that it says it is permissible to mark on it (see sample), but *do not* mark the FAA question booklet. It is suggested that you put the answers on the Question Selection Sheet (1, 2, 3, or 4 as applicable) before filling in the circles on the official answer sheet that is described next. This could save a lot of problems such as inaccurately marked answers. (The minimum passing grade is 70%.)

AIRMAN WRITTEN TEST APPLICATION. You'll fill in your vital statistics on the Airman Written Test Application before taking the test and then fill in the proper answer circle for each question (see sample). (As another example, you'd read question 1123 carefully and then fill in the proper circle item 35 on that page.) Knowing the material thoroughly but marking the wrong item or circling an item isn't the way to let the FAA know how sharp you really are.

WRITTEN TEST QUESTIONS. Probably the biggest problem the average written-test taker has (besides marking the answer in the wrong place) is that of misreading the question *and* the answer choices. As noted in Chapter 1, you'll have 4 hours to complete the test, but sometimes that seems little enough time when you get stuck on a particularly tough question. Also, don't waste time on a question that seems to have *no* correct answer or that is (to you) extra complicated. *Move on.* Answer the questions that you are able to and come back to the tough ones last. Some of the "easier" questions may trigger responses for the ones that produced a blank mind.

References will be given by the FAA for the questions that you missed.

ANSWERS. The 60 answers (there are 10 extra questions here) are given in two ways. Another Question Selection Sheet has been inserted in the back of the book with the proper answers written in. Following that is a Written Test Application, also with the correct answer selections filled in.

After you've checked the questions and seen what you've missed (or maybe you didn't miss any), look at the areas in which you're weak.

Review these weak areas in particular but don't neglect the other questions when getting ready for the real thing.

When your flight or ground instructor feels that you are ready for the test, he or she will endorse you to that effect. (There is a form provided in the back of *SPFM.*) Okay, get started.

1014. With a reported wind of north at 20 knots, which runway (6, 14, 24, or 32) is appropriate for an airplane with a 13-knot maximum crosswind component? (See Figure 27-C.)

1—Runway 6.
2—Runway 14.
3—Runway 24.
4—Runway 32.

1032. What is the approximate ground roll distance after landing under the following conditions? (See Figure 27-D.)

OAT . . . . .90°F
Pressure altitude .4,000 feet
Weight . . . . .2,800 pound
Tailwind component. . . . . .5 knots

1—1,200 feet
2—1,575 feet
3—1,725 feet
4—1,950 feet

1045. What effect does higher density altitude have on propeller efficiency?

1—Increased efficiency due to less friction on the propeller blades.
2—Reduced efficiency because the propeller exerts less force than at lower density altitudes.

Chapter 27. The Written Test

DEPARTMENT OF TRANSPORTATION · FEDERAL AVIATION ADMINISTRATION

QUESTION SELECTION SHEET
PA-3A

◀ USE WITH QUESTION BOOK PA-3 ONLY!

TITLE: **PRIVATE PILOT - AIRPLANE**   TEST NO.

NAME _____

NOTE: IT IS PERMISSIBLE TO MARK ON THIS SHEET.

On Answer Sheet For Item No.	Answer Question Number	On Answer Sheet For Item No.	Answer Question Number	On Answer Sheet For Item No.	Answer Question Number
1	1014	21	1424	41	1700
2	1032	22	1427	42	1717
3	1045	23	1429	43	1725
4	1061	24	1437	44	1732
5	1062	25	1438	45	1739
6	1101	26	1441	46	1762
7	1123	27	1469	47	1764
8	1168	28	1472	48	1783
9	1172	29	1474	49	1794
10	1178	30	1475	50	1827
11	1228	31	1491	51	1832
12	1247	32	1502	52	1833
13	1274	33	1554	53	1836
14	1276	34	1569	54	1863
15	1278	35	1574	55	1864
16	1346	36	1595	56	1867
17	1348	37	1622	57	1871
18	1359	38	1648	58	1872
19	1361	39	1665	59	1902
20	1421	40	1674	60	1907

Fig. 27-A.

DEPARTMENT OF TRANSPORTATION — FEDERAL AVIATION ADMINISTRATION

AIRMAN WRITTEN TEST APPLICATION

DATE OF TEST	TITLE OF TEST	TEST NO.
MONTH 12 DAY 14 YEAR 83	PRIVATE PILOT - AIRPLANE	PAR-003

PLEASE PRINT ONE LETTER IN EACH SPACE—LEAVE A BLANK SPACE AFTER EACH NAME

NAME (LAST, FIRST, MIDDLE): DOE JOHN ROCHESTER

DATE OF BIRTH: MONTH 09 DAY 27 YEAR 29

MAILING ADDRESS NO. AND STREET, APT. #, P.O. BOX, OR RURAL ROUTE: 1427 COMMERCE STREET

CITY, TOWN OR POST OFFICE, AND STATE: SEWANEE TENNESSEE   ZIP CODE: 37375

DESCRIPTION — HEIGHT: 72" WEIGHT: 180 HAIR: Brown EYES: Grey

BIRTHPLACE (City and State, or foreign country): CLARKSVILLE, TENNESSEE

CITIZENSHIP: USA   SOCIAL SECURITY NO.: 123456789

IF A SOCIAL SECURITY NUMBER HAS NEVER BEEN ISSUED CHECK THIS BLOCK → ☐

Is this a retest? ☒ No ☐ Yes, date of last test _____

Have you taken or are you taking an FAA approved course for this test? ☒ No ☐ Yes (If "yes" give details below)

Graduation date: _____ NAME OF SCHOOL: _____ CITY AND STATE: _____

CERTIFICATION: I CERTIFY that all of the statements made in this application are true, complete, and correct to the best of my knowledge and belief and are made in good faith. Signature: *John R. Doe*

— — DO NOT WRITE IN THIS BLOCK — — FOR USE OF FAA OFFICE ONLY — —

Applicant's identity established by: _____

CARD A					CARD B			
CATEGORY	TEST NUMBER	TAKE NO.	SECTIONS 1 2 3 4 5 6 7	EXPIRATION MONTH DAY YEAR	CERTIFICATED SCHOOL NUMBER	MECH EXP DATE BY SECTION 1 2 3	ID	FIELD OFFICE DESIGNATION

SIGNATURE of FAA Representative

INSTRUCTIONS FOR MARKING THE ANSWER SHEET. Completely darken only one circle for each question. DO NOT USE (X) OR (✓) Use black lead pencil furnished by examiner. To make corrections, open answer sheet so erasure marks will not show on page 2. Then erase incorrect response on page 4. On page 2 (copy) mark the incorrect response with a slash (/). Questions are arranged in VERTICAL sequence as indicated by the arrows.

Fig. 27-B.

WIND COMPONENTS
Demonstrated Crosswind Component is 17 kts

EXAMPLE:
WIND SPEED	20 KTS
ANGLE BETWEEN WIND DIRECTION AND FLIGHT PATH	50°
HEADWIND COMPONENT	13 KTS
CROSSWIND COMPONENT	15 KTS

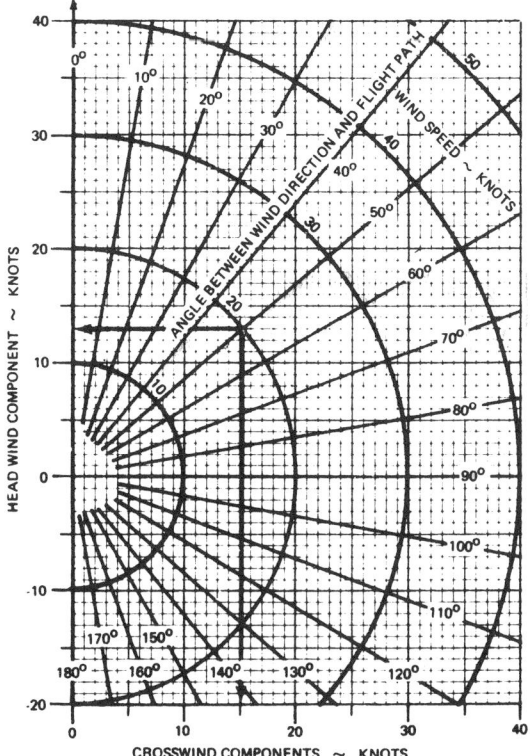

Fig. 27-C.

3—Reduced efficiency due to the increased force of the thinner air on the propeller.

4—Increased efficiency because the propeller exerts more force on the thinner air.

1061. The use of carburetor heat tends to

1—decrease engine output and increase operating temperature.
2—decrease engine output and decrease operating temperature.
3—increase engine output and increase operating temperature.
4—increase engine output and decrease operating temperature.

1062.—If an engine continues to run after the ignition switch is turned to the OFF position, the probable cause may be

1—the mixture is too lean and this causes the engine to diesel.
2—the voltage regulator points are sticking closed.
3—a broken magneto ground wire.
4—fouled spark plugs.

1101. In the Northern Hemisphere, a magnetic compass will normally initially indicate a turn toward the east if

1—an aircraft is decelerated while on a south heading.

LANDING DISTANCE

ASSOCIATED CONDITIONS:
POWER	RETARDED TO MAINTAIN 900 FT/ on FINAL APPROACH
FLAPS	DOWN
LANDING GEAR	DOWN
RUNWAY	PAVED, LEVEL, DRY SURFACE
APPROACH SPEED	IAS AS TABULATED
BRAKING	MAXIMUM

WEIGHT ~ POUNDS	SPEED AT 50 FT	
	KNOTS	MPH
2950	70	80
2800	68	78
2600	65	75
2400	63	72
2200	60	69

EXAMPLE:
OAT	25°C (77°F)
PRESSURE ALTITUDE	3965 FT
WEIGHT	2814 LBS
WIND COMPONENT	9.0 KNOTS (HEADWIND)
GROUND ROLL	1080 FT
TOTAL OVER 50 FT OBSTACLE	1700 FT
APPROACH SPEED	68 KNOTS (78 MPH)

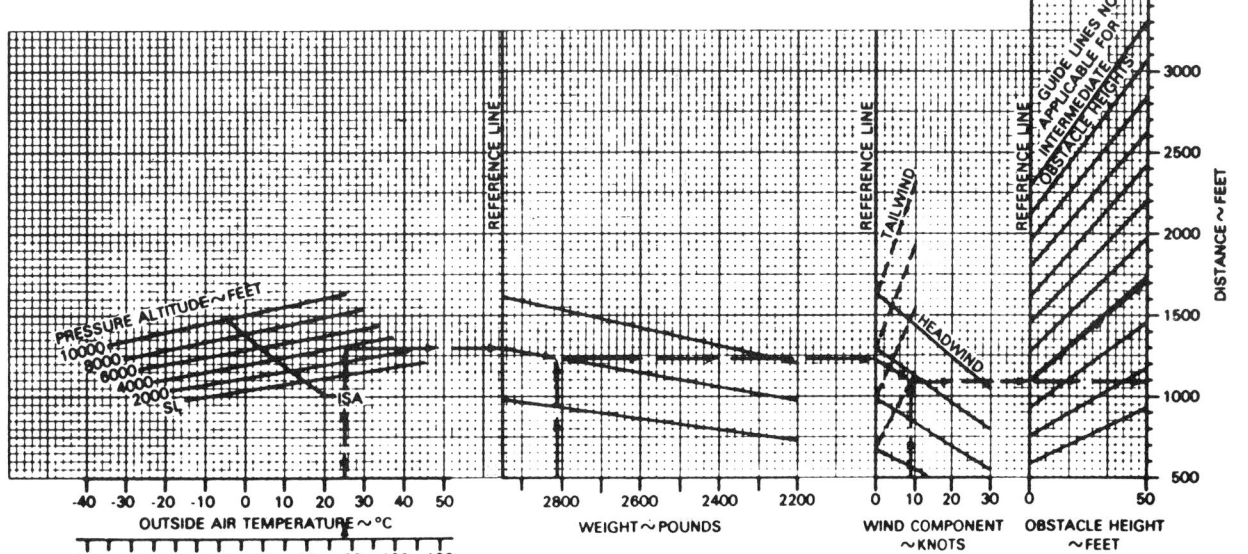

Fig. 27-D.

2—an aircraft is accelerated while on a north heading.
3—a right turn is entered from a north heading.
4—a left turn is entered from a north heading.

1123. What is an important airspeed limitation that is not color coded on airspeed indicators?

1—Never-exceed speed.
2—Maximum structural cruising speed.
3—Maneuvering speed.
4—Maximum flaps-extended speed.

1168. What is one advantage of an airplane said to be inherently stable?

1—The airplane will not spin.
2—The airplane will be difficult to stall.
3—The airplane will require less effort to control.
4—The airplane will return to its original condition after being disturbed.

1172. What effect does loading an airplane to the most aft CG have on the airplane stability?

1—The airplane will be less stable at slow speeds, but more stable at high speeds.
2—The airplane will be less stable at high speeds, but more stable at low speeds.
3—The airplane will be more stable at all speeds.
4—The airplane will be less stable at all speeds.

1178. As altitude increases, the indicated airspeed at which a given airplane stalls in a particular configuration will

1—decrease as the true airspeed decreases.
2—decrease as the true airspeed increases.
3—remain the same as at low altitude.
4—increase because the air density becomes less.

1228. Upon landing, the front passenger (180 pounds) departs the airplane. A rear passenger (204 pounds) moves to the front passenger position. What effect does this have on the CG if the airplane weighed 2,690 pounds and the MOM/100 was 2260 just prior to the passenger transfer? (See Figures 27-E and 27-F.)

1—The weight changes but the CG is not affected.
2—The CG moves forward approximately 0.1 inch.
3—The CG moves forward approximately 2.4 inch.
4—The CG moves forward approximately 3 inches.

1247. Refer to Figure 27-G. An aircraft departs an airport in the central standard time zone at 0730 CST for a 3-hour flight to an airport located in the mountain standard time zone. What should the landing time be?

1—0830 MST.
2—0930 MST.
3—1000 MST.
4—1030 MST.

1274. What minimum altitude is requested for aircraft over National Wildlife Refuges such as the one depicted at (b)? (See Figure 27-H.)

1—500 feet AGL.
2—1,000 feet AGL.
3—2,000 feet AGL.
4—3,000 feet AGL.

1276. The lighting at Rock County Airport (i) in Figure 27-H is

1—pilot controlled.
2—operated part time.
3—available on request.
4—limited to the beacon light.

1278. What UNICOM frequency, if any, is indicated for Rock County Airport (i) in Figure 27-H?

1—None is listed.
2—118.8 MHz.
3—122.8 MHz.
4—122.95 MHz.

1346. Which RMI indication in Figure 27-I represents the aircraft tracking to the station with a right crosswind?

1—A.
2—B.
3—C.
4—D.

1348. The first action after starting an aircraft engine should be to

1—adjust for proper RPM and check for desired indications on the engine gauges.
2—check the magneto or ignition switch momentarily in the OFF position for proper grounding.
3—test each brake and the parking brake.
4—visually clear the area for people and obstacles.

1359. Which wind condition would be most critical when taxiing a nosewheel-equipped high-wing airplane?

1—Direct headwind.
2—Direct crosswind.
3—Quartering headwind.
4—Quartering tailwind.

1361. Is it necessary to preflight an aircraft that was hangared the night before in ready-to-fly condition?

1—No, if the aircraft has not been handled since hangaring.
2—Yes, because fuel contamination from condensation is possible.
3—Yes, because the oil level should always be checked.

USEFUL LOAD WEIGHTS AND MOMENTS

OCCUPANTS

FRONT SEATS ARM 85		REAR SEATS ARM 121	
Weight	Moment/100	Weight	Moment/100
120	102	120	145
130	110	130	157
140	119	140	169
150	128	150	182
160	136	160	194
170	144	170	206
180	153	180	218
190	162	190	230
200	170	200	242

BAGGAGE OR 5TH SEAT OCCUPANT ARM 140

Weight	Moment/100
10	14
20	28
30	42
40	56
50	70
60	84
70	98
80	112
90	126
100	140
110	154
120	168
130	182
140	196
150	210
160	224
170	238
180	252
190	266
200	280
210	294
220	308
230	322
240	336
250	350
260	364
270	378

USABLE FUEL

MAIN WING TANKS ARM 75

Gallons	Weight	Moment/100
5	30	22
10	60	45
15	90	68
20	120	90
25	150	112
30	180	135
35	210	158
40	240	180
44	264	198

AUXILIARY WING TANKS ARM 94

Gallons	Weight	Moment/100
5	30	28
10	60	56
15	90	85
19	114	107

*OIL

Quarts	Weight	Moment/100
10	19	5

*Included in Basic Empty Weight

Empty Weight – 2015

MOM/100 – 1554

MOMENT LIMITS vs WEIGHT

Moment limits are based on the following weight and center of gravity limit data (landing gear down).

WEIGHT CONDITION	FORWARD CG LIMIT	AFT CG LIMIT
2950 lb. (take-off or landing)	82.1	84.7
2525 lb.	77.5	85.7
2475 lb. or less	77.0	85.7

Fig. 27-E.

4—No, if the same person who hangared the aircraft will act as pilot in command.

1421. What is the general direction of movement of the other aircraft if during a night flight you observe steady red and green lights ahead and at the same altitude?

1—The other aircraft is crossing to the left.

2—The other aircraft is crossing to the right.
3—The other aircraft is approaching head-on.
4—The other aircraft is headed away from you.

1424. Wingtip vortices, the dangerous turbulence that might be encountered behind a large aircraft, are created only when that aircraft is

1—operating at high speeds.

MOMENT LIMITS vs WEIGHT (Continued)

Weight	Minimum Moment 100	Maximum Moment 100	Weight	Minimum Moment 100	Maximum Moment 100
2100	1617	1800	2600	2037	2224
2110	1625	1808	2610	2048	2232
2120	1632	1817	2620	2058	2239
2130	1640	1825	2630	2069	2247
2140	1648	1834	2640	2080	2255
2150	1656	1843	2650	2090	2263
2160	1663	1851	2660	2101	2271
2170	1671	1860	2670	2112	2279
2180	1679	1868	2680	2123	2287
2190	1686	1877	2690	2133	2295
2200	1694	1885	2700	2144	2303
2210	1702	1894	2710	2155	2311
2220	1709	1903	2720	2166	2319
2230	1717	1911	2730	2177	2326
2240	1725	1920	2740	2188	2334
2250	1733	1928	2750	2199	2342
2260	1740	1937	2760	2210	2350
2270	1748	1945	2770	2221	2358
2280	1756	1954	2780	2232	2366
2290	1763	1963	2790	2243	2374
2300	1771	1971			
2310	1779	1980	2800	2254	2381
2320	1786	1988	2810	2265	2389
2330	1794	1997	2820	2276	2397
2340	1802	2005	2830	2287	2405
2350	1810	2014	2840	2298	2413
2360	1817	2023	2850	2309	2421
2370	1825	2031	2860	2320	2428
2380	1833	2040	2870	2332	2436
2390	1840	2048	2880	2343	2444
2400	1848	2057	2890	2354	2452
2410	1856	2065	2900	2365	2460
2420	1863	2074	2910	2377	2468
2430	1871	2083	2920	2388	2475
2440	1879	2091	2930	2399	2483
2450	1887	2100	2940	2411	2491
2460	1894	2108	2950	2422	2499
2470	1902	2117			
2480	1911	2125			
2490	1921	2134			
2500	1932	2143			
2510	1942	2151			
2520	1953	2160			
2530	1963	2168			
2540	1974	2176			
2550	1984	2184			
2560	1995	2192			
2570	2005	2200			
2580	2016	2208			
2590	2026	2216			

Fig. 27-F.

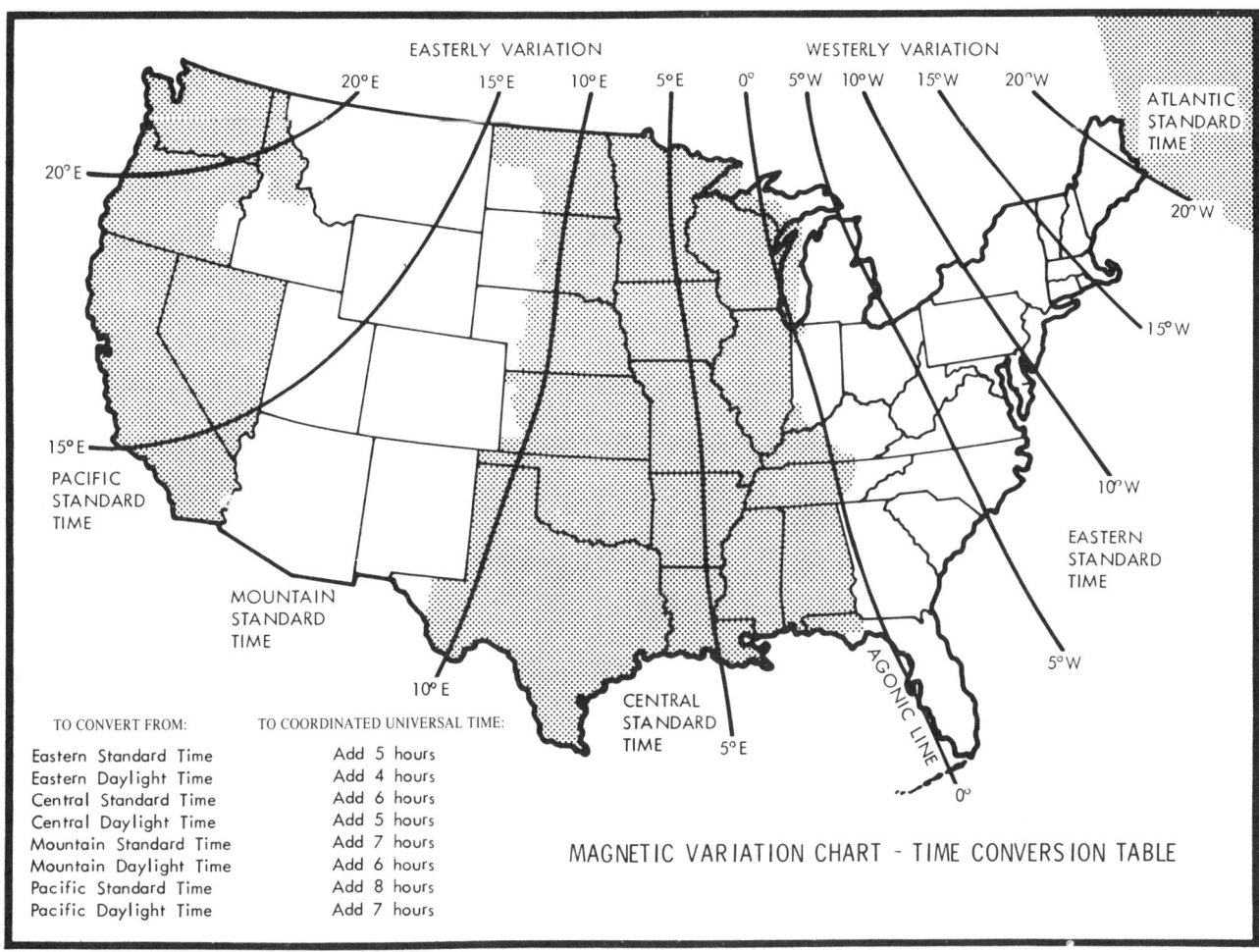

Fig. 27-G.

2—heavily loaded.
3—developing lift.
4—using high-power settings.

1427. What action can a pilot take to aid in cooling an engine that is overheated during a climb?

1—Lean the mixture to best power condition.
2—Increase RPM and reduce climb speed.
3—Reduce rate of climb and increase airspeed.
4—Increase RPM and climb speed.

1429. The most important rule to remember in the event of a power failure after becoming airborne is to

1—quickly check the fuel supply for possible fuel exhaustion.
2—determine the wind direction to plan for the forced landing.
3—turn back immediately to the takeoff runway.
4—maintain safe airspeed.

1437. Select the proper traffic pattern and runway for a landing as indicated on the airport diagram in Figure 27-J.

1—Right-hand traffic and Runway 4.
2—Right-hand traffic and Runway 18.
3—Left-hand traffic and Runway 22.
4—Left-hand traffic and Runway 36.

1438. If the wind is as shown by the landing direction indicator in Figure 27-J, the pilot should land to the

1—north on Runway 36 and expect a crosswind from the right.
2—south on Runway 18 and expect a crosswind from the right.
3—southwest on Runway 22 directly into the wind.
4—northeast on Runway 4 directly into the wind.

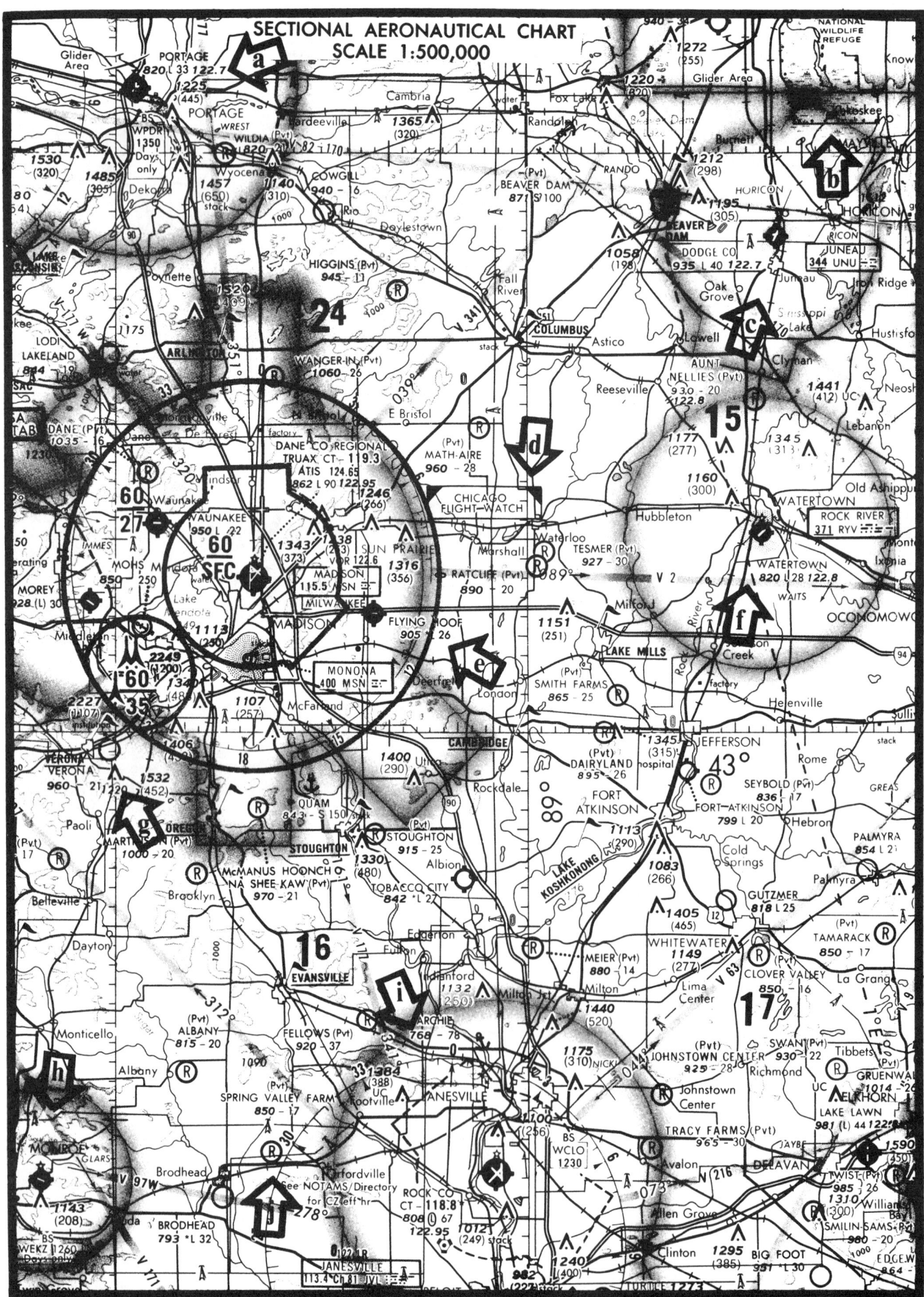

Fig. 27-H.

Chapter 27. The Written Test 125

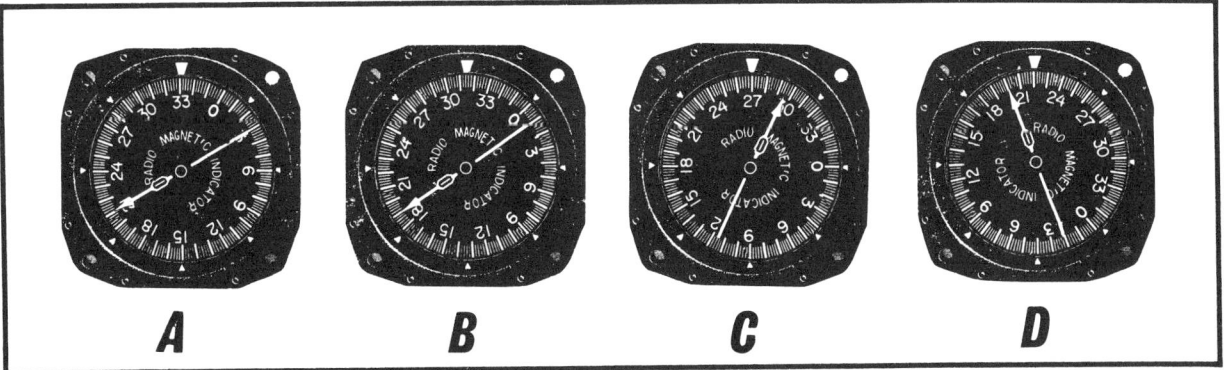

Fig. 27-I.

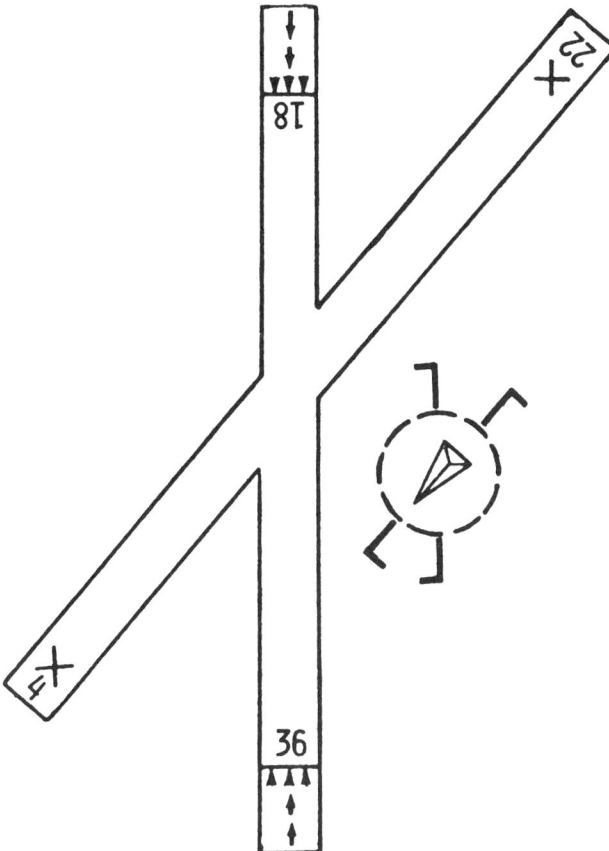

Fig. 27-J.

1441. How can a military airport be identified at night?

1—Alternate white and green beacon light flashes.
2—Dual peaked (two quick) white flashes between intermittent green flashes.
3—White flashing beacon lights with steady green at the same location.
4—Alternate white and red beacon light flashes.

1469. If air traffic control advises that radar service is being terminated when the pilot is departing a terminal radar service area, the transponder should be set to code

1—0000.
2—1200.
3—4096.
4—7700.

1472. When the approaching Abilene Municipal at 7,500 feet from the west, the initial contact with approach control should be on (see Figure 27-K)

1—121.3 MHz.
2—124.1 MHz.
3—125.0 MHz.
4—126.5 MHz.

1474. Which runways at Abilene Municipal have right-hand traffic patterns? (See Figure 27-K.)

1—Rwy 17L-35R.
2—Rwy 17R-35L.
3—Rwys 17R, 35R, and 22.
4—All runways.

1475. How can a pilot receive transcribed weather broadcasts at Abilene Municipal? (See Figure 27-K.)

1—Local telephone call to ABI FSS.
2—Monitor ABI VORTAC on 113.7 MHz.
3—Monitor TQA VOR on 111.6 MHz.
4—Monitor ABI LOM on 353 kHz.

1491. While flying north, a radar ATC facility issues the following warning:

"TRAFFIC 10 O'CLOCK, 2 MILES, SOUTHBOUND."

The pilot would look for this traffic in a direction approximately

1—10° behind the left wing of the airplane.
2—60° to the left of the nose of the airplane.

3—30° to the right of the nose of the airplane.
4—20° to the left of the nose of the airplane.

1502. The letters VHF/DF, appearing in the *Airport/Facility Directory* for a certain airport, indicate that

1—this airport is designated as an airport of entry.
2—the flight service station has equipment with which to determine your direction from the station.
3—this airport has a direct-line phone to the flight service station.
4—this airport is a defense facility.

TEXAS

```
    ABERNATHY MUNI    (F83)   4.3 E   GMT−6(−5DT)   33°50'45"N 101°45'45"W        DALLAS-FT. WORTH
    3327   B   S4                                                                 L-13A
    RWY 17-35: H4000X75 (ASPH)    S-8   LIRL
       RWY 17: Road.         RWY 35: Road. Rgt tfc.
    RWY 03-21: H3235X75 (ASPH)    S-8
       RWY 21: P-line. Rgt tfc.
    AIRPORT REMARKS: Attended continuously.
    COMMUNICATIONS: UNICOM 122.8
       LUBBOCK FSS (LBB) Toll free call dial 0, ask for ENTERPRISE 84044.
    RADIO AIDS TO NAVIGATION:
       LUBBOCK (L) ABVORTAC 110.8   ■ LBB   Chan 45   33°42'18"N 101°54'49"W   031° 11.3 NM to fld.
          3310/11E. General outlook only 0400-1100Z‡.
```

ABILENE

```
  §  ABILENE MUNI    (ABI)   2.6 SE   GMT−6(−5DT)   32°24'41"N 99°40'53"W         DALLAS-FT. WORTH
     1790   B   S4   FUEL 100LL, JET A, A1 +   OX 1    CFR Index A                H-2H, L-13B, 15C
     RWY 17L-35R: H7199X150 (ASPH)     S-80, D-110, DT-160   HIRL   .39% up N     IAP
        RWY 17L: VASI(V4L) − GA 3.0° TCH 43'.        RWY 35R: SSALR. Pole. Rgt tfc.
     RWY 17R-35L: H7201X150 (ASPH)     S-75, D-100, DT-160   MIRL   .32% up S
        RWY 17R: VASI(V4L) − GA 3.0° TCH 58'. Rgt tfc.    RWY 35L: VASI(V4L) − GA 3.0° TCH 49'.
     RWY 04-22: H3686X100 (ASPH)   S-35, D-44, DT-68   MIRL
        RWY 22: Rgt tfc.
     AIRPORT REMARKS: Attended continuously. Parachute Jumping. Prior Permission Required for certificated air carrier
        operations 0400-1200Z‡.
     COMMUNICATIONS: UNICOM 122.95
        ABILENE FSS (ABI) on arpt. 122.65, 122.2, 122.1R, 120.1  (915) 677-4336
     ®  APP/DEP CON 126.5 (5500-10,000') 121.3 (5500' & blo) 161-350°, 124.1 (5500' & blo) 351-160°, 125.0
           (1300-0500Z‡)
     ®  FORT WORTH CENTER APP/DEP CON 127.45 (0500-1300Z‡)
        TOWER 120.1 (1500-0100Z‡)   GND CON 121.9
        STAGE II SVC ctc APP CON within 20 NM
     RADIO AIDS TO NAVIGATION:
        (H) ABVORTAC 113.7    ■ ABI    Chan 84    32°28'53"N 99°51'47"W    105° 10 NM to fld. 1810/10E.
        TUSCOLA (L) VOR 111.6    TQA    32°14'08"N 99°48'59"W    020° 13.5 NM to fld.
        TOMHI NDB (LOM) 353    AB    32°17'55"N 99°40'26"W    350° 5.4 NM to fld.
        ILS 110.3 I-ABI Rwy 35R LOM TOMHI NDB
        ASR
     COMM/NAVAID REMARKS: ABI FSS will provide AAS 0500-1300Z‡ 120.1.
```

```
    ELMDALE AIRPARK    (6F4)   5.2 E   GMT−6(−5DT)   32°27'00"N 99°39'00"W        DALLAS-FT. WORTH
    1775   S4   FUEL 100LL   TPA− 2175(400)                                       L-13B, 15C
    RWY 17-35: H2950X25 (ASPH)    S-4    LIRL
       RWY 17: Thld dsplcd 180'. Trees.        RWY 35: Thld dsplcd 50'. Road. Rgt tfc.
    AIRPORT REMARKS: Attended dalgt hours. Parachute Jumping. TPA 400' or lower unless authorized by Abilene
       RAPCON/tower. Ngt lndgs not recommended for pilots unfamiliar with arpt. Rwy condition poor on South half of
       runway.
    COMMUNICATIONS:
       ABILENE FSS (ABI)
    RADIO AIDS TO NAVIGATION:
       ABILENE (H) ABVORTAC 113.7    ■ ABI    Chan 84    32°28'53"N 99°51'47"W    090° 11.0 NM to fld.
          1810/10E.
```

```
    ZIMMERLE    (6F2)   13.9 SE   GMT−6(−5DT)   32°16'13"N 99°35'51"W             DALLAS-FT. WORTH
    2057                                        Not insp.
    RWY 15-33: 1200X100 (TURF)
       RWY 15: Rgt tfc.         RWY 33: Rgt tfc
    AIRPORT REMARKS: Unattended
    COMMUNICATIONS:
       ABILENE FSS (ABI)
```

```
    ACTON    32°26'04"N 97°39'49"W                                                DALLAS-FT. WORTH
    (L) VORTAC 110.6    AQN    Chan 43    173° 12.5 NM to Cleburne Muni. 848/09E   L-13C, 15D, 17A
    LRCO 122.1R 110.6T (FORT WORTH FSS)
```

```
    ADDISON    (See DALLAS)
```

Fig. 27-K.

Chapter 27. The Written Test

1554. To act as pilot in command of an aircraft, one must show by logbook endorsement the satisfactory (1) accomplishment of a flight review or (2) completion of a pilot proficiency check within the preceding

1—6 months.
2—12 months.
3—24 months.
4—36 months.

1569. If an in-flight emergency requires immediate action, a pilot in command may

1—deviate from FARs to the extent required to meet the emergency, but must submit a written report to the Administrator within 24 hours.
2—not deviate from FARs unless prior to the deviation approval is granted by the Administrator.
3—deviate from FARs to the extent required to meet that emergency.
4—not deviate from FARs unless permission is obtained from air traffic control.

1574. In addition to other preflight actions for a VFR flight away from the vicinity of the departure airport, regulations require the pilot in command to

1—file a flight plan.
2—check each fuel tank visually to ensure that it is full.
3—check the accuracy of the omninavigation equipment and the emergency locator transmitter.
4—determine runway lengths of airports of intended use and the airplane's takeoff and landing distance data.

1595. What is the fuel requirement for flight under VFR at night?

1—Full fuel tanks.
2—Enough to complete the flight at normal cruising flight with adverse wind conditions.
3—Enough to fly to the first point of intended landing and to fly after that for 30 minutes at normal cruising speed.
4—Enough to fly to the first point of intended landing and to fly after that for 45 minutes at normal cruising speed.

1622. When are nonrechargeable batteries of an ELT (emergency locator transmitter) required to be replaced?

1—Every 24 months.
2—When 50 percent of their useful life expires or they were in use for a cumulative period of 1 hour.
3—At the time of each 100-hour or annual inspection.
4—Annually.

1648. While on the final approach for landing, an alternating green and red light followed by a flashing red light is received from the control tower. Under these circumstances the pilot should

1—land and clear the runway in use as safely and quickly as possible.
2—discontinue the approach, fly the same traffic pattern and approach again, and land.
3—abandon the approach, realizing the airport is unsafe for landing.
4—abandon the approach, circle the airport to the right, and expect a flashing white light when the airport is safe for landing.

1665. When is an airport traffic area in effect?

1—From 1 hour before sunrise to 1 hour after sunset.
2—When the associated control tower is in operation.
3—When the associated FSS is in operation.
4—From sunrise to sunset.

1674. The minimum flight visibility required for VFR flights above 10,000 feet MSL and more than 1,200 feet AGL is

1—1 SM.
2—3 SM.
3—5 SM.
4—not specified by regulation.

1700. What are the minimum requirements for airplane operations under special VFR in a control zone at night?

1—The minimum visibility is 3 miles and the airplane must operate clear of clouds.
2—The airplane must be under radar surveillance at all times while in the control zone.
3—The airplane must be equipped for IFR and with an altitude-reporting transponder.
4—The pilot must be instrument rated and the airplane must be IFR equipped.

1717. How long does the airworthiness certificate of an airplane remain valid?

1—As long as the aircraft has a current registration certificate.
2—Indefinitely, unless the aircraft suffers major damage.
3—As long as the airplane is maintained and operated as required by FARs.
4—Indefinitely, unless the prescribed operating limitations are exceeded.

1725. A temperature inversion would most likely result in which of the following weather conditions?

1—Clouds with extensive vertical development above an inversion aloft.

2—Good visibility in the lower levels of the atmosphere and poor visibility above an inversion aloft.
3—An increase in temperature as altitude is increased.
4—A decrease in temperature as altitude is increased.

1732. If, without adjusting the altimeter setting, a flight is made from an area of high pressure into an area of lower pressure and a constant altitude is maintained, the altimeter would indicate

1—higher than the actual altitude above sea level.
2—lower than the actual altitude above sea level.
3—the actual altitude above sea level.
4—the actual altitude above ground level.

1739. Determine the density altitude for the following conditions (see Figure 27-L):

Altimeter setting........................29.25
Rwy temperature........................+81°F
Airport elevation.......................5,250 feet

1—4,600 feet.
2—5,877 feet.
3—8,400 feet.
4—7,700 feet.

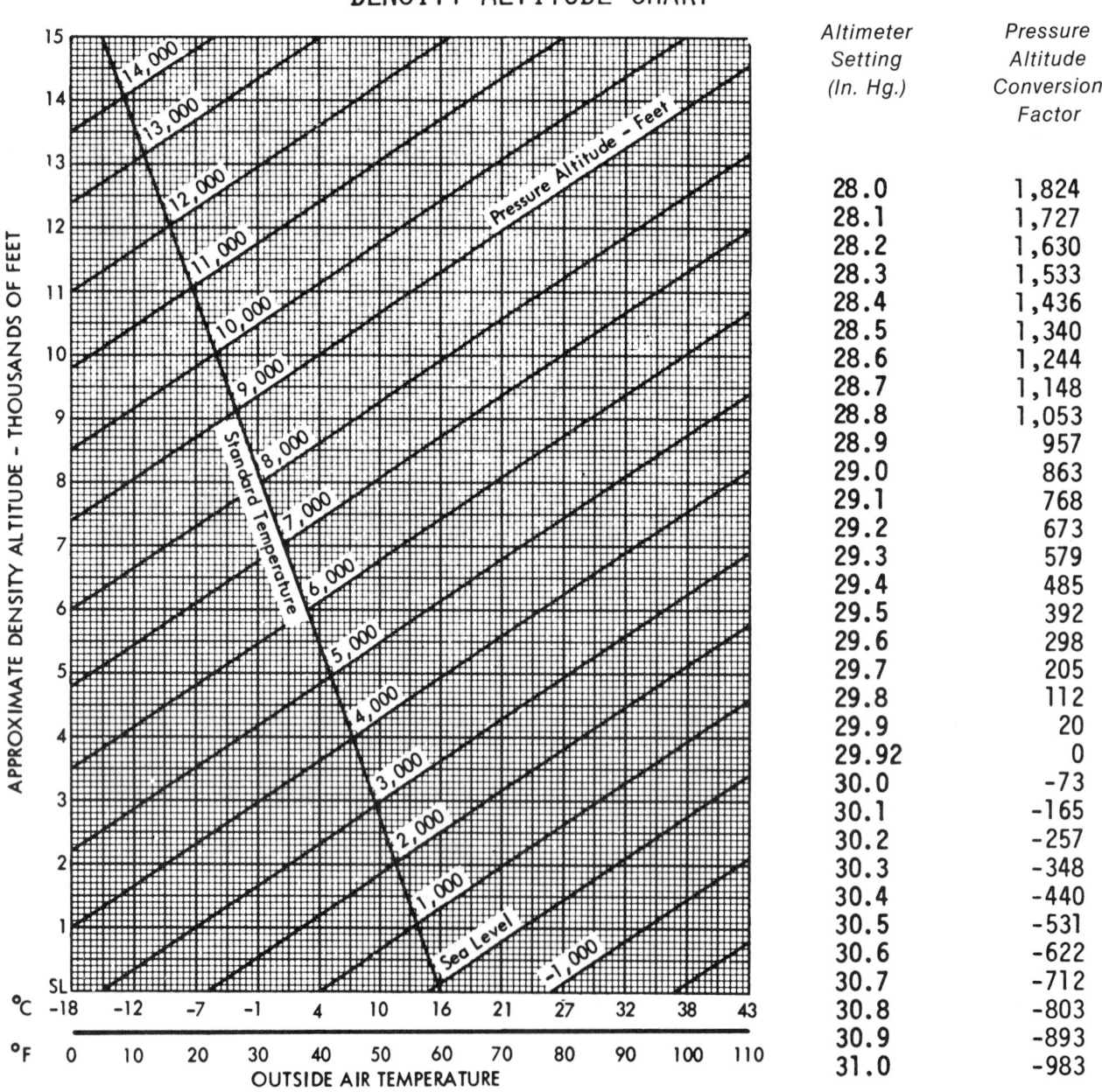

Fig. 27-L.

1762. Which of the following would decrease the stability of an air mass?

1—Warming from below.
2—Cooling from below.
3—Decrease in water vapor.
4—Sinking of the air mass.

1764. What is a characteristic of stable air?

1—Stratiform clouds.
2—Unlimited visibility.
3—Fair weather cumulus clouds.
4—Temperature decreases rapidly with altitude.

1783. When flying at a low altitude across a mountain range the greatest potential danger, caused by descending air currents, will usually be encountered on the

1—leeward side when flying into the wind.
2—windward side when flying into the wind.
3—leeward side when flying with the wind.
4—windward side when flying with the wind.

1794. Frost which has not been removed from the lifting surfaces of an airplane before flight

1—may prevent the airplane from becoming airborne.
2—will change the camber (curvature of the wing) thereby increasing lift during the takeoff.
3—may cause the airplane to become airborne with a lower angle of attack and at a lower indicated airspeed.
4—would present no problems, since frost will blow off when the airplane starts moving during takeoff.

1827. What is the sky condition depicted for Chicago Midway Airport (MDW) in Figure 27-M?

1—Thin overcast, measured ceiling 700 feet, overcast 1,100 feet, visibility 2 miles in rain plus fog.
2—Sky partially obscured, measured ceiling 700 overcast, visibility 1½, heavy rain, fog.
3—Thin overcast measured 700 feet overcast, visibility 1½, heavy rain, fog.
4—Sky partially obscured, measured ceiling 700 overcast, visibility 11, occasionally 2, with rain and heavy fog.

1832. From which primary source should information be obtained regarding expected weather at your destination and estimated time of arrival?

1—Low-Level Prog Chart.
2—Weather Depiction Chart.
3—Terminal Forecast.
4—Radar Summary and Weather Depiction Chart.

1833. According to the Terminal Forecast for Oklahoma City (OKC) in Figure 27-N, the cold front should pass through

1—between 21Z and 02Z the next day.
2—between 18Z and 21Z with heavy thunderstorms.
3—between 1515Z and 18Z.
4—after 09Z the next day.

```
INK SA 1854 CLR 15 106/77/63/1112G18/000
BOI SA 1854 150 SCT 30 181/62/42/1304/015
LAX SA 1852 7 SCT 250 SCT 6HK 129/60/59/2504/991
MDW RS 1856 -X M7 OVC 11/2R+F 990/63/61/3205/980/RF2 RB12
JFK RS 1853 W5 X 1/2F 180/68/64/1804/006/R04RVR22V30 TWR VSBY 1/4
```

Fig. 27-M.

```
OK FT 011447

GAG FT 011515 100 SCT 250 SCT 2610. 16Z 60 SCT C100 BKN 3315G22 CHC C50
  BKN 5TRW. 01Z 250 SCT 3515G25. 09Z VFR WIND..

HBR FT 011515 C120 BKN 250 BKN 3010. 17Z 100 SCT C250 BKN 3215G25 CHC C30
  BKN 3TRW. 00Z 250 SCT 3515G25. 09Z VFR WIND..

MLC FT 011515 C20 BKN 1815 BKN OCNL SCT. 20Z C30 BKN 1815G22 CHC C20 BKN
  1TRW. 03Z C30 BKN 2015 CHC C7 X 1/2TRW+G40. 09Z MVFR CIG TRW..

OKC FT 011515 C12 BKN 140 BKN 1815G28 LWR BKN V SCT. 18Z C30 BKN 250 BKN
  2315G25 LWR BKN OCNL SCT CHC C7 X 1/2TRW+G40. 21Z CFP 100 SCT C250
  BKN 3315G25 CHC C30 BKN 5TRW-. 02Z 100 SCT 250 SCT 3515G25. 09Z VFR
  WIND..

PNC FT 011515 C100 BKN 250 BKN 1810. 16Z CFP 20 SCT C100 BKN 3115 SCT V
  BKN. 00Z 250 SCT 3515G25. 09Z VFR WIND..

TUL FT 011515 C20 BKN 1915G22. 19Z C30 BKN 1815G25 CHC 3TRW. 23Z CFP C100
  BKN 250 BKN 3215G25 CHC C30 BKN 5TRW. 09Z VFR WIND..
```

Fig. 27-N.

1836. What is the outlook for weather conditions at McAlester (MLC)? (See Figure 27-N.)

1—Ceilings 2,000–3,000 feet with southerly winds.
2—Ceiling 700 feet, sky obscured, visibility ½ mile in the thundershowers.
3—VFR except in the thundershowers, peak wind gusts 40 knots.
4—Marginal VFR due to low ceilings and thundershowers.

1863. To determine the freezing level and areas of probable icing aloft, the pilot should refer to the

1—Radar Summary Chart.
2—Weather Depiction Chart.
3—Area Forecast.
4—Surface Analysis.

1864. To obtain a continuous transcribed weather briefing including winds aloft and route forecasts for a cross-country flight, a pilot could monitor

1—a TWEB on a low-freqency radio or VOR receiver.
2—a VHF radio receiver tuned to an ATIS frequency.
3—the regularly scheduled weather broadcast on a VOR frequency.
4—a high-frequency radio receiver tuned to the En Route Flight Advisory Service (Flight Watch) station.

1867. SIGMET's are issued as a warning of potentially hazardous weather conditions

1—particularly to light aircraft.
2—to all aircraft.
3—only to light aircraft operations.
4—particularly to heavy aircraft.

1871. What information is provided by the Radar Summary Chart that is not shown on other weather charts?

1—Lines and cells of hazardous thunderstorms.
2—Ceilings and precipitation between reporting stations.
3—Types of precipitation between reporting stations.
4—Areas of cloud cover and icing levels within the clouds.

1872. What values are used for Winds Aloft Forecasts?

1—Magnetic direction and knots.
2—Magnetic direction and miles per hour.
3—True direction and knots.
4—True direction and miles per hour.

1902. How should you establish contact with an EFAS (En Route Flight Advisory Service) station, and what service would you normally expect?

1—Call EFAS on 122.2 for routine weather, current reports on hazardous weather, and altimeter settings.
2—Call flight assistance on 122.5 for advisory service pertaining to severe weather.
3—Call flight watch on 122.0 for information regarding actual weather and thunderstorm activity along your route.
4—Call ARTCC on assigned frequency and ask for flight watch services.

1907. Rapid or extra deep breathing while using oxygen can cause a condition known as

1—hypoxia.
2—aerosinusitis.
3—aerotitis.
4—hyperventilation.

28

THE PRACTICAL TEST

This chapter is intended to review the practical test requirements and to hammer home some points made in earlier chapters of this book and *SPFM*. Figure 28-1, *SPFM*, the Applicant's Practical Test Checklist, lays out what's needed when you go for the test. One of the biggest gripes of examiners is that applicants report for the test with incomplete paperwork or haven't flown the hours of various phases as required by FAR Part 61.

Be sure to be fully familiar with the publication *Private Pilot—Practical Test Standards*, FAA-S-8081-1A. (It may be 1B or 1C by the time you read this.)

V SPEEDS

2801. The max angle of climb speed is designated

1—V_X.
2—V_Y.
3—V_{SO}.
4—V_A.

2802. V_{NE} is marked on the airspeed indicator as

1—the junction of the green and yellow arcs.
2—the top of the white arc.
3—a red radial line.
4—the bottom of the green arc.

GENERAL PROCEDURES

2803. You took the private pilot written test on December 17, 1988. You may take the practical test no later than

1—December 17, 1989.
2—December 31, 1990.
3—December 17, 1990.
4—December 31, 1989.

PREFLIGHT OPERATION

2804. Aviation fuel is considered to weigh

1—6 pounds per gallon.
2—7.5 pounds per gallon.
3—6 pounds per cubic foot.
4—8.5 pounds per gallon.

2805. A moment, as defined for airplane weight and balance work here, is

1—a distance times a weight or force and in calculations is expressed in foot-pounds.
2—always measured from the leading edge of the wing.
3—a distance times a weight or force and in calculations is expressed as pounds per furlong.
4—a distance times a weight or force and is expressed as pound-inches.

2806. In preparing for the cross-country portion of the practical test, you are required to demonstrate your ability to analyze weather information. Which of the following would be a good operating practice?

1—In addition to checking all available information concerning the destination(s), also check actual weather reports at stations west of the airports to be used.
2—A good check of the terminal forecasts for the route points (airports) will make checking the actual weather reports unnecessary.
3—Have the briefer at the FSS or Weather Service Office give you the go or no-go decision.

4—Get the opinion of the examiner for a go or no-go decision to show that you want all possible inputs.

2807. You are running well behind time in the period allowed for the practical test. The examiner says that you may skip the preflight check since you had checked the fuel and oil just before the 30-minute flight to this airport. What do you do in this case?

1—You need not preflight the airplane since the examiner is automatically pilot in command for the flight.
2—You need not preflight the airplane, since you are pilot in command and can make this decision based on the shortage of time available.
3—You should always preflight the airplane, even if time for the practical test is running out.
4—Preflight checks, like checklists, are for people who are unfamiliar with a particular airplane and may be used at the discretion of the pilot in command (you).

2808. The primary responsibility for assuring that the proper amount and grade of fuel and oil are in the airplane to be flown on the check ride belongs to the

1—pilot in command (you).
2—owner-operator (the FBO).
3—mechanic(s) at the airport holding an inspection authorization.
4—examiner, since he is automatically pilot in command on a check flight.

AIRPORT AND TRAFFIC PATTERN OPERATIONS

2809. The in-flight light signal used by the tower to indicate that you should give way to other aircraft and continue circling is a

1—steady green.
2—flashing white.
3—flashing red.
4—steady red.

2810. The two-bar visual approach slope indicator (VASI) indicates the condition as shown in Figure 28-A when you are on final approach.

Choose the correct statement.

1—The airplane is too low.
2—The lights indicate an impossible situation.
3—The airplane is too high.
4—The airplane is on the proper glide slope.

Fig. 28-A.

FLIGHT MANEUVERING BY REFERENCE TO GROUND OBJECTS

2811. Which of the following is the most common error for student pilots performing a rectangular course?

1—Gaining altitude.
2—Losing altitude.
3—Overcorrecting for the wind.
4—Carrying too much power.

2812. Which of the following would most likely result in the failure of the ground reference maneuvers portion of the practical test?

1—Gaining altitude.
2—Undercorrecting for the wind.
3—Failure to look around for other aircraft.
4—Poor initial positioning with the reference.

FLIGHT AT CRITICALLY LOW AIRSPEEDS

2813. Flight at minimum controllable airspeed is a condition in which

1—the airplane is flown at approximately 10 knots above the normal power-on stall speed.
2—an increase in the angle of attack by adding load factor or by slowly applying back pressure will result in a stall.
3—the airplane is in the stalled condition, or past the critical angle of attack.
4—the airplane is flown at the highest certificated weight.

2814. Imminent stalls may be required (at a safe altitude) on the practical test in which of the following configurations or flight situations?

1—Takeoff, climb, or approach.
2—Cruise, approach, takeoff, and departure.

3—During wind drift correction maneuvers, takeoff, departure, and landing approaches.
4—Takeoff, departure, cruise, and accelerated maneuvers.

2815. Which of the following statements is correct concerning full stalls? A full stall is a situation in which

1—the angle of attack is increased until the first buffeting or decay of control effectiveness is noted.
2—the stall break occurs with the nose at an attitude of at least 30° above the horizon (power on *or* power off).
3—a stall occurs as indicated either by a sudden loss of control effectiveness or uncontrollable pitching.
4—a spin occurs.

2816. At a safe altitude during the practical test the examiner tells you to "do a takeoff and departure stall straight ahead." That's his only statement. Your procedure should be to

1—clear the area, set up the stall, and recover with power at idle.
2—set up the stall and recover with all power safely available.
3—clear the area, set up the stall, and recover with all power safely available.
4—set up the stall and recover with power at idle.

2817. Which of the following may be required on the practical test?

1—Short-field approach and landing.
2—A forward slip to a landing with flaps or no flaps if the manufacturer does not prohibit such operations.
3—At least one landing in sufficient crosswind to require crosswind techniques but not to exceed the limitations of the airplane.
4—All the above.

MANEUVERING BY REFERENCE TO INSTRUMENTS

2818. You will be expected to do turns by reference to instruments, rolling out on a prechosen heading within

1—plus or minus 20°.
2—plus 10°.
3—plus or minus 10°.
4—plus or minus 15°.

2819. You are doing hood work on the private practical test, and the examiner has to take control to keep you from exceeding the red line in what started out to be a 500 fpm descending turn. Which of the following statements is correct?

1—If the other portions of the practical test were satisfactory, the examiner will issue the private certificate with a limitation of "VFR flight only."
2—You have failed the practical test, will not be issued a private certificate, and on the next check will be given credit only for those parts or phases satisfactorily completed.
3—You have failed the practical test and will have to satisfactorily pass *all* parts or phases again.
4—None of the above statements is correct.

2820. Which of the following could be required for an applicant to accomplish under the hood on the private practical test?

1—Follow a VOR radial, complete an ILS approach, or demonstrate the use of the VHF/DF procedures.
2—Complete a VOR or ADF approach or demonstrate the use of VHF/DF procedures.
3—Follow a VOR radial or, using an ADF, home to a radio beacon or commercial broadcast station or demonstrate the proper procedure to get emergency assistance from approach control or an FSS.
4—Make a VHF/DF approach.

CROSS-COUNTRY FLYING

2821. Which of the following statements concerning the cross-country portion of the practical test is correct?

1—You will not be required to divert to an alternate.
2—You may use VOR or ADF equipment as aids to navigation.
3—Dead reckoning navigation may not be used.
4—You will work out the ETA to the selected destination airport to the nearest 20 minutes.

MAXIMUM PERFORMANCE TAKEOFFS AND LANDINGS

2822. Which statement concerning short-field takeoffs or landings is correct?

1—The manufacturer's recommendations for your airplane supersede any suggestions made in the flight test guide.
2—The maximum angle of climb airspeed is *always* greater than the maximum rate of climb at sea level.

3—Holding the control wheel or stick back, using full brake pressure, and locking the main wheels is the most efficient way to have the shortest landing roll.
4—Carry 50 percent power throughout the landing to allow the airplane to touch down as slowly as possible to minimize the total distance required.

2823. Which of the following statements concerning soft-field takeoffs or landings is correct?

1—On a soft-field takeoff the airplane should be held on the ground until V_x is attained, then climbed at that value.
2—The soft-field takeoff run should be done at a higher angle of attack than that of a short-field run to aid in decreasing ground drag.
3—On a soft-field takeoff the airplane should be held on the ground until V_y is attained, then climbed at that value.
4—It is more efficient to land an airplane on a soft area if the power is at idle to ensure the lowest touchdown speed.

NIGHT FLYING, NIGHT VFR NAVIGATION

2824. Which one of the following statements is correct concerning the night flying requirements of the practical test?

1—If you do not demonstrate actual night flying ability on the practical test, your private certificate will have a notation, "Night flying prohibited."
2—The night flying experience requirement for the private certificate is 3 hours and five takeoffs and landings to a complete stop in a period from 1 hour after sunset to 1 hour before sunrise.
3—The examiner is prohibited from having you demonstrate night flying under conditions as cited for night operations in FAR 61.57(d).
4—You may be asked to plan either a local or a cross-country night flight on the practical test.

EMERGENCY OPERATIONS

2825. Which of the following will *not* be a required demonstration on the practical test?

1—Partial or complete loss of power.
2—Pilot incapacitation.
3—Fuel starvation.
4—Fire in the engine compartment.

2826. Which of the following emergency operations will you be expected to demonstrate your ability to handle on the practical test?

A. Alternator inoperative.
B. Structural failure of the wing or horizontal stabilizer.
C. Gear or flap malfunctions.
D. Landing short of the runway.
E. Door opening in flight.
F. Midair collision.
G. Inoperative elevator trim.
  1—ACEG.
  2—ABCDG.
  3—ACDF.
  4—BCFG.

2827. Choose the correct statement concerning checkitis. Checkitis is characterized by

1—shaking knees.
2—a knotted stomach.
3—loss of memory.
4—all the above symptoms.

29

REVIEW OF FEDERAL AVIATION REGULATIONS

Just as an individual must know the regulations and pass a test on them to earn a license to drive a car, the prospective private pilot must also master the regulations that govern the kind of flying he or she plans to do. Whether the regulations concern cars or airplanes, each was designed to increase safety.

Private pilots need to be familiar with appropriate sections of three chapters, or "parts," of the Federal Aviation Regulations (FARs). Part 1 lists definitions, abbreviations, and symbols; Part 61 concerns the requirements for the various pilot certificates; and Part 91 deals with general operating and flight rules. In addition, private pilots need to know the provisions of Part 830 of the National Transportation Safety Board rules, which pertain to the notification and reporting of aircraft accidents or incidents and overdue aircraft as well as the preservation of aircraft wreckage, mail, cargo, and records.

FARs can be pretty dry (some people read them on those nights they can't seem to get to sleep), but this chapter is intended to bring out some points in general language.

PART 1

As you read the FARs for the first time, you will probably be struck by the precise language used. The technical terms in Parts 61 and 91 have very specific meanings, so Part 1 is a valuable reference for any student who needs to understand the other parts of the FARs. For example, there are several speeds that a pilot needs to know; Part 1 notes that V_A means design maneuvering speed, and V_{so} means the stalling speed or minimum steady-flight speed in the landing configuration. Table 29.1 lists the speeds most frequently used by the beginning pilot and their definitions. Many of the standard abbreviations that most pilots learn by listening to other pilots are also defined clearly in Part 1, such as CAS for calibrated airspeed, MSL for mean sea level, or VFR for visual flight rules.

TABLE 29.1. Summary of Symbols for V-Speeds

Symbol	Meaning
V_A	Design maneuvering speed
V_{FE}	Maximum flap extended speed
V_{NE}	Never-exceed speed
V_{NO}	Maximum structural cruising speed
V_{SO}	Stalling speed or minimum steady-flight speed in the landing configuration
V_{S1}	Stalling speed or minimum steady-flight speed in a specified configuration
V_X	Speed for best angle of climb
V_Y	Speed for best rate of climb

PART 61 — CERTIFICATION: PILOTS AND FLIGHT INSTRUCTORS

Part 61 covers the information you need to become a student pilot or a private pilot as well as the requirements for several other certificates. The student who is working toward the private pilot certificate will find that most or all of subparts A, B, C, and D are important. Subparts E, F, and G concern certification of commercial pilots, airline transport pilots, and flight instructors respectively. The following discussion is designed to amplify some of the important portions of Part 61 that relate to student and private pilots.

Category and Class

Category and class are defined according to whether the words apply to an aircraft or a pilot's certificate. These terms are defined in Part 1 but are discussed in more detail in Part 61. (See Table 29.2.)

TABLE 29.2. Examples of Category, Class, and Type

Term	Aircraft	Pilot Certification
Category	Normal Utility Acrobatic Limited	Airplane Rotorcraft Glider Lighter-than-air
Class	Airplane Rotorcraft Glider Lighter-than-air	Single-engine land Single-engine sea Multiengine land Multiengine sea
Type	*Specific make and basic models* Cessna 152 Piper Arrow Beech Sundowner	*Aircraft over 12,500 pounds or a turbojet* DC 3 Convair 440 Lear jet

On a pilot's certificate, "category" means airplane, rotorcraft, glider, or lighter-than-air. Category as applied to aircraft is based on use of operating limitations such as normal, utility, acrobatic, or restricted.

"Class" on a pilot certificate may be either single- or multiengine land and single- or multiengine sea. *Class* for an aircraft follows the same pattern as the pilot *categories*, that is, airplane, rotorcraft, glider, or lighter-than-air. This sometimes causes confusion

If you were discussing the trainer you use in learning to fly, it would probably be listed in the utility category because of the stresses involved in the maneuvers you perform. It would be in the airplane class, and the type might be a Cessna 152, Piper Cherokee, etc. On your pilot's certificate you would be qualified to fly an airplane as the category and single-engine land as the class. Because the gross weight of the airplane is below 12,500 pounds and it is not a jet, there would be no type rating required.

Certificates—Pilot and Medical

Although there are many ratings that can be given, there are only four pilot certificates. These are student, private, commercial, and airline transport pilot (FAR 61.5).

To be eligible for a student pilot certificate, a person must be at least sixteen years of age and be able to read, speak, and understand English (FAR 61.83). The applicant must also pass a medical examination by a physician designated by the Federal Aviation Administration (FAA) (FAR 61.3c). Such physicians, Designated Medical Examiners (DMEs), have the necessary forms and know about the special requirements of flying. There are three types of medical certificates (FAR 61.23); the most common is the *third-class*, and it is effective until the last day of the month, 24 months after it is obtained. An example would be getting the medical certificate on March 10, 1989, which would mean that it would be valid until midnight March 31, 1991. This certificate is used with student and private pilot privileges. That means a person having an effective third-class medical certificate may not receive compensation for flying. In addition, as a student pilot, you may not carry a passenger or fly in furtherance of a business.

A student certificate is normally issued when you get your medical examination. This is a form printed on the back of a special medical certificate that has space for the endorsement of your instructor when you are found competent to solo or to go solo cross-country. Designated flight examiners and FAA personnel can also give you a student certificate if it is not on the back of your medical certificate. Other medical certificates are *first-class* (valid for six months to the end of the last month—March 10, 1989 through September 30, 1989) or *second-class* (good for one year to the end of the last month). However, these certificates will be valid for 24 months to the end of the last month if they are used by a private or student pilot. For instance, if you obtained a first-class medical certificate on March 10, 1989, just to find out if you could pass the first-class medical requirements but had only a private pilot airman's certificate, it would still be valid through March 31, 1991.

Student Pilot Endorsements

As a student pilot you will not be endorsed for solo flying by your flight instructor until you have shown that you understand the General Operating and Flight Rules (Part 91 of the FARs) that pertain to solo flight (FAR 61.87).

GENERAL SOLO ENDORSEMENTS. Other requirements for student solo flight described in Part 61 are that student pilots must have had instruction on how to conduct a preflight inspection, how to taxi and run up, and how to perform normal takeoffs and landings as well as on operating the airplane in straight and level flight, climbs, turns, descents, flight at minimum controllable airspeeds, and stall recognition and recovery. A student must also understand airport traffic patterns, wake turbulence problems, and emergencies. Your student's certificate must be endorsed by an instructor for every type of airplane you will solo. In addition, your logbook should also be endorsed.

Every 90 days, to be legally qualified for solo flight, a student must have an endorsement in the logbook by an authorized flight instructor who has given instruction in the airplane and finds that he or she meets the requirements for solo flight and is competent to make a safe solo flight in that aircraft (FAR 61.87).

Chapter 29. Review of Federal Aviation Regulations 137

SOLO CROSS-COUNTRY. To be endorsed for solo cross-country flight, the student pilot must have received instruction by an authorized instructor in the use of charts, pilotage, dead reckoning, and radio navigation along with flight by reference to flight instruments and instruction in short-field, soft-field, and crosswind takeoffs and landings. Critical weather recognition and use of weather reports and forecasts and emergencies are also to be covered. If the instructor feels the student has this knowledge, he or she will endorse the student certificate for solo cross-country flight. A cross-country flight is considered to be one for which the landing is over 25 nautical miles from takeoff (FAR 61.93).

For *each* solo cross-country flight, you should understand that you must also carry an endorsement by an instructor in your logbook that the cross-country planning for that trip was reviewed with you and that conditions are suitable for safe flight (FAR 61.93c).

The instructor may also endorse your logbook for repeated flights between two airports that are *not* more than 50 nautical miles apart if instruction has been given over this stipulated course and you have demonstrated competence to fly the route safely (FAR 61.93c).

In general, as a student, you may not land or take off from any airport other than your home base, except in an emergency, until you have been found competent to fly solo cross-country. However, you may also practice solo takeoffs and landings at an airport *within* 25 nautical miles if the instructor feels you are able to do this safely (FAR 61.93). *To count as cross-country experience for the private certificate, a 50-nautical-mile leg is considered a minimum,* as will be noted later.

■ Minimum Requirements for the Private Certificate

To be eligible for the flight test to become a private pilot, a person must be at least seventeen years of age, have at least a current third-class medical certificate, have passed a written examination given by the FAA, and have the required hours of flight time logged (FAR 61.103, 61.109).

THE WRITTEN TEST. The FAA written examination will cover the aeronautical knowledge needed such as the Federal Aviation Regulations, use of *AIM*, and the FAA Advisory Circulars. In addition, the applicant should (1) have a satisfactory knowledge of VFR navigation, using pilotage, dead reckoning, and radio aids; (2) be able to recognize critical weather situations from the ground and in flight and procure and use aeronautical weather reports and forecasts; and (3) be familiar with the safe and efficient operation of airplanes, including high-density airport operations, collision avoidance precautions, and radio communication procedures (FAR 61.105).

To be eligible to take this written examination, evidence must be presented that the student has successfully passed a course of instruction or home study or has logged ground instruction from an authorized instructor. This is to show that you're prepared for the examination and aren't just taking it on a whim.

AERONAUTICAL EXPERIENCE. The aeronautical experience required of a private pilot is a minimum of 40 hours flight time (FAR 61.109). Twenty of these flight hours must be with an appropriate flight instructor, including 3 hours of cross-country instruction (with at least one flight lasting 2 hours) (FAR 61.107), 3 hours at night with ten takeoffs and landings, and 3 hours in preparation for the flight test within 60 days prior to that test. Also, instruction is required in using only flight instruments and navigational aids. These hours are in addition to those required for solo flight. If the night requirements are not met, the private pilot certificate may be issued prohibiting night flying. Most students require more than 40 hours of flight time before the flight test because of delays or layoffs due to weather and other factors.

The other 20 hours shall be solo, and include at least 10 hours of cross-country flights. Again, to be counted as cross-country flight to satisfy this requirement, each flight shall have a landing *more than 50 nautical miles from the point of departure.* One flight must be of at least 300 nautical miles with landings at a *minimum of three points, one* of which is at least 100 nautical miles from the original departure point. (The 100-mile minimum can be on an outbound or inbound leg.) Three solo takeoffs and landings to a full stop must be at an airport with an operating control tower. This last requirement was imposed because many pilots were having trouble understanding what the tower personnel expected of them when they landed at controlled fields. (Also, pilots were getting lost once they ventured out of their immediate training area.) See Figure 29-A.

Some flight schools are approved by the FAA and follow the regulations in Part 141. Only 15 hours of solo flight time are required to get a private certificate under Part 141, 5 hours less than under Part 61. Therefore, Part 141 requires only a total of 35 hours of flight time. However, each approved school curriculum allocates considerable ground time to its program as well as preflight and postflight discussions for each lesson.

THE PRACTICAL TEST. The practical test for the private pilot consists of an oral examination, maneuvers listed in the private pilot practical test standards and in Part 61, and an example of a cross-country with simulated emergency operations (FAR 61.107). All the requirements are discussed in the *Private Pilot Practical Test Standards* (FAA-T-8081-1) published by the FAA and in *SPFM*. The object of the flight test is to demonstrate that the candidate can perform all tasks of basic airmanship safely.

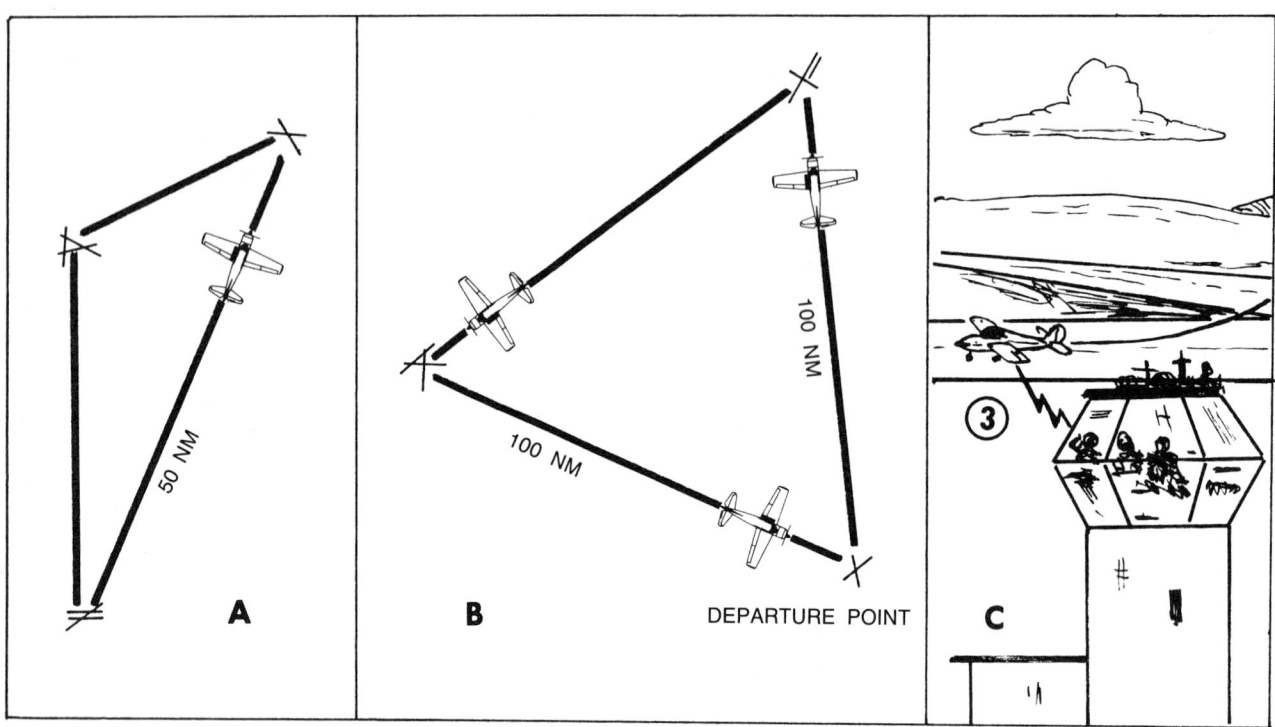

Fig. 29-A. (A) To count as a cross-country, a landing must be made at a point more than 50 NM from the point of departure. The route does not have to be a triangle as shown but may be a 50 + NM leg with a direct return. (B) One flight must be at least 300 nautical miles with landings at a *minimum of three points, one* of which is at least 100 nautical miles from the original departure point. (The 100-mile minimum can be on an outbound or inbound leg.) (C) Three solo landings to a full stop must be made at an airport with an operating control tower.

■ Some Added Points

LOSS OF CERTIFICATE. If you should misplace your medical or pilot's certificate, Part 61 also states that the FAA in Oklahoma must be notified in addition to sending a check or money order for $2.00 for a new copy (FAR 61.29). If you change your address, the FAA must be notified within 30 days or you lose the privileges of your certificate (FAR 61.60). If you want a certificate with the new address, you must send $2.00 for the new copy.

PILOT RECORDS. Pilot logbooks must be a reliable record showing the training and experience needed to meet the aeronautical requirements for a certificate or rating. The logbooks will also verify the recurrency requirements that may be necessary as well as the conditions of each flight (FAR 61.51).

Every 24 calendar months you must pass a flight review with an appropriate flight instructor and have your logbook endorsed that you have successfully passed this review. If a new certificate or rating has been received, this will act as a flight review. This flight review, commonly called the Biennial Flight Review (BFR), covers the maneuvers required by your certificate, and you must show you are proficient and safe in performing them (FAR 61.57).

PRIVATE PILOT PRIVILEGES AND RESPONSIBILITIES. As a private pilot you may carry passengers and property but may not do so for compensation or hire. However, a private pilot may *share* the operating expenses of a flight with passengers. When you were a student pilot, you could not fly an airplane in furtherance of business. Now, as a private pilot you can use your airplane for business and even be paid if the airplane is only incidental to that business and you do not carry passengers or property for pay (FAR 61.89, 61.118).

To carry passengers, a private or commercial pilot must have made three takeoffs and three landings within the preceding 90 days in an aircraft of the same category and class (and type if a type rating is required for that aircraft). If night flying with passengers, three takeoffs and three landings must have been made to a *full stop* at night in the same category and class of aircraft (see Fig. 29-B). To carry passengers in a *tailwheel* airplane, the three *day* landings must be made to a *full stop* also (FAR 61.57).

Chapter 29. Review of Federal Aviation Regulations 139

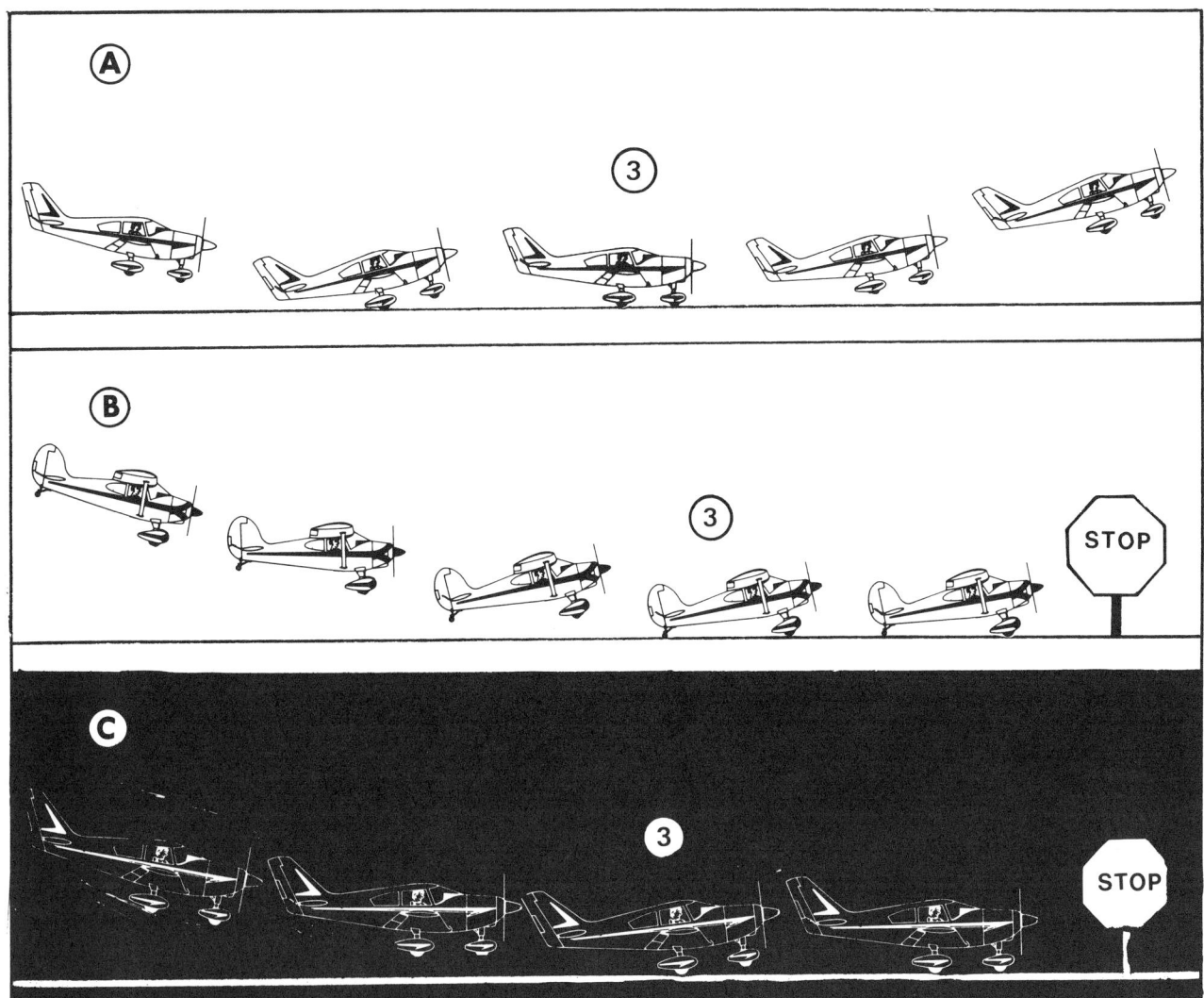

Fig. 29-B. To carry passengers, a pilot must have made three takeoffs and landings within the past 90 days in an aircraft of the same category and class (and type if a type rating is required for that aircraft). (A) For a tricycle-gear airplane, landings may be touch and go during official daylight. (B) For tailwheel airplanes, the landings must be full stop, night or day. (C) For all airplanes three full-stop landings are required at night.

HIGH-PERFORMANCE AIRPLANES. As a private or commercial pilot you may want to fly larger aircraft to make longer trips faster and more comfortably. To fly high-performance airplanes, you must have an endorsement in your logbook that you have received flight instruction in the same kind of airplane and are competent to fly it. A high-performance aircraft is one with more than 200 horsepower *or* one with retractable landing gear, flaps, and a controllable-pitch propeller. The one exception to the endorsement would be the case of a pilot who had logged time as pilot in command in high-performance airplanes before November 1, 1973, which would be accepted as prior knowledge and experience (FAR 61.31e).

PART 91—GENERAL OPERATING AND FLIGHT RULES

■ Responsibilities and Authority of the Pilot

In everyday terms, Part 91 contains the "rules of the road," or how to fly safely. This section is divided into four subparts: general, flight rules, maintenance, and larger multiengine airplanes. The private or student pilot should be very familiar with the first three. Later, when you get that corporate flying job, the last section will be more important to you.

In Part 91 you, as pilot in command, are given the final authority for operating your aircraft. This authority implies that you may deviate from these operating rules when an in-flight emergency arises. This is a serious responsibility, and if you deviate you will have to write a report of that deviation to the FAA administrator if requested to do so. You are in command, but you must also be responsible for the operation of the aircraft (FAR 91.3).

As pilot in command, you must ensure that the flight is safe from beginning to end. You are required to be familiar with all available information concerning the flight. This includes information on weather reports and forecasts and alternatives if the flight is away from the vicinity of the airport. Information on runway lengths for takeoffs and landings should also be known for any flight (FAR 91.5). You must not operate an aircraft in a careless or reckless manner (FAR 91.9). While in flight, when you are performing as pilot in command or as a required member of a flight crew, safety regulations require that your seat belts must be fastened at all times. During takeoffs and landings the shoulder harness must be fastened also. It is your duty as pilot in command to inform all passengers to fasten their seat belts for takeoffs and landings, and the passengers are obligated to do so (FAR 91.7, 91.14).

■ Medical Factors

DRUGS AND ALCOHOL. Flying an airplane requires a clear head. You should therefore preflight yourself as well as the plane. Before serving as pilot or a required crew member, you must wait at least 8 hours after consumption of any alcoholic beverage and must not have .04 percent or more of alcohol by weight in the blood. (When that state trooper asks you to take this test for percentage of weight of alcohol in your blood, FAR 91 says you *shall* submit to this test.) Because alcohol and drugs have been known to affect behavior even more adversely at altitude, the consumption of these are strictly prohibited before a flight. Also, if you have been convicted of any federal or state statute relating to narcotic drugs (including possession or transportation of narcotic drugs, marijuana, or depressant or stimulant drugs), you will be ineligible for any pilot certificate or rating for one year after final conviction (FAR 61.15). Except in an emergency the pilot in command may not allow any intoxicated passenger or one under the influence of drugs to be carried aboard for a flight. If you are sick enough to take medicine, you should be sure you are in condition to fly safely; check with your local aviation medical examiner. If you are tired or worried, you may get between a rock and a hard place. Be sure you can perform as the pilot in command. Read "Medical Facts for Pilots" in the *AIM*.

PERSONAL CHECKLIST. A personal checklist is given in the chapter "Fitness for Flight," *AIM:* I'm physically and mentally safe to fly, not being impaired by *I*llness, *M*edication, *S*tress, *A*lcohol, *F*atigue, *E*motion—I M S A F E.

HYPOXIA. One of the items discussed in *AIM* is hypoxia (lack of oxygen), which can cause dangerous problems, even permanent brain damage, when flying at high altitudes without supplemental oxygen. The *AIM* and Part 91 have incorporated rules about the use of supplemental oxygen (FAR 91.32). Over 12,500 and including 14,000 feet MSL, supplemental oxygen is required by the pilot and crew for flight time exceeding 30 minutes. This means you could, for instance, go up to 13,500 feet for 25 minutes and not have to use oxygen. If your flight is above 14,000 feet MSL, oxygen is required for the pilot and crew for the entire time. Because problems are even more severe above 15,000 feet, oxygen *must be provided* for all persons aboard the airplane for flights above 15,000 feet MSL. You can see these are minimums. It would be safer to use oxygen at even lower altitudes.

HYPERVENTILATION. Under emotional stress or pain, hyperventilation (overbreathing) can occur. The breathing rate may increase, giving rise to symptoms similar to hypoxia. If you are not sure which is the problem, since hypoxia is more dangerous, a simple test may be helpful. Take three or four breaths of pure oxygen if available. No improvement suggests that the problem is hyperventilation, *not* hypoxia. To relieve hyperventilation, slow your breathing rate and breathe into a bag if available (a Sic-Sac can be pressed into service). Slowing down your breathing and rebreathing used air will often make a rapid improvement. (Hyperventilation creates a carbon dioxide *deficiency*.)

■ Aircraft Inspections and Documents

As the pilot in command you are responsible for seeing that your aircraft is in a condition for safe flight and is airworthy. The airplane must also have on board all the required documents and placards. One way to remember the required documents needed in an airplane is to remember the word *ARROW: A*irworthiness certificate, *R*egistration certificate issued to the owner, *R*adio license required by the Federal Communications Commission (FCC), *O*perations placards, and *W*eight and Balance for that particular airplane. The last two may be included in an approved flight manual for the specific aircraft, containing the weight, operating speeds, and performance charts.

INSPECTIONS. An annual inspection is required within the last 12 calendar months, and the specified information must be entered in the aircraft and engine logs (FAR 91.169). If the aircraft is for hire, it must also have an inspection every 100 hours of time in service.

This 100-hour period may be extended up to 10 hours if it is necessary to take the plane to the place where the maintenance is to be done, but those hours in excess of 100 are then to be deducted from the next 100-hour inspection time. For example, if it took 3 hours more to get the plane to the airplane mechanic, the next 100-hour inspection will actually be due 97 hours from the time of the inspection. If an annual inspection is done, this automatically starts another 100-hour period, since the annual requires more work and must be signed off in the aircraft logs by an inspector, not just the airframe and powerplant (A/P) mechanic as for the 100-hour inspection.

Anything that is done to the aircraft must be entered in the aircraft logbook, and maintenance to the engine must be recorded in the engine logbook with a description of the work, date of completion, and the signature of the person who approved its return to service. The A/P mechanic also certifies that all airworthiness directives (ADs) are complied with, keeping the plane's airworthiness certificate current (FAR 91.173).

■ Airplane Equipment

Equipment requirements are also given in Part 91, listed according to how and when the aircraft is used. Basically, for daylight VFR flight you need an airspeed indicator, altimeter, and magnetic compass and for each engine, a tachometer, oil pressure and temperature gauge, and engine temperature gauge. If a high-performance aircraft, it will also need a landing gear position indicator and a manifold pressure gauge. This is just the minimum equipment. Most airplanes have much more (FAR 91.33).

If it is to be flown at night, you will also need approved position lights and an anticollision light. Because these lights may be a drain on the battery, you will need an adequate source to handle the electrical and radio equipment. You'll also need one spare set of fuses in case of emergency. When the plane is for hire, an electric landing light is also required (FAR 91.33).

TRANSPONDERS. Equipment in the aircraft also has to meet certain qualifications. Since some transponders were found to emit spurious signals that created problems with air traffic control radar stations, all transponders are now required to meet TSO (Technical Standard Order) type standards. They also must be checked every 24 months for accuracy by an approved repair station.

If you fly in controlled airspace above 10,000 feet MSL or in Terminal Control Areas (TCAs), your transponder must have the 4096 code capability (that is, digits from 0000 to 7777) and have automatic altitude reporting capability, Mode C (FAR 91.24). Air traffic control authorizes some deviations from the automatic altitude reporting equipment requirement in TCAs and under certain circumstances. If your trans-

Fig. 29-C. View of an aircraft without adequate lighting over the Arizona desert at midnight.

ponder is inoperative or if only your automatic altitude reporting equipment is not operating, ATC may authorize a deviation.

PORTABLE ELECTRONIC DEVICES. Some portable electronic devices emit signals that may cause interference with navigation or communication systems in an aircraft. These could cause dangerous navigation problems and are therefore prohibited. The exceptions allowed on an aircraft are portable voice recorders, hearing aids, heart pacemakers, and electric shavers, which generally do not cause such interference. It would be wise to check any of these electronic devices for interference with your radios (FAR 91.19).

EMERGENCY LOCATOR TRANSMITTERS. To help find downed aircraft, emergency locator transmitters (ELTs) must be installed in airplanes and be in operating condition. ELTs are battery-operated transmitters that send out an emergency signal on 121.5 MHz and/or 243.0 MHz. Batteries must be replaced if they have been in use for more than 1 cumulative hour or whenever 50 percent of their useful life has expired. (The expiration date must be clearly marked on the outside of the transmitter and also entered in the aircraft maintenance records so that it is easy to check when batteries should be replaced.) These precautions will ensure at least 45 hours of operation if needed. If an aircraft is to be ferried or is used only for training within a 50-mile radius, an ELT need not be in the aircraft (FAR 91.52).

To be sure your aircraft's ELT is operational, tests may be conducted on the ground only, for no more than three sound sweeps and during the first 5 minutes of each hour, in cooperation with the nearest FSS or control tower. When flying, it is a good practice to monitor 121.5 MHz occasionally to see if you can identify a possible emergency. Because some ELTs go off inadvertently, you can check yours by tuning to 121.5 MHz before shutting off radios.

■ Avoiding Other Aircraft

The flight rules of Part 91 concern many aspects of safe flying practice, including right-of-way rules (FAR 91.67). One of the rules is that you should see and avoid another aircraft and give way when it has the right-of-way. For instance, if two aircraft are converging at the same altitude, the one on the right has the right-of-way. That is, if you are converging with another airplane and it's on your right, it has the right-of-way. If it's to your left, *you* have the right-of-way, but don't contest it. If the aircraft are in different categories, the less maneuverable has the right-of-way; that is, a balloon has the right-of-way over a glider, a glider has the right-of-way over a gyroplane or an airplane. If two aircraft are approaching head-on, each pilot must change course to the right. If you are overtaking an airplane, you should go to the right until you are well clear to avoid a collision. The aircraft on final approach or landing has the right-of-way over the aircraft either landing or taking off. So if you see another airplane either enroute or in the traffic pattern, these rules should help avoid a bad situation. Even if you have the right-of-way, remember that other pilots may not have seen you. Keep scanning for other aircraft.

AIRCRAFT SPEEDS. At certain altitudes or areas, maximum speed restrictions have been imposed (FAR 91.70). Below 10,000 feet MSL the maximum speed is 250 knots; if you are inside a TCA, it is also 250 knots. You cannot operate an aircraft in the airspace underlying a TCA or in a VFR corridor designated through a TCA at an indicated airspeed of more than 200 knots. In an airport traffic area, jets must be at 200 knots or less, while reciprocating engines have a maximum speed of 156 knots. These speeds are intended to help you see and avoid other aircraft in the congested areas. More about TCAs later.

In choosing an altitude to fly when going cross-country, you need to consider both the wind and the hemispheric rule, which states that if your magnetic *course* is between North (360°) to 179°, you should fly at odd thousands plus 500 feet. If your *course* is from South (180°) to 359°, you should be at even thousands plus 500 feet. This rule is in effect if you are flying more than 3000 feet above the surface (FAR 91.109). The reason wind was mentioned is that it affects the *heading* required to get a particular *course*. Your heading may lead you to believe that you should be flying an even plus 500 altitude when the course, or track, you are making would require an odd thousands plus 500 feet altitude.

WEATHER FACTORS. Avoiding other aircraft (and TV towers) also depends on visibility and your clearance from the clouds. A summary of this criteria is given in Figure 29-D. You should be thoroughly familiar with these requirements.

MINIMUM VFR VISIBILITY AND DISTANCE FROM CLOUDS

ALTITUDE	UNCONTROLLED AIRSPACE		CONTROLLED AIRSPACE	
	Flight Visibility	Distance From Clouds	** Flight Visibility	** Distance From Clouds
1200' or less above the surface, regardless of MSL Altitude	*1 statute mile	Clear of clouds	3 statute miles	500' below 1000' above 2000' horizontal
More than 1200' above the surface, but less than 10,000' MSL	1 statute mile	500' below 1000' above 2000' horizontal	3 statute miles	500' below 1000' above 2000' horizontal
More than 1200' above the surface and at or above 10,000' MSL	5 statute miles	1000' below 1000' above 1 statute mile horizontal	5 statute miles	1000' below 1000' above 1 statute mile horizontal

* Helicopters may operate with less than 1 mile visibility, outside controlled airspace at 1200 feet or less above the surface, provided they are operated at a speed that allows the pilot adequate opportunity to see any air traffic or obstructions in time to avoid collisions.

** In addition, when operating within a control zone beneath a ceiling, the ceiling must not be less than 1000'. If the pilot intends to land or takeoff or enter a traffic pattern within a control zone, the ground visibility must be at least 3 miles at that airport. If ground visibility is not reported at the airport, 3 miles flight visibility is required. (FAR 91.105)

Fig. 29-D. Review of minimum VFR visibility and distance from clouds. (*AIM*)

Chapter 29. Review of Federal Aviation Regulations 143

AIRCRAFT LIGHTING. During the time from official sunset to sunrise, position lights are required as well as an anticollision light (FAR 91.73). Sometimes the anticollision lights cause flicker vertigo due to reflections from haze and clouds. Also, strobes might interfere with other pilots during ground operations. (Under these circumstances it may be safer to turn them off.) At official sunset, airports turn on their rotating beacons and runway lights.

The operating time for aircraft position lights from official sunset to sunrise is sometimes confused with the time to be logged as night flying time in your logbook. Night time may not be logged for a flight unless the flight takes place between 1 hour after sunset and 1 hour before sunrise.

AIRPORT LIGHTING. The lighting around airports is discussed in *AIM*. For instance, it notes the use of Visual Approach Slope Indicators (VASIs)—if you are above the indicator light beam, it shows a white light; if you are below, it gives a red light (showing danger). *SPFM* has a discussion of VASIs and their use. Usually you want to approach "above" the near light and "below" the far light, giving an indication of red light over white light. When the heavy jets used this two-bar light system, they found themselves landing short, so systems with three light bars are installed at some airports for large jet aircraft. In haze and dust, the white lights may sometimes appear yellow.

Rotating beacons at lighted land airports are a combination of white and green lights, or green only if there is a nearby airport using a green and white beacon system. If the rotating beacon is on in a control zone during the daytime hours, it means the field is below VFR. Military airport beacons flash green and white but are distinguished from civil airports by a pattern of two quick white flashes alternating with a longer green flash. There was an accident reported of a land airplane landing on what appeared at night to be a fine long runway with lights, etc., with an accompanying rotating beacon of yellow and white. This resulted in a very short landing "roll" and a watery environment. (See Chapter 26 in this book and *SPFM*.)

■ **Enroute Considerations**

MINIMUM SAFE ALTITUDES. When you get ready for cross-country flight, there are several safety factors to be considered. Minimum safe altitudes should be observed, which means that in the event of a power failure you should be flying at an altitude that is not a hazard to persons or property on the ground.

1. Over congested areas, as a town, you should be at least 1000 feet above the highest obstacles within 2000 feet horizontal to the aircraft.

2. Over other areas, except over open water or sparsely populated areas, you should fly at least 500 feet above the surface.

3. Over open water or sparsely populated areas, the aircraft must not be operated closer than 500 feet to any person or structure. (This could mean a horizontal distance.)

4. Over mountainous areas, a minimum altitude of 2000 feet above ground level is recommended (FAR 91.79).

To be sure you are above these minimum altitudes, your altimeter should be set accurately to the current altimeter setting of an FAA Flight Service Station or tower along your route. This should be done at least every 100 miles or more often if it seems necessary due to terrain or weather changes. If no altimeter setting is available at the beginning of your flight, your altimeter should be set to field elevation before takeoff (FAR 91.81).

RESTRICTED AND OTHER AIRSPACE. When plotting your cross-country, you may see restricted and prohibited areas on the chart. These are not to be used unless you have permission from the controlling agency (FAR 91.95). These restrictions are listed on sectional charts along with the times they are effective. Some other areas are assigned for military training. These are called Military Operations Areas (MOAs). Although not restricted, MOAs should be regarded with caution, since they contain fast-moving jet traffic and jets cannot always see light aircraft. For information, contact the nearest FSS as indicated by Figure 29-E.

FLIGHT PLANS. Although a flight plan is not required, it's strongly recommended for cross-country flight. If you've filed (and activated) a flight plan, checking procedures will be started when your flight plan is not closed within 30 minutes after your estimated time of arrival. *You* will have to activate your flight plan (by radio, normally), since an FSS will hold it for 1 hour after proposed departure time and then automatically cancel it if not activated. Required flight plan information is listed in FAR 91.83.

RESERVE FUEL. For many years, only pilots flying under IFR were required to have enough fuel on board to fly to their destination and to an alternate if one was required and to have reserve fuel on board equivalent to 45 minutes of flight at normal cruise. Accident reports demonstrated that private pilots were not using good judgment on the amount of fuel they might need. Some pilots forgot to provide for changes in flight plans and were running out of fuel enroute. Based on this the FAA decided a regulation was needed for VFR pilots also. You are now required under VFR to have enough fuel to fly at normal cruising speed to your destination and for an additional 30 minutes during the day or 45 minutes at night (FAR 91.22).

VOR RECEIVERS. During your cross-country flights you will be using pilotage, dead reckoning, and radio navigation. These methods of navigation are dis-

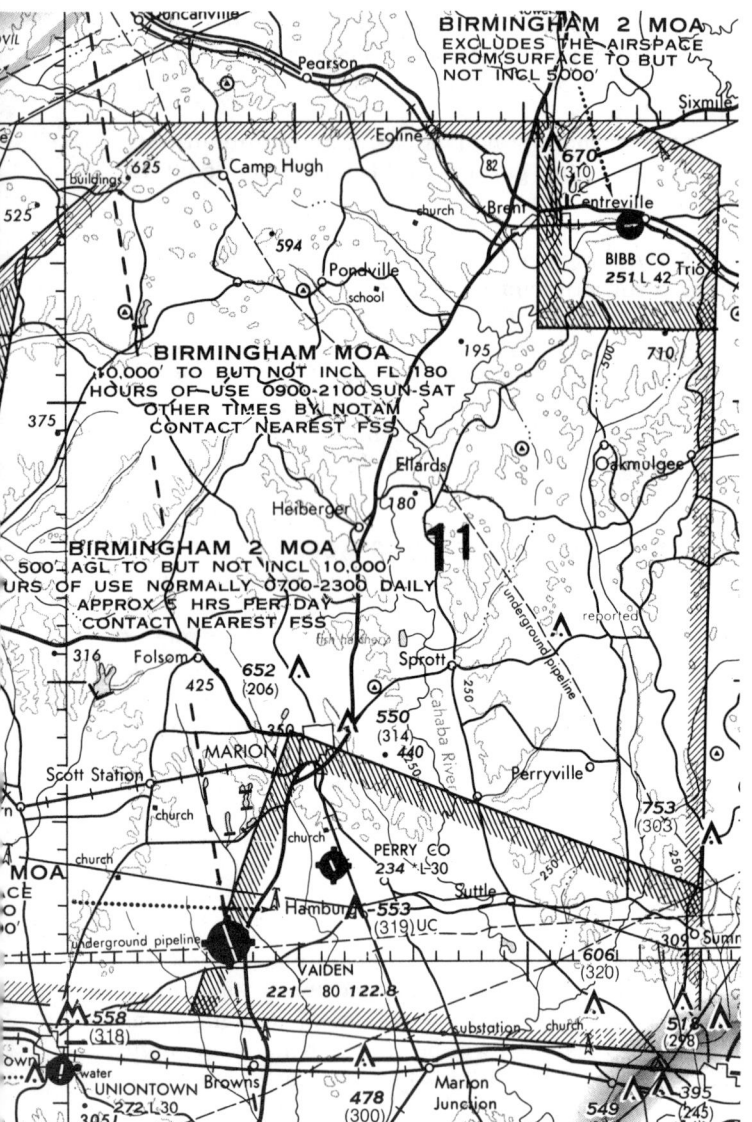

Fig. 29-E. Portions of Military Operation Areas (MOAs) near Birmingham, Alabama, on the sectional chart. Note the times, altitudes, and contact information.

cussed in *SPFM*. Regulations require that the calibration of the bearing selector of the Very High Frequency Omnirange (VOR) receiver be checked every 30 days if the flight is to be conducted under IFR. It might help you in flying VFR if you also check that your VOR calibration falls within these same limits (FAR 91.25).

■ Operation around Airports

Airports without control towers have a standard pattern consisting of left-hand turns. If because of noise abatement or obstructions a right-hand pattern is specified as part of your preflight planning, you can find this information in the *Airport/Facility Directory* before you take off. Most airports recommend a pattern altitude of 1000 feet above the elevation of the airport. Figure 20-1, *SPFM* is a depiction of recommended pattern procedure for a noncontrolled airport.

AIRPORT TRAFFIC AREAS. When there is an operating control tower, you need to know that an airport traffic area (ATA) is in effect. This is an area normally with a horizontal radius of 5 statute miles from the center of the airport up to but not including 3000 feet above the surface. Don't enter airport traffic areas unless you intend to land at or take off from an airport in the ATA and have clearance from the tower if operating into or from the primary (tower-controlled) airport. If the radio fails in flight, the aircraft may be operated and landed there if weather conditions are at or above VFR weather minimums (FAR 91.85, 91.87). These areas are not drawn on maps, so you need to find out if a control tower is in operation from data on your aeronautical chart (noting whether the airport symbol is colored blue) or from the *Airport/Facility Directory*. The airport traffic area exists because of communications requirements. If the control tower is *not* operating (for instance, it's normally shut down for some period during the day), the *airport traffic area does not exist* during that period.

LIGHT SIGNALS. A pilot should also know the light signals given by control towers in case of radio failure. (See Fig. 21-16, *SPFM*.)

Radio failures are not confined to aircraft. One instructor taxiing out at a controlled field received a flashing white light from the tower. It happened that a construction worker had accidentally cut the electrical power for the tower transmitter, and no one in the tower could transmit to the airplanes. The white light was the way of informing airplanes to return to their starting points until the tower could get emergency power to the communications equipment. Use of light signals at controlled airports generally arises from some unusual, even emergency, situation; therefore, a pilot should know these signals and be able to respond to them.

CONTROL ZONES. Control zones are established around some airports and are shown on sectional charts with dashed lines marking the boundaries (see item 1, Fig. 29-F). They are usually 5 statute miles in radius from the center of the airport, with extensions for instrument approaches. Control zones are set up to protect IFR traffic in marginal weather. Sometimes control zones and airport traffic areas may be located at the same airport, and sometimes one may be found without the other. Control zones are a special type of controlled airspace, and weather is the criterion. The airport must have at least 3 miles visibility and a 1000 feet ceiling for VFR operations.

Fig. 29-F. Airspace restrictions in the vicinity of the Atlanta Terminal Control Area on the sectional chart. (1) A "standard" control zone boundary is marked by dashed lines. (2) The control zone prohibiting special VFR is indicated by "Ts." (3) Transition areas. (4) A section of the TCA extending from 3500 feet MSL to the top at 12,500 feet MSL.

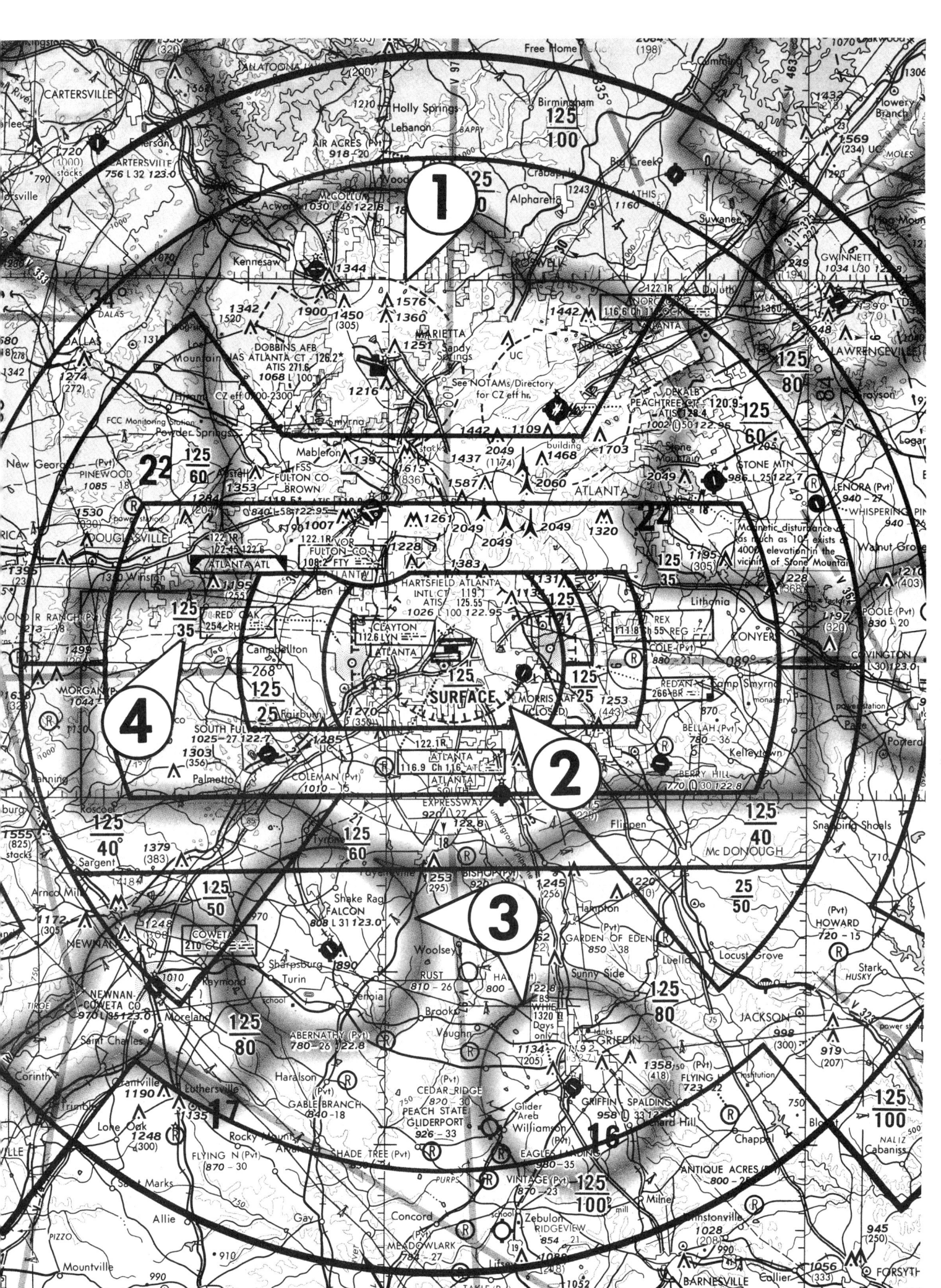

If the ceiling and visibility in a control zone fall below the minimums for VFR, you may request a special VFR clearance from Air Traffic Control (ATC) to enter the area. ATC can give you permission to enter the control zone to land or to take off. With this clearance, you must remain clear of any clouds and have at least 1 mile visibility. Certain control zones, because of their high volume of traffic, are not able to handle special VFR traffic; these are marked on charts with a series of Ts instead of dashes—TTTT (see item 2, Fig. 29-F). Also, because it is so easy to get vertigo or become disoriented in such limited visibility, special VFR clearances may not be issued at night unless the pilot is IFR rated and in an IFR-equipped aircraft (FAR 91.107).

TERMINAL CONTROL AND AIRPORT RADAR SERVICE AREAS. Terminal Control Areas have been established at the busiest major airports to provide traffic separation. Airplanes operated within a TCA must be equipped with a Mode C (altitude reporting) transponder with a 4096 code capability, maintain two-way communications with ATC, and have a VOR or Tactical Air Navigation (TACAN) receiver (FAR 91). You are required to have authorization from ATC before operating in a TCA. (Unless ATC says the magic words, "Cleared into the TCA," you'd better stay outside the boundaries.)

A private certificate is required to operate in TCA airspace or to take off or land at an airport within the area. There are exceptions, however. Except for 12 primary TCA airports where student pilot flying is prohibited, student pilots are permitted to fly solo in a TCA *if* they have received specified training and have had a logbook endorsement by a certified flight instructor before the fact. Training operations in or through a TCA may be required to be conducted along routes and/or in accordance with procedures developed and specified by the ATC facility having jurisdiction over the TCA. These procedures may take the form of a memorandum issued by that facility, and the word may be passed by a letter to airmen or a letter of agreement between ATC and a flight school or flying club.

The Airport Radar Service Area (ARSA) is set up at tower-controlled airports, which are busy but not so active as those in TCAs, as a replacement for the earlier developed Terminal Radar Service Areas (TRSAs). The TRSAs took in more volume of airspace, but the service was voluntary. The ARSA is smaller in volume but is more restrictive. ARSAs are discussed in more detail in Figures 29-G and 29-H and accompanying text for those figures.

OTHER CONTROLLED AIRSPACE. Controlled airspace usually starts 1200 feet above the ground if an area is bounded by a blue tint on a sectional chart. If the area is shaded magenta, it means that controlled airspace starts at 700 feet above the ground and is a transition area. These areas usually help IFR traffic

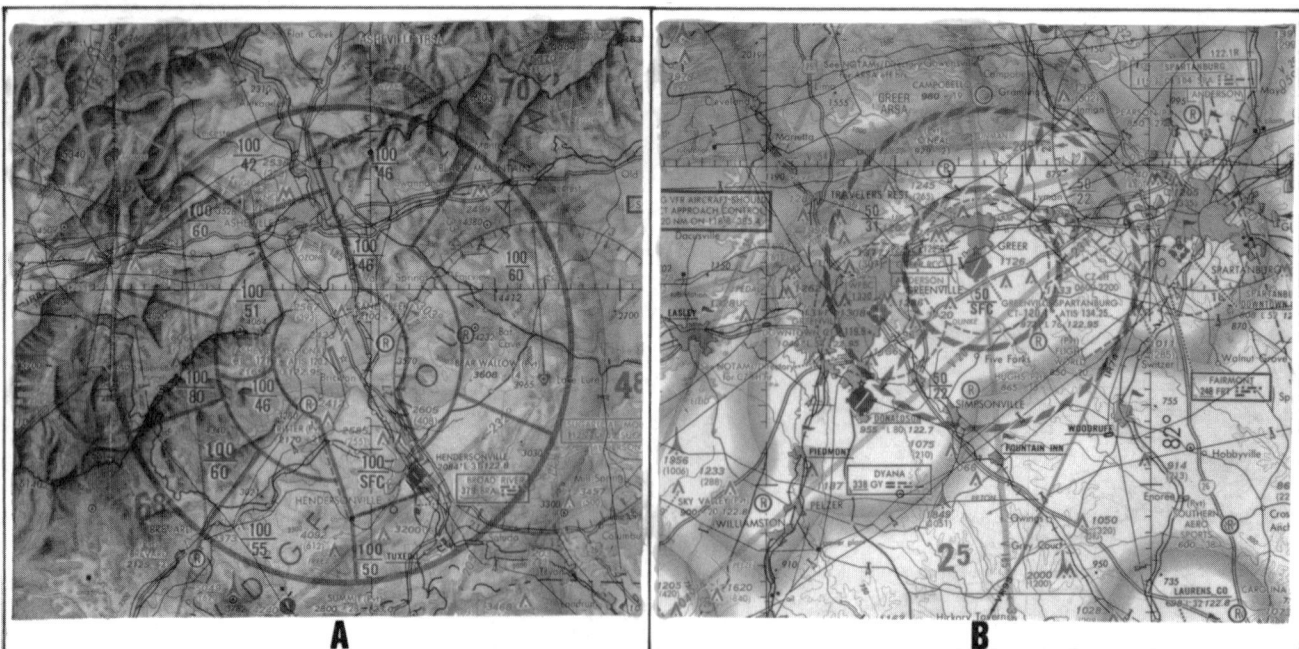

Fig. 29-G. (A) The TRSA at Asheville, North Carolina, as depicted on the sectional chart. Note that the top of the TRSA is 10,000 MSL, with segments having various base altitudes as required by the mountainous terrain. (B) The ARSA at Greenville-Spartanburg Airport as depicted on the sectional chart. For more details on ARSAs in general, read the accompanying text.

move from airways and other controlled airspace (with a minimum height of 1200 feet) through the 700-foot transition area to control zones around airports or to airports with IFR approaches. In other words, it permits smooth transition in controlled airspace from enroute to terminal areas (item 3, Fig. 29-F).

To summarize, there are five types of controlled airspace listed in *AIM:* continental control areas, control areas, control zones, terminal control areas, and transition areas. These are all areas in which aircraft may be subject to ATC, either for safety or because of the high volume of air traffic. Usually it means to you, the VFR pilot, that if the area goes below certain minimums, you must land (FAR 91.105), since you can no longer see other air traffic because of clouds or restricted visibility. Controlled airspace and requirements for different altitudes are confusing to most pilots. *AIM* and *SPFM* (Figure 21-14) have charts that display in detail the different types of airspace and their requirements. (Also see Figures 20-P and 20-Q in this book.) Table 29.3 may help to summarize the main features as well as other regulations concerning altitudes in the air space.

TABLE 29.3. Summary of Altitude Regulation Requirements

Altitude	Requirements
No upper limit	Continental control area (a control zone has no upper limit if there is no CCA above it); aircraft equipped with 4096 code, Mode C transponder
FL 600	Top of the positive control area
FL 450	Top of jet routes
FL 240	Distance measuring equipment required for operation at or above this altitude when operating with VOR navigational equipment
FL 180	Bottom of positive control area, bottom of jet routes
Below 18,000 MSL	Top of airway structure shown on sectional charts, low enroute IFR charts
Above 15,000 MSL	Oxygen required for all passengers aboard aircraft
14,500 MSL	Bottom of the continental control area, top of control zone
Above 14,000 MSL	Oxygen required for pilot and required crew for duration of flight
Above 12,500 MSL	Oxygen required for pilot and required crew if flight lasts over 0.5 hour; aircraft equipped with 4096 code
10,000 MSL and above	Basic VFR—1000 feet above, 1000 feet below, 1 mile horizontally from clouds, 5 miles visibility. Mode C transponder in controlled airspace
Below 10,000 MSL	Basic VFR—1000 feet above, 2000 feet horizontally, 500 feet below clouds, 3 miles visibility (1 mile visibility in uncontrolled airspace); maximum speed—250 knots (under TCAs, 200 knots)
Above 3000 AGL	Bottom of VFR cruising altitudes (hemispherical rule)
Below 3000 AGL	Top of airport traffic area; maximum speed in traffic area (turbine engine 200 knots, reciprocating engine 156 knots)
1200 AGL	Bottom of federal airways (blue tint on sectional chart)
700 AGL	Bottom of the transition area (magenta tint on sectional chart)
Ground level	Bottom of control zone; bottom of traffic area

■ Airport Radar Service Area (ARSA)

Airport Radar Service Areas (ARSAs) are replacing TRSAs around the United States. As shown in Figures 29-G and H and the discussion below there are some changes in requirements and dimensions.

a. **Operating Rules and Pilot/Equipment Requirements**
  (1) **Pilot Certifications:** Student Pilot or better.
  (2) **Equipment:** Two-Way Radio.
  (3) **Arrivals and Overflights:** No person may operate an aircraft in an airport radar service area unless two-way radio communication is established with ATC prior to entering that ARSA and is thereafter maintained with ATC, while within that area.
  (4) **Departures:**
    (a) **Primary Airport:** No person may operate an aircraft within the ARSA unless two-way radio communication is maintained with ATC while within that ARSA.
    (b) **Satellite Airports:** Aircraft departing satellite airports/heliports within the ARSA surface area shall establish two-way communication with ATC as soon as possible. Pilots must comply with approved FAA traffic patterns when departing these airports.
  (5) **ULTRALIGHT VEHICLES:** No person may operate an ultralight vehicle within an airport radar service area unless that person has prior authorization from the air traffic control facility having jurisdiction over that airspace. (FAR-103)
  (6) **Parachute Jumps:** No person may make a parachute jump and no pilot in command may allow a parachute jump to be made from that aircraft in or into an airport radar service area without, or in violation of, the terms of an ATC authorization. (FAR-105)

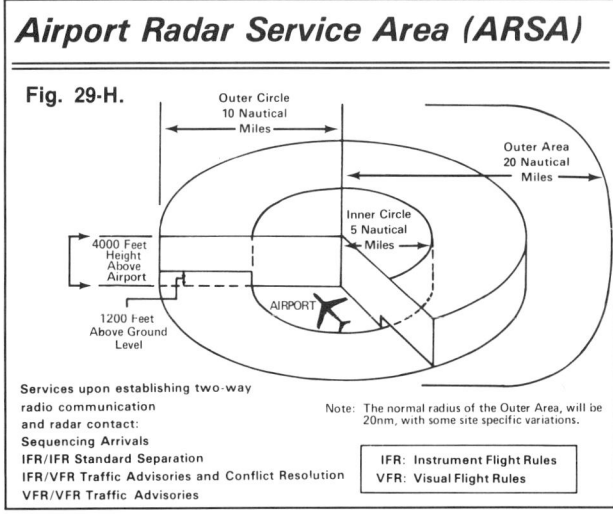

Fig. 29-H.

(7) Hot Air Balloons: No person may operate a hot air balloon within an airport radar service area unless that person has prior authorization from the air traffic control facility having jurisdiction over that airspace. (FAR-91)

b. ATC Services

  (1) Within The ARSA:

   (a) Sequencing of all aircraft arriving the primary/ARSA airport.

   (b) Standard IFR separation between IFR aircraft.

   (c) Between IFR and VFR aircraft-traffic advisories and conflict resolution so that radar targets do not touch, or 500 feet vertical separation.

   (d) Between VFR aircraft-traffic advisories and as appropriate, safety advisories.

  (2) Within The Outer Area:

   (a) The same services are provided for aircraft operating within the outer area, as within the ARSA, *when two-way communication and radar contact is established.*

   (b) While pilot participation in this area is strongly encouraged, it is not a VFR requirement.

  (3) Beyond The Outer Area:

   (a) Standard IFR separation.

   (b) Basic Radar Service.

   (c) Stage II/Stage III Service, where appropriate.

   (d) Safety Advisory, as appropriate.

c. Since this is a radar program ARSA services will only be provided within radar/radio coverage. In the event of a radar outage, separation and sequencing of VFR aircraft will be suspended. The pilot will be advised that the service is not available and issued wind, runway information and the time to contact the tower.

d. While pilot participation is required within the ARSA, it is voluntary within the outer area and can be discontinued, within the outer area, at the pilot's request.

e. Traffic advisories and conflict resolution will be provided in the outer area unless the pilot requests to discontinue the service.

f. Service provided beyond the outer area will be on a workload permitting basis and can be terminated by the controller if the IFR/ARSA workload increases to a point that approaches controller/position capacity.

g. ARSA service will not be provided to an aircraft operating in a satellite airport's traffic area (ATA) and in communication with that satellite airport's air traffic control tower even though that airport underlies the ARSA. When an aircraft is instructed to contact the tower of a satellite airport, ARSA service automatically stops and *Airport* Traffic Control Service begins.

h. Two-way communication with a satellite control tower does not authorize an aircraft to enter the ARSA. A pilot who wishes to exit a satellite ATA into an ARSA must establish two-way communication with the ARSA facility, prior to entering the ARSA.

i. Aircraft proceeding to a satellite airport or to a VFR practice area within the outer area can expect to have radar service terminated at a sufficient distance to allow time to change to the appropriate frequency for traffic/airport information.

j. Some approach control facilities shut down for portions of the night. When this occurs at an ARSA facility, ARSA service will not be provided during those periods even though radar service is provided to that airport by an air route traffic control center.

SUMMARY

Knowledge of these regulations will help you to be a safer pilot. Most of these came about because of an accident or incident where more control was seen to be necessary. They are really minimum requirements because they cover all types of pilots with different qualifications. As a student or private pilot you may want to be more conservative than required by regulations to help you have a long and safe flying life.

These questions will be the last look at FARs before the "real" written and/or flight test. Some questions on material in *AIM* are also included here.

2901. You just took your private flight test in a Piper Tomahawk. The category and class listed on your private pilot certificate will be

1—utility and airplane.
2—restricted and airplane if you have not fulfilled the night requirement.
3—airplane and single-engine land.
4—aircraft, tricycle gear only.

2902. Because you feel it will make you a safer pilot, you have decided to get an instrument rating. To find the necessary requirements, you will look in the

1—*Airman's Information Manual*, "Basic Flight Information."
2—FARs, Part 61.
3—FARs, Part 1.
4—FARs, Part 91.

2903. To act as pilot in command or as a required flight crew member of an airplane, you must have in your personal possession

1—a current pilot certificate and logbooks to show recent flight experience.
2—your pilot logbooks that show three takeoffs and landings to a full stop within the last 90 days.
3—an appropriate current medical certificate.
4—proof of instruction by a certified flight instructor within the past 90 days.

2904. *Pilot* certificates issued under FAR Part 61 are

1—student, private, commercial, airline transport.
2—private, instrument, commercial.
3—airplane, rotorcraft, glider, lighter-than-air.
4—instrument airplane, instrument helicopter.

2905. According to the regulations governing drugs and alcoholic beverages,

1—a person convicted of violating any federal or state law concerning narcotic drugs may hold a pilot's certificate for *only* 1 year after the date of the final conviction.
2—any conviction for violating either federal or state laws concerning narcotic drugs is ground for suspending or revoking a pilot's certificate.
3—a person convicted of violating any federal or state laws concerning narcotic drugs need not report this on their next medical examination.
4—these rules do not apply to pilots flying under Federal Aviation Regulation.

2906. Some pilot or flight instructor certificates may have certain restrictions placed upon them. Pick the correct statement.

1—Your student pilot's certificate is good until you obtain your private pilot's certificate and as long as the instructor endorses you for solo flight.
2—The flight instructor certificate has no expiration date but is only effective while the instructor holds a current pilot certificate.
3—Any certificate, other than student pilot or flight instructor, is issued without an expiration date.
4—Commercial and private certificates are current for 1 or 2 years, depending on what privileges are exercised.

2907. If you are a private pilot, which one of the following statements concerning medical certificates applies?

1—Your medical certificate issued on July 16, 1989, will expire on June 30, 1991.
2—Your second-class medical certificate issued on January 15, 1989, will expire on January 31, 1991.
3—If you received a first-class medical certificate, it will expire at the end of the last day of the sixth month after the date of the examination.
4—Your second-class medical certificate can be used with commercial pilot's privileges, so you may charge for taking your friends up for a trip.

2908. If, as a private pilot, you want to take a friend along on a cross-country flight, you'll have to meet certain requirements. These are:

1—During the day you must have made three takeoffs and landings to a full stop within 90 days in any category, class, and type if required.
2—At night you must have made three takeoffs and landings within the past 90 days in the category of aircraft that is to be used.
3—If you have made three takeoffs and landings to a full stop during the day within 90 days in the same category, class, and type to be used, these may qualify you for currency at night.
4—If you have made three takeoffs and landings to a full stop at night within 90 days in the same category, class, and type to be used, these may also qualify for the currency requirement to carry passengers during the day.

2909. You started flying in 1984 and earned your private certificate in 1986, having done *all* your flying in a Cessna 150. Now, to save time on business trips, you decide to buy a Piper Dakota. It has 235 horsepower and fixed landing gear. To legally fly this type of aircraft you will need to

1—do three takeoffs and landings solo to be able to take passengers along on business trips.

Chapter 29. Review of Federal Aviation Regulations 149

2—have a minimum of 10 hours with a flight instructor, since this type of airplane is considered a high-performance airplane.
3—read the approved flight manual, since this type of airplane does not have a retractable landing gear so is not considered a high-performance airplane.
4—receive instruction from a flight instructor and have it entered in your logbook and have been found competent to fly this high-performance airplane.

2910. To have a reliable record, you should log your flight time in a logbook. The term "pilot in command" means that

1—you are the only occupant in the aircraft.
2—you are responsible for the operation and safety of an aircraft during flight time.
3—your instructor is with you in the aircraft, but you, as a student pilot, are manipulating the controls.
4—the person in the left seat is in command of the aircraft.

2911. To remain current after you have received your private pilot certificate on June 10, 1989, which of the following statements applies?

1—When flying as pilot in command, you must have in your *personal possession* a current medical and pilot certificate and have successfully passed a flight review within the preceding 12 months.
2—You must have your logbook endorsed by an appropriately certificated person within the preceding 24 calendar months, stating that you have successfully passed the BFR.
3—You should only fly solo in an aircraft until you have acquired a flight review endorsement.
4—You should obtain a flight review before June 30, 1990.

2912. The FAA recommends teaching attitude instrument flying. To be endorsed for the private pilot flight test by your instructor, you should be able to

1—fly into clouds and get out of them successfully.
2—do proficient VOR approaches.
3—fly solely by reference to the instruments, in a safe manner.
4—recover from Lomcevaks while under the hood, in a safe manner.

2913. Several endorsements must be made for a student pilot; pick the correct one of the choices below:

1—As a student pilot you must demonstrate that you are familiar with the flight rules of Part 91 of the FARs and have received flight instruction in (1) stall recovery in airplanes, (2) collision avoidance procedures, and (3) emergencies before the flight instructor can endorse you for solo flight.
2—Every 60 days the student pilot's certificate must

be endorsed for solo flight by an authorized flight instructor.
3—To be endorsed for solo cross-country in airplanes, a student pilot must have received instruction in procedures pertaining to celestial navigation, pilotage, and dead reckoning.
4—As a student pilot you may go cross-country without the endorsement of your certified flight instructor as long as you remain within 50 nautical miles of the airport.

2914. When you are ready to take the private flight test, some of the experience you must have logged as an applicant includes

1—3 hours of solo night flight, including 10 takeoffs and landings.
2—a dual cross-country flight lasting at least 2 hours.
3—at least 10 hours of solo cross-country flight, with each flight having a landing at least 25 nautical miles from the point of departure.
4—three dual takeoffs and landings at an airport with an operating control tower.

2915. There are certain privileges and limitations for the private pilot. To act as pilot in command as a private pilot, you may

1—be able to accept pay for flying if you have logged over 200 hours.
2—have your friends pay for the cost of renting an airplane to go to Florida for a vacation, since you will be donating your services to fly them down.
3—be able to share the operating costs of the airplane with your passengers.
4—be able to act as an aircraft salesman if you have over 100 hours logged.

2916. A friend of yours wants to learn to fly. To be eligible for a student certificate in airplanes, she

1—must hold at least a third-class medical certificate.
2—will have to be at least 17 years of age.
3—must be able to speak Spanish as a second language because she hopes to fly in South America after getting her certificate.
4—must be endorsed for solo flight before she obtains a student certificate.

2917. To be eligible for a private pilot certificate, you must

1—have logged 40 hours of dual instruction in the aircraft to be used for the flight test.
2—be at least 18 years of age if you intend to fly airplanes.
3—be able to speak Spanish as a second language, because you hope to fly in South America after you get your certificate.
4—hold at least a third-class current medical certificate.

2918. In an airplane only one person can be responsible for the operation of the aircraft. If an emergency should arise, as pilot in command you know that

1—the only persons to give instructions will be the tower personnel.
2—you can deviate from any clearance or rule to the extent that is necessary to meet the emergency.
3—if you deviate from any rule you must immediately send a report of this deviation to the FAA.
4—you are required to call ATC and wait until they give you a new clearance that will help you deal with the emergency.

2919. As pilot in command you have certain preflight requirements that you must meet. These actions will include

1—a preflight inspection of the airplane to determine if it is in an airworthy condition.
2—knowing the takeoff and landing distance for all the airports that will be used.
3—knowing the current weather and forecasts for airports where you intend to land.
4—All the above statements are correct.

2920. Because altitude and alcohol are a deadly combination, the regulations have been changed over the years. You must now

1—wait 8 hours before flying, with no other restrictions.
2—wait at least 8 hours between bottle and throttle and have less than .04 percentage by weight of alcohol in your blood.
3—tell the trooper that you are not required to take a test for alcohol except by a representative of the FAA administrator.
4—wait 12 hours between bottle and throttle.

2921. Concerning the use of drugs, the safest rule is to take no medicine unless

1—it is advised by any doctor.
2—you use simple over-the-counter drugs.
3—they are simple antihistamines for allergies.
4—advised by an aviation medical examiner.

2922. As pilot in command you will have the responsibility of not acting in a careless or reckless manner. To ensure this, you should

1—not drop any object from an airplane that might cause damage or injury.
2—be able to legally drop objects as long as you file notice with the nearest FSDO at least 24 hours before such action.
3—be careful in taxiing around other planes, but you are only responsible for the safety of the aircraft occupants, not outsiders.
4—yell "Clear" whenever you start an airplane's

Chapter 29.   Review of Federal Aviation Regulations   151

engine and hold the taxi to 15 mph on the ramp and no more than 30 mph on the taxiway.

2923. You should never fly an airplane in an intentional manner involving an abrupt change in the aircraft's attitude not necessary for normal flight unless you

1—have at least 5 miles flight visibility.
2—are flying above 2000 feet above the ground.
3—are outside control zones and federal airways.
4—have a waiver issued by the NTSB.

2924. Considering the wind and forecast weather information, to be legal flying a VFR cross-country you will need enough fuel to fly

1—to your destination and then for 1 hour at normal cruise.
2—to your destination, then to an alternate, and for another 45 minutes as a reserve.
3—to your destination, using 65 percent power settings.
4—to your destination and still have 30 minutes reserve at normal cruise if the flight is during the day.

2925. Transponders are to be tested and inspected every 24 months. If you are using a transponder, you must also be aware that

1—in controlled airspace above 10,000 feet MSL, except airspace at or below 2500 AGL, your transponder must have 4096 code, Mode C capability.
2—your transponder must meet the requirements of TSO standards only if it is older than 5 years.
3—ATC will not authorize any deviations from the requirement of a Mode C transponder in any of the Terminal Control Areas.
4—Mode C transponder means that it has only 64 codes.

2926. Acrobatic flight can teach you to deal with unexpected unusual attitudes. To accomplish these maneuvers under safe conditions, you should

1—practice near populated areas so that people can see you perform.
2—wear a properly packed parachute if the maneuver exceeds a bank of 60° or a pitch (up or down) of over 30° and is not required for certification.
3—have practiced parachute jumps to be prepared to jump in case of an emergency.
4—always begin your maneuver at 1500 feet above the ground.

2927. When filing your day VFR flight plan, the amount of fuel *required* to be on board the aircraft prior to takeoff must be

1—the full amount the tanks will hold.
2—the amount of fuel required to arrive at your destination.
3—the amount needed for the trip as well as 30 minutes of reserve at normal cruising speed.
4—only the fuel needed to go to your destination and then to an alternate.

2928. Lack of oxygen (hypoxia) is a very dangerous condition and could, in extreme cases, cause permanent brain damage. Oxygen-use regulations require that for any flight over

1—14,000 feet oxygen is to be provided for all the people aboard the aircraft.
2—12,500 feet oxygen is to be used by everyone for the duration of the flight.
3—10,000 feet oxygen should be only used by the pilot if the flight is over 30 minutes at that altitude.
4—15,000 feet oxygen must also be provided for any passengers on the aircraft.

2929. Certain minimum altitudes are required when flying enroute (except for takeoff or landing). Pick the correct statement.

1—Over Los Angeles you need to be at least 1000 feet above the tallest obstacle, building, or tower listed on the sectional chart for that city.
2—Over the ocean, you should stay at least 50 feet above any ship or swimmers in your path.
3—Regardless of where you are, you should be at an altitude to execute an emergency landing, if necessary, without undue hazard to those on the ground.
4—If you are over a sparsely populated area, you should fly at least 1000 feet above any obstacle and 2000 feet horizontally from any tower or building.

2930. Emergency locator transmitters are used as a means of locating downed aircraft. ELTs

1—emit an audio tone on 121.5 MHz.
2—can be tested at any time to ensure that they are operating properly.
3—are to be used only as in-flight emergencies.
4—require a battery that will provide power for many weeks in case of a crash.

2931. Certain maximum airspeeds have been imposed in busy, potentially dangerous areas. The maximum airspeed you can operate an aircraft

1—is 250 knots below 12,500 feet.
2—in an airport traffic area is 156 knots when flying an airplane with a reciprocating engine.
3—under a terminal control area would be 110 knots, since there will be many other airplanes going under the TCA also.
4—below 10,000 MSL will be 200 knots.

2932. A VFR flight plan must be closed by the pilot according to the regulations. The proper way to close the flight plan is to

1—request the tower to close it.
2—call the nearest FSS station prior to landing.
3—call the nearest FSS on the telephone after landing.
4—have the tower automatically close it.

2933. Accidents occur because pilots do not set their altimeters correctly or fail to read them properly. To ensure that your altimeter is correct,

1—set it to field elevation when you leave so that it will always remain correct upon landing at your destination.
2—obtain a current altimeter setting within 100 nautical miles of your position while enroute.
3—call an enroute FSS and request its field elevation.
4—none of the above actions apply, according to FARs.

2934. Filing and activating a VFR flight plan gives you additional assistance in case of an emergency landing. When you do not cancel a VFR flight plan within 30 minutes of the estimated time of arrival, the FSS personnel will initiate search procedures. Therefore, when filing a flight plan,

1—don't worry about details of routing as long as you have the destination listed correctly.
2—put down the total amount of fuel on board in hours and minutes, so they can estimate how long you could remain airborne.
3—make sure that you put down your pilot certificate number correctly to help Search and Rescue if you have an accident enroute.
4—list a time of arrival that has 30 minutes extra figured in the estimate, so if you are late, the FSS will not start a search.

2935. To enter an airport traffic area, one requirement is to have

1—at least 3 miles visibility and 1000 feet between the ground level and the lowest cloud base that constitutes a ceiling.
2—two-way radio communication.
3—an operating transponder.
4—an annual inspection within the last 12 months and a 100-hour inspection if the airplane is used for hire.

2936. To enter a control zone, a requirement is to have

1—at least 3 miles visibility and 1000 feet between the ground level and the lowest cloud base that constitutes a ceiling.
2—two-way radio communication.
3—an operating transponder.
4—an annual inspection within the last 12 months and a 100-hour inspection if the plane is used for hire.

2937. While on a cross-country flight from Knoxville, Tennessee, to Chattanooga, you notice a large cumulus cloud at about your flight altitude. You are flying at 4500 MSL (3500 AGL) and should remain

1—500 feet under, 1000 feet over, or 2000 feet horizontally from the cloud.
2—500 feet over, 1000 feet under, or 2000 feet horizontally from the cloud.
3—1000 feet over, 1000 feet under, or 1 mile away from the cloud.
4—always to the left of the cloud, so other traffic will pass to the right.

2938. Some of the busiest airports are in Terminal Control Areas. When can you penetrate a TCA?

1—Anytime you like, as long as you are in VFR conditions.
2—As for an ARSA (Airport Radar Service Area—see page 147), you may enter if two-way communications have been established.
3—No student pilot may enter a TCA under any circumstances.
4—Only when the controller gives a definite clearance to enter the TCA.

2939. Terminal Control Areas consist of controlled airspace extending upward from the surface or higher to specified altitudes. In this airspace, aircraft are subject to operating rules that apply to

1—participating aircraft on a voluntary basis.
2—to IFR traffic only.
3—to VFR traffic only.
4—all aircraft.

2940. Between 1200 feet AGL and 10,000 MSL in controlled airspace the VFR clearance from clouds is

1—500 feet below, 500 feet above, 2000 feet horizontally.
2—500 feet below, 1000 feet above, 2000 feet horizontally.
3—1000 feet below, 1000 feet above, 1 statute mile horizontally.
4—500 feet above, 1000 feet below, 2000 feet horizontally.

2941. Flying on a magnetic course of 280°, what is the lowest recommended altitude that you should fly when the surrounding terrain is approximately 1000 feet?

1—4500 MSL.
2—5500 MSL.
3—6500 MSL.
4—7500 MSL.

Chapter 29.   Review of Federal Aviation Regulations   153

2942. Control zones are

1—depicted by a magenta line on navigational charts.
2—only available for IFR traffic during hours of tower operation.
3—only effective up to but not including 3000 feet AGL.
4—concerned with weather minimums.

2943. Stage III is a radar service provided in Terminal Radar Service Areas. This service

1—is mandatory for all aircraft operating within the TRSA.
2—is provided only for IFR traffic.
3—is voluntary for IFR traffic.
4—is given all aircraft communicating with "the system" in that airspace, unless pilots state they do not want to participate in TRSA service ("negative stage III").

2944. Approach control advises you to SQUAWK VFR. You should

1—turn on your transponder to STANDBY, since you do not have VFR on your receiver.
2—set the transponder code on 7700.
3—set the transponder code on 1200.
4—say "VFR."

2945. Among requirements to fly in a TCA is

1—an instrument rating.
2—a private pilot certificate or better if landing at the main airport.
3—RNAV equipment.
4—over 2000 hours as pilot in command.

2946. A special VFR clearance is only applicable in a control zone and requires

1—at least 1 mile visibility, and you must stay clear of clouds.
2—that there is an operating control tower.
3—a clearance from an operating control tower.
4—at least 3 miles visibility.

2947. Certain documents are required to be present on board an aircraft. These include

1—airworthiness and registration certificates, radio license, operation placards, and weight and balance information.
2—flight manual, which will have all the necessary information.
3—aircraft logbooks, registration, airworthiness, operations placards.
4—an approved manufacturer's certificate for that particular aircraft.

2948. The FARs require certain maintenance on transponders. This includes

1—an annual inspection on the transponder to be sure that it is operating properly.
2—an inspection every 24 months by a certified repair station.
3—transponders that have Mode D capability.
4—transponders that are used in IFR conditions only.

2949. Hypoxia, in simple terms, is a lack of sufficient oxygen to keep the brain functioning properly. You know from medical facts that

1—your body has a built-in alarm system that indicates a lack of oxygen.
2—an early symptom is a sense of well-being, euphoria.
3—symptoms are most marked at 5000 feet during the day and 10,000 feet at night.
4—alcohol increases the brain's tolerance to hypoxia.

2950. Hyperventilation is overbreathing and may result from emotional tension or anxiety. Hyperventilation

1—symptoms include dizziness, tingling hands, and blue fingernails.
2—can slow your breathing rate.
3—may be eliminated by breathing into a paper bag.
4—results in too little oxygen in your system.

2951. Choose the correct statement.

1—Lack of oxygen can bring on a feeling of euphoria.
2—The effects of carbon monoxide can be easily overcome.
3—Bends only occur after scuba diving if the dive has been over 100 feet, and you will be flying over 5000 feet.
4—The symptoms of hyperventilation are quite different from hypoxia.

2952. Vertigo (spatial disorientation) has been responsible for many airplane accidents in restricted visibilities. If you feel you may be experiencing vertigo, you should

1—try to land as soon as possible.
2—turn your head often to clear it.
3—try flying into the sun to reduce your visibility.
4—believe your instruments and fly in reference to them.

2953. If you have been subjected to carbon monoxide, prior to flying again you should

1—take at least a 1-hour rest on the ground.
2—get a good night's sleep before flying.
3—use oxygen for at least 30 minutes before flying again.
4—know that it takes several days to clear the body.

APPENDIX

UNITED STATES GOVERNMENT FLIGHT INFORMATION, PUBLICATION
AIRPORT/FACILITY DIRECTORY
SOUTHEAST U.S.   SE

EFFECTIVE 0901Z 21 NOV 19 TO 0901Z 16 JAN 19

Consult NOTAMS for latest information

DIRECTORY LEGEND   1
TABLE OF CONTENTS

General Information	Inside Front Cover
Abbreviations	1
Legend, Airport/Facility Directory	2
Airport/Facility Directory	11
Heliports	247
Seaplane Bases	249
Notices	251
FSS and National Weather Service Telephone Numbers	269
Air Route Traffic Control Centers	273
GADO and FSDO Addresses/Telephone Numbers	276
Preferred IFR Routes	277
VOR Receiver Check	282
Parachute Jumping Areas	287
Aeronautical Chart Bulletin	291
Tower Enroute Control (TEC)	297
National Weather Service (NWS) Upper Air Observing Stations	312
Enroute Flight Advisory Service (EFAS)	Inside Back Cover

ABBREVIATIONS

The following abbreviations are those commonly used within this Directory. Other abbreviations may be found in the Legend and are not duplicated below.

AAS	airport advisory service	ldg	landing
acft	aircraft	med	medium
apch	approach	NFCT	non-federal control tower
arpt	airport	ngt	night
avbl	available	ntc	notice
bcn	beacon	opr	operate
blo	below	ops	operates operation
byd	beyond	ovrn	overrun
clsd	closed	p-line	power line
ctc	contact	PPR	prior permission required
dalgt	daylight	req	request
dsplc	displace	rqr	requires
dsplcd	displaced	rgt tfc	right traffic
durn	duration	rwy	runway
emerg	emergency	svc	service
extd	extend, extended	tmpry	temporary, temporarily
fld	field	tkf	take off
FSS	Flight Service Station	tfc	traffic
ints	intensity	thld	threshold
lgtd	lighted	twr	tower
lgts	lights		

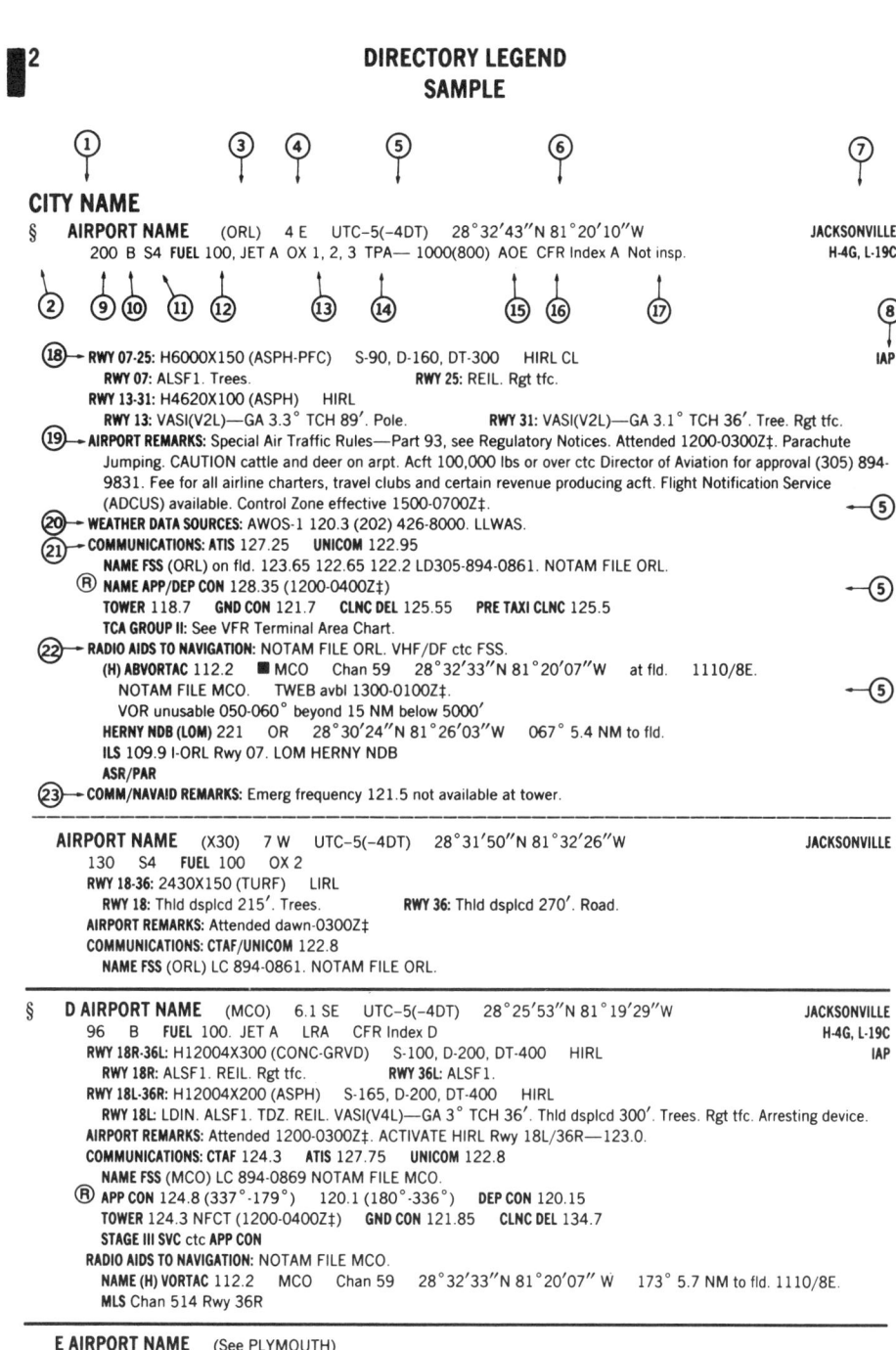

DIRECTORY LEGEND 3

LEGEND

This Directory is an alphabetical listing of data on record with the FAA on all airports that are open to the public, associated terminal control facilities, air route traffic control centers and radio aids to navigation within the conterminous United States, Puerto Rico and the Virgin Islands. Airports are listed alphabetically by associated city name and cross referenced by airport name. Facilities associated with an airport, but with a different name, are listed individually under their own name, as well as under the airport with which they are associated.

The listing of an airport in this directory merely indicates the airport operator's willingness to accommodate transient aircraft, and does not represent that the facility conforms with any Federal or local standards, or that it has been approved for use on the part of the general public.

The information on obstructions is taken from reports submitted to the FAA. It has not been verified in all cases. Pilots are cautioned that objects not indicated in this tabulation (or on charts) may exist which can create a hazard to flight operation.

Detailed specifics concerning services and facilities tabulated within this directory are contained in Airman's Information Manual, Basic Flight Information and ATC Procedures.

The legend items that follow explain in detail the contents of this Directory and are keyed to the circled numbers on the sample on the preceding page.

① CITY/AIRPORT NAME

Airports and facilities in this directory are listed alphabetically by associated city and state. Where the city name is different from the airport name the city name will appear on the line above the airport name. Airports with the same associated city name will be listed alphabetically by airport name and will be separated by a dashed rule line. All others will be separated by a solid rule line.

② NOTAM SERVICE

§—NOTAM "D" (Distance teletype dissemination) and NOTAM "L" (local dissemination) service is provided for airport. Absence of annotation § indicates NOTAM "L" (local dissemination) only is provided for airport. Airport NOTAM file identifier will be shown as "NOTAM FILE IAD" for all public-use airports. See AIM, Basic Flight Information and ATC Procedures for detailed descriptions of NOTAM.

③ LOCATION IDENTIFIER

A three or four character code assigned to airports. These identifiers are used by ATC in lieu of the airport name in flight plans, flight strips and other written records and computer operations.

④ AIRPORT LOCATION

Airport location is expressed as distance and direction from the center of the associated city in nautical miles and cardinal points, i.e., 4 NE.

⑤ TIME CONVERSION

Hours of operation of all facilities are expressed in Coordinated Universal Time (UTC) and shown as "Z" time. The directory indicates the number of hours to be subtracted from UTC to obtain local standard time and local daylight saving time UTC−5(−4DT). The symbol ‡ indicates that during periods of Daylight Saving Time effective hours will be one hour earlier than shown. In those areas where daylight saving time is not observed that (−4DT) and ‡ will not be shown. All states observe daylight savings time except Arizona and that portion of Indiana in the Eastern Time Zone and Puerto Rico and the Virgin Islands.

⑥ GEOGRAPHIC POSITION OF AIRPORT

⑦ CHARTS

The Sectional Chart and Low and High Altitude Enroute Chart and panel on which the airport or facility is located.

⑧ INSTRUMENT APPROACH PROCEDURES

IAP indicates an airport for which a prescribed (Public Use) FAA Instrument Approach Procedure has been published.

⑨ ELEVATION

Elevation is given in feet above mean sea level and is the highest point on the landing surface. When elevation is sea level it will be indicated as (00). When elevation is below sea level a minus (−) sign will precede the figure.

⑩ ROTATING LIGHT BEACON

B indicates rotating beacon is available. Rotating beacons operate dusk to dawn unless otherwise indicated in AIRPORT REMARKS.

⑪ SERVICING

S1: Minor airframe repairs.
S2: Minor airframe and minor powerplant repairs.
S3: Major airframe and minor powerplant repairs.
S4: Major airframe and major powerplant repairs.

DIRECTORY LEGEND

4

⑫ FUEL

CODE	FUEL
80	Grade 80 gasoline (Red)
100	Grade 100 gasoline (Green)
100LL	Grade 100LL gasoline (low lead) (Blue)
115	Grade 115 gasoline
A	Jet A—Kerosene freeze point $-40°$ C.
A1	Jet A-1—Kerosene, freeze point $-50°$ C.
A1+	Jet A-1—Kerosene with icing inhibitor, freeze point $-50°$ C.
B	Jet B—Wide-cut turbine fuel, freeze point $-50°$ C.
B+	Jet B—Wide-cut turbine fuel with icing inhibitor, freeze point $-50°$ C.

⑬ OXYGEN

OX 1 High Pressure
OX 2 Low Pressure
OX 3 High Pressure—Replacement Bottles
OX 4 Low Pressure—Replacement Bottles

⑭ TRAFFIC PATTERN ALTITUDE

Traffic Pattern Altitude (TPA)—The first figure shown is TPA above mean sea level. The second figure in parentheses is TPA above airport elevation.

⑮ AIRPORT OF ENTRY AND LANDING RIGHTS AIRPORTS

AOE—Airport of Entry—A customs Airport of Entry where permission from U.S. Customs is not required, however, at least one hour advance notice of arrival must be furnished.

LRA—Landing Rights Airport—Application for permission to land must be submitted in advance to U.S. Customs. At least one hour advance notice of arrival must be furnished.

NOTE: Advance notice of arrival at both an AOE and LRA airport may be included in the flight plan when filed in Canada or Mexico, where Flight Notification Service (ADCUS) is available the airport remark will indicate this service. This notice will also be treated as an application for permission to land in the case of an LRA. Although advance notice of arrival may be relayed to Customs through Mexico, Canadian, and U.S. Communications facilities by flight plan, the aircraft operator is solely responsible for insuring that Customs receives the notification. (See Customs, Immigration and Naturalization, Public Health and Agriculture Department requirements in the International Flight Information Manual for further details.)

⑯ CERTIFICATED AIRPORT (FAR 139)

Airports serving Department of Transportation certified carriers and certified under FAR, Part 139, are indicated by the CFR index; i.e., CFR Index A, which relates to the availability of crash, fire, rescue equipment.

FAR-PART 139 CERTIFICATED AIRPORTS
INDICES AND FIRE FIGHTING AND RESCUE EQUIPMENT REQUIREMENTS

Airport Index	Required No. Vehicles	Aircraft Length	Scheduled Departures	Agent + Water for Foam
A	1	$\leq 90'$	≥ 1	500#DC or 450#DC + 50 gal H_2O
AA	1	$> 90'$, $\leq 126'$	< 5	300#DC + 500 gal H_2O
B	2	$> 90'$, $\leq 126'$	≥ 5	Index A + 1500 gal H_2O
		$> 126'$, $\leq 160'$	< 5	
C	3	$> 126'$, $\leq 160'$	≥ 5	Index A + 3000 gal H_2O
		$> 160'$, $\leq 200'$	< 5	
D	3	$> 160'$, $\leq 200'$	≥ 5	Index A + 4000 gal H_2O
		$> 200'$	< 5	
E	3	$> 200'$	≥ 5	Index A + 6000 gal H_2O

$>$ Greater Than; $<$ Less Than; $\geq$ Equal or Greater Than; $\leq$ Equal or Less Than; H_2O–Water; DC–Dry Chemical.

NOTE: If AFFF (Aqueous Film Forming Foam) is used in lieu of Protein Foam, the water quantities listed for Indices AA thru E can be reduced $33^1/_3\%$. See FAR Part 139.49 for full details. The listing of CFR index does not necessarily assure coverage for non-air carrier operations or at other than prescribed times for air carrier. CFR index Ltd.—indicates CFR coverage may or may not be available, for information contact airport manager prior to flight.

DIRECTORY LEGEND 5

⑰ FAA INSPECTION

All airports not inspected by FAA will be identified by the note: Not insp. This indicates that the airport information has been provided by the owner or operator of the field.

⑱ RUNWAY DATA

Runway information is shown on two lines. That information common to the entire runway is shown on the first line while information concerning the runway ends are shown on the second or following line. Lengthy information will be placed in the Airport Remarks.

Runway direction, surface, length, width, weight bearing capacity, lighting, gradient (when gradient exceeds 0.3 percent) and appropriate remarks are shown for each runway. Direction, length, width, lighting and remarks are shown for sealanes. The full dimensions of helipads are shown, i.e., 50X150.

RUNWAY SURFACE AND LENGTH

Runway lengths prefixed by the letter "H" indicate that the runways are hard surfaced (concrete, asphalt). If the runway length is not prefixed, the surface is sod, clay, etc. The runway surface composition is indicated in parentheses after runway length as follows:

- (AFSC)—Aggregate friction seal coat
- (ASPH)—Asphalt
- (CONC)—Concrete
- (DIRT)—Dirt
- (GRVD)—Grooved
- (GRVL)—Gravel, or cinders
- (PFC)—Porous friction courses
- (RFSC)—Rubberized friction seal coat
- (TURF)—Turf
- (TRTD)—Treated
- (WC)—Wire combed

RUNWAY WEIGHT BEARING CAPACITY

Runway strength data shown in this publication is derived from available information and is a realistic estimate of capability at an average level of activity. It is not intended as a maximum allowable weight or as an operating limitation. Many airport pavements are capable of supporting limited operations with gross weights of 25-50% in excess of the published figures. Permissible operating weights, insofar as runway strengths are concerned, are a matter of agreement between the owner and user. When desiring to operate into any airport at weights in excess of those published in the publication, users should contact the airport management for permission. Add 000 to figure following S, D, DT, DDT and MAX for gross weight capacity:

S—Runway weight bearing capacity for aircraft with single- wheel type landing gear, (DC-3), etc.
D—Runway weight bearing capacity for aircraft with dual-wheel type landing gear, (DC-6), etc.
DT—Runway weight bearing capacity for aircraft with dual-tandem type landing gear, (707), etc.
DDT—Runway weight bearing capacity for aircraft with double dual- tandem type landing gear, (747), etc.

Quadricycle and dual-tandem are considered virtually equal for runway weight bearing consideration, as are single-tandem and dual-wheel.

Omission of weight bearing capacity indicates information unknown.

RUNWAY LIGHTING

Lights are in operation sunset to sunrise. Lighting available by prior arrangement only or operating part of the night only and/or pilot controlled and with specific operating hours are indicated under airport remarks. Since obstructions are usually lighted, obstruction lighting is not included in this code. Unlighted obstructions on or surrounding an airport will be noted in airport remarks.

Temporary, emergency or limited runway edge lighting such as flares, smudge pots, lanterns or portable runway lights will also be shown in airport remarks.

Types of lighting are shown with the runway or runway end they serve.

- LIRL—Low Intensity Runway Lights
- MIRL—Medium Intensity Runway Lights
- HIRL—High Intensity Runway Lights
- REIL—Runway End Identifier Lights
- CL—Centerline Lights
- TDZ—Touchdown Zone Lights
- ODALS—Omni Directional Approach Lighting System.
- AF OVRN—Air Force Overrun 1000' Standard Approach Lighting System.
- LDIN—Lead-In Lighting System.
- MALS—Medium Intensity Approach Lighting System.
- MALSF—Medium Intensity Approach Lighting System with Sequenced Flashing Lights.
- MALSR—Medium Intensity Approach Lighting System with Runway Alignment Indicator Lights.
- SALS—Short Approach Lighting System.
- SALSF—Short Approach Lighting System with Sequenced Flashing Lights.
- SSALS—Simplified Short Approach Lighting System.
- SSALF—Simplified Short Approach Lighting System with Sequenced Flashing Lights.
- SSALR—Simplified Short Approach Lighting System with Runway Alignment Indicator Lights.
- ALSAF—High Intensity Approach Lighting System with Sequenced Flashing Lights
- ALSFl—High Intensity Approach Lighting System with Sequenced Flashing Lights, Category I, Configuration.
- ALSF2—High Intensity Approach Lighting System with Sequenced Flashing Lights, Category II, Configuration.
- VASI—Visual Approach Slope Indicator System.

VISUAL APPROACH SLOPE INDICATOR SYSTEMS

- VASI—Visual Approach Slope Indicator
- SAVASI—Simplified Abbreviated Visual Approach Slope Indicator

DIRECTORY LEGEND

6

S2L	2-box SAVASI on left side of runway
S2R	2-box SAVASI on right side of runway
V2R	2-box VASI on right side of runway
V2L	2-box VASI on left side of runway
V4R	4-box VASI on right side of runway
V4L	4-box VASI on left side of runway
V6R	6-box VASI on right side of runway
V6L	6-box VASI on left side of runway
V12	12-box VASI on both sides of runway
V16	16-box VASI on both sides of runway
*NSTD	Nonstandard VASI, VAPI, or any other system not listed above

VASI approach slope angle and threshold crossing height will be shown when available; i.e., GA 3.5° TCH 37.0'.

PILOT CONTROL OF AIRPORT LIGHTING

Key Mike	Function
7 times within 5 seconds	Highest intensity available
5 times within 5 seconds	Medium or lower intensity (Lower REIL or REIL-Off)
3 times within 5 seconds	Lowest intensity available (Lower REIL or REIL-Off)

Available systems will be indicated in the Airport Remarks, as follows:

ACTIVATE MALSR Rwy 7, HIRL Rwy 7-25-122.8.
or
ACTIVATE MIRL Rwy 18-36-122.8.
or
ACTIVATE VASI and REIL, Rwy 7-122.8.

Where the airport is not served by an instrument approach procedure and/or has an independent type system of different specification installed by the airport sponsor, descriptions of the type lights, method of control, and operating frequency will be explained in clear text. See AIM, "Basic Flight Information and ATC Procedures," for detailed description of pilot control of airport lighting.

RUNWAY GRADIENT

Runway gradient will be shown only when it is 0.3 percent or more. When available the direction of slope upward will be indicated, i.e., 0.5% up NW.

RUNWAY END DATA

Lighting systems such as VASI, MALSR, REIL; obstructions; displaced thresholds will be shown on the specific runway end. "Rgt tfc"—Right traffic indicates right turns should be made on landing and takeoff for specified runway end.

⑲ AIRPORT REMARKS

Landing Fee indicates landing charges for private or non-revenue producing aircraft, in addition, fees may be charged for planes that remain over a couple of hours and buy no services, or at major airline terminals for all aircraft.
Remarks—Data is confined to operational items affecting the status and usability of the airport.

⑳ WEATHER DATA SOURCES

AWOS—Automated Weather Observing System

AWOS-1—reports altimeter setting, wind data and usually temperature, dewpoint and density altitude.
AWOS-2—reports the same as AWOS-1 plus visibility.
AWOS-3—reports the same as AWOS-1 plus visibility and cloud/ceiling data.
See AIM, Basic Flight Information and ATC Procedures for detailed description of AWOS.

SAWRS—identifies airports that have a Supplemental Aviation Weather Reporting Station available to pilots for current weather information.
LAWRS—Limited Aviation Weather Reporting Station where observers report cloud height, weather, obstructions to vision, temperature and dewpoint (in most cases), surface wind, altimeter and pertinent remarks.
LLWAS—indicates a Low Level Wind Shear Alert System consisting of a center field and several field perimeter anemometers.
HIWAS—See RADIO AIDS TO NAVIGATION

DIRECTORY LEGEND 7

㉑ COMMUNICATIONS

Communications will be listed in sequence in the order shown below:

Common Traffic Advisory Frequency (CTAF), Automatic Terminal Information Service (ATIS) and Aeronautical Advisory Stations (UNICOM) along with their frequency is shown, where available, on the line following the heading "COMMUNICATIONS." When the CTAF and UNICOM is the same frequency, the frequency will be shown as CTAF/UNICOM freq.

Flight Service Station (FSS) information. The associated FSS will be shown followed by the identifier and information concerning availability of telephone service, e.g., Direct Line (DL), Local Call (LC-384-2341), Long Distance (LD 202-426-8800 or LD 1-202-555-1212) etc. The airport NOTAM file identifier will be shown as "NOTAM FILE IAD." Where the FSS is located on the field it will be indicated as "on arpt" following the identifier. Frequencies available will follow. The FSS telephone number will follow along with any significant operational information. FSS's whose name is not the same as the airport on which located will also be listed in the normal alphabetical name listing for the state in which located. Remote Communications Outlet (RCO) providing service to the airport followed by the frequency and name of the Controlling FSS.

FSS's provide information on airport conditions, radio aids and other facilities, and process flight plans. Airport Advisory Service is provided on the CTAF by FSS's located at non-tower airports or airports where the tower is not in operation.

(See AIM, Par. 157/158 Traffic Advisory Practices at airports where a tower is not in operation or AC 90 - 42C.)

Aviation weather briefing service is provided by FSS specialists. Flight and weather briefing services are also available by calling the telephone numbers listed.

Remote Communications Outlet (RCO)—An unmanned air/ground communications facility, remotely controlled and providing UHF or VHF communications capability to extend the service range of an FSS.

Civil Communications Frequencies—Civil communications frequencies used in the FSS air/ground system are now operated simplex on 122.0, 122.2, 122.3, 122.4, 122.6, 123.6; emergency 121.5; plus receive-only on 122.05, 122.1, 122.15, and 123.6.

a. 122.0 is assigned as the Enroute Flight Advisory Service channel at selected FSS's.
b. 122.2 is assigned to all FSS's as a common enroute simplex service.
c. 123.6 is assigned as the airport advisory channel at non-tower FSS locations, however, it is still in commission at some FSS's collocated with towers to provide part time Airport Advisory Service.
d. 122.1 is the primary receive-only frequency at VOR's. 122.05, 122.15 and 123.6 are assigned at selected VOR's meeting certain criteria.
e. Some FSS's are assigned 50 kHz channels for simplex operation in the 122-123 MHz band (e.g. 122.35). Pilots using the FSS A/G system should refer to this directory or appropriate charts to determine frequencies available at the FSS or remoted facility through which they wish to communicate.

Part time FSS hours of operation are shown in remarks under facility name.

Emergency frequency 121.5 is available at all Flight Service Stations, Towers, Approach Control and RADAR facilities, unless indicated as not available.

Frequencies published followed by the letter "T" or "R", indicate that the facility will only transmit or receive respectively on that frequency. All radio aids to navigation frequencies are transmit only.

TERMINAL SERVICES

CTAF—A program designed to get all vehicles and aircraft at uncontrolled airports on a common frequency.
ATIS—A continuous broadcast of recorded non-control information in selected areas of high activity.
UNICOM—A non-government air/ground radio communications facility utilized to provide general airport advisory service.
APP CON—Approach Control. The symbol ® indicates radar approach control.
TOWER—Control tower
GND CON—Ground Control
DEP CON—Departure Control. The symbol ® indicates radar departure control.
CLNC DEL—Clearance Delivery.
PRE TAXI CLNC—Pre taxi clearance
VFR ADVSY SVC—VFR Advisory Service. Service provided by Non-Radar Approach Control.
 Advisory Service for VFR aircraft (upon a workload basis) ctc APP CON.
STAGE II SVC—Radar Advisory and Sequencing Service for VFR aircraft
STAGE III SVC—Radar Sequencing and Separation Service for participating VFR Aircraft within a Terminal Radar Service Area (TRSA)
ARSA—Airport Radar Service Area
TCA—Radar Sequencing and Separation Service for all aircraft in a Terminal Control Area (TCA)
TOWER, APP CON and DEP CON RADIO CALL will be the same as the airport name unless indicated otherwise.

DIRECTORY LEGEND

8

㉒ RADIO AIDS TO NAVIGATION

The Airport Facility Directory lists by facility name all Radio Aids to Navigation, except Military TACANS, that appear on National Ocean Service Visual or IFR Aeronautical Charts and those upon which the FAA has approved an Instrument Approach Procedure.

All VOR, VORTAC ILS and MLS equipment in the National Airspace System has an automatic monitoring and shutdown feature in the event of malfunction. Unmonitored, as used in this publication for any navigational aid, means that FSS or tower personnel cannot observe the malfunction or shutdown signal. The NAVAID NOTAM file identifier will be shown as "NOTAM FILE IAD" and will be listed on the Radio Aids to Navigation line. When two or more NAVAIDS are listed and the NOTAM file identifier is different than shown on the Radio Aids to Navigation line, then it will be shown with the NAVAID listing. Hazardous Inflight Weather Advisory Service (HIWAS) will be shown where this service is broadcast over selected VOR's.

NAVAID information is tabulated as indicated in the following sample:

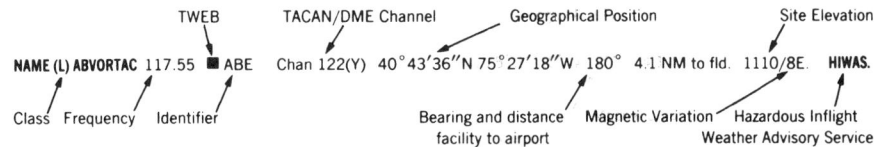

VOR unusable 020°-060° beyond 26 NM below 3500'

Restriction within the normal altitude/range of the navigational aid (See primary alphabetical listing for restrictions on VORTAC and VOR/DME).

Note: Those DME channel numbers with a (Y) suffix require TACAN to be placed in the "Y" mode to receive distance information.

HIWAS—Hazardous Inflight Weather Advisory Service is a continuous broadcast of inflight weather advisories including summarized SIGMETs, convective SIGMETs, AIRMETs and urgent PIREPs. HIWAS is presently broadcast over selected VOR's and will be implemented throughout the conterminous U.S.

ASR/PAR—Indicates that Surveillance (ASR) or Precision (PAR) radar instrument approach minimums are published in U.S. Government Instrument Approach Procedures.

RADIO CLASS DESIGNATIONS

Identification of VOR/VORTAC/TACAN Stations by Class (Operational Limitations):

Normal Usable Altitudes and Radius Distances

Class	Altitudes	Distance (miles)
(T)	12,000' and below	25
(L)	Below 18,000'	40
(H)	Below 18,000'	40
(H)	Within the Conterminous 48 States only, between 14,500' and 17,999'	100
(H)	18,000' FL 450	130
(H)	Above FL 450	100

(H) = High (L) = Low (T) = Terminal

NOTE: An (H) facility is capable of providing (L) and (T) service volume and an (L) facility additionally provides (T) service volume.

The term VOR is, operationally, a general term covering the VHF omnidirectional bearing type of facility without regard to the fact that the power, the frequency protected service volume, the equipment configuration, and operational requirements may vary between facilities at different locations.

AB	Automatic Weather Broadcast (also shown with ■ following frequency.)
DF	Direction Finding Service.
DME	UHF standard (TACAN compatible) distance measuring equipment.
DME(Y)	UHF standard (TACAN compatible) distance measuring equipment that require TACAN to be placed in the "Y" mode to receive DME.
H	Non-directional radio beacon (homing), power 50 watts to less than 2,000 watts (50 NM at all altitudes).
HH	Non-directional radio beacon (homing), power 2,000 watts or more (75 NM at all altitudes).
H-SAB	Non-directional radio beacons providing automatic transcribed weather service.
ILS	Instrument Landing System (voice, where available, on localizer channel).
ISMLS	Interim Standard Microwave Landing System.
LDA	Localizer Directional Aid.

DIRECTORY LEGEND 9

LMM	Compass locator station when installed at middle marker site (15 NM at all altitudes).
LOM	Compass locator station when installed at outer marker site (15 NM at all altitudes).
MH	Non-directional radio beacon (homing) power less than 50 watts (25 NM at all altitudes).
MLS	Microwave Landing System
S	Simultaneous range homing signal and/or voice.
SABH	Non-directional radio beacon not authorized for IFR or ATC. Provides automatic weather broadcasts.
SDF	Simplified Direction Facility.
TACAN	UHF navigational facility-omnidirectional course and distance information.
VOR	VHF navigational facility-omnidirectional course only.
VOR/DME	Collocated VOR navigational facility and UHF standard distance measuring equipment.
VORTAC	Collocated VOR and TACAN navigational facilities.
W	Without voice on radio facility frequency.
Z	VHF station location marker at a LF radio facility.

FREQUENCY PAIRING PLAN AND MLS CHANNELING

MLS CHANNEL	VHF FREQUENCY	TACAN CHANNEL	MLS CHANNEL	VHF FREQUENCY	TACAN CHANNEL	MLS CHANNEL	VHF FREQUENCY	TACAN CHANNEL
500	108.10	18X	568	109.45	31Y	634	114.05	87Y
502	108.30	20X	570	109.55	32Y	636	114.15	88Y
504	108.50	22X	572	109.65	33Y	638	114.25	89Y
506	108.70	24X	574	109.75	34Y	640	114.35	90Y
508	108.90	26X	576	109.85	35Y	642	114.45	91Y
510	109.10	28X	578	109.95	36Y	644	114.55	92Y
512	109.30	30X	580	110.05	37Y	646	114.65	93Y
514	109.50	32X	582	110.15	38Y	648	114.75	94Y
516	109.70	34X	584	110.25	39Y	650	114.85	95Y
518	109.90	36X	586	110.35	40Y	652	114.95	96Y
520	110.10	38X	588	110.45	41Y	654	115.05	97Y
522	110.30	40X	590	110.55	42Y	656	115.15	98Y
524	110.50	42X	592	110.65	43Y	658	115.25	99Y
526	110.70	44X	594	110.75	44Y	660	115.35	100Y
528	110.90	46X	596	110.85	45Y	662	115.45	101Y
530	111.10	48X	598	110.95	46Y	664	115.55	102Y
532	111.30	50X	600	111.05	47Y	666	115.65	103Y
534	111.50	52X	602	111.15	48Y	668	115.75	104Y
536	111.70	54X	604	111.25	49Y	670	115.85	105Y
538	111.90	56X	606	111.35	50Y	672	115.95	106Y
540	108.05	17Y	608	111.45	51Y	674	116.05	107Y
542	108.15	18Y	610	111.55	52Y	676	116.15	108Y
544	108.25	19Y	612	111.65	53Y	678	116.25	109Y
546	108.35	20Y	614	111.75	54Y	680	116.35	110Y
548	108.45	21Y	616	111.85	55Y	682	116.45	111Y
550	108.55	22Y	618	111.95	56Y	684	116.55	112Y
552	108.65	23Y	620	113.35	80Y	686	116.65	113Y
554	108.75	24Y	622	113.45	81Y	688	116.75	114Y
556	108.85	25Y	624	113.55	82Y	690	116.85	115Y
558	108.95	26Y	626	113.65	83Y	692	116.95	116Y
560	109.05	27Y	628	113.75	84Y	694	117.05	117Y
562	109.15	28Y	630	113.85	85Y	696	117.15	118Y
564	109.25	29Y	632	113.95	86Y	698	117.25	119Y
566	109.35	30Y						

㉓ **COMM/NAVAID REMARKS:**
Pertinent remarks concerning communications and NAVAIDS.

Bibliography and Recommended Reading

Here are some books suggested for further reading on the various areas covered.

Airframe and Powerplant Mechanics Powerplant Handbook (AC 65-12). Washington, D.C.: USGPO, 1971.
Airman's Information Manual. Washington, D.C.: USGPO, 1989.
Aviation Weather (AC 00-6A). Washington, D.C.: USGPO, 1975.
Aviation Weather Services (AC 00-45C). Washington, D.C.: USGPO, 1979.
Bent, McKinley. *Aircraft Powerplants.* New York: McGraw-Hill, 1978.
Boyne, Walter J. *Flying: An Introduction to Flight, Airplanes, and Aviation Careers.* Englewood, N.J.: Prentice-Hall, 1980.
Collins, Leighton. *Take-offs and Landings.* New York: Delacorte, 1981.
Flight Training Handbook (AC 61-21A). Washington, D.C.: USGPO, 1980.
Flying Magazine, 1st ed. *Back to Basics: Aircraft Construction, Cockpit Mechanics, & Flight Procedures.* New York: Van Nostrand Reinhold, 1977.
Garrison, Peter. *Flying Airplanes: The First Hundred Hours.* Garden City, N.Y.: Doubleday, 1980.
How to Obtain a Good Weather Briefing. FAA, GAMA, and Ohio State University, 1980.
Kershner, William K. *Advanced Pilot's Flight Manual,* 5th ed. Ames: Iowa State University Press, 1985.
_____. *Flight Instructor's Manual,* 2nd ed. Ames: Iowa State University Press, 1981.
Langewiesche, Wolfgang. *Stick and Rudder.* New York: McGraw-Hill, 1944.
Maher, Gay Dalby. *The Joy of Learning to Fly.* New York: Delacorte, 1977.
Pilot's Handbook of Aeronautical Knowledge (AC 61-23B). Washington, D.C.: USGPO, 1980.
Smith, Robert T. *How to Fly Light Planes.* Blue Ridge Summit, Pa.: Tab Books, 1979.

Information received from companies and *Pilot's Operating Handbooks* referred to:

Bendix Avionics Division, Ft. Lauderdale, Fla., TPR-2060.
Cessna Aircraft Co., Wichita, Kans. *Pilot's Operating Handbook* for Cessna 150, 152, 172.
King Radio Corp., Olathe, Kans. KX 170B, KI 208, KI 209.
Lycoming Flyer. AVCO-Lycoming, Williamsport, Pa.
NARCO Avionics, Fort Washington, Pa. ADF equipment information.
Safetech, Inc., Newtown, Pa. Information on E-6B and FDF-57B computers.

Answers and Explanations to Chapter Questions

CHAPTER 2 — THE AIRPLANE AND HOW IT FLIES

201. 4. See Figure 2-3, *SPFM*.
202. 2. See Figure 2-5, *SPFM*.
203. 1. See page 6, *SPFM*.
204. 3. The 55 pounds is raised 6 feet in 3 seconds, which would be 330 foot-pounds in 3 seconds, or 110 foot-pounds per second. Since 1 horsepower is 550 foot-pounds per second, the answer works out to be 110/550 = 1/5 horsepower.
205. 1. Page 6, *SPFM*.
206. 2. Figure 2-9, *SPFM*.
207. 3. Figures 2-14 and 2-16, *SPFM*.
208. 3. Figure 2-15, *SPFM*. Interference drag is worse for sharp junction angles. The F4U Corsair, with its inverted gull wings, had lower interference drag because the wing root joined the fuselage at a 90° angle (Fig. 2-A).
209. 2. Parasite drag increases as the square of the airspeed. See "Drag," *SPFM*.

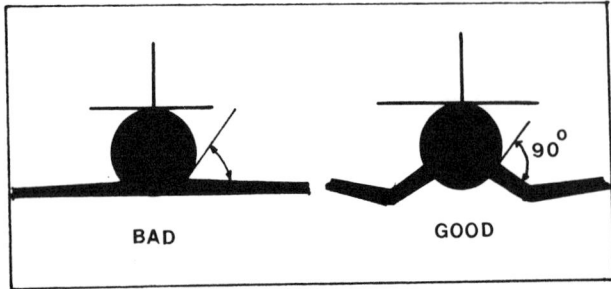

Fig. 2-A.

210. 4. See "Weight," *SPFM*. The people in Australia fly upside down all the time as far as people in the United States are concerned (and vice versa), but since gravity acts toward the center of the earth, it hasn't bothered either group.

CHAPTER 3 — COCKPIT: INSTRUMENTS AND SYSTEMS

301. 3. *True* altitude is the height above sea level, and the *absolute* altitude is the height *above* the surface. This example airplane is flying at both altitudes.
302. 1. The airplane performs according to the density altitude.
303. 2. Calibrated is the answer. It used to be called "true indicated airspeed," but this caused some confusion and was changed.
304. 3. In Chapter 3, *SPFM* it is indicated that the correction for calibrated airspeed (CAS) to equivalent airspeed (EAS) is not needed for the lower airspeeds and altitudes used by light trainers, and it's assumed that CAS equals EAS.
305. 2. Using the rule of thumb of adding 2 percent per thousand feet, you'd add (6 × 0.02) × 120 = 0.12 × 120 = 14.4. Add 14.4 knots to the indicated (calibrated) airspeed to get 134.4 (call it 134) knots.
306. 4. The pitot tube has both dynamic *and* static pressures existing when the airplane is in motion. The static pressure in the static tube "cancels" that in the pitot tube, leaving only the dynamic pressure being accurately measured (it says here).

307. 2. As noted in Chapter 3, *SPFM*, oil pressure gauges sometimes fail and indicate trouble when there isn't any. Watch that oil temperature gauge as you fly toward better terrain.
308. 1. The memory aid ANDS will help you here. While on an easterly or westerly heading: Accelerate—North (the compass indicates a more northerly heading); Decelerate—South (the compass indicates a more southerly heading).
309. 2. Three of the instruments in Figure 3-A indicated a turn to the right, and in B and C the ball has "fallen into the turn." They indicate a slipping right turn. A skidding right turn is indicated by D.
310. 1. Note that the instrument in Figure 3-B has "doghouses" to indicate the deflection for a standard rate turn. The needle is deflected one-half that required for a standard rate of turn and has a rate of 1½° per second. The 180° turn would take 120 seconds.
311. 3. Without going into electrical theory, the job of the alternator is to run the electrical components and to keep the battery charged. If you lost the alternator, you'd cut electrical use to a minimum and land at an airport as soon as practicable. Check your *Pilot's Operating Handbook* for the procedure for your airplane.
312. 4. In nearly every case the turn and slip, or turn coordinator, is electrically driven as separate from the attitude indicator (A/I) and heading indicator (H/I), which are normally driven by an engine-driven vacuum or pressure pump. Check this for your airplane.
313. 1. See Figure 3-23, *SPFM*.
314. 3. The A/I and H/I are operated by the engine-driven vacuum pump on most trainers. (See Fig. 3-22, *SPFM*.)
315. 1. The clock is the culprit.
316. 2. A calibrated airspeed of 150 knots would be about 174 knots true airspeed at 10,000 feet; using the rule of thumb of dividing that by 10 and adding half to that, you'd get 17.4 + 17.4/2 = 26.1°. This is approximately 25°, which certainly would be as close as you could fly the altitude indicator practically.
317. 1. There are no numbers given in *SPFM*, but for the record, the landing light is by far the biggest user of electric current.

CHAPTER 4—PREFLIGHT CHECK

401. 3. See the text at the beginning of this chapter.
402. 2. As indicated in this chapter, worn or broken piston rings may allow oil to get into the combustion chamber and be burned. A coagulated frammis (4) is not the answer because it is a factor that makes dentures slip and also may cause the heartbreak of psoriasis.
403. 2. IO-470. The engine is opposed (O) and has fuel injection (I). The bore of 5 inches would mean a piston surface area of πr^2 or $(2.5)^2 \times \pi$. Using 3.1416 for π, the area is 19.635 square inches. The stroke (piston movement) is 4 inches so that each cylinder displaces $4 \times 19.635 = 78.54$. There are six cylinders, so that the total displacement is 471.24 cubic inches. The engine is direct drive (not geared), so a "G" wouldn't be part of the numbers. Your numbers may differ slightly from the above answers, depending on how far you take the decimal points.
404. 3. Chapter 4, *SPFM*. The warmer air is less dense, so for the same weight of fuel being metered the mixture is richened. If, say at cruise, you need to use carburetor heat (and in trainers you should use *full* heat if you use *any*), you'll have to re-lean the mixture to get smooth running.
405. 1. The fuel injection system has better fuel distribution because the mixing is done just before it enters the cylinders. Because of this, the system is less susceptible to carburetor ice. Induction icing (caused by visible moisture freezing in the intake area) can still occur however.
406. 4. Because of possible restart problems, a good all-around philosophy is *never* to deliberately run a tank dry, particularly with a fuel injection system.
407. 3. The carburetor is not getting heat. In *SPFM* it was noted that the warmer air is less dense and a slight power loss would result. (A figure of 100 rpm was given as an average, but it could vary among airplanes.) If no ice was present, the rpm would stay at the lower value as long as the heat was ON. If ice had been present when the heat was applied, the rpm would drop initially because of the warmer air and then pick up *above* the first setting as the ice cleared out. This question ties in with question 413 in that there is a good possibility that the heat hose is detached at one or both ends. (See item G in Fig. 4-M and also see Fig. 4-2, *SPFM*.) You may have missed this in the preflight check but might catch it here, since that's the purpose of pulling the heat ON. *Don't* pull the carburetor heat ON and quickly shove it OFF. Leave it ON for 10 seconds to check an initial drop in rpm and to see if it has cleared out ice. As the answer to question 413 notes, without an operating carburetor heat you might get into icing conditions that could cause a forced landing. Taxi back to have the problem checked if the heat isn't working properly during the pretakeoff check.
408. 3. Students fall into categories. Some students have fallen out of airplanes (or were pushed) when they smoked and contributed to vacuum-system air-filter problems.
409. 2. That's the oil cooler.
410. 1. If item B ruptures, you can expect to have a large oil leak, a rapidly rising oil temperature, and possible engine stoppage.
411. 4. That's the oil breather line. If you picked the first choice, it's possible that you are overwhelmed by technical gobbledygook. (A magneto overflow simplex routing system?) As far as filling the nosewheel tire in flight is concerned, when you get the private certicate you can send out that passenger who is always making sneering comments about your landings.
412. 1. Item D is the oil sump where the engine oil is stored.
413. 3. That's the carburetor heat hose, and during your preflight you should check it for attach-

414. 1. It's the right magneto.
415. 4. Exhaust manifold. In the picture, you might initially mistake it for an intake manifold, but look at it disappearing into the carburetor heat muff. When looking at an actual engine, you could readily see evidence of prior heating, whereas the intake manifold usually stands (or sits) in unheated glory.
416. 2. That's an ignition lead going to the bottom plug of the right front cylinder. The engine would still run on BOTH with that lead cut, but a mag check would show a problem. This particular installation has the right mag firing the lower right and upper left plugs. Selecting the right mag would show a prodigious drop, since on that mag one cylinder would be totally out of action. Remember that different engines have different ignition wire routings.
417. 2. E is the alternator and F is the carburetor.

CHAPTER 5—STARTING THE AIRPLANE

501. 3. The engine is pulling in "extra" fuel through the primer line. See Figure 23-17, *SPFM* for a primer system.
502. 1. You might have answered (2), which is the *air-to-fuel* ratio. The best fuel-to-air ratio is sometimes called the stoichiometric mixture, which term, if used at the proper time, can cause your fellow student pilots to fall back in admiration.
503. 2. The airplane has just come down after a flight on a very hot day. Engines tend to get loaded (flooded) under these conditions. This would be the *first* assumption about the problem. Use the hot start procedure.
504. 4. Thirty seconds is a normal time for the oil pressure to come up. Oswald Zilch always misses this question; he thinks the answer should be (1).
505. 3. You'll want to keep the engine turning over to pull the fire up into the cylinders, but you should also turn off the mixture and fuel to stop the source. It may then be necessary to get out of the airplane and use a fire extinguisher. Put this book down and look up the recommended procedure for this situation in the *Pilot's Operating Handbook now* before you forget it.
506. 4. *Cancel the flight.* The first choice is out of the question; there have actually been cases where a pilot propped an airplane and it got away with a nonpilot passenger on board. In one known case the passenger was airborne for a long period before the fatal crash occurred. The second choice is as bad and just as illegal because the passenger could hit the throttle after the start and run over *you* and *then* get airborne. Number (3) also stinks because all you need is a nonpilot milling around an airplane with the engine running. The nonpilot isn't as aware of propeller danger as you are. Probably (4) was pretty obvious, but this question was brought in so that you might remember if you run into such a situation later.

An added note about propping an airplane: it sounds dramatic to be using CONTACT instead of ON, but at a noisy airport ON can sound like OFF or vice versa, and communications can break down between the propper and proppee.

CHAPTER 6—TAXIING

601. 4. You are on a left base at a 90° angle to the runway heading of 050°, so your heading is 90° more than that, or 140°.
602. 2. Taxiway lines are solid yellow. That's what choice (2) said, but this is known as "repeating to reinforce learning"—or something like that.
603. 3. Hold lines are placed at a position away from the runway so that if you stop there you can check traffic without getting clobbered by a large (or small) airplane. Do as your mother used to tell you years ago—stop and look both ways before crossing. Also see Chapter 25 of this book.
604. 1. Pump the brakes. You'll feel them get firm and the braking effectiveness increase. Don't wait until too late though. Get them fixed as soon as possible.
605. 2. Another way to remember what to do with the stick or wheel when taxiing in a strong quartering tailwind is to "dive and turn away from the wind." With a quartering headwind, "climb and turn into the wind."

CHAPTER 7—PRETAKEOFF OR COCKPIT CHECK

701. 2. Closing the throttle usually prevents any backfiring, which happens at higher power settings when the ignition is turned back on. Your instructor may show you a "deliberate" check of the mag ground wires after the run-up or just before shutting the engine down after a flight. He'll pull the throttle to idle and turn the mag switch to OFF (the mixture is still rich). If the engine starts shutting down, both mag ground wires are working properly (and he'll turn the switch back to BOTH). If the engine doesn't have any reaction to the mag switch being turned OFF, then one or both of the ground wires is detached or the switch is faulty and should be reported for repair. As indicated in *SPFM*, this situation can be dangerous, since one mag (or both) is "hot," and someone moving the propeller could be hit as it kicks over.
702. 3. Switch tanks and run the engine up to ensure that the tank is feeding properly. This is discussed in more detail under "Fuel Management" in Chapter 23, *SPFM.*
703. 1. *Maintain control of the airplane.* Get some alti-

tude so that you can get organized. The chances are good that it's the right (or rear) seat belt or harness sticking out and banging on the side of the fuselage, but it sure sounds like the engine is giving up the ghost.

704. 1. The worst combination is a high density-altitude (high elevation and high outside air temperatures) plus a full-rich mixture setting and carburetor heat ON, giving an even richer mixture. The other choices lack one or more of the extremes given in (1).

705. 2. Until you've tried to touch down on a short strip, you don't realize how far an engine idling too fast can pull an airplane down a landing area. Even at an airport with plenty of runway length you can tell a noticeable difference. (You'll be hauling the throttle back against the stop in an unconscious, or conscious, attempt to reduce the power.) The high-idle rpm problem plus a thermal or two could eat up a short field. To take off *anytime* with a known problem can cause some tough questions to be directed at you if an incident or accident occurs during the flight.

CHAPTER 8—EFFECTS OF CONTROLS

801. 1. You may have missed this one, but the point is for you to remember the correct answer for use later. The job of any trim tab is to *relieve control pressures* for the pilot; it's a poor man's autopilot. At the low airspeeds of landing, the pressures are very light, so you need more control *area* to keep the elevators effective and to hold the nose off at the lowest airspeed possible. By trimming nose *up* (the logical assumption) you are *not* getting as much effective area as you would by trimming nose *down* (Fig. 8-A). Check with your instructor on this for *your* airplane.

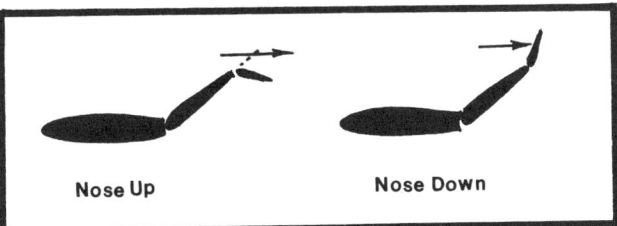

Fig. 8-A.

802. 2. The airflow moving against a down tab will move the elevators up, raising the nose and possibly causing a stall. Also see Chapter 14, *SPFM*, "Stabilator or Elevator Trim Tab Stall."

803. 3. Don't think of the elevators as up or down controls because (as noted in Chapter 8, *SPFM*) if the airplane is inverted, pulling back on the wheel or stick would mean a severe altitude loss. An old flying truism is "Pull back on the wheel to go up, pull back more to go down (stall)."

804. 4. The longitudinal axis runs through the fuselage, and ailerons control lateral movement (roll) around that axis. Of course, the longitudinal (pitch) control, the elevator, controls motion around the lateral axis. (Got that?) This has been a source of confusion for students since Orville and Wilbur did their work at Kitty Hawk. The engineers use an X, Y, Z axis system, which is less confusing (see Fig. 8-B).

805. 3. The airplane wants to roll to the right, so you need left aileron application or you would have to hold left wheel or stick to keep the wings level. The tab is on the left aileron, so you would bend it *down*, making that aileron come up. The right aileron (which is connected, you hope) will go down, both surfaces producing a counterroll or balance.

806. 2. Remember again that a tab is bent or moved opposite to the way you want the control surface to move. It's a (small) control surface on the larger control surface.

807. 3. See Figure 8-B again.

CHAPTER 9—THE FOUR FUNDAMENTALS

901. 4. Figure 9-A shows that the stall speed multiplier is (about) 1.15; $72 \times 1.15 = 82.8$ or 83 knots.

902. 2. The airplane had an engine of 200 brake horsepower with an efficiency of 75 percent at the best rate of climb speed, which meant that 150 THP is being produced. To maintain level flight at that speed requires 100 THP, so that an excess 50 THP is available for climb. Using the climb equation in Chapter 9, *SPFM*:

$$\text{Rate of climb} = \frac{\text{excess THP} \times 33{,}000}{\text{weight}}$$

$$= \frac{50 \times 33{,}000}{2000} = 825 \text{ fpm}$$

903. 4. Look at Figure 9-C. In any steady-state condition the forces acting fore and aft along the flight path must be balanced as well as those acting perpendicular to the flight path. Lift acts perpendicular to the flight path, but here in the climb, weight has components acting rearward *and* perpendicular to the flight path. Lift is less than weight (component C is less than the weight itself) and lift (D) must equal that (C = D). Thrust must equal the rearward component of weight *plus* drag, so it is greater than drag (A = B).

904. 3. See "Normal Glide" in Chapter 9, *SPFM*.

905. 3. The 2000-pound airplane is descending at a rate based on the deficit thrust horsepower. Brake horsepower being used is 80 HP; however, the prop is only 50 percent efficient, so 40 *thrust* horsepower is being developed. The airplane needs 100 THP to maintain level flight, so it's 60 THP shy. Using the equation:

$$\text{Rate of descent} = \frac{\text{deficit THP} \times 33{,}000}{\text{weight}}$$

$$= \frac{60 \times 33{,}000}{2000} = 990 \text{ fpm } down$$

168 ANSWERS/EXPLANATIONS TO QUESTIONS

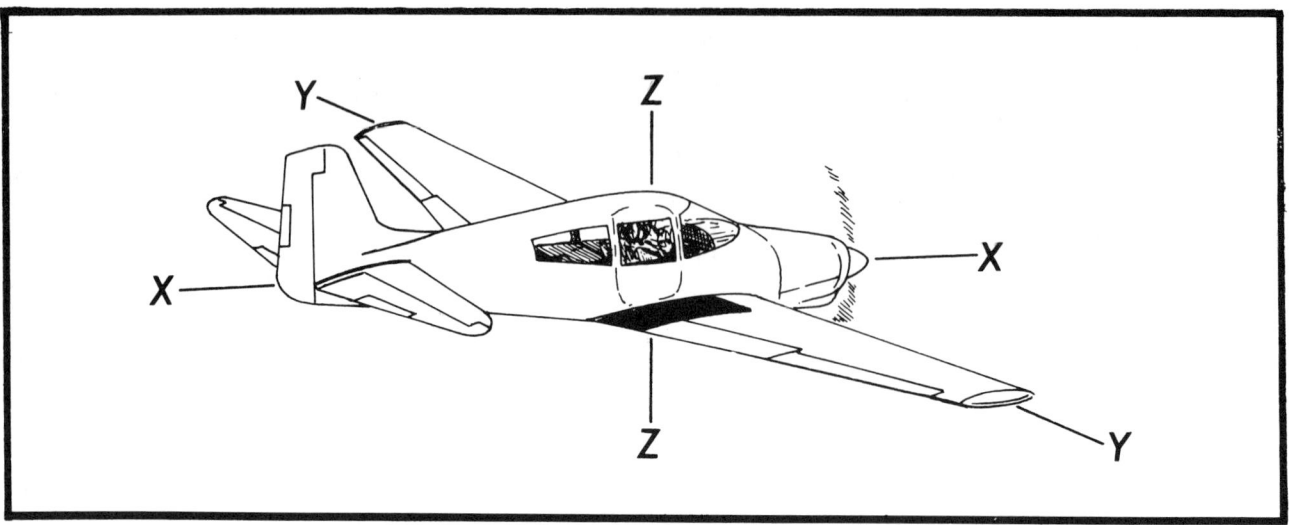

Fig. 8-B.

906. 1. The load factor is 2 at a 60° bank. The stall speed increases as the square root of the load factor. (Read "Load Factors in the Turn" in Chapter 9, *SPFM*.) The square root of 2 was shown as 1.414 there, so the stall speed in a 60° bank is 1.414 × 70 = 98.98 knots. (Call it 99 knots.) Also see "Accelerated Stalls" in Chapter 14, *SPFM*.
907. 2. Read the "Normal Climb" section in Chapter 9, *SPFM*.
908. 4. Any of the first three answers *could* be correct, but Airplane A could be flying straight and level just above the stall instead of climbing. Airplane B could be descending in a flat attitude (and low airspeed) or it could be flying straight and level at cruise. The point is that nothing was mentioned about power in any of the statements.
909. 4. In a balanced level turn at a given bank all pilots in all types of airplanes will be pulling the same number of g's. The faster airplane will have a much larger radius of turn. See Figures 9-2 and 9-4, *SPFM*. Airspeed is not a factor; the angle of bank controls the g's imposed. The figures are valid for any airplane.

CHAPTER 10 — ELEMENTARY PRECISION MANEUVERS

1001. 2. You'll have to shallow the bank first because added back pressure would increase drag (induced drag), and the horsepower deficit (and rate of descent) would be even greater. (See question 905.) For Pete's sake, don't use top rudder; it *does not* act as the elevator in any kind of turn.
1002. 4. You wouldn't be worried about wind drift in this maneuver. Of course, if you did a number of 720s with a very strong wind and weren't watching, you could drift well out of the practice area.
1003. 3. Check Figure 10-5, *SPFM*.
1004. 3. At point (3), the groundspeed is the greatest of the four points of turn. Also the airplane in Figure 10-A at (3) has the steepest bank shown.
1005. 4. The groundspeed would be slowest at this point, so since the angle of bank is proportional to the groundspeed, the bank will be the shallowest at point (7).

CHAPTER 11 — ELEMENTARY FORCED LANDINGS

1101. 1. The propeller windmills after power is lost, and the engine will pick up power within seconds after things (fuel, carb heat) are set to rights. If the engine has seized (it got so hot that it "froze

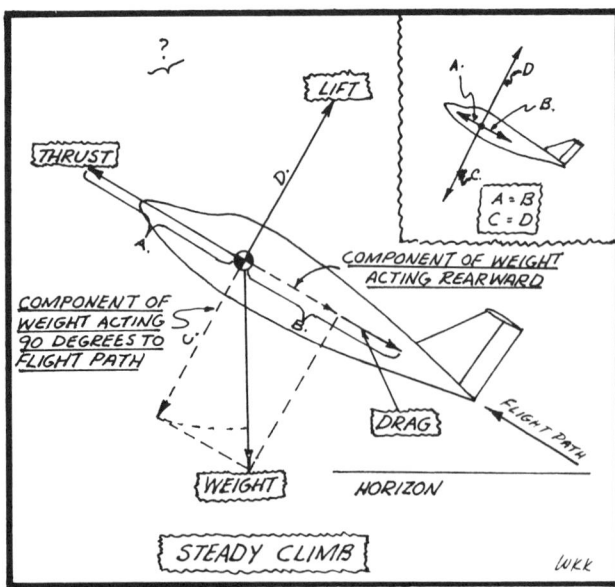

Fig. 9-C.

ANSWERS/EXPLANATIONS TO QUESTIONS   169

1102. 3. The more or less gradual loss of power is a classic sign of carburetor icing. In this case you would get the carb heat on right away to get the most from the residual engine heat. If you wait *too* long, the engine exhaust system won't have the heat to clean out the ice, which means... (etc.). Look at Chapter 4, *SPFM* again. As noted, you'd also switch tanks, turn on electric fuel pumps, and perform other cockpit chores. Of course, the first order in any emergency situation is to maintain control of the airplane, which would mean that in the event of a total power loss the first move is to establish a normal glide. But that wasn't one of the choices in the question. Answer (4) was obviously wrong; do any reading of the *Pilot's Operating Handbook* procedures *before* a flight.

1103. 2. Terrain or obstructions may very well require a downwind landing. The engine may fail at a point where it will take too much altitude to get around into the wind. The most important point is to maintain control of the airplane at all times. No stalling around until you are touching down.

CHAPTER 12—STALLS AND SLOW FLIGHT

1201. 4. To recover from a stall, you have to decrease the angle of attack or, as Chapter 2, *SPFM* says, point the airplane where it's going. In any airplane recover from a stall by moving the stick or wheel forward (assuming that the airplane is right side up).

The stall is a function of angle of attack; a particular airplane at a given flap setting and power will always stall at the same angle of attack. Stall speed always increases with added weight and, most times, with a forward center of gravity position. More about this later.

1202. 3. As indicated in the preceding answer, the angle of attack is the critical factor. The stall *speed* goes up as a function of the *square root* of the weight change or load factor as noted in Chapter 9, *SPFM*. Chapter 23, *SPFM* goes into more detail about how a more forward center of gravity position may raise the stall speed.

1203. 2. The odds are that in a right takeoff and departure stall, "torque" effects would cause the airplane to be slipping to the right as the break occurs. As a *general* rule the ball will move away from the wing that's going to drop and cause trouble as the stall approaches (and occurs) in unbalanced flight. The ball, wishing to avoid controversy, disassociates itself from the instigator of trouble.

1204. 1. See Figure 12-12, SPFM.

1205. 2. Look at Figure 12-8, *SPFM* and read the first part of the section on "Flight at Minimum Controllable Airspeed (Slow Flight)." The "other factors" mentioned might include the center of gravity position (fore or aft).

1206. 4. Check the same references as indicated for 1205.

1207. 4. There's not enough information here to confirm whether the pilot should move the wheel or stick back to climb (see point 1 in Fig. 12-13, *SPFM*) or ease the nose over to climb as would be the case if the airplane were at point 5 in Figure 12-13. Push or pull to climb? The elevators are the angle of attack (airspeed) control used to get the airplane to the best rate (or angle) of climb airspeed that you desire. Power or lack of it at a particular airspeed controls the vertical performance of the airplane.

1208. 3. The manufacturer of a single-engine normal category airplane is only required to demonstrate that it will recover from a one-turn spin or a 3-second spin, whichever takes longer, in not more than one additional turn, with the controls operated in the manner normally used for recovery. The regulations (FAR 23) cover flaps and control requirements too, but basically the first sentence covers the main situation. It's generally agreed in the industry that a spin is not developed until after *two* turns (the first two turns are considered the incipient spin, with comparatively easy recovery), so the manufacturer is not required to prove that a normal category single-engine airplane can recover from a fully developed spin. *Don't spin an airplane that is in the normal category.*

1209. 2. These are the classic indications of a left spin. The rate of sink for some light trainers may be from 5000 to 8000 fpm (that's no misprint), depending on the steepness, or mode, of the spin. The vertical speed indicator usually will be pegged full down, which is not always the case for a spiral, although a very steep spiral could produce such a reading. The airspeed is the best reference, since it will be very low in the spin. The needle, or small airplane, shows the direction of rotation.

1210. 1. This is a typical indication of a spiral. The ball may be close to the center, though usually slightly to the left. (The airplane with a U.S.-built engine tends to yaw to the right in a dive.) The needle, or small airplane, may or may not be pegged. The airspeed is high, usually well above cruise.

1211. 1. This is the best *general* spin recovery method but is not intended to replace the specifics as cited by your instructor or the *Pilot's Operating Handbook* for a particular airplane. The reason for retracting the flaps is that some airplanes may have poor spin recovery characteristics with flaps extended, and the maximum flaps-extended speed also could be exceeded in the recovery dive. A quick review of recovery from an accidental spin:

1—Throttle closed.
2—Ailerons neutral.
3—Flaps full up, if extended.
4—Opposite rudder, then forward motion of the wheel or stick.
5—When rotation stops, neutralize the rudder and ease out of the dive.

CHAPTER 13 — TAKEOFFS AND LANDINGS

1301. 1. Remember that when the nosewheel is eased off the ground, you'll lose the traction and will need to use more right rudder deflection to fight the torque. Pushing forward (3) can cause wheelbarrowing and directional control problems. Answer (2) is no good, and if in (4) you expect the tricycle-gear airplane to fly itself off, you'd better be using Muroc Lake at Edwards Air Force Base.

1302. 2. If you *start* the rotation at about 1 foot above the surface (1), you'll have to be pretty quick. Answers (3) and (4) never happen.

1303. 4. The chances are that you are subconsciously turning the control wheel while bringing it back. You might sit in the airplane on the ground and "practice" landings to see if you are using asymmetric back pressure.

1304. 2. Providing a steeper descent angle at the same airspeed is *one* of the purposes. The main purpose is to provide a higher maximum coefficient of lift so that the landing airspeed is lower. *Don't* let the tricycle-gear airplane touch down on all three wheels at once (4).

1305. 3. Power will keep you flying, but keep that airspeed under control. *Don't* try to stretch the approach.

1306. 2. Get that power on to stop further descent. Get the carb heat OFF, and get the flaps up in increments. Don't pull the flaps up in one move; you may get a sink that could cause problems.

1307. 4. A probable cause of your problem is that you are scanning too close to the airplane. (See "Where to Look," Chapter 13, *SPFM.)*

1308. 1. The maximum crosswind component is 0.2 V_{so}, or 20 percent of the stall speed with landing flaps at max certificated weight, so 0.2 × 50 = 10 knots.

1309. 3. As the airplane slows during the landing process, the controls become less effective and need to be deflected more, as indicated in this choice. (See "Crosswind Landings," Chapter 13, *SPFM.)*

1310. 4. The engineers say that wake turbulence (vortex strength) has to do with span loading, or how much each foot of wing span is carrying. Figure 13-A shows that with no flaps the vortices are concentrated (and strong at the wing tips), assuming the same airplane and weight. Vortices are strongest at the lower airspeeds, that is, higher angles of attack, so that flying at an indicated airspeed near the bottom of the green arc would satisfy this condition.

CHAPTER 14 — ADVANCED STALLS

1401. 2. Two points are to be made here: (1) the standard traffic pattern has left turns, so you'd have to know this in order to answer the question. (See Fig. 6-2, *SPFM.*) You need to analyze what control positions would be necessary to make you want to slide to the right or outside the turn. The only combination that could do this is answer (2). Another factor: It was mentioned that you were on your first solo cross-country. The strange situation would more likely cause distractions, with a resulting inattention to coordination. (That last sentence sounds like something a bureaucrat would write, but the point is to *fly the airplane.)*

1402. 1. The airplane will tend to roll toward the inside wing (the left one here) since it is in a skidding turn. The ball will move away from the wing that is about to cause trouble, as noted in the answer to question 1203.

1403. 1. As the section "Cross-Control Stall" in Chapter 14, *SPFM* indicates: *Neutralize the ailerons, use right (opposite) rudder to stop rotation, while relaxing the back pressure.* Each of the other answers has an incorrect procedure. In your mind go through the correct steps to use if you get into a cross-control situation. Instinct and prior nonstalled experience will try to persuade you to use full aileron against the roll. *Don't.*

1404. 4. The 45° bank angle is steep enough that the stall will occur at a noticeably higher airspeed. A 90° bank would be too steep. A shallow bank might result in the nose being pulled up too high, and a whip stall (or tail slide) could occur.

1405. 2. The load factor is a function of the square of the stall speed ratio. The airplane is stalled at an airspeed 1.5 times normal (105/70)², and squaring this results in (1.5)² = 2.25 g's (positive). Since the positive load factor for a normal category is 3.8 g's, the airplane is well within the bounds.

1406. 3. The term "in theory" was used because mathematically the airplane would pull 16 g's, (240/60)² = (4)². In actuality the airplane would "relieve the stress" (something major would

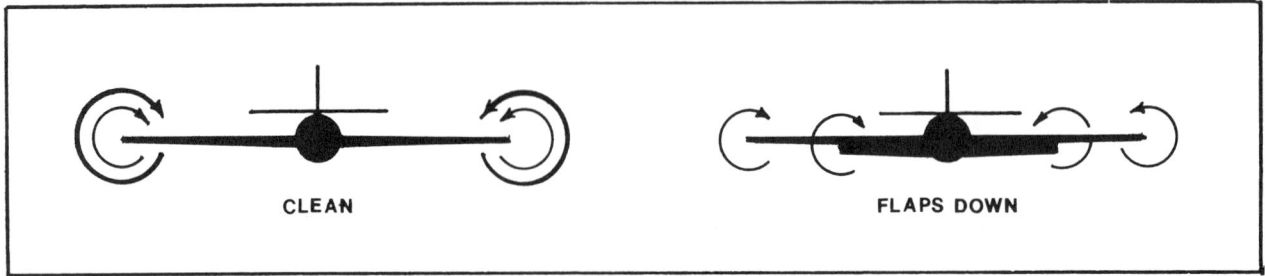

Fig. 13-A.

break off), probably at around 6–8 g's for normal and utility categories and at about 9–10 g's for most aerobatic airplanes. The main thing to remember is that problems of stress go up as the *square* of the airspeed.

1407. 4. The first sentence under the heading "Accelerated Stalls" (Chapter 14, *SPFM*) says it all.

1408. 2. Elevators or stabilators control the angle of attack (airspeed) and acceleration (positive and negative g forces). Elevators also control pitch or movement around the lateral (Y) axis. To think of elevators controlling altitude can be confusing at a critical point. Look at Figure 12-13, *SPFM* again: If an airplane is at point (1) carrying full power, "pulling" back on the control wheel or stick will result in a climb. If the airplane is at point (5), staggering along at full power (in level flight), the pilot would "push" (ease the nose over) to get to the max rate of climb speed. Do you "pull" or "push" to climb? It depends on where the airplane is on the power curve, but the elevators control the airspeed at any point on the power curve.

1409. 3. Pilots are sometimes puzzled about where the 1.76 negative g figure comes from. Normal and utility category load factors are prescribed by FAR 23; after the positive load factor is established (4.4 + g's for utility category), the negative load factor must be 4/10, or 0.4, of that. So 0.4 × 4.4 = 1.76 g's. The positive-limit load factor for a normal category airplane is 3.8; 0.4 × 3.8 = 1.52 g's, which is the negative-limit load factor.

1410. 1. The surprise is the main danger in this problem. The airplane lifts off and the nose pitches up before you realize what is happening. As noted in the section on the "Trim Tab Stall" (Chapter 14, *SPFM*), you'll normally be able to handle the wheel force in such a situation in a *trainer* (sometimes two hands may be required at first), but a larger airplane could be uncontrollable. A forward center of gravity would help the situation (some). The runway length has little or nothing to do with the problem, since the airplane is airborne when the trouble occurs. Of course, if the runway is very short, you may hit the trees or that drive-in theater screen *before* getting a pitch-up and stall. The answer is, of course, to spend a couple of seconds more with the checklist to ensure that the pitch trim is set properly and avoid the problem.

CHAPTER 15—EMERGENCY FLYING BY REFERENCE TO INSTRUMENTS

1501. 3. Turns with 60° banks (B) and accelerated stalls (D) are not realistic training in preparation for getting yourself out of an accidental encounter with actual instrument conditions. If you really get into the soup, you'll want to keep banks shallow and pitch control movements *easy*.

1502. 1. Take a look at the information accompanying Figure 15-1, *SPFM*.

1503. 4. Retard the throttle, level the wings with coordinated controls, use back pressure as necessary to ease the nose up to level (it will start moving up of its own accord as the wings are leveled), and stop the altimeter. Selections B and F would be more useful in a *spin* recovery and would cause problems in a spiral.

1504. 4. One instrument alone doesn't tell what is happening. The *attitude indicator* is just that. It tells the bank or pitch attitude of the airplane but doesn't say anything about performance.

1505. 3. Again, the attitude indicator doesn't show anything except *attitude*. What the airplane is doing about that attitude depends on the other instruments.

1506. 1. While the text in *SPFM* mentions that full power is applied (to reduce the altitude loss during the recovery), the main move in any near-stall situation is to get that back pressure off (lower the nose). The elevators (or stabilator) stall and unstall the airplane. If you can simultaneously apply power as you get the nose down, fine.

1507. 2. The recovery was made on a heading of 135°, and the shortest way around to 270° is a 135° turn to the *right*. At 3° per second (standard rate), *45 seconds* would be required to complete the turn. At 900 fpm, a climb from 3300 to 4500 (1200 feet) would require *1 minute and 20 seconds*.

1508. 1. The airplane nose is passing through Magnetic West, so the compass will be approximately correct. Remember it lags about 30° when turning through Magnetic North and leads about the same amount when turning through South. (It depends on the latitude.) Answer 4 is incorrect because at B the compass will be indicating approximately 150°, which is 120° from the heading (270°) at A.

1509. 1. In the left turn as shown, the magnetic compass, which lags by 30° when the airplane is pointed at Magnetic North, will be indicating 030°.

1510. 3. *Never* exceed a standard-rate turn when you've gotten into the soup and need to extricate yourself. In a climb, a steeply banked turn results in little or no climb and could cause a loss of control. See the thumb rule in Chapter 3, *SPFM* (under "Attitude Indicator") about the bank required for a standard-rate turn.

1511. 4. The safest area to be in the situation noted is in the middle of the green arc (85 knots), that is the point where you aren't apt to stall or get into the yellow (caution) range where higher velocity gusts could cause problems. You certainly wouldn't dive at the red line, because of possible overstress, or at 50 knots, where a stall is imminent. Letting down at 110 knots puts you on the edge of the yellow, and the airspeed could slip over into that area. Also note that 85 knots is within the flap-operating range for this airplane, and you could be ready to extend the flaps if needed after breaking out. This is a canned problem, but you might look at the airspeed indicator in your airplane to get some ideas.

1512. 3. South, because the magnetic compass leads and exaggerates the turn (and reaction to bank). Don't get caught on top of an overcast anyway.

CHAPTER 16—POSTSOLO PRECISION MANEUVERS

1601. 4. The angle of bank is directly proportional to the groundspeed.
1602. 2. Same as the explanation above.
1603. 1. The banks will be of similar steepness, but at B the airplane will be crabbed inside the circle and at D the nose will be pointed away from the circle (balanced flight).
1604. 3. See Figure 16-7, *SPFM*.
1605. 1. See Figure 16-8, *SPFM* and read "Eights across a Road."

CHAPTER 17—SPECIAL TAKEOFF AND LANDING PROCEDURES

1701. 4. Okay, a little arithmetic is involved here. The climb part of the exercise requires a distance of 600 feet (1360 − 760 = 600) to clear the 50-foot obstacle. The ratio of required height (at the obstacle) to the distance traveled is 50/600 = 1/12, or a foot of altitude for each 12 feet of horizontal distance. If the airplane had lifted off 36 feet sooner and set up in the climb, it would be approximately 3 feet higher at the original obstacle. Three feet (or even 1 foot) could mean the difference between success and an accident; use all the available takeoff area.

1702. 2. The horizontal distance during the climb portion is 2500 − 1300 = 1200 feet. This gives a height-to-distance ratio of 50/1200 = 1/24. You'd have another 2 feet of altitude when you got to the *original* 2500-foot point (before you used more runway). These examples in questions 1701 and 1702 are to show that for every 12 feet of added ground run at sea level density, or every 24 feet at 6000 feet density altitude, a foot of altitude is added at a particular point in the climb for the sample airplane used here. The numbers were rounded off slightly for arithmetical purposes.

As you can see, at higher altitudes the climb angle is less (1–24 at 6000 feet, as compared to 1–12 at sea level for this airplane) because of the loss of power and thrust. The best rate of climb of an airplane (for a given altitude and weight) is found at the airspeed where the most *excess thrust horsepower* is available (see "Normal Climb" in Chapter 9, *SPFM* again). The max *angle* of climb is obtained at the airspeed at which the most *excess thrust* is available. The airspeed for max rate is always greater than that for max angle and *decreases* with altitude. The airspeed for max angle *increases* with altitude, and the two speeds come together at the absolute ceiling of the airplane. (There's just one speed there at which the airplane can fly without losing altitude.) As a rule of thumb, the airspeed for best rate *decreases* about 1 percent per thousand feet of density altitude and the airspeed for best angle *increases* about 0.5 percent per thousand feet.

Notes on technique—The short-field takeoff requires the best combination of takeoff *and* climb. Some pilots advocate keeping the flaps up until reaching a certain airspeed, then extending them abruptly (usually full down) to get off early. This distracts from flying the airplane, and the full flaps may hurt the climb portion of the exercise so that the obstacle isn't cleared. It's best to set the flaps as indicated in the *Pilot's Operating Handbook* and use recommended techniques.

1703. 1. See Figure 17-2, *SPFM*. You will touch down well past the spot.
1704. 3. Hold that wheel or stick full back as you brake to get the best braking effectiveness. Retracting the flaps about halfway during the roll puts more weight on the main wheels for braking, but in a retractable-gear airplane moving the wrong handle can give you an answer like (4).
1705. 1. *Don't* stop in a soft area, but keep the airplane moving as you taxi onto the takeoff area. Use flaps as recommended by the manufacturer and hold that wheel or stick back to keep the nosewheel from digging in (or to keep the tailwheel from ending up ahead of the airplane).
1706. 3. The lowest air density (or highest density-altitude) would result from this combination of pressure and temperature. In Chapter 17, *SPFM* it was shown that for every 15°F (8½°C) *above* standard temperature for a particular altitude, the density altitude is raised by 1000 feet. *The warmer air is less dense.* To get this 1000 feet by a *lowered pressure*, pressure would have to be approximately 1 inch of mercury lower than standard, or corrected it would, for instance, be 28.92 inches of mercury, not 29.92. But such a low pressure of 28.92 or lower rarely exists from natural causes (except in the vicinity of hurricanes). Standard temperature at sea level is 59°F, with a lapse rate of 3.5°F per 1000 feet.

Looking at the four answers one by one: (1) Altimeter setting 29.92 and temperature of 74°F. The barometric pressure is normal and the temperature is 15°F above normal. The density-altitude is *1000 feet*. (Disregard any moisture effects.) (2) Altimeter 30.42 and temperature 74°F. The higher pressure makes for higher density (500 feet below sea level), but the higher temperature lowers the density by adding about 1000 feet of "altitude" so that the density-altitude is about *500 feet* above standard sea level. (3) Altimeter 30.42 and temperature 89°F. The higher pressure took you down to a higher density of about 500 feet below sea level, but the temperature of 89°F (30°F above normal for sea level) pulled the situation up by 2000 feet. Density-altitude is approximately *1500 feet. This is the correct answer.* (4) The altimeter setting 29.42 pulled you up to a 500-foot density-altitude, but the temperature lowered it by about 1000 feet. The airplane is "operating" at 500 feet below sea level.

ANSWERS/EXPLANATIONS TO QUESTIONS 173

1707. 2. High temperatures and moist conditions make for higher density-altitudes (thinner air) and longer takeoff rolls.

1708. 3. This was a straightforward question that could be answered directly from the chart. Note that the numbers are for short-field techniques.

1709. 2. You'll have to do a little interpolating here, since 15°C is exactly between 10°C and 20°C. Looking first at the *ground rolls* for those two temperatures at 4000 feet, 10°C = 1030 feet, 20°C = 1115 feet. Taking the exact average you'd get 2145/2 = 1072.5 feet (which was called 1075 to be slightly on the conservative side).

For the total distance over a 50-foot obstacle at 4000 feet, 10°C = 1965, 20°C = 2125 feet. Again averaging, an answer of 2045 feet is obtained. If the question had asked to find the distances required at, say, 17°C at 4500 feet, the interpolation chore involved would have probably kept you off the golf course for several days while you worked it out. If the temperature at 4000 feet is 17°C, you'd be better off in actual practice to use the figures for 20°C, which would be a conservative approach. Suppose, however, you have a problem that requires finding the ground roll and total distance at 4500 feet and 15°C. In this case the altitudes *and* temperatures are between those given on the chart. You would obtain the values at 4000 feet at 15°C, as was just done, and then do the same for 5000 feet at 15°C, which would be (looking at the chart):

5000 feet: at 10°C distances are 1140 and 2185
          at 20°C distances are 1230 and 2360
                                2370   4545

Averaging the distances (adding and dividing by 2), you'd get 1185 and 2275 feet (rounded off) at 5000 feet pressure altitude and 15°C. To find the distances at 4500 feet and 15°C, you would average the numbers for 15°C at 4000 and 5000 feet:

At 4000 feet and 15°C: 1075 and 2045 feet
At 5000 feet and 15°C: 1185 and 2275
                        2260   4320 feet

Dividing each of the sums by 2, the rounded-off result for 4500 feet pressure altitude and 15°C would be 1130 ground roll and 2160 feet total respectively. If there was a 9-knot headwind, you'd decrease these distances by 10 percent, as the notes to Figure 17-A say, to get a final answer of 1017 and 1944 feet. Again, practically speaking, you'd be better off to use the numbers for 5000 feet and 20°C, since the distances often depend on maximum performance by an experienced test pilot. But the point here, too, is to get you used to using the takeoff and landing distance charts.

The Take-off Data Chart shown in Figure 17-D is from an earlier (FAA) Private Pilot—Airplane Written Test and so is the following question:

Existing Situation:
Gross weight   1700 pounds
Outside temperature   66°F
Pressure altitude   5000 feet
Wind (headwind)   20 knots

The total takeoff distance required to clear a 50-foot obstacle is
1—575 feet.
2—633 feet.
3—518 feet.
4—930 feet.

Looking at Figure 17-D, you see that at a weight of 1700 pounds and 5000 feet (41°F) the distance required with a 20-knot headwind is 575 feet (which is "incidentally" one of the answers). The problem is not complete because the temperature given was 66°F, not 41°F as shown on the chart. However, the notes to Figure 17-D indicate that you are to increase the distance by 10 percent for each 25°F above the standard for a particular altitude. The given temperature of 66°F is exactly 25°F higher than the standard at 5000 feet (41°F), so 10 percent is added to the 575 feet gotten earlier and an answer of 632.5 (633) feet is given in (2), which is the correct answer. In using these types of charts on the written test, carefully work out the problem *fully*, then compare your answer with the choices. By looking at the choices first, you might be tempted to give the answer "575" and

TAKE-OFF DATA
TAKE-OFF DISTANCE FROM HARD SURFACE RUNWAY WITH FLAPS UP

GROSS WEIGHT POUNDS	IAS AT 50' MPH	HEAD WIND KNOTS	AT SEA LEVEL & 59°		AT 2500 FT. & 50°F		AT 5000 FT. & 41°F		AT 7500 FT. & 32°F	
			GROUND RUN	TOTAL TO CLEAR 50 FT OBS	GROUND RUN	TOTAL TO CLEAR 50 FT OBS	GROUND RUN	TOTAL TO CLEAR 50 FT OBS	GROUND RUN	TOTAL TO CLEAR 50 FT OBS
2300	68	0	865	1525	1040	1910	1255	2480	1565	3855
		10	615	1170	750	1485	920	1955	1160	3110
		20	405	850	505	1100	630	1480	810	2425
2000	63	0	630	1095	755	1325	905	1625	1120	2155
		10	435	820	530	1005	645	1250	810	1685
		20	275	580	340	720	425	910	595	1255
1700	58	0	435	780	520	920	625	1095	765	1370
		10	290	570	355	680	430	820	535	1040
		20	175	385	215	470	270	575	345	745

NOTES: 1. Increase distance 10% for each 25°F above standard temperature for particular altitude.
2. For operation on a dry, grass runway, increase distances (both "ground run" and "total to clear 50 ft. obstacle") by 7% of the "total to clear 50 ft. obstacle" figure.

Fig. 17-D.

1710. 4. The *calm-wind* correct answer was 1075 and 2045 feet. The 9-knot headwind, according to the notes in Figure 17-A, would decrease the numbers by 10 percent, giving distances of 968 and 1841 feet.

1711. 1. Looking at the distances for the ground roll and total distance for a pressure altitude of 2000 feet and a temperature of 30°C, you see a straightforward 505 ground roll and 1165 feet. Since the airplane was landing on a dry grass runway, the notes to Figure 17-B required that *both* distances be increased by *45 percent of the ground roll figure* (505 here). Okay, 45 percent of 505 is $0.45 \times 505 = 227$ feet. This figure is added to 505 and 1165 to get *732 and 1392* feet. The ground roll is the only portion of the landing affected by the runway surface, naturally, but this effect must be added to *both* figures.

    The question probably arises now as to why distance was added by the dry grass on the *takeoff* roll. (More rolling friction as compared to dry pavement is the answer; the airplane is "held back.") Wait a minute; if there is all that drag caused by the dry grass, *why is the ground roll distance increased on the landing also?* It would seem that the landing ground roll would be shorter because of the added rolling friction, but the answer is that these landing distances are found using *short-field* procedures, which means that a *maximum braking effort* is involved and dry grass is "slicker" than pavement.

1712. 2. You would interpolate between 4000 and 5000 feet pressure altitude and 10 and 20°C to get 525 and 1195 feet. The headwind of 14 knots would shorten the distances by 15 percent (each 9 knots equals 10 percent) so that $0.85 \times 525 = 446$ and $0.85 \times 1195 = 1016$ (rounded off).

1713. 4. The Wind Component Chart can be hard to read, but by following the 20-knot circle around to a 26° wind angle (344° to 010° = 26° angle), you'd see that the wind components are approximately 18 knots (headwind) and 9 knots (crosswind).

CHAPTER 18—HIGH-ALTITUDE EMERGENCIES

1801. 3. See Figure 18-2, *SPFM*.
1802. 2. The more you can turn an unusual situation into a more normal one, the better off you are. You are hitting the Key Position at a slightly higher altitude to compensate for the drag effects of a windmilling propeller on the glide distance.
1803. 3. Checking the Glide Performance Chart, you can see that the glide distance is approximately 10 nautical miles. In writing this type of question, there are pitfalls; the original question was, "From an altitude of 7000 feet above the ground *you* can cover a ground distance of approximately . . ." (italics added). Actually, *you* would cover little distance since the unaided human body has the glide ratio of a wheelbarrow full of wet cement.

CHAPTER 19—THE NAVIGATION IDEA

1901. 2. Pilotage (flying by reference to landmarks) is the answer here. You should use pilotage with dead reckoning (computed heading and groundspeed) *and* radio navigation. These three methods enhance each other and can make you a more accurate pilot. It's especially helpful to have been relying on all three methods in case the radios fail or you are flying over areas that have few recognizable landmarks.

    When using pilotage, try to look as far as visibility will allow, then correlate this with what you see on the chart.

1902. 1. As Figure 19-1, *SPFM* shows, meridians are imaginary lines extending around the earth through the geographic north and south poles. You use meridians and parallels (also shown in Fig. 19-1, *SPFM*) to locate a position. Measure up or down a meridian for latitude and along a parallel to get longitude.

    Locating the Sparta-White Co. Airport (see Fig. 19-B) becomes a matter of getting the coordinates (36°04′N and 85°32′W). Read that as 36 degrees, 4 minutes North and 85 degrees, 32 minutes West. You'd find 36°04′ and draw a line along that latitude (A-A). You'd then locate 85°32′ West and draw a line on that longitude (B-B). The airport should be where the lines cross.

1903. 3. Parallels are equidistant apart, but meridians converge at the geographic poles. Only at the equator would a minute of longitude equal 1 nautical mile. A knot is 1 nautical mile per hour, and the term was developed in the olden days of sailing when a log or other drag device with a line attached (and knots in the line at specific intervals) was thrown overboard. The number of knots were counted for a given time as the drag of the log pulled the line out. So the ship was making "2 knots" or "4 knots," etc.

1904. 1. You can figure the difference between Coordinated Universal Time (UTC) in the United States by dividing the longitude by 15. So if you're at 90° west longitude, your standard time is 6 hours behind Greenwich, England (where the prime meridian is located). The earth actually turns about 15.04° per hour, but who's counting?

1905. 2. *Variation* is the magnetic angle between the geographic north pole and Magnetic North Pole. Draw a course line on your chart, measure the true course with the plotter, and convert to the magnetic course by adding or subtracting variation.

1906. 4. You should know the directions of the compass so you can approximate courses or headings. Figure 19-C may help you to understand these points, with East 090°, South 180°, West 270°,

ANSWERS/EXPLANATIONS TO QUESTIONS 175

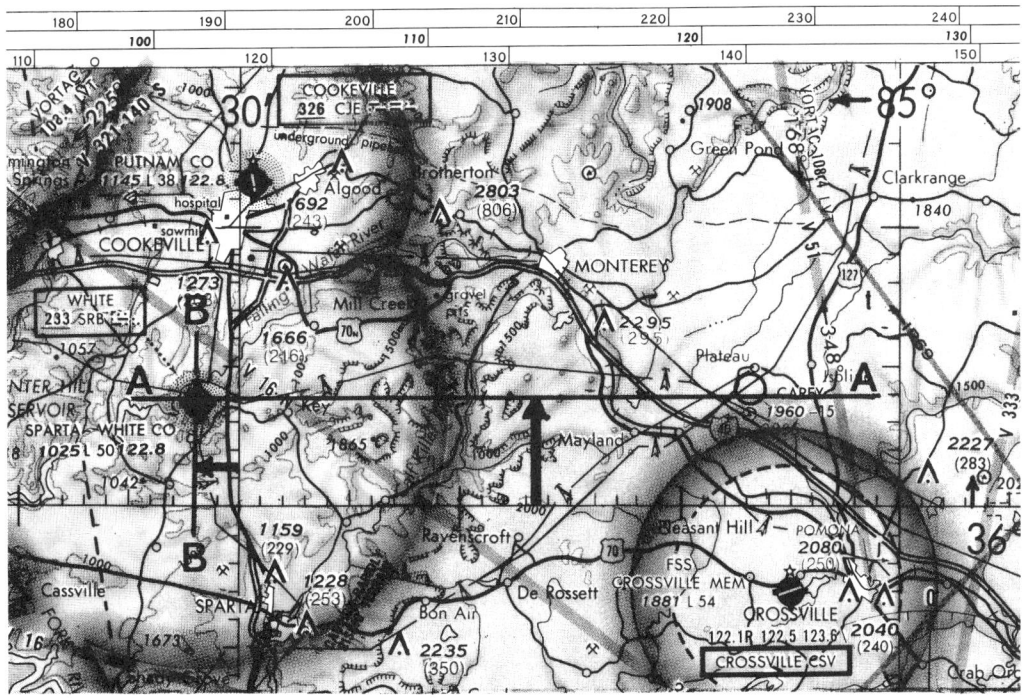

Fig. 19-B.

and North 360°. If you like to play with numbers, the following would be of interest. The first numbers of the prime points are 0, 1, 2, 3; the second numbers read down 9, 8, 7, 6, with the last digit being 0. Northeast is 045, Southeast 135, Southwest 225, and Northwest 315. Those first numbers are 0, 1, 2, 3, with the second numbers reading down 4, 3, 2, 1, and the last digit being 5 in each case.

1907. 4. There are a number of types of plotters on the market. A composite one is illustrated in Figures 19-D and 19-E. You can read the *true course* on the two outer scales when the grommet or hole is over a meridian (North-South line) as shown in Figure 19-D. You will notice that the two numbers are exactly 180° apart. This gives a reading of outbound and reciprocal true courses. Again, to avoid misreading the course and going hell-bent for election in the wrong direction, you should estimate the approximate direction on the chart.

If your course does not intercept a meridian, you can use the center scales that are shaped like a quarter-circle. (See Fig. 19-E.) By estimating the course from the points of a compass, it's easier to know which scale to use on the plotter.

1908. 2. You can look at the course and tell that it's a few degrees West of South.

1909. 2. The direction is between Southwest (or 225°) and West (or 270°). Read the correct scale; it could be bad news to end up flying either 90 or 180° from the required course.

1910. 1. Select a constant CAS and a constant pressure altitude (PA). Change the temperature and see how it changes the TAS.

Example: (1) CAS = 150 knots, PA = 5000 feet, temperature = −10°C, TAS = 157 knots (see Fig. 19-F). (2) CAS = 150 knots, PA = 5000 feet, temperature = +35°C, TAS = 170 knots (see Fig. 19-G). (The temperature is exaggerated to make a point.)

1911. 4. The CAS is read on the middle scale. The TAS will be directly above the CAS on the outer scale.

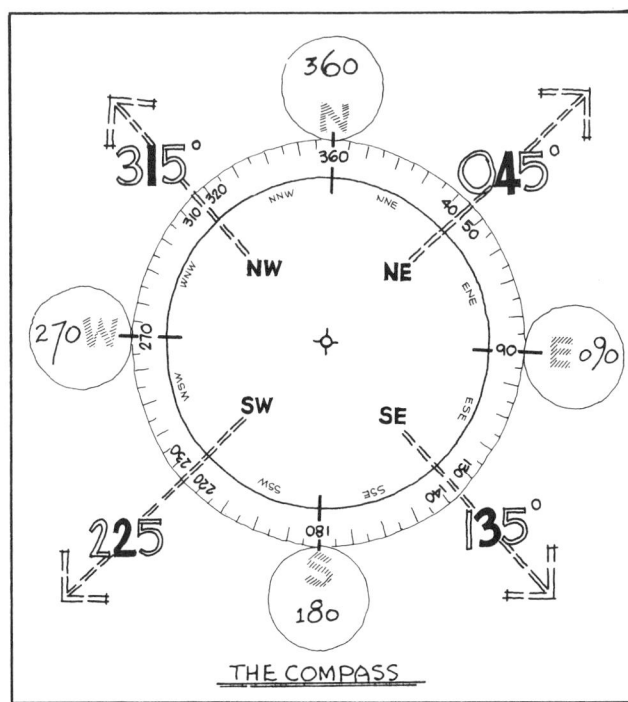

Fig. 19-C.

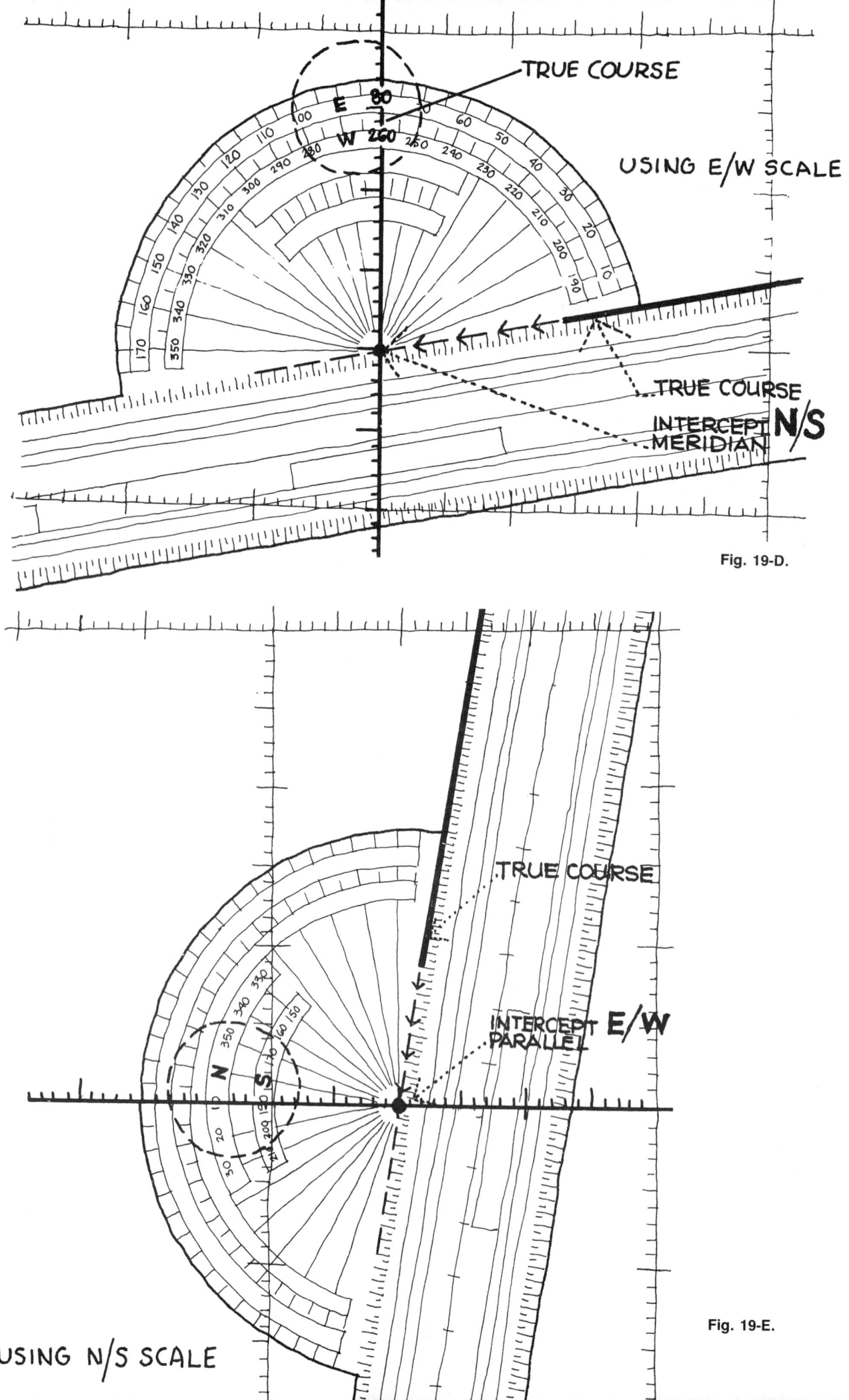

Fig. 19-D.

Fig. 19-E.

ANSWERS/EXPLANATIONS TO QUESTIONS 177

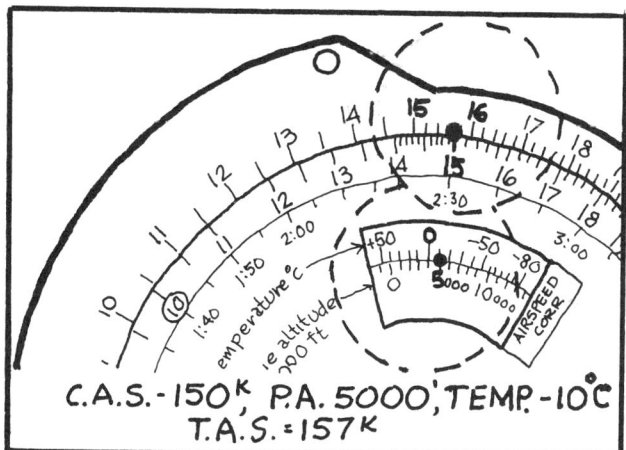

Fig. 19-F.

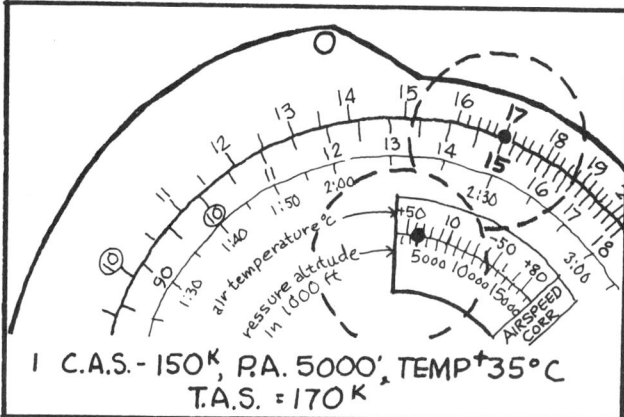

Fig. 19-G.

Use the correct window on the calculator side of the computer. One side is to compute true altitude; the other is used with TAS computations (see Fig. 19-H).

One other problem error is not setting the correct temperature over the right altitude. The altitudes are given in 1000-foot increments, and sometimes the plus and minus temperature indications are portrayed in reverse order.

1912. 3. The standard adiabatic lapse rate is a decrease in temperature of 2°C per thousand feet increase in altitude. To see the effect of altitude changes at the same CAS, use a temperature of +10°C at 5000 feet and a temperature of 0°C at 10,000 feet and notice the increase in TAS.

Example: (1) CAS = 120 knots, PA = 5000 feet, temperature = +10°C, TAS = 130 knots. (2) CAS = 120 knots, PA = 10,000 feet, temperature = 0°C, TAS = 141 knots. (See Fig. 19-I.)

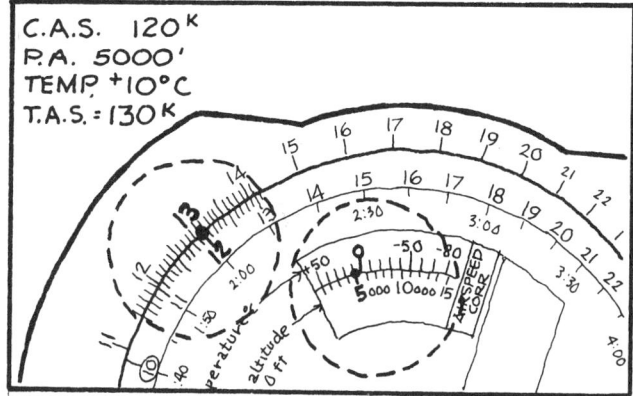

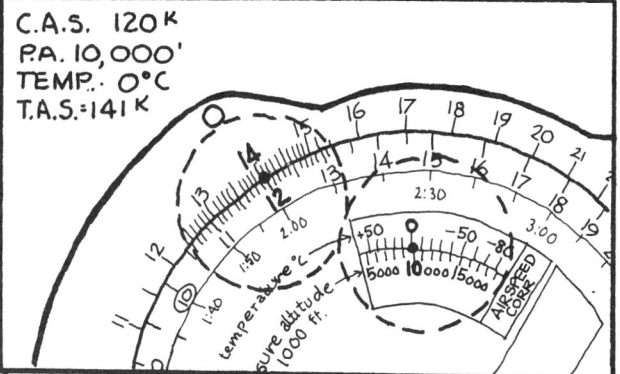

Fig. 19-I.

1913. 4. True altitude is computed in the true altitude window, placing the PA under the temperature. The indicated altitude is found around the middle scale. True altitude is read directly over the indicated altitude on the outside scale (see Fig. 19-J).

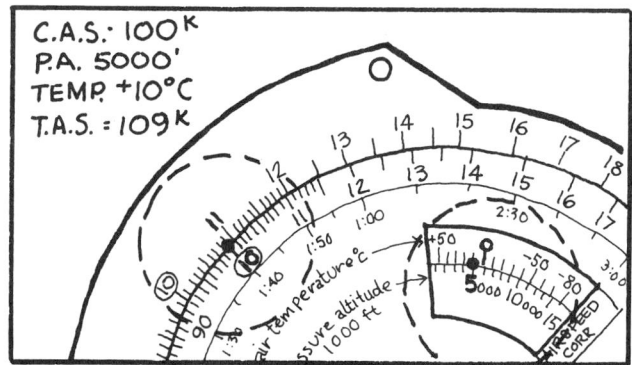

Fig. 19-H.

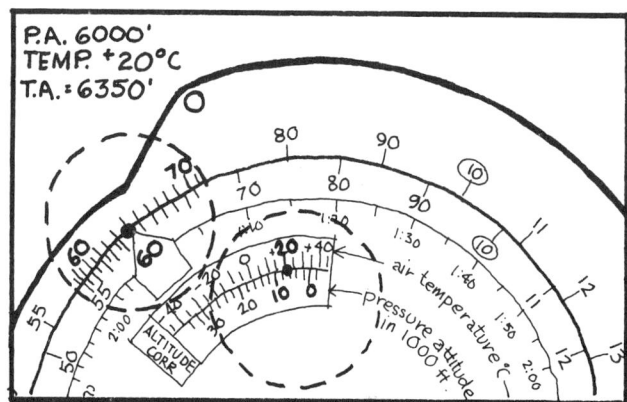

Fig. 19-J.

1914. 1. If you place +15°C (standard sea level temperature) over the sea level pressure altitude in the altitude correction window, you will find that the PA will agree with the true altitude. Also you might note that the standard temperature will decrease with altitude, with the standard adiabatic lapse rate of 2°C per thousand feet. At 10,000 feet the standard temperature will be −5°C.

When the temperature is more or less than standard, the pressure altitude will differ from the true altitude. At 10,000 feet, with a higher than normal temperature of +5°C, the true altitude will be 10,400 feet (see Figs. 19-K, 19-L). You should remember HALT (*High Altimeter because of Low Temperature*). HALT, before you hit something, because if the outside temperature is lower than standard, the altimeter will be indicating higher than the airplane is actually flying (see Fig. 19-M).

1915. 1. The PA is the altitude read with the pressure set at 29.92 inches of mercury. If the pressure is less than 29.92, turn the Kollsman window indication up to get to 29.92, and the altitude indicated by the instrument will increase accordingly (and vice versa).

For a constant PA your computer will show that the density-altitude (DA) will increase when temperature increases. (The air will get thinner.) *Example:* (1) PA = 5000 feet, temperature = −10°C, DA = 3150 feet. (2) PA = 5000 feet, temperature = +30°C, DA = 7800 feet (see Fig. 19-N).

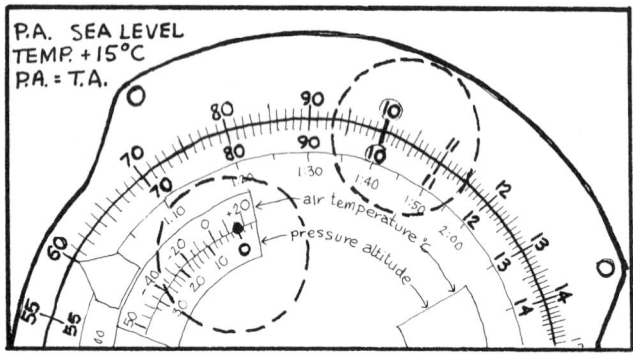

Fig. 19-K.

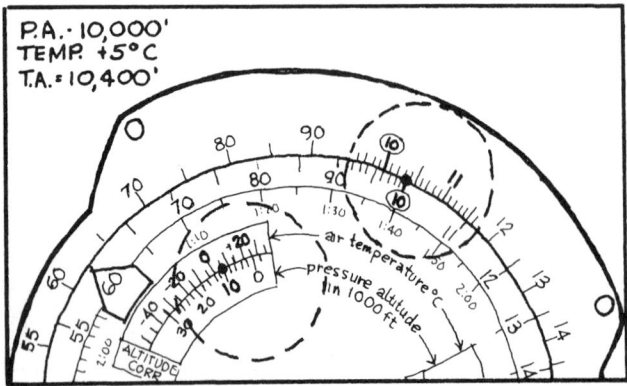

Fig. 19-L.

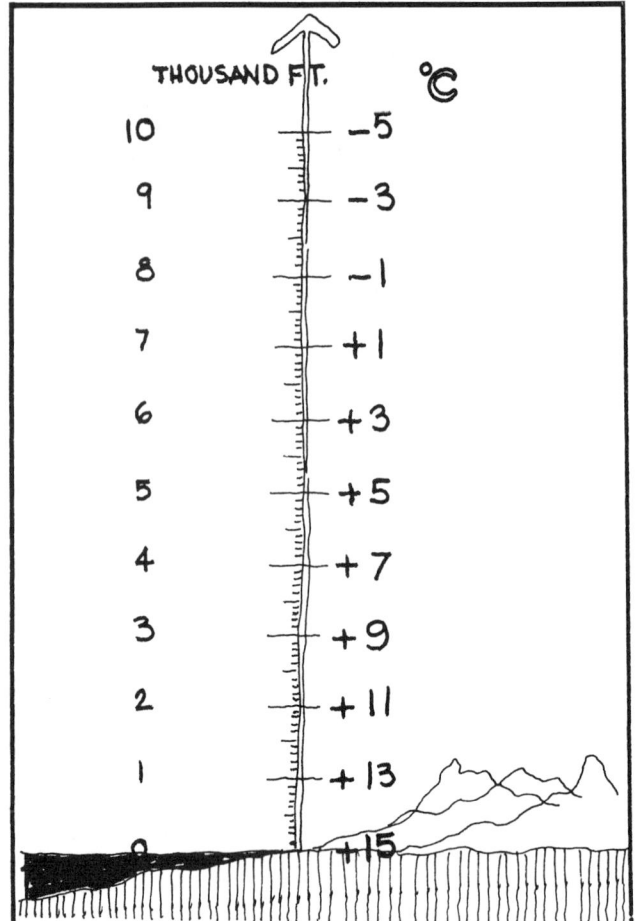

Fig. 19-M.

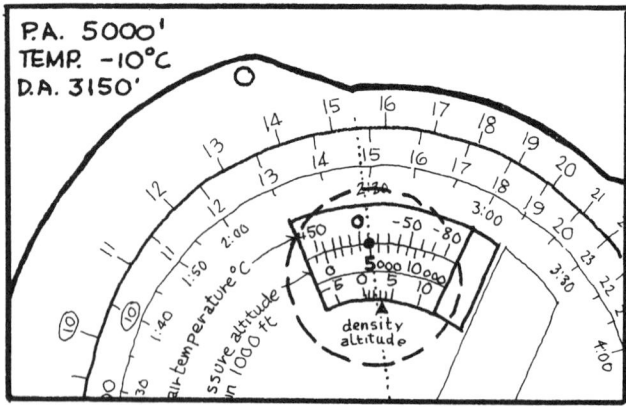

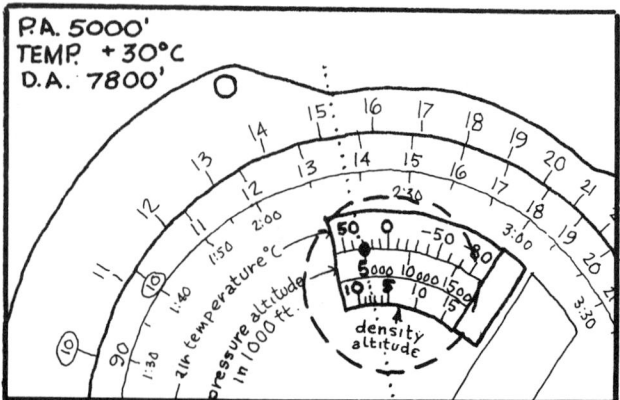

Fig. 19-N.

ANSWERS/EXPLANATIONS TO QUESTIONS 179

Warm air is less dense and weighs less. Air that is denser weighs more for a given volume. As altitude increases, the air is less dense. Humidity also changes density-altitude. Water vapor has a molecular weight that is less than that of dry air, so its density is less. Lower pressure, higher temperature, and high humidity will increase density-altitude.

1916. 4. A to B (see Figs. 19-O, 19-P).

True course (TC)	090°	Distance	49 miles
True heading (TH)	088°	Groundspeed	95 knots
Variation	−14°	Estimated time enroute	31 minutes
Magnetic heading (MH)	074°		
Deviation	−2°		
Compass heading (CH)	072°		

1917. 3. B to C (see Figs. 19-Q, 19-R).

True course	225°	Distance	57 miles
True heading	218°	Groundspeed	140 knots
Variation	−14°	Wind correction angle	−7°
Magnetic heading	204°	Estimated time enroute	24.5 minutes (call it 25)
Deviation	+4°		
Compass heading	208°		

Magnetic course = true course ± variation; MC = 225° − 14° = 211°. The other calculations were put in to complete the problem.

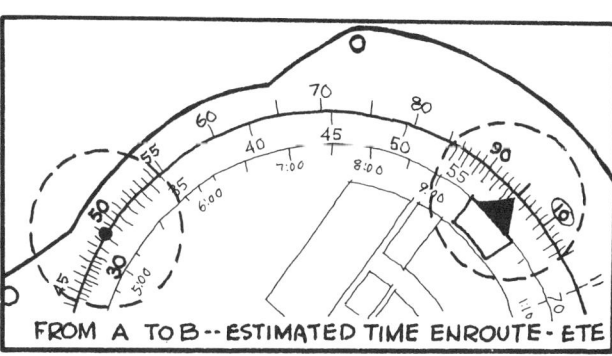

Fig. 19-P.

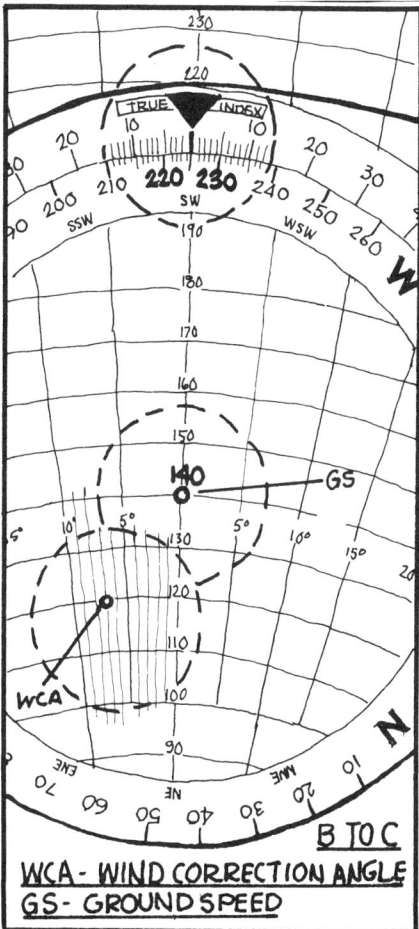

Fig. 19-Q.

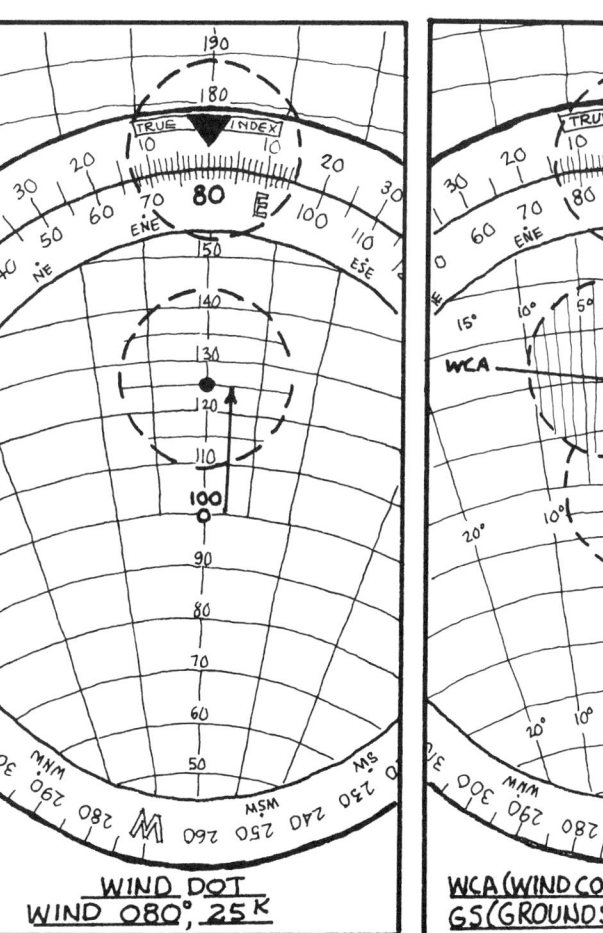

Fig. 19-O.

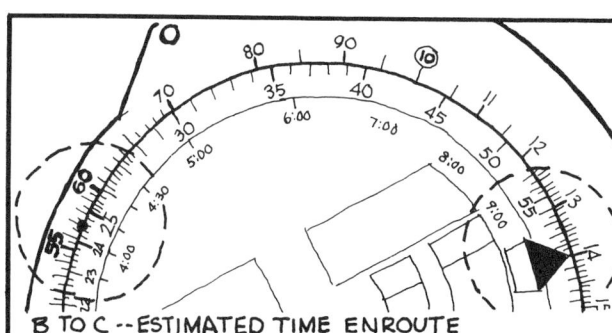

Fig. 19-R.

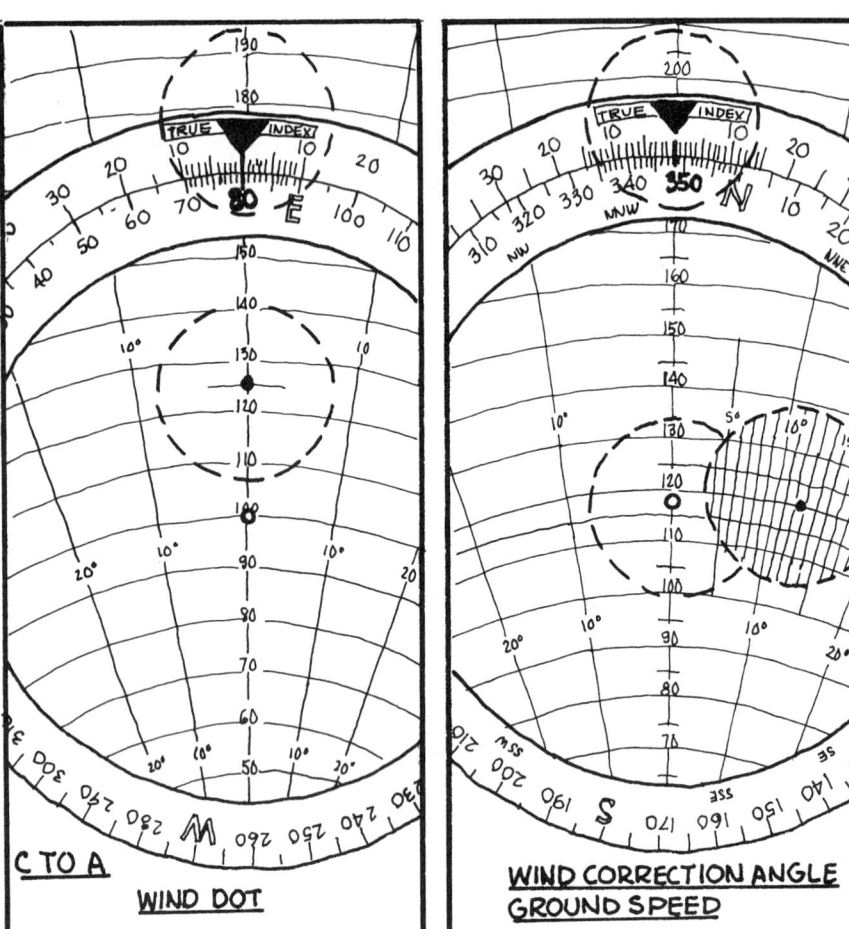

Fig. 19-S. **Fig. 19-T.**

1918. 2. C to A (see Figs. 19-S, 19-T).

True course	348°	Distance	40 miles
True heading	360°	Groundspeed	118 knots
Variation	−14°	Wind correction	
Magnetic heading	346°	angle	+12°
Deviation	+1°	Estimated time	
Compass heading	347°	enroute	20.3 minutes (call it 20)

Then, finally, A to B to C to A = total time enroute = 1 hour and 16 minutes.

You might find that the wind correction angle (WCA) may be computed at any one of three steps during the process of going from true course to compass heading.

In most cases it won't make any measurable (or flyable) difference, but for the sake of establishing good habits of accuracy for use later when you are commander of a space shuttle, the generally accepted and most accurate method is to use the WCA to find true heading, then correct for variation and deviation to get the *compass heading.* In this procedure, since aloft wind is forecast, or given, as a true direction (and in knots), the first step is to get the true heading and make the corrections as necessary.

The source of possible problems is that the compass deviation varies with the magnetic heading and is noted on the compass correction card for every 30° (see Fig. 19-4, *SPFM*). You might work a particular problem, using magnetic and compass courses for wind correction (remembering that you'll have to convert the wind to magnetic and compass directions), and compare the final compass headings to see the difference, if any.

1919. 1. To compute the actual time elapsed from one checkpoint to another, place the elapsed time under the distance between the checkpoints. In this case place 11 minutes under 20 nautical miles. Read the groundspeed of 109 knots over the rate index (or 60) on the middle scale (see Fig. 19-U).

Actual groundspeed is something that should be computed soon after takeoff and several times enroute, to be sure of your groundspeed and actual time enroute. It is *important* to be sure of the flight time and gas consumption for the trip. It would be tough to run out of fuel because the winds changed.

1920. 1. Place 7.5 under the rate index (or 60). Read the time under 48 on the outer scale = 384 minutes, or 6 hours and 24 minutes (see Fig. 19-V). This is the total time you have available, consuming all the usable fuel. You should not calculate based on the total fuel capacity (50 gallons)

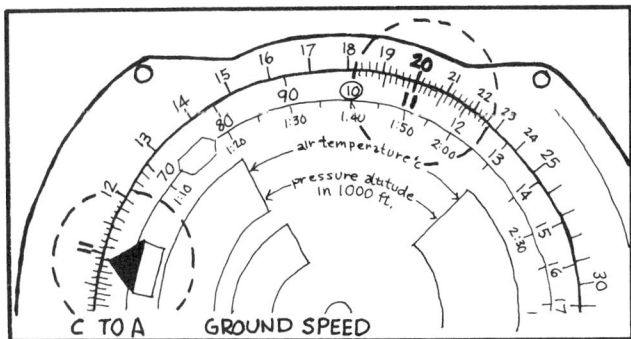

Fig. 19-U.

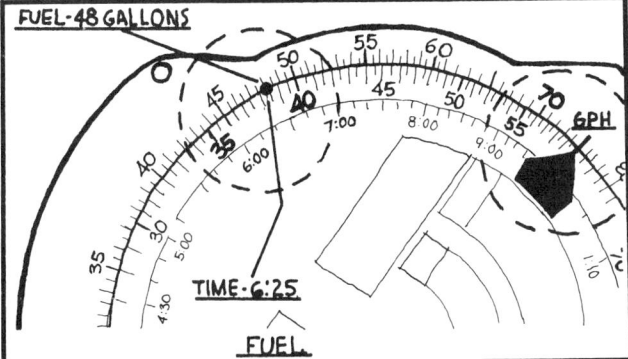

Fig. 19-V.

since 2 gallons are unusable, that is, not available for flight. This is the "time available in your tanks." It is a good idea to check the actual fuel used on a trip and calculate your actual fuel consumption rate in gallons per hour. Take your total flight time and compute this against the amount of fuel used (amount needed to refill the tank). *Example:* The flight was 3 hours and you used a total of 27 gallons. Using your performance charts for taxi, takeoff, climb, cruise, and landing, you can get an accurate picture of the amount of fuel you really consumed for each segment.

Regulations require that before beginning a VFR flight, you should have enough fuel to complete your trip plus being able to fly at normal cruise at least 30 minutes more during the day and 45 minutes at night.

1921.   4.   Figure 19-W shows that you have to place the known factor under its scale, and the conversion is read directly under the other arrow.

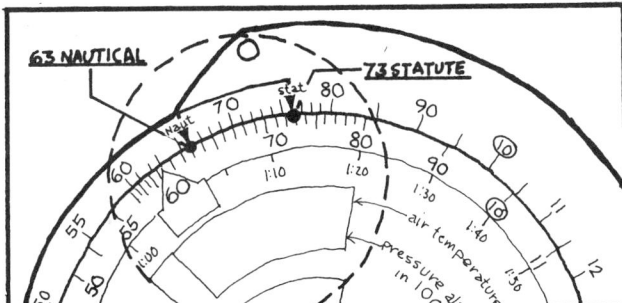

Fig. 19-W.

1922.   1.   The conversion table in Figure 19-X is read on some computers. ATIS gives the surface temperature in Fahrenheit. The charts and windows on most computers use Celsius, since the temperature is given in Celsius above ground level in the Winds Aloft Charts.

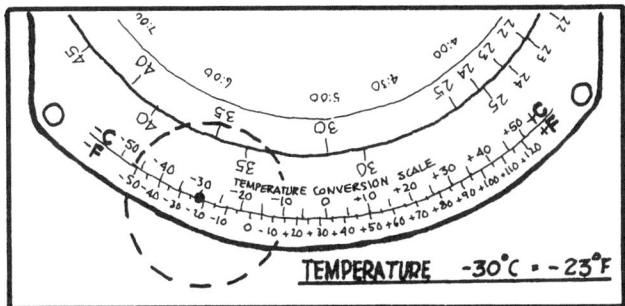

Fig. 19-X.

Your computer will have an instruction manual and sample problems, and you should practice with it until you fully understand how it works.

You may have an electronic computer that will work problems down to 5 figures, but for practical application it's best to call times to the nearest half-minute, fuel to the nearest 0.1 of a gallon, and headings or courses to the nearest degree. You need to be accurate but also practical.

ANSWERS TO COMPUTER EXERCISES

Exercise A: Computation of True Airspeed

Pressure Altitude	Free Air Temperature	Calibrated Airspeed (knots)	True Airspeed (knots)
3,000 feet	0°C	140	144
8,000 feet	−5°C	160	179
12,000 feet	−10°C	190	226
5,000 feet	+30°C	140	157

Exercise B: Time-Speed-Distance Problems

Time (hours:minutes)	Groundspeed (knots)	Distance (NM)
6:11	104	643
3:32	159	563
0:45	167	125
4:17	133	570

Exercise C: Fuel Consumption Problems

Time (hours:minutes)	Rate (gph)	Usable Fuel (gallons)
7:44	7.5	58
4:25	11.5	50.8
1:20	9.4	12.5
3:45	18.5	69.4

Exercise D: True Altitude

Free Air Temperature	Pressure Altitude	True Altitude
+15°C	6,000 feet	6250
−10°C	10,000 feet	9800

Exercise E: Wind Vectors

Wind Direction	Wind-speed	True Course	True Airspeed	True Heading	Ground-speed
(from) 350°	30	075°	140	063°	134
115°	28	240°	155	231°	169
100°	32	310°	140	317°	167
170°	26	080°	160	089°	158

Exercise F: Wind Vectors (continued)

Wind Direction	Wind-speed	Variation	True Course	True Airspeed	True Heading	Ground-speed	Magnetic Heading
078°	30	3E	190°	175	181°	184	178°
110°	38	8E	028°	200	039°	191	031°
060°	35	10W	130°	180	119°	165	129°
045°	25	1E	292°	165	300°	173	299°

Exercise G: Wind Vectors Corrected to Compass Heading

Wind Direction	Wind-speed	Variation	True Course	Deviation	True Airspeed	True Heading	Ground-speed	Compass Heading
220°	20	2E	340°	+1	160	334°	169	333°
150°	25	0	183°	+3	135	177°	113	180°
230°	10	7W	005°	−2	154	002°	161	007°
070°	20	12W	112°	+2	126	106°	110	120°

Exercise H: Conversion Problems

Statute Miles	Nautical Miles
160	139
276	240
8	7

Celsius	Fahrenheit
+32°	90°
−20°	−4°

CHAPTER 20 — THE CHART AND OTHER PRINTED AIDS

2001. 2. Your problem when using the sectional chart is that of finding the primary meridians and parallels. Figure 20-B shows how, and you can see the meridian 36° and parallel 86° near the top of the chart. You'd move down 15′ from the 36° line to 35°45′N and add 02′ to the 86° mark and find that Sheybogan is the spot. If you *misread* the longitude you might end up 35°45′ and 85°32′, which is closest to Spencer, and is, naturally, one of the answer choices.

2002. 4. The line under the frequency of the radio beacon (326 CJE) indicates that there is *no voice*. You can't transmit on 326 kHz *or*, in this *particular* case, listen on 326 MHz. Note that the box gives the frequency and identification plus the Morse code for that identification. You'd listen to a dash-dot-dash-dot, dot-dash-dash-dash, dot, to check that it is CJE, or Cookeville radio beacon.

2003. 4. Note the box symbols. Each of the three NDBs cited have a line under the frequency, denoting *no* voice transmission capability.

2004. 2. Laying out the routes with a straight-edge, you'd find that the Ellington-Murfreesboro trip would take you right by Puckett and its glider area. The order of right-of-way (assuming that none are in distress) is balloon, glider, airship (blimp or dirigible), airplane or rotorcraft. You're more likely to encounter glider (sailplane) traffic on weekend days of good weather. You'll have to give way to any gliders you encounter on the trip. An aircraft in distress has right-of-way over all other air traffic.

2005. 2. Ellington wins this one at 707 feet above sea level (see the chart in the back of the book).

2006. 4. Since the people on the ground think that *they* are the center of things, the information given is what they can do. So 122.1R means that the facility *receives only* on that frequency. You can't transmit on 110.2 MHz, since it is a VOR frequency.

2007. 1. The 530/02E (third line from the bottom in the Anniston-Calhoun County information) indicates the answer. Note that Runway 5 requires a right traffic pattern; your heading on base would be approximately 320°, not 140° as given by (4).

2008. 4. Since you are approaching on a magnetic course of 080°, you're 260° from the airport and would fall into the frequency required for the area, 226° −007° (counting clockwise, naturally).

2009. 2. Any signals you would get in this area and altitude would be inaccurate.

2010. 1. The notation is "GA 3.0°TCH 26′," which means that the proper glide angle is 3.0°, and on that path the aircraft will cross the runway threshold at a height of 26 feet. This is giving more details than the average student pilot needs, but it is included here to help you get used to using the *Airport/Facility Directory*.

2011. 3. Runway 01L-19R is concrete and grooved to aid in water runoff (to decrease hydroplaning tendencies).

2012. 1. Nashville (BNA) has PATWAS or TIBS.

2013. 2. The printed matter talks in terms of azimuth *from* the VOR (radials).

2014. 1. For the answer to this one, review Figures 20-P and Q and Figure 21-14, *SPFM*.

2015. 3. Although your MSL altitude is high, you are 700 feet above the surface, so you would need 1 statute mile visibility and should remain clear of clouds.

2016. 2. The 20° wind correction to the right would mean that on a magnetic heading of 194° you would be tracking 174° magnetic; the altitude requirements hinge on your ground track, or course, not heading.

2017. 4. See Figure 20-S.

CHAPTER 21 — USING THE RADIO

2101. 1. Best signal strength for most ADFs is found on ANT or REC functions. After you've gotten the best reception, switch to the ADF mode or function.

2102. 4. The ADF receives in the LF/MF range of frequencies, which are noted as kiloHertz (kHz). LF = 30–300 kHz; MF 300–3000 kHz.

2103. 2. Figure 21-3, *SPFM* shows the homing idea.

2104. 3. The magnetic heading is 090° with a relative bearing of 060°. The magnetic bearing to the station is 090° + 060° = 150°.

2105. 3. Since nothing was mentioned about heading, a relative bearing of 290° would require a 70° left turn to have a zero relative bearing to the station. (You'll have to make wind corrections as necessary to *track* to the station.)

2106. 3. The magnetic bearing to the station is 150° + 120° = 270°. You'll have to turn to a heading of 270°, or West, to point the airplane to the station, so you and the airplane are *east* of it.

2107. 4. The first three answers are correct.

2108. 3. The VOR *receiver* is just that and has a spread of from 108.00 to 117.95 MHz, so none of the other frequencies could be picked up.

2109. 2. If your OBS setting and heading are close, you'd "fly" toward the needle. See Figures 21-B and 21-C.

2110. 1. See Figures 21-B and 21-C again.

2111. 1. The VHF frequencies are static-free as compared to lower frequencies, and VOR cross-checks can be a good navigation aid in flat areas of sparse checkpoints. As noted in Chapter 25, *SPFM*, the cross-checks give you an idea of the *area* you're in.

2112. 4. Radials are numbered as *outbound* from the VOR, so the 045 radial is northeast of the station.

2113. 4. All the statements are correct. Maybe answer 3 needs clarifying. Assume A, B, and C in Figure 21-J are positions of an airplane as it flies from south to north. When the 270 radial is selected at A, the TO-FROM indicator will indicate FROM and the needle will be to the right (toward the station). As the airplane progresses, the needle will center when the selected radial is reached and then indicate left, *away* from the station. One technique when taking a VOR cross-bearing (as being done here) is to "turn" the airplane in your mind to the selected bearing (270) and note that the needle always "points" to the radial. ("Turn" airplanes A–F to 270° and note the needle position for each.) Instrument pilots, when getting VOR cross-bearing information, select the radial (so the TO-FROM says FROM) and note that if the relative position of the needle and of the VOR station are the same, the radial has not been reached. Note that at A the needle and station are to the right. At D *both* are to the left. C and F needles and VOR relative positions don't match, so the selected radial has been passed.

2114. 2. This one is close to question 2113. Note that the station is off to the left (090 FROM is being indicated). The needle (left) and VOR relative positions match so that the selected radial has not been passed.

2115. 1. If you set up a needle-centered FROM reading, it's easy to draw lines outward from the VOR rose. Usually two VORs are sufficient to get your area of position, but three could be better. You'd tune in the stations *one at a time* unless your trainer is so well equipped as to have three VOR receivers. Don't land in the nearest pasture because (a) it could be dangerous and (b) the farmer might not be at home anyway.

2116. 2. One memory aid in using a VOT is to think of the Cessna 182 airplane (180-TO). Then "obviously" it should be 360-FROM. If your airplane has an RMI (Radio Magnetic Indicator), it will indicate 180° on any OBS setting. One instructor tells his students to assume that all VOTs are at the South Pole. Some of the airplanes at the airport will have an RMI, and you might ask your instructor to discuss how it works.

2117. 1. Transmitting on 122.1 MHz and listening on a local VOR frequency usually cuts down on interference of transmissions from other FSSs.

2118. 3. Note that "emergency situation" was used. If you need help and can't communicate, the procedure indicated would be valid. If you're flying out of the local uncontrolled airport on a sunny afternoon, find you can't get anybody on the Unicom, and use the transponder in such a fashion, you could lose friends in nearby FAA facilities. If you are on the way in to a busy, controlled airport and lose communications on that sunny day, why not land at a less-congested airport in the area and, if you *have* to go on in, discuss the matter by phone. *Always* keep looking for other airplanes, communications or not.

2119. 1. Look back at Figure 21-G.

2120. 1. See Figure 21-F.

2121. 4. The majority of ground control frequencies are 121.7, 121.8, or 121.9 MHz. The controller may eliminate the "121" part of the frequency. Change over to ground control *only* after the tower says to do so.

2122. 3. You'd listen to ATIS and get the word on the wind, weather, and runway(s) and, when approach control is contacted, would tell them you have "Delta" (or "Foxtrot," etc.). You'll be switched to tower frequency and, later, ground control when applicable.

2123. 1. As the name implies, it's essential but routine information for that *terminal*.

2124. 2. You'll transmit *and* receive on this frequency.

2125. 3. Only answer 3 would be pertinent to Flight Watch. An FSS would have (or would get) the information to the services in the other three answers.

2126. 2. Check the explanation for question 2122.

2127. 1. The sectional chart *and* the *Airport/Facility Directory* have the Unicom frequency for a particular airport.

2128. 4. If you ask for a *weather briefing*, the FSS can give you the details needed for your trip, including any severe weather or navigation problems you might encounter. Telling them the route, time of departure, and expected time enroute will help. (Tell them that you are a student pilot.)

2129. 3. This answer makes common sense, but some-

184

ANSWERS/EXPLANATIONS TO QUESTIONS

times student pilots think the system is more complex than it is. The other answers are wrong because: (1) the Center doesn't need anybody crying on its shoulder (except in an emergency); (2) it may be very important for you to talk to the FSS and, after all, the facility exists only to help pilots; and (4) *don't assume anything in aviation.*

2130. 3. The Airport Advisory Service preferred frequency is 123.6 MHz, but you may use others available; 122.2 MHz is a frequency common to all FSSs for transmitting *and* receiving. The frequencies for a particular FSS are given in the *Airport/Facility Directory.*

2131. 2. Look at Figure 21-H for the pronunciation of the various numbers. (*Niner* is used to keep it from being confused with five or *fife.*) Again, you should tell the FSS on what frequency you'll be listening. (An FSS gives *advisories,* not takeoff clearances.)

2132. 4. This answer was pretty obvious since, as you know, 121.5 MHz is the emergency frequency.

2133. 3. This is given in Chapter 21, *SPFM,* but for more detail on the VASI you might want to review *AIM.*

2134. 2. You must taxi clear of the landing area now in use (runway). Answer 3 would be bad because that's what you are *not* supposed to do. (*Stop there,* that is.) Answer 4 *is for airborne aircraft* and doesn't mean that on the ground you would stay out of everybody's way and taxi in circles. (See Fig. 21-16, *SPFM.*)

CHAPTER 22—WEATHER INFORMATION

2201. 3. Standard sea level may be expressed in many ways, as in the question. The correct answers could be: 29.92 inches Hg, 1013.2 mb, 760 mm Hg, 14.7 psi, and 2116 psf.

2202. 3. A high-pressure area *usually* means good weather but always has clockwise circulation in the Northern Hemisphere.

2203. 4. The cold front as depicted by the symbol shown in (4) normally moves faster than a warm front and has a comparatively narrow band of weather and cumulus clouds. These are not the only features; you should also be aware of heavy precipitation and turbulence as important factors.

2204. 2. In the Northern Hemisphere the Coriolis force deflects the winds to the right; in the Southern Hemisphere it deflects them to the left. Torque and P-factor are forces that affect engine/propeller-driven airplanes.

2205. 2. All these characteristics are usually apparent on the passage of a fast-moving cold front. The warm front usually involves a slow clearing process.

2206. 4. See Figure 22-2, *SPFM* for the frontal system symbols. The warm front normally moves about one-half the speed of a cold front (see Fig. 22-H).

2207. 4. The weather is generally similar to a warm front, usually not as intense but of longer duration.

Fig. 22-H. Characteristics of "typical" warm and cold fronts. The vertically developed clouds may produce clear ice, whereas the status type (stable air) clouds usually associated with warm fronts may produce rime icing at or above the freezing level.

ANSWERS/EXPLANATIONS TO QUESTIONS 185

2208. 3. *Families* of clouds are distinct from *types* of clouds, which are described by form and appearance.
2209. 2. The higher clouds—cirrus, cirrostratus, and cirrocumulus—are composed of extremely fine ice crystals.
2110. 3. The normal lapse rate of air is 2°C (3.5 °F) per 1000 feet. The lapse rate could vary depending on the moisture in the air, but the figures given are for "average air."
2211. 1. If you look at the various illustrations of fronts, you'll see that all the diagrams show the warm air above the cold.
2212. 2. Isobars are lines joining points of equal pressure. (See Fig. 22-3, *SPFM*.)
2213. 3. Stratus clouds are layered.
2214. 4. Check Figure 22-I for the stages of hail production.

2215. 2. Mature stage. Incidentally, what is a peristatic genesis?
2216. 1. Trying to outclimb one of these is a losing proposition for most light aircraft.
2217. 4. See Figure 22-J.

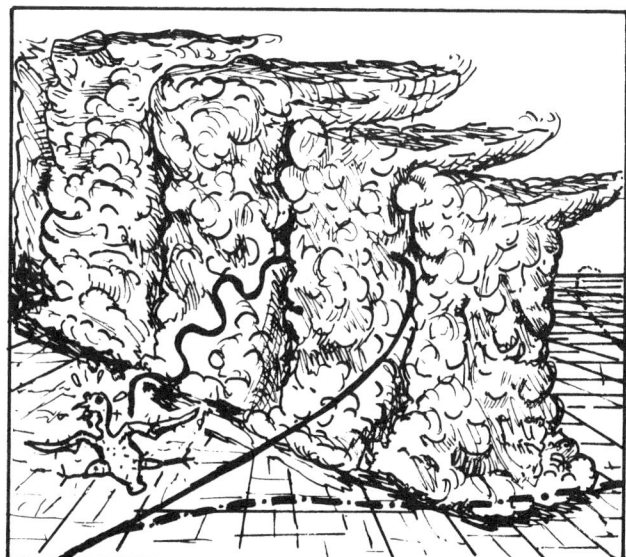

Fig. 22-J. An airplane should fly the dashed-line route, staying safely away (at least 5 miles) from the cloud and overhang, or complete the 180° turn well *before* getting to the squall line. Note that the turkey who tried to go through lost some feathers.

2218. 4. This might be a good conversation starter at your next party.
2219. The numbers in the blanks should read, starting from the top: 1, 5, 4, 3, 2.
2220. 3. Euphoria's borders are closed to tourists so (4) couldn't be the answer although euphoria (good feelings) *is* a symptom of hypoxia; that's why it's dangerous.
2221. 1. See Figure 22-K.
2222. 4. 15°C at sea level. The answer of 59°C would be hot indeed.
2223. 1. °C = 5/9(°F − 32); °F = (9/5 × °C) + 32.
2224. 4. Indicated altitude.
2225. 2. See Figure 22-L.
2226. 2. The Coriolis force is directly proportional to the wind speed as mentioned in *Aviation Weather*.
2227. 1. Wind shear has caused airliners (and other airplanes) to crash on takeoff or approach. See Figure 13-35, *SPFM*.
2228. 2. The rough surface of the frost causes early separation of the air over the wing, resulting in a loss of lift.
2229. 4. Answer (1) would seem like a logical choice, but read the question again carefully.
2230. 1. Read the section on "Weather Sequences" in *SPFM*.
2231. 4. This seems like a simple question, but the term is used fairly often on aviation weather reports, particularly in winter snow showers. Incidentally, the process of a substance going from a solid directly to a gas, bypassing the liquid stage, is called *sublimation*. You may have

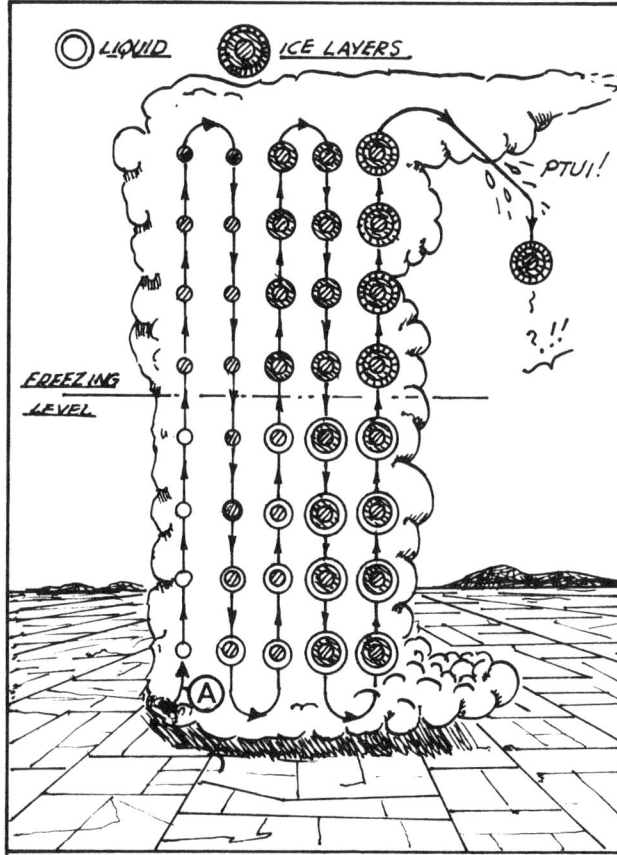

Fig. 22-I. The strong vertical currents of the cumulonimbus cloud can cause overstress of the airplane, and hail is created as an additional hazard. Shown here is a stylized version of how hail is formed. The cycle starts at (A) with rain being lifted and frozen; it then falls, picking up more liquid at the lower altitudes. The pellet is raised and that new liquid is frozen. This cycle may be repeated several times, resulting in the "layered" look of hail. The bird shown is in the clear, but it may have a midair with a goodly sized hailstone that has been spat out of the anvil head. Stay well away when circumnavigating thunderstorms, not only because of the hail but also because of turbulent air nearby. Needless to say, the bird and hailstones are not to scale with each other or to the cloud.

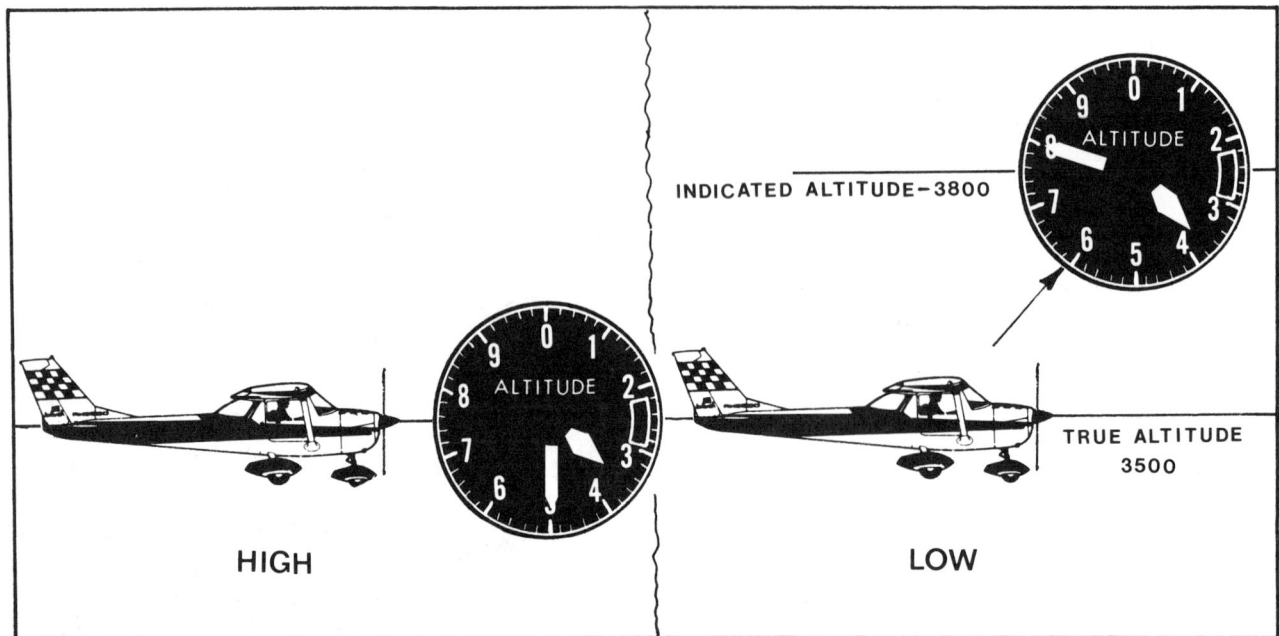

Fig. 22-K. Flying from a high-pressure area to a low-pressure area without resetting the altimeter results in the altimeter indicating erroneously high.

Fig. 22-L. Convection currents are good for sailplanes, but on summer days they can cause some too-high approaches.

missed this one since it wasn't stated in *SPFM*, but you'll know it now, right?

2232. 2. This one was so obvious that it may have fooled you.
2233. 3. You can tell your airsick passengers that unstable air, not your flying, caused their misery. If, however, they get sick in stable air, better check your flying.
2234. 2. You might check Figure 22-11, *SPFM*.
2235. 4. If that layer had been *thin* broken it would not have been given as the ceiling.
2236. 2. Visibility is given in *statute* miles. See Figure 22-11, *SPFM*.
2237. 1. See Figure 22-11, *SPFM*.
2238. 1. See Figure 22-11, *SPFM*. The peak wind or windshift time is recorded.
2239. 4. It's "less than 6 knots."
2240. 4. 6 statute miles.
2241. 2. Review "terminal forecasts" in *SPFM*.
2242. 4. These are the minimums for marginal VFR.
2243. 3. See Figure 22-11, *SPFM*.
2244. 3. Review AIRMETS in *SPFM*.
2245. 1. Review SIGMETS in *SPFM*.
2246. 2. UA has to mean that the report came from Up in the Air. (See Fig. 22-M.)
2247. 3. The best way to remember the temperature effects on the altimeter is to remember HALT. (*High Altimeter because of Low Temperature.*) In that case, the altimeter indicates *higher* than the actual altitude of the airplane, so HALT before you fly into that mountain you think will be cleared so well. Remembering HALT, you can go the other way and know that a higher temperature would mean that the altimeter would read *low*, a safer condition for terrain clearance. These temperature corrections can be done on most computers (see Fig. 22-N).
2248. 4. 0204 is 020° (true) at 4 knots.
2249. 1. The designation RS (Record Special) is a scheduled observation indicating a significant change in one or more of the reporting elements. That's Zulu time for HSV tower operating hours.
2250. 2. A Beech 90 made the report of light to moderate turbulence to CSV. The ceiling (1) at MKL is *ragged*. Runway 02 Left at BNA has a visual range of 6000 feet and answer (3) had nothing to do with drizzle or rain beginning. The altimeter setting at MEM (4) is 30.06 inches Hg.
2251. 2. A special was put out at 1712Z indicating such a visibility and ceiling drop.

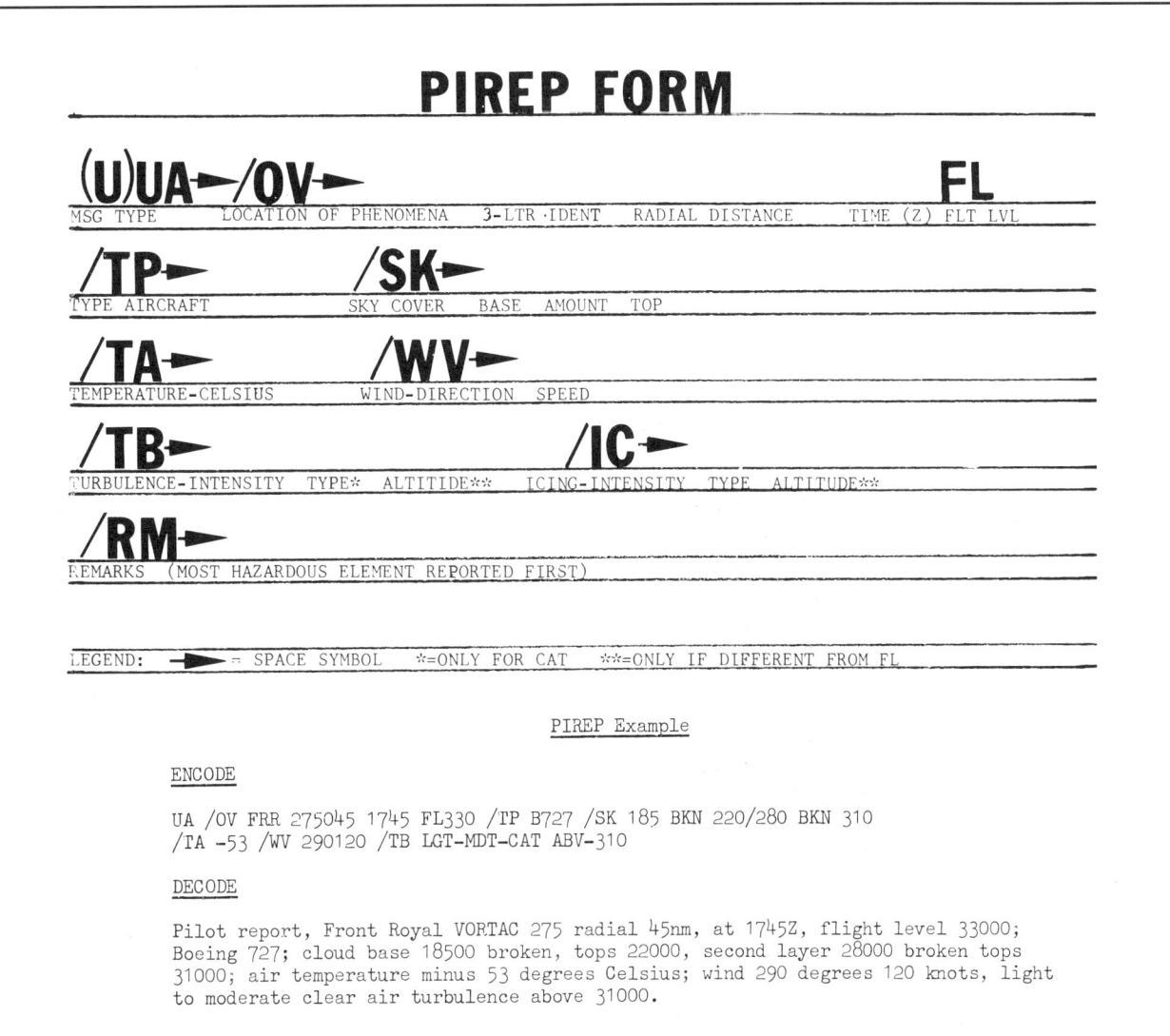

Fig. 22-M. Pilot report form and example.

2252. 4. The drizzle ended at 30 minutes past the last hour.

2253. 3. 0400 CST is 1000Z, and the forecast is as given in that choice.

2254. 1. Huntsville. Between 1000Z (0400 CST) and 1600Z (1000 CST), HSV is forecast to have a ceiling of 500 overcast, 2 miles in light rain and fog. (2) Crossville, between 0900Z (0300 CST) and 1600Z (1000 CST), is forecast to have a ceiling of 800 overcast and 3 miles in light drizzle and fog. (3) McKellar, between 1000Z (0400 CST) and 1600Z (1000 CST), is forecast to have a ceiling of 800 overcast, 3 miles in light rain and fog. (4) Nashville, between 1100Z (0500 CST) and 1600Z (1000 CST), is forecast to have a ceiling of 1200 overcast, 2 miles in light rain and fog. So . . . Huntsville is forecast to have the worst weather at 0600 CST.

2255. 1. This one needs a little discussion. In *SPFM* it's noted that a ceiling of less than 500 feet and/or visibility of less than 1 mile constitute the condition LIFR (Low IFR). The visibility of ¾ mile is the factor here. The point is that the weather was forecast to be IFR, which is too bad for a student or a noninstrument rated pilot to try to fly in.

2256. 4. LLWS stands for Low-Level Wind Shear. (If you didn't know the answer earlier, now you do, and can check for this on your future cross-countries.)

2257. 2. The conditions are forecast to be continuing beyond 2200Z. The other answers don't match the conditions cited.

2258. 3. Reading the area forecast carefully, you see that the coastal waters will have scattered to broken clouds at 2000-3000 feet, layered to 12,000 feet in the eastern portion. The other portions listed have layers starting at 3000-5000 feet, are clear, or have cirrus (CI) clouds.

2259. 2. There will occasionally be ceilings below 1000 feet and visibilities below 3 miles in stratus, fog, and precipitation.

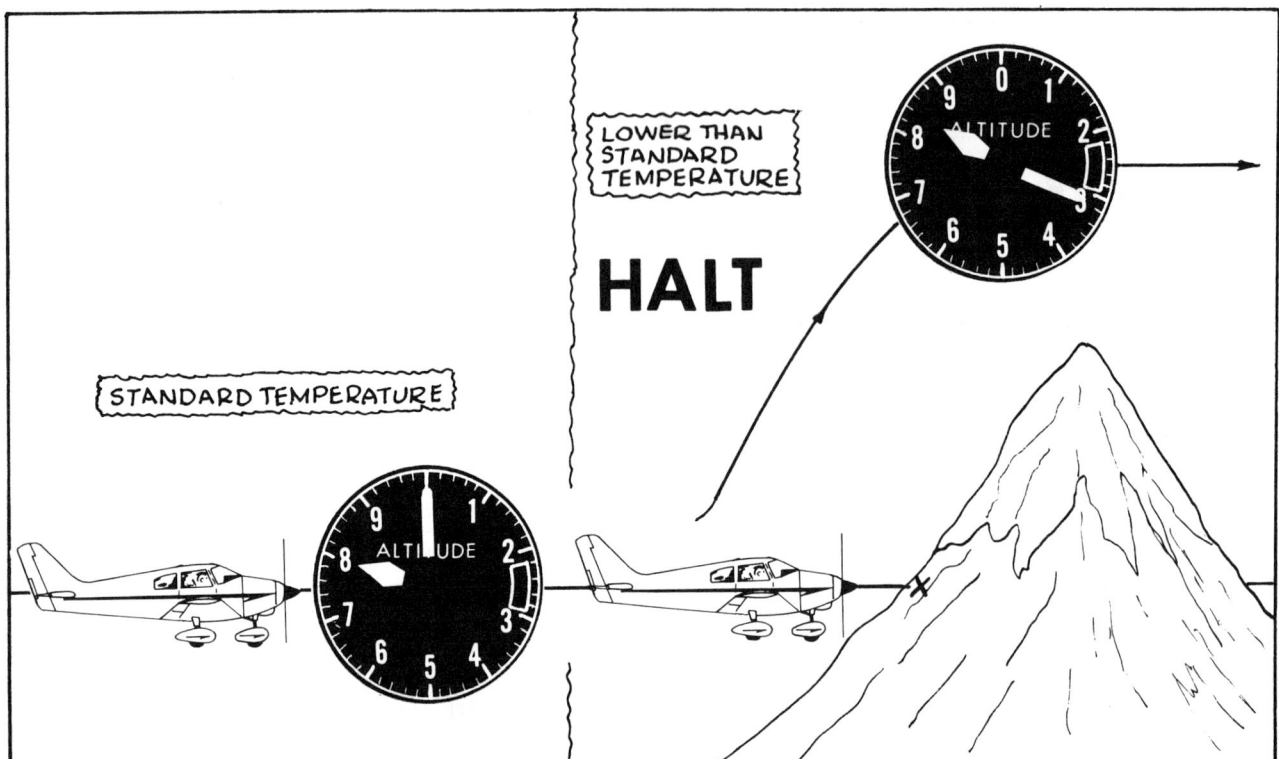

Fig. 22-N. HALT. There is a *H*igh *A*ltimeter because of *L*ow *T*emperature. The altimeter shows that the airplane could clear that mountain when actually it wouldn't. This will be of even more importance when you start working on that instrument rating and are concerned about terrain clearance when on solid instruments.

2260.   3.   9900 means less than 5 knots and is described as light and variable.

2261.   2.   As *SPFM* indicates, there isn't any 750° direction, so you'd subtract 50 from the 75 to get 25 (250°) and add 100 to the 02 to get 102 knots. The temperature is −51° *Celsius*.

2262.   4.   30 (300°) true at 09 (9) knots and a temperature of +1° *Celsius*.

2263.   1.   The Surface Analysis Chart is the winner here.

2264.   3.   The front (a warm front here) moves in the direction in which the projections are pointing, so it's moving northwest.

2265.   2.   The Low north of Montana has a pressure of 997.0 mb. You might mistakenly want to call it 29.97 inches of mercury.

2266.   4.   Note that the isobars are closest together on route A to C, indicating a faster rate of change of pressure.

2267.   2.   On the route from A to B the isobars are relatively the farthest apart, showing a slow rate of change of pressure enroute.

2268.   3.   AVL, STL, and IND are within a smooth-line boundary that encloses areas of IFR conditions (ceiling less than 1000 feet and/or visibility less than 3 miles).

2269.   1.   DSM, BNA, and HAR are in areas enclosed by the scalloped line and are in MVFR conditions (ceiling 1000–3000 feet inclusive and/or visibility 3–5 miles inclusive).

2270.   4.   GFK, PHX, and CRP are not in an outlined area and have ceilings of 3000 feet, or unlimited, and visibility greater than 5 miles.

CHAPTER 23 — THE CROSS-COUNTRY:
KNOWING YOUR AIRPLANE

2301.   2.   The airworthiness certicate is the only document required to be *displayed*. The aircraft and engine logbooks must be available for inspection, so for local flights most schools keep them in the office. In Chapter 21, *SPFM* under "Distance Measuring Equipment" it was indicated that equipment had to be listed on the radio station license because a signal was being transmitted from the airplane. This would go for the transponder also.

2302.   1.   The measure of the load factor is the lift-to-weight ratio. The lift (6000 pounds) is 3 times the weight (2000 pounds).

2303.   2.   The maneuvering speed, by definition, is found as the stall speed (flaps up) times the square root of the airplane's limit load factor. A normal category airplane with a limit load factor (positive) of 3.8 g's and a 60-knot stall speed at maximum weight would have a maneuvering speed of

$\sqrt{3.8} \times 60 = 1.95 \times 60 = 117$ knots. The maneuvering speed would decrease as weight went down because the stall speed decreases with lighter weights. At a lighter weight, the stall speed might be down to 50 knots so that the maneuvering speed would be $1.95 \times VS_1 = 1.95 \times 50 = 97.5$ knots. A quick rule of thumb to find V_A at lighter weights is to decrease the maneuvering speed by *one-half* the percentage of airplane weight decrease. As an example, suppose for an airplane at its maximum certificated weight of 3000 pounds the published V_A is 120 knots. At 2400 pounds (a decrease in weight of 20 percent) the maneuvering speed would be decreased by one-half that percentage, or 10 percent. The maneuvering speed for that airplane is $120 - (10$ percent of $120) = 120 - 12 = 108$ knots. If you're flying at 2400 pounds, you'd have to slow it up to *108* knots (*not* 120 knots) to avoid exceeding the (positive) limit load factor of 3.8 g's.

Again, the *limit* load factor is the number of g's that can be imposed on the airframe without permanent deformation occurring. The *ultimate* load factor is 50 percent higher (5.7 g's positive for the normal category airplane), and above that the structure will fail. In other words, you'll bend it above 3.8 g's and break it above 5.7 g's. The limit and ultimate load factors on the *negative* side for a normal category airplane are -1.52 g's and -2.28 g's respectively. These numbers are for a new airplane that hasn't been landed many times by students.

If you stay below the pertinent V_A, the airplane will stall before you are able to exert over 3.8 g's (or 4.4 g's for the utility category).

Lower weight, *lower* maneuvering speed. Also see "Load Factors in the Turn" in Chapter 9, *SPFM*.

2304.   3.   A normal category airplane has a positive load factor of 3.8 g's. The square root of 3.8 is 1.95 and, as shown in the last answer, is the multiplier of the stall speed to get V_A.

2305.   4.   The weight has decreased 20 percent from 4000 pounds, so the maneuvering speed should be decreased by 10 percent, or by 14 knots, to 126 knots. The *Pilot's Operating Handbook* lists the lower maneuvering speeds for lower weights, but you should have a rough idea of how weight affects V_A.

2306.   1.   Multiply each weight by its arm, getting a moment. Add the moments together and divide the total moment by the total weight.

Weight (lb)	Arm (inches)	Moment (pound-inches)
10	10	100
15	18	270
5	28	140
30		510

510/30 = 17 inches

2307.   2.   Review Figure 23-5, *SPFM*. Working the problems and starting with airplane A, assume that the lift is a string holding the airplane up in straight and level cruising flight and that all moments and forces must be balanced. The nose-down moment is 3000 pounds $\times$ 2 inches = 6000 pound-inches. This must be balanced by a tail-down moment of 6000 pound-inches. With an arm of 150 inches, in order to get the proper moment, the tail-down *force* must be 40 pounds $(6000/150 = 40)$. Summing up the vertical forces, it's found that $3000 + 40 = 3040$ pounds of lift required.

Solving for *your* airplane (B), you'll find that the tail-down force must be 200 pounds or your airplane must "carry" 3200 pounds and fly at an angle of attack (with added drag) to do it. Your competitor will be faster under the requirements established here, since her airplane only "weighs" 3040 pounds.

Because airplane A is carrying less of a load, it will stall at a lower airspeed (but at the same angle of attack as yours).

Your airplane (B) with a more forward CG will be more stable in turbulent air than your competitor's. This is not to imply that airplane A is *unstable*, but yours will be easier to fly under those conditions. Figure 23-J is an actual stall-speed chart for most forward and rearward angles of attack. Note in this case that only a small difference is made, but it's there.

2308.   4.   You'd multiply each weight by its arm from the datum.

$$570 \text{ pounds} \times 40 \text{ inches} = 22{,}800$$
$$(640 + 630) \times 100 \text{ inches} = \underline{+127{,}000}$$
$$149{,}800 \text{ pound-inches}$$

The center of gravity position is moment/weight $= 149{,}800/1840 = 81.4$ inches (rounded off).

STALL SPEEDS

CONDITION: Power Off

MOST REARWARD CENTER OF GRAVITY

WEIGHT LBS	FLAP DEFLECTION	ANGLE OF BANK							
		0°		30°		45°		60°	
		KIAS	KCAS	KIAS	KCAS	KIAS	KCAS	KIAS	KCAS
1600	UP	46	48	49	52	55	57	65	68
	10°	44	45	47	48	52	54	62	64
	40°	42	42	45	45	50	50	59	59

MOST FORWARD CENTER OF GRAVITY

WEIGHT LBS	FLAP DEFLECTION	ANGLE OF BANK							
		0°		30°		45°		60°	
		KIAS	KCAS	KIAS	KCAS	KIAS	KCAS	KIAS	KCAS
1600	UP	47	49	51	53	56	58	66	69
	10°	45	46	48	49	54	55	64	65
	40°	42	42	45	45	50	50	59	59

Fig. 23-J. Actual stall-speed variations with CG positions. Calibrated airspeed and 0° angle of bank with zero degrees flaps is underlined, but you can make comparisons in any configuration and bank.

ANSWERS/EXPLANATIONS TO QUESTIONS

2309. 2. Adding the empty weight, passengers, and baggage (1840 + 732 + 80 = 2652 pounds), you'd have 348 pounds left for fuel. Since aviation gasoline weighs 6 pounds per gallon, there would be 58 gallons (nearly a full load) available.

2310. 3. Adding up people (290 pounds), BAGGAGE (90 pounds), FUEL (90 pounds), and the airplane (1120 pounds), you get 1590 pounds. Using the loading graph for each "item," you'd find

Item	Weight (lb)	Moment (pound-inches)
Airplane	1120	37,200
People	290	11,300
Baggage	90	5,800
Fuel (15 gallons)	90	3,800
	1590	58,100

58,100/1590 = *36.5* inches aft of datum (rounded off). Looking at the CG limits, you see that you are safe. Be sure to double check and use the proper slope line in the Loading Graph (Fig. 23-D) when establishing the moment. (This is one of the most common errors.)

Note that the destination and time of year of the flight was not indicated. Why are you two taking swim suits and snorkeling gear to International Falls, Minnesota, in January?

2311. 1. Checking the moments first and again assuming that lift is a "string holding the airplane up," note that the nose-down moment is 2000 pounds × 6 inches = 12,000 pound-inches. The tail-down moment must also be 12,000 pound-inches, and the arm of 200 inches requires a force of *60 pounds* tail-down force to get that moment. Lift must equal the weight (2000) and downforce (60) and is *2060 pounds*. The area of the horizontal tail is 30 square feet, so that 60/30 = *2 psf*.

2312. 3. As *SPFM* says, people can get into trouble in an aft-loaded airplane when it climbs out of ground effect.

2313. 1. Continue the preflight check and make your flight. Green (in the United States) is the color of Grade 100/130. You wouldn't want to replace it with red-dyed fuel (Grade 80) because this *could* cause detonation (answer 2). Answer (3) is wrong because why should you drain 100/130 and replace it with 100/130? Answer (4) is wrong because you have the proper fuel and should operate the airplane normally.

2314. 4. Aviation 80 is SAE 40 and is "thinner" than Aviation 100. The others are all oils of higher viscosity (heavier), which would not be desirable in colder temperatures.

2315. 1. You would find the time, fuel, and distance for a climb from sea level to 7500 feet (interpolating between 7000 and 8000 feet). You'd then find the numbers for sea level to 1500 feet (again interpolating). Subtract the 1500-foot figures from the 7500-foot figures to get the answer.

2316. 2. The *rule of thumb* in *SPFM* indicates that 25 rpm should be added per thousand feet. At 6000 feet you would require an extra 150 rpm (6 × 25) to maintain 65 percent. The sea level value is 2400 rpm, so the answer is 2550 rpm.

2317. 2. The engine uses the same amount of fuel at 65 percent at any altitude if properly leaned. Go forward and check Figure 23-G.

2318. 4. Answer (1) can't be correct because the battery in an airplane has nothing to do with ignition. If you chose this answer, move back to Chapters 3 and 4 of this book and *SPFM*. Answer (2) should have been eliminated by the long discussion of "how dry the air is." However, you should use carburetor heat, switch tanks, and go through your recommended checklist for engine problems, as always. Answer (3) wouldn't cut it because you are at a low altitude and the density altitude should be low, so even if the mixture is full rich, there shouldn't be any problem. The probable cause, based on the information here, is answer (4); you forgot to richen the mixture before or during the descent.

2319. 1. You'll have to interpolate here. The temperature (+5°C) is standard for 5000 feet; but 5000 feet is not given, so you'd go to 4000 feet standard temperature and split the difference between 2700 and 2600 rpm to get an answer of 5.5 gallons per hour (gph). Doing the same for 6000 feet, the answer is halfway between 4.8 gph at 2600 rpm and 5.4 gph at 2700 rpm, or *5.1* gph. Finally, you'd get the average of consumption at 4000 feet (5.5 gph) and 6000 feet (5.1 gph) to find an answer of *5.3 gph*.

2320. 2. The standard temperature at 6000 feet is +3°C. (Sea level standard + 15°C; the normal lapse rate is −2°C per thousand feet, so at 6000 feet the temperature is 15°C − 12°C = +3°C.) The temperature given is +13°C, or 10°C above standard, at 6000 feet. You would find the fuel consumption at 2400 and 2500 rpm at the standard temperature and split the difference for a value of *4.1* gph. The same would be done for 20°C above standard for 2400 and 2500 rpm, again finding the average fuel consumption for 2450 rpm to be *3.9 gph*. Since the question asks for the *fuel consumption at a value of 10°C above normal* an answer (finally) is obtained of 4.0 gph (answer 2). (It's easier to make up these questions than to answer them.)

2321. 2. Looking in Figure 23-G at the standard temperature column and (once more) interpolating to get the true airspeed of 98 knots, you move to Figure 23-H for 98 knots at 4000 feet to get a range of 370 NM.

2322. 3. Answer (1) is wrong because, as indicated in *SPFM*, you might find out that tank wasn't working right at a bad time right after the lift-off. Answer (2) is not a good procedure because that other tank may give a problem when you are low during the climbout (crunch). Answer (4), for all its pontifical declaration, could cause real problems as noted in "Fuel Management" in Chapter 23, *SPFM*.

2323. 4. A careful check shows that an electric fuel pump is a part of the system for this low-wing airplane.

2324. 3. Note in fuel system (A) that if the mixture is pulled to idle cutoff, or "pulled out of the socket," the carburetor is not sending any fuel to the cylinders. The primer furnishes a separate source of fuel and may be used to get intermittent bursts of power at the throttle setting given. (You'd pull it out, let it fill, then push it in for a jackrabbit sort of progress.) This might stretch the descent some, but the idea is brought up here to make you aware of the components of the fuel system.

2325. 4. The order is mixture, prop, and throttle.
2326. 1. Throttle back, prop control back (reduce rpm), and then set (lean) the mixture.

CHAPTER 24—NAVIGATION PLANNING

2401. 1. The isogonic line (1° W) crosses the course to Crossville so that a true course of 041° gives a magnetic course of 042°. Your measurement may be off 1° either way. As noted in *SPFM*, estimate the course line so that you won't read the plotter backward and start off in the general direction of Huntsville (Alabama).
2402. 4. You'll cross U.S. Interstate 24 and U.S. 41. You may have to look on the chart along any major highway to find the number; the point is for you to be aware that such information is available on the sectional chart.
2403. 2. That's Coalmont and it has a road, abandoned railroad, and a power line running through it.
2404. 4. Sandy is listed as a private airport and is not hard-surfaced, but note that it's 4000 feet long. As you turn west toward it, you will be flying toward better terrain (farming land) west of the Cumberland Plateau. If you see that Sandy, which is on the plateau, is unsuitable, you'll have better landing areas just west of it. Or you might then work your way back to Sewanee over good terrain.
2405. 1. BCEG.
   B. Beersheba Springs is on top of the escarpment (Fig. 24-E).

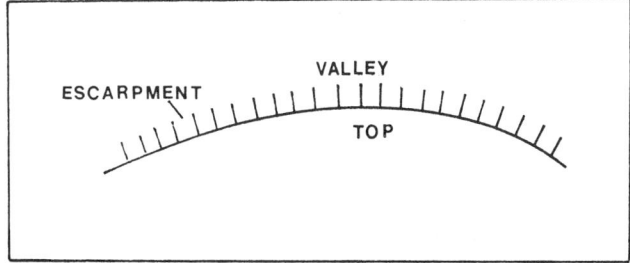

Fig. 24-E. Symbol for an escarpment on the sectional chart.

   C. Looking at the chart you can see Tarlton is at the bottom of the escarpment.
   E. Altamont has a water tank just southeast of town.
   G. Looking at the chart and comparing the markings to Figure 24-B, you can see that there is a valley (or cove, as the mountain people call it) that you'll cross southeast and east of Beersheba Springs.
2406. 2. Use the corner of a sheet of paper to check the 90° angle from the course.
2407. 3. Shortly after this you will fly over a strip mine.

2408. 1. You should be abeam of a dam (and lake), which is about 1½ miles right of course.
2409. 3. The average IAS (CAS) during the climb is 65 knots for a TAS of 69 knots at 4000 feet density altitude. Using a computer with an average wind for the climb of 210° at 13 knots, the groundspeed is found to be 82 knots. The time to climb, using Figure 24-B, is 7 minutes for a distance of 9.6 NM (call it 10).
2410. 4. At 64 percent at standard temperature at 5500 feet the TAS is 99 knots. After using the computer for the wind at 6000 feet (2616), the true heading and groundspeed respectively are 036° and 111 knots. The variation for this leg is 0°; looking at the compass card in Figure 24-B, you see that 4° is to be subtracted to give a compass heading of 032°.
2411. 3. The airplane took off at 1128 CST and required 7 minutes to climb from 2000 feet to 5500 feet (see Fig. 24-B) and required 10 NM in the climb. The cruise and letdown portion (49 NM) required 27 minutes, for a total of 34 minutes; 1128 + 34 = 1202 CST.
2412. 3. The fuel used for the climb from Sewanee (2000 feet) to cruise altitude (5500 feet) would be (see Fig. 24-B):
   a. Fuel required to climb from sea level to 2000 feet = 0.5 gallons.
   b. Fuel required to climb from sea level to 5500 feet (interpolate between 5000 and 6000 feet to get a total of 1.5 gallons)—since you are *starting* at 2000 feet altitude, the amount required is 1.5 − 0.5 = *1.0 gallons*. Start, taxi, and takeoff require *0.8 gallons*. The distance required for the climb is 10 miles at a groundspeed of 82 knots, leaving 49 miles to be flown at cruise (111 knots). This cruise portion would require 27 minutes. At 64 percent the fuel consumption is 4.8 gph, and 27 minutes of cruise operation would require *2.2 gallons*. So . . .

Start, taxi, and take off	0.8
Climb	1.0
Cruise	2.2
	4.0 gallons

2413. 2. Figure 24-A and the chart have the elevation as 1881 feet. The VOR (Hinch Mountain) used at Crossville is at an elevation of *3040 feet*. Don't be thinking in terms of the airport elevation if you are flying toward the VOR in less than good visibility conditions.
2414. 2. Okay, you may want to go back through all your calculations on this one, but broken down it's this:

   Time and distance to climb from Sewanee Airport to 5500 feet = 7 minutes and 10 NM
   Time in cruise = 27 minutes (49 NM at 111 knots)
   Total time enroute = 34 minutes
   Departure time = 1128 CST; arrival time 1202 CST.

   You'll be descending from 5500 MSL to 3500 MSL, or descending 2000 feet at 500 fpm. You'll have to start 4 minutes before the ETA, or at 1158 CST. Of course, on the trip itself you'd start the descent at a position or time based on actual groundspeed and other factors.

2415. 4. The recommended Airport Advisory Service frequency for talkin' *and* listenin' is 123.6 MHz. The FSS doesn't transmit on 122.1 MHz or on Unicom; 121.5 MHz is the emergency frequency, and you wouldn't use it for routine communications. Other frequencies are listed in the *A/FD*. If you are in doubt, 122.2 MHz is assigned to the majority of FSSs as a common enroute frequency.

2416. 1. As the *Airport/Facility Directory* (Fig. 24-A) indicates, the telephone number to call at Crossville from Sewanee for filing a flight plan is 1-484-9541. The other telephone number is fictitious (555, etc.), and you couldn't call on the radio to a point 59 NM away while sitting on the ground. (See Chapter 21, *SPFM* and the discussion of VHF and line-of-sight transmissions.)

2417. 2. The three legs add up to 204 NM (59 + 78 + 67 = 204 NM).

2418. 4. 278° is the measurement here.

2419. 3. This is not a particularly good question, since most people don't worry about *compass course* in a practical situation, but finding it here is *good for you*. See Chapter 19 here for some problems in this area.

2420. 4. True course = 278°, wind 190° at 12 knots, true airspeed = 69 knots. Using the computer, you find that the true heading = 268° and groundspeed = 68 knots. True heading = 268°, variation 1° W, deviation +5° (see Fig. 24-B), so that the compass heading = 274°.

2421. 1. Your groundspeed is 68 knots. The climb is from 1881 feet (call it 2000 feet) to 4500 feet. Using the same procedure as for question 2412, you'll find that in Figure 24-B it requires 3 minutes to climb from sea level to 2000 feet and 8 minutes to climb from sea level to 4500 feet. The difference is 5 minutes, so this is the time required to climb from 2000 feet to 4500 feet MSL.

At a groundspeed of 68 knots in the climb, a time of 5 minutes would cover a distance of 6 NM. Laying out 6 NM on course from Crossville, you find that you would be approximately abeam of Pleasant Hill.

2422. 3. Split the wind between 3000 and 6000 feet to get a value at 4500 feet of 225° at 14 knots. (Winds 3000—1912, 6000—2616.)

True airspeed = 93 knots (Fig. 24-B)
Groundspeed = 84 knots
True heading = 271°
Magnetic heading = 272°; compass heading = 277°

2423. 2. The high-tension line is crossed near DeRossett at 10 NM enroute. (1) You'll fly toward rapidly *descending* terrain. (3) The isogonic line is hard to spot on the ground. (4) You should pass about 3 miles south of the Sparta–White County Airport.

2424. 4. Check Figure 24-A. First, listen to ATIS on 120.0 MHz to get wind and runway (and other) information. Note that the approach control data indicates "124.0 (016°-196°)" and "120.6 (197°-015°)." This indicates that if you are approaching in the semicircle of 016° to 196° (magnetic) *from* the airport, you would contact approach control on 124.0 MHz. The magnetic course from Crossville to Nashville is 278°, which means that you are 098° *from* the airport and would communicate on 124.0 MHz.

2425. 3. Checking the chart, you'd see that a distance of 25 NM out of Nashville on the route would put you about 2 NM southwest of Watertown. (1) Runway 13-31 is asphalt and has been grooved to cut down on hydroplaning (skidding) problems. (2) *Airport Remarks* at BNA says that landing fees will be charged to *commercial* users only. (4) Norene isn't at the position indicated in this choice.

2426. 2. Runway 13-31 indicates S-129 (third line down), or it can take airplanes with single main wheels weighing up to 129,000 pounds. It can take dual main wheel airplanes up to 151,000 pounds and dual tandem up to 229,000 pounds. The more wheels, the less concentration of the weight, so the airplane can weigh more. Runway 02L-20R can take only 100,000 pounds for single main wheels, and 2R and 20L can take only 60,000 pounds for a single main wheel configuration.

2427. 1. Don't switch to ground control while still on the runway and under the jurisdiction of the tower. The tower might need to contact you about that wide-bodied jet about to use your airplane for a landing site—and you're fumbling around, trying to contact ground control.

2428. 2. Call the FSS and extend your ETA to Sewanee (or wherever) because your estimated time enroute (ETE) takes into account the entire time elapsed.

2429. 4. First, you'd use the climb chart to work out the time, fuel, and distance to climb from 500 feet to 5500 feet. This turns out to be 9 minutes, 1.4 gallons, and 11 NM. The notes in the climb chart indicate that 10 percent must be added to the 3 factors for each 8°C above standard, as thoughtfully indicated in the question. So, you'd add 10 percent to get 10 minutes, 1.5 gallons, and 12 NM for fuel; however, you'd have to add 0.8 gallons for start, taxi, and takeoff to get 10 minutes, 2.3 gallons, and 12 NM respectively.

2430. 1. The true airspeed at 2600 rpm (see Fig. 24-B) is 99 knots. True course is 146° and wind 260° at 16 knots. The true heading is 153° and magnetic heading is 153°. Looking at the compass deviation card, you see that in the area of 150° magnetic, no deviation is indicated, so the compass heading is 153°.

2431. 3. The groundspeed for that leg is 105 knots.

2432. 2. The compass heading is 151°, so checking Figure 24-B you note the magnetic heading is 151° also. At your geographic position the variation is 1° W, so the true heading is 150°. (A canned problem, all right, since few people can hold a CH of exactly 151°.)

The relative bearing is 288° for a true bearing of 078° TO the station. You'll use the plotter to draw a line 258° (the reciprocal of 078°) FROM the radio beacon on the Warren County Airport. You'll find that it crosses the course line at Beechgrove. Hint: To help the process, draw your own meridian through the radio beacon symbol on the chart and use the plotter to get the 258° (true) line. Charts for use with automatic direction finder equipment help-

ANSWERS/EXPLANATIONS TO QUESTIONS

fully have compass roses around the radio beacons (similar to those found at VORs on the chart) so that lines may be drawn outward on the required bearings (see Fig. 24-F).

2433. 3. Measuring the distance, it's found to be 27 miles. Seventeen minutes have elapsed between the check points, and a look at the computer gives a groundspeed of 95 knots.

2434. 4. You'll be descending from 7500 MSL to 3500 MSL at 500 fpm, requiring 8 minutes. Solving for groundspeed: true airspeed = 99 knots, wind 260° at 16 knots, so that groundspeed is 105 knots. At 105 knots the 8-minute descent will require a distance of 14 NM and "backtracking" from Sewanee-Franklin County Airport. You'll find that the point for starting descent is directly abeam of the Arnold Air Force Base runway.

2435. 3. 20.3 gallons. While working wind triangles based on estimated winds may be an exercise in futility, it's a very good practice to estimate the fuel to be consumed for a trip by checking the no-wind requirements and considering that as a *minimum*.

If there is any wind (except on a one-legged flight with a tailwind), more time and fuel are required than for a no-wind trip.

Looking at the various legs, using the information given for the question, and checking the fuel:

Sewanee to Crossville:
Start, taxi, and takeoff	0.8
Climb (2000–5500 feet) (7 min) (8 NM)	1.0
Cruise—total distance 59 NM with 8 NM used for climb = 51 NM for cruise and descent. Cruise at 99 knots at 64 percent at 5500 feet = 31 minutes. At 4.8 gph 31 minutes, fuel consumed	2.5
Taxi in	0.4
TOTAL	4.7 gal

Crossville to Nashville Metro:
Start, taxi, and takeoff	0.8
Climb (2000–4500 feet) (5 min) (5 NM)	0.7
Cruise, 78 − 5 NM = 73 NM at 98 knots = (45 minutes at 4.8 gph)	3.6
Taxi in	0.4
TOTAL	5.5 gal

Nashville to Sewanee:
Start, taxi, and takeoff	0.8
Climb (500–5500) (9 min) (11 NM)	1.4
Cruise at 5500 feet, 67 − 11 = 56 NM at 99 knots (34 minutes at 4.8 gph)	2.7
Taxi in	0.4
TOTAL	5.3 gal

The total estimated fuel to be consumed on the trip is 4.7 + 5.5 + 5.3 = *15.5 gallons*.

Well, that's answer 4, but you need an hour reserve at 4.8 gph, to make a total of 20.3 gallons. You got answer 1 if you had forgotten the reserve and fuel required to taxi in. You chose answer 2 if you forgot the fuel required to taxi in. People who make up questions for written tests have a natural mean streak in them.

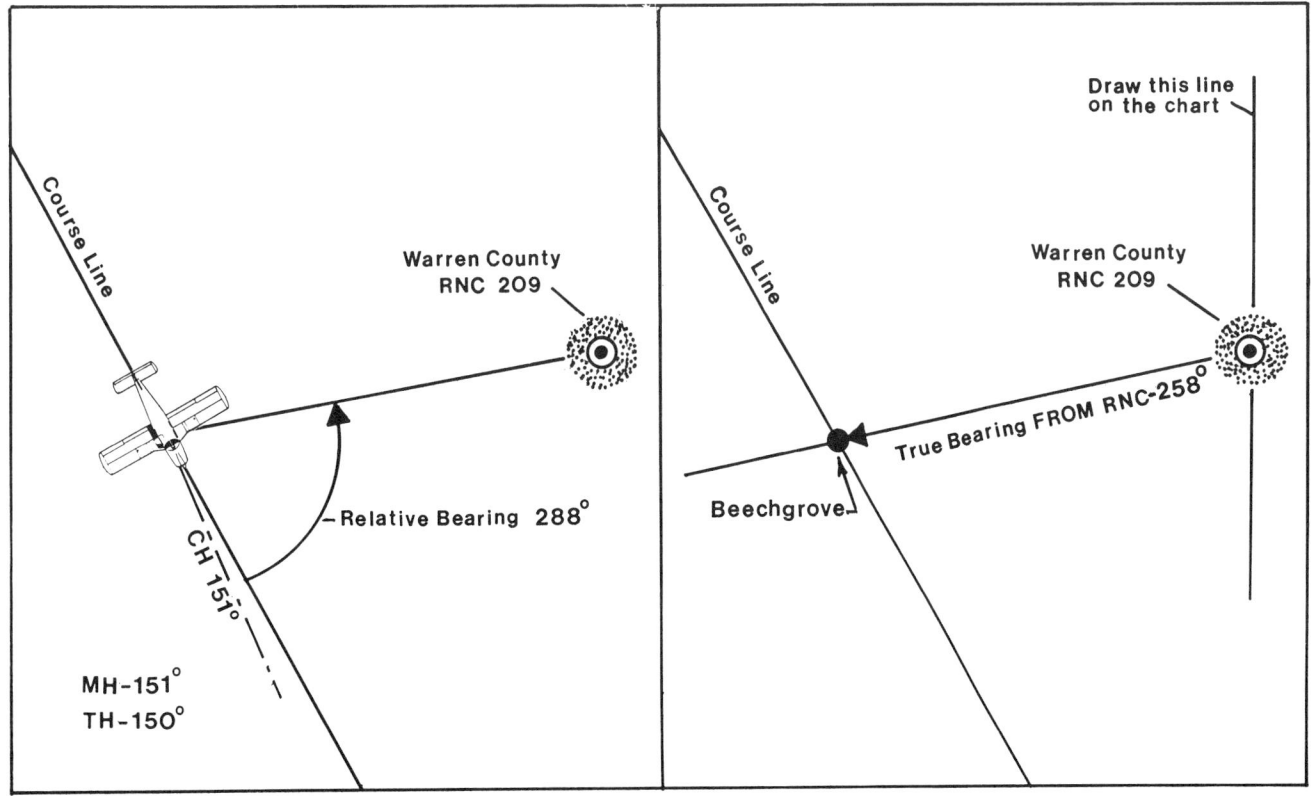

Fig. 24-F. Steps in finding the true bearing from a radio beacon.

2436. 1. The climbs would require (total) :21
Total at cruise 1:50
30 minutes at each stop 1:00
3:11

2437. 3. All the stations reporting show a deterioration of weather in the 0900, 1000, and 1100 CST reports. (1) The weather at Nashville is going down faster than forecast. For instance, BNA is forecast to have 5000 scattered and 5 miles visibility in haze until 18Z (1200 CST). The ceiling and visibility even at 1000 CST and 1100 CST are signicantly worse than that. (2) The weather reports of MKL, west of Nashville, are *very important*, since weather in the United States moves west to east. The weather at MKL will probably be Nashville's weather in a few hours. (4) Chattanooga is forecast to be IFR after 0900Z (0300 CST or 0400 EST), not 0900 CST.

2438. 1. Look at the temperature/dewpoint spread decreasing at all stations as the reports come out. When the spread is 4°F or less, visible moisture (drizzle, rain, fog) will likely be present. The pressure is dropping at the stations, another general sign of worsening weather.

2439. 2. Extrapolating the 0900, 1000, and 1100 CST reports, you would probably get a value pretty close to that cited. Answer (1) is most unlikely since it is an actual improvement over the 1100 CST weather and is reversing the general trend. Answer (3) is even more of a reversal of trend. Answer (4) shows too rapid deterioration, based on reported weather at the other stations for the 3 hours.

2440. 4. The visibilities are too bad at Crossville (and between) for a low-time pilot to be blundering around over strange and rough terrain like the Cumberland Plateau. The visibility at Nashville has been 3 miles all morning. Even if good ceilings were expected, 3 miles is not enough visibility for a student pilot to be flying into a major airport. A little more deterioration and you could find yourself in an actual IFR situation.

At 1100 CST the weather at MKL is less than VFR, and it is deteriorating at an accelerating rate. (The ceiling dropped by 1500 feet, and the visibility came down by 1½ miles from a marginal 4 miles.) Light drizzle has started and the pressure is falling rapidly (PRESFR). That weather will most likely be in the Nashville area by 1300–1400 CST. And so will you, if you leave Sewanee around 1130 CST as planned.

If you were leaving a small airport such as Sewanee, weather depiction and surface analysis charts and other such information wouldn't be available. You can copy the terminal forecasts and hourly reports over the phone and can ask the briefer about the locations of fronts and MVFR and IFR weather, but there may be times when the material as given for questions 2437–2440 is all you can get.

Chances are that the terminal forecasts would be revised as the weather changed and there would not be such a variation between the forecast and actual weather as shown here, but the main point is for you to check *trends;* don't just look at the latest weather.

Answer (2), to leave 2 hours later, would mean that the weather will be even worse, as the trend shows, and you would be getting fairly close to dark on your return to Sewanee, depending on the time of year. That's all you'd need all right, worsening weather and darkness coming on. Flying to Crossville (answer 3) would give you a chance of getting stuck there, or leaving the airplane and coming back by bus. There's little point of starting a trip that is not likely to be completed as planned.

The best judgment here, based on your (fictional) experience and the weather information available, is to cancel the flight. It looks like tomorrow won't be good either, but you can check the weather then. Meanwhile, you might want to review a few chapters in *SPFM*. . . .

NOTES

After you get the private certicate, you sure won't be likely to work the computer in as much detail as done here, but the point is that you *could* work these navigation problems if you had to. As mentioned in *SPFM*, working out a compass heading to the nearest degree and groundspeed to the nearest knot (using forecast winds) and blindly following the numbers can lead to landings in exotic places. As a VFR pilot you'll pay close attention to physical references on the chart and if all that careful computer, performance chart, and deviation card work disagrees with what's happening in flight, well, you can say that doing all that calculating was good for "self-discipline."

Also, as noted in *SPFM*, try to picture what the wind effect is. For instance, if your true course is 150° and the wind is from 210° at 20 knots (or any speed for that matter), you'll have to correct to the right (true heading will be greater than 150°) and there will be a headwind component (groundspeed less than true airspeed) no matter what numbers you work out to 12 places on a computer. The old computer saying is GIGO—*Garbage In, Garbage Out*—so make sure that you have an idea of what's happening before throwing in numbers.

CHAPTER 25—FLYING THE CROSS-COUNTRY

2501. 2. Set the heading indicator with the magnetic compass at least once during each leg, and every 15 minutes is better; set it when the compass has settled down.

2502. 2. Don't get *on top* of a broken layer, though; it could become an overcast. (1) Don't stick your hand out the window to check the wind; that should have been settled back in Chapter 18. (3) Watching smoke, etc., on the ground doesn't indicate what the wind is at your altitude. (4) The airspeed indicator shows the dynamic pressure being generated as the airplane is traveling within the air mass (and not always accurately

ANSWERS/EXPLANATIONS TO QUESTIONS   195

at that). At a constant 100 knots indicated airspeed you might have a calibrated airspeed of, say, 80 *or* 120 knots and could be standing still, or moving at 200 knots *over the ground*. One TV aviation series of some years back had a scene with two brave pilots leading a flight of B-17s on their way over to bomb Germany. "Look at the airspeed indicator," says one high-ranking aviator. "It shows that we have a tremendous tailwind!" (All it showed was that better technical advice was needed.)

2503. 4. This area is unusable because of its structure. You could ding an airplane using it.

2504. 1. The displaced threshold may be used for taxiing, takeoffs, or landing roll-out but may *not* be used for soccer, volleyball, picnicking, or general messing around.

2505. 2. The runway is closed.

2506. 2. That's what *AIM* says.

2507. 3. Start a right turn. Don't lock that right wheel (see Chapter 6, *SPFM*).

2508. 1. The terms used for the markings are *holding position markings* or the more popular *hold line*. See questions in Chapter 6 again.

2509. 3. This is *generally* the best action because if you've been doing well heretofore the chances are good that checkpoints will show up as you progress. It's possible that a wind shift could have moved you slightly to, say, the right of course so that good checkpoint isn't just off the right as planned but could be *directly below* the airplane, while you are nervously looking in all directions for it. Bank the airplane and look directly underneath too.

Answer (1) is wrong because taking a 30° change in heading in what you *consider* the right direction may cause problems. (2) Circling for the sake of circling isn't getting you anywhere, but if there is an unfamiliar but outstanding reference on the ground nearby, you might circle it enough to get a good look and locate it on the chart with respect to your route—that's legitimate circling. Usually one 360° turn in this situation is enough to get an idea of what and where it is. (4) Making a 180° to go back to pick up an earlier known checkpoint could mean that you couldn't find it and, because of a different wind correction required on the return, might miss it by a wide margin. Also, a checkpoint could look different from this side, and you wouldn't recognize it even if you flew back to it. Backpackers have a habit of looking behind them as they move through the forest to see how the landmarks will appear on the return trip.

2510. 4. As *SPFM* says, the VOR cross bearings show only the *area* you are in, but this is to give you practice in drawing cross bearings on the chart. The nearest airport should be Smithville, on a true course of approximately 074° from your cross bearing position.

2511. 1. Confess, Climb, Communicate, Comply, Conserve, and Cool, keeping of. Some of the other choices might be used in explaining how you got the problem in the first place.

2512. 2. The turn radius of an airplane at a given angle of bank is a function of the square of the airspeed.

That's why it's suggested in *SPFM* that you slow down when blundering along in marginal weather. At 120 knots the turn radius in a 45° bank is about 1279 feet. At a speed of 80 knots (two-thirds of 120) the turn radius at that same bank angle is about 568 feet, or well less than half. Slow down, but don't get into a marginal control situation.

Answer (3) is refuted in *SPFM*. If you and the airplane are down in one piece, *don't* take off until you've discussed the situation with your instructor. Don't turn a forced landing into a tragedy by attempting to fly the airplane out on your own. (4) It is considered *good* technique to follow a known road if one is available (answer 4).

2513. 4. Be prepared for strong and shifting winds. You may have to go on to another airport if the thunderstorm hangs around. The fuel remaining will be the deciding factor. Don't count on landing straight in—who knows what the wind direction and speeds are in this situation. Carefully check the airport's wind indicator(s); the wind may be too strong for you to handle.

2514. 2. *Don't* take a chance that the gauge is lying, but turn toward better terrain or an airport for landing and watch the oil temperature gauge. See Chapter 3 questions again.

2515. 1. The chances are that the heavy rain may be partially blocking the carburetor air intake screen so that using an alternate air source (carburetor heat) will let air get to the engine. This was brought up so that you might think of it in an actual situation. *Your flight instructor and the Pilot's Operating Handbook will be the final sources of information*, since a textbook has to have a general approach. It's an outside chance that you would run a tank dry exactly as you get into the rain, but if the carb heat move doesn't seem to be working, you might switch to another tank.

A NOTE ON SURVIVAL

The chances of your having a crash enroute and needing to survive for several days waiting for rescuers are remote indeed, but it has happened and could happen to you.

There are reports of pilots and passengers who crashed while flying over the Rockies or other mountainous areas in winter and were wearing (and carrying aboard) only light clothing and no food, water, or means of building a fire. After all, they were going to Las Vegas or places in California that were warm and the airplane heater was working fine, so what was the big deal about carrying along a lot of extra junk?

A survivable crash in itself is a traumatic experience, but the shock is multiplied many times when, in addition to injuries, the occupants are suddenly thrust from the warm cabin environment to outside temperatures perhaps 80°F (or more) lower. Even if you are on a flight plan, which gets the search started sooner, the airplane may be hard to spot and several days may pass before the wreckage is found. (A mostly white airplane in the snow in a remote area is indeed a problem, and a lot of our airplanes are primarily white with a relatively small amount of color trim.) The authors' participation in searches in the Cumberland and Appalachian mountains has shown that an airplane that goes down into the woods may be hidden because the trees snap back to cover it. In these wooded areas searchers look for freshly broken limbs to indicate a crash site. Also, many crashed airplanes that land in comparatively open areas don't retain their airplane shape and may be broken up so that the shadows blend well with the background. (The worst crashes may appear as a pile of junk that someone has dumped from a truck out in the boonies.) People who have not had experience in air search don't understand why the aircraft can't be located in a few minutes or, at worst, a couple of hours. Search planes may fly right overhead and miss it.

If you don't file a flight plan or didn't leave word about your route and times with somebody, the *start* of the search may be delayed for a couple of days or more. You owe it to yourself and later to your passengers to have the best chance for making it after surviving the impact. Of course, the news media, usually inaccurate about aviation occurrences (particularly crashes), are always quick to add knowingly at the end of a TV report or newspaper article that "the airplane was *not* on a flight plan." The implication is that if the pilot had been on a flight plan he would not have had the problem in the first place. Or that the airplane that spun in during a wrapped-up turn to final might have defied the laws of aerodynamics if the pilot had filed a flight plan. But getting back to reality. . . .

You should file a flight plan on a cross-country so that search and rescue operations may begin as soon as possible. That's one of the jobs of the FSS people, and they are glad to do it.

But, talking about surviving until the St. Bernard and keg arrive, you should make up a small basic kit to keep in the airplane. You might consider matches (kitchen matches with the heads dipped in paraffin or kept in a moistureproof container such as some pill bottles), a short length of candle (light the candle to start a fire rather than using up all the matches), a small mirror for signaling, a packet of hard candy and raisins, a reasonable water supply, a folded piece of plastic 4 feet by 4 feet for use as a solar still or water collector, and other items that might stretch your life span a few days. (Stuffing charts and other paper inside your clothing can help fight hypothermia.) Commercial low-weight survival kits are available through aviation suppliers, as are books on survival, and you might want to put a kit and book in your airplane. As noted in Chapter 26, *SPFM* under night flying, Cyalume sticks are light and safe; they could be used for night signaling if necessary.

For some reason, some people consider planning for survival after a crash as being "old maidish." These are the same individuals who have egg on their face when the engine quits on takeoff, since the idea was not considered previously, or when a tank runs dry, and a procedure must be developed on the spot. Airline and military pilots prepare for emergencies while still on the ground, have survival equipment on board, and consider *that* is a professional attitude. You owe it to your passengers to give them a chance after the expensive crunching sounds have stopped.

This is not intended to replace any of the information in survival books but to bring some ideas to mind. One last item: sometimes it's tempting to leave the airplane and strike out for help. Statistics have argued against this, and there have been a number of cases where one of the survivors left to get help and was never seen again, whereas the people who stayed with the airplane were spotted and rescued. There are exceptions in individual situations, of course, but even a beat-up airplane is usually easier to spot than a person out on his or her own.

CHAPTER 26 — INTRODUCTION TO NIGHT FLYING

2601. 4. Deer can't separate colors, so the orange won't be outstanding to them.
2602. 4. The statements are all correct.
2603. 2. It's been found that about 30 minutes is required to become mostly night adapted. The *AIM* states that a *moderate* degree of dark adaptation may be attained in 20 minutes under dim red cockpit lighting. Under red lighting the magenta markings on the charts may be hard to see. You'd better have a white light available and, since night vision is the third item to go with age (memory is one of the other two), you'd better carry an extra pair of eyeglasses along if you are a wearer.

(1) There's a blind spot in the daytime, also. (See Fig. 26-3, *SPFM*.) (3) Oxygen helps vision if taken before and during the night flight. Use of alcohol and tobacco hurts. (Don't drink within 8 hours before a flight or while flying. It's stupid in the daytime and suicidal for night flying.) (4) Turn *up* the brightness of the instrument lighting when over a brightly lighted city.
2604. 1. The period in question requiring position lights is from *sunset to sunrise.* This requirement is often confused with the requirement for pilot night flying experience as cited in FAR 61.57d, which says "*1 hour after sunset to 1 hour before sunrise.*" Note that each requirement is on the conservative side; for instance, if the pilot experience requirement started at sunset, some pilots (not you, of course) might fly only from sunset until darkness set in and get credit for night experience. On the other hand, for safety's sake, it's best to have the *aircraft position lights on at sunset.*
2605. 3. If another aircraft on the horizon remains in the same relative position to your airplane and, as the statement indicates, is getting closer (the light is getting brighter), a collision threat exists. Turn to break that relative-position line.
2606. 2. *Military airports*—Green-white-white-green. They have a *dual* flash of white between the greens. *Civilian airports*—Green-white-green. These airports have a *single* white flash between the greens. (See Fig. 26-B.)
2607. 1. Red lights are generally used for nearby obstructions at night. Flashing high-intensity white lights may be used for daytime conditions but are reduced in intensity for twilight and nighttime operation.
2608. 4. The chimney will have high-intensity *flashing* white lights. Steady white lights wouldn't get your attention as well.
2609. 2. The weather is below VFR conditions (1000 and 3).
2610. 4. As noted in *SPFM,* turning the position lights on takes a comparatively small amount of power and warns people nearby that the airplane is occupied (and to avoid the propeller arc), when other airplanes' engine noises might drown out your "CLEAR." If you turn the landing lights on

Fig. 26-B.

(1), you may not have enough electric power to start and could distract pilots in other airplanes. Turning up the cockpit lights (2) probably wouldn't show up well enough to warn people outside, and (3) strobe lights can be a distraction to other pilots also (*AIM*).

2611. 3. Landing lights and strobes, in addition to using electrical power, can be distracting to pilots, who are landing. Don't turn the position lights off unless you want another airplane sharing the cockpit with you. Review the answer to question 2604.

2612. 1. *Blink* the position or landing lights. Don't (3) turn the position lights off for any period because it's dangerous and you'll be in violation of FARs (see the answer to question 2604 again, if this isn't clear) and your airplane would be an unlighted obstruction on the taxiway. (2) Turning up the cockpit lighting won't be seen by the tower and would mean nothing anyway. (4) Moving the ailerons is a good arm exercise but is hard to see.

2613. 2. Give yourself a little more time in the pattern. Answer (3) is talking about judgment factors, not Operation Lights On.

CHAPTER 27 — THE WRITTEN TEST

1. Question Selection Sheet, with correct answers written in. (See p. 198.)

2. Airman Written Test Application—answer section with answers filled (in circles). (See p. 199.)

PRIVATE PILOT - AIRPLANE

On Answer Sheet For Item No.	Answer Question Number	On Answer Sheet For Item No.	Answer Question Number	On Answer Sheet For Item No.	Answer Question Number
1	1014 – 4	21	1424 – 3	41	1700 – 4
2	1032 – 2	22	1427 – 3	42	1717 – 3
3	1045 – 2	23	1429 – 4	43	1725 – 3
4	1061 – 1	24	1437 – 2	44	1732 – 1
5	1062 – 3	25	1438 – 2	45	1739 – 3
6	1101 – 4	26	1441 – 2	46	1762 – 1
7	1123 – 3	27	1469 – 2	47	1764 – 1
8	1168 – 4	28	1472 – 4	48	1783 – 1
9	1172 – 4	29	1474 – 3	49	1794 – 1
10	1178 – 3	30	1475 – 2	50	1827 – 2
11	1228 – 4	31	1491 – 2	51	1832 – 3
12	1247 – 2	32	1502 – 2	52	1833 – 1
13	1274 – 3	33	1554 – 3	53	1836 – 4
14	1276 – 1	34	1569 – 3	54	1863 – 3
15	1278 – 4	35	1574 – 4	55	1864 – 1
16	1346 – 4	36	1595 – 4	56	1867 – 2
17	1348 – 1	37	1622 – 2	57	1871 – 1
18	1359 – 4	38	1648 – 3	58	1872 – 3
19	1361 – 2	39	1665 – 2	59	1902 – 3
20	1421 – 3	40	1674 – 3	60	1907 – 4

CHAPTER 28 – THE PRACTICAL TEST

Note: Any chapter references with the answers apply to both *SPFM* and this book.

2801. 1. V_X is the max *angle* of climb. People confuse this with V_Y, max *rate*, but remember that an X has more *angles* than a Y (Chapter 3).

2802. 3. V_{NE} is the *never exceed speed*, or the red line. The junction of the green and yellow arcs is V_{NO} (Chapter 3).

2803. 2. The validity of the written test is for 24 calendar months, so it's good until midnight of the last day of that month (FAR 61.39).

2804. 1. Chapter 23.

2805. 4. Chapter 23.

2806. 1. Chapter 22 and Chapter 24. This one is fairly obvious, since in the United States weather moves from west to east. The weather at the stations west of the route or destination(s) will usually foretell what will be happening in a few hours at the areas of real interest. You need to check as many different sources as possible, not just the terminal forecast as noted in (2). As far as (3) and (4) are concerned, the examiner knows that you will be on your own after getting the private certificate and wants to see your decision making.

2807. 3. Chapter 4. Throughout the practical test the examiner will be looking at your judgment, and part of that judgment is whether you can be

CHAPTER 27 ANSWERS
FINAL EXAM

#	Ans	#	Ans	#	Ans	#	Ans	#	Ans	#	Ans	#	Ans
1	4	23	4	45	3	67	—	89	—	111	—	133	—
2	2	24	2	46	1	68	—	90	—	112	—	134	—
3	2	25	2	47	1	69	—	91	—	113	—	135	—
4	1	26	2	48	1	70	—	92	—	114	—	136	—
5	3	27	2	49	1	71	—	93	—	115	—	137	—
6	4	28	4	50	2	72	—	94	—	116	—	138	—
7	3	29	3	51	3	73	—	95	—	117	—	139	—
8	4	30	2	52	1	74	—	96	—	118	—	140	—
9	4	31	2	53	4	75	—	97	—	119	—	141	—
10	3	32	2	54	3	76	—	98	—	120	—	142	—
11	4	33	3	55	1	77	—	99	—	121	—	143	—
12	2	34	3	56	2	78	—	100	—	122	—	144	—
13	3	35	4	57	1	79	—	101	—	123	—	145	—
14	1	36	4	58	3	80	—	102	—	124	—	146	—
15	4	37	2	59	3	81	—	103	—	125	—	147	—
16	4	38	3	60	4	82	—	104	—	126	—	148	—
17	1	39	2	61	—	83	—	105	—	127	—	149	—
18	4	40	3	62	—	84	—	106	—	128	—	150	—
19	2	41	2	63	—	85	—	107	—	129	—		
20	3	42	3	64	—	86	—	108	—	130	—		
21	3	43	3	65	—	87	—	109	—	131	—		
22	3	44	1	66	—	88	—	110	—	132	—		

199

ANSWERS/EXPLANATIONS TO QUESTIONS

2808. 1. Chapter 23. Also see FAR 61.47. (The examiner is normally *not* pilot in command but may be by prior arrangement.)
2809. 4. A steady red in the air means "Don't land but give way to other aircraft and continue circling" (Chapter 21.)
2810. 2. The indication as shown won't exist in a properly operating VASI system. It shows that you are too high for the far lights and too low for the near lights. An impossible combination, but it will make you read the following questions more carefully anyway. Review the VASI in Chapter 21, also read *AIM* Chapter 2 (and see illustration's of VASI types in that publication).
2811. 1. Gaining altitude is *the* most common error for student pilots performing a rectangular course, though any instructor can tell you that the other three errors (and more) are done also. Watch for this on the check. (Chapter 10.)
2812. 3. You may get by with a semipoor job on the other three items, but have a midair collision or even a near collision and see what it does to the flight test results.
2813. 2. See Chapter 12 of *The Student Pilot's Flight Manual*. (The key is the angle of attack.)
2814. 1. These are the flight situations where a critically slow airspeed could (and has) caused accidents.
2815. 3. The *attitude* at the stall has nothing to do with the type of stall. As Chapter 12, *SPFM* notes, an airplane may be stalled at any attitude. Answer (1) describes an imminent or partial stall; if (4) happens, it means that you've missed the idea. (If the examiner has to take over in that spin, you are in a heap of trouble.)
2816. 3. Use all the power safely available in a stall recovery unless the examiner tells you otherwise on the check ride. (He or she may want to check that you know that a stall may be recovered with power at idle.) If you don't use power, based on the statement given, the examiner might think you wouldn't use it in a real situation. CLEAR THE AREA.
2817. 4. The answer to this one was pretty obvious, but you need a break once in a while.
2818. 3. Chapter 15. Plus or minus 10°. This requirement should give you no trouble.
2819. 2. You might have checked answer (4) again (because "none of the above" or "all of the above" is the right answer too many times), but read again the "General Procedures for Practical (Flight) Tests" in Chapter 28, *SPFM*.
2820. 3. Answers (1) and (2) indicate the need to make an *approach*, which is not required. A VHF/DF approach (4) is not on an agenda either.
2821. 2. You may use VOR or ADF equipment to help navigate during the cross-country portion of the test.
2822. 1. The manufacturer gives specifics for a particular airplane. The Practical Test Standards, this book, and *SPFM* are, by their nature, required to have general information. Answer (2) is wrong; the max rate of climb airspeed is always higher there. Answer (3) is wrong because locking the wheels not only results in squared-off tires and wheels but is less effective braking than an incipient (near) skid condition. Answer (4) gives a good procedure for a *soft*-field landing.
2823. 2. You'll want to get the weight off the wheels to decrease the increased ground drag.
2824. 4. While the night flying portion of the practical test is usually completed through oral questioning and few check rides are given at night, the examiner could legally have you plan and fly an actual local or cross-country night flight.
2825. 2. A demonstration of pilot incapacitation is *not* required, although some people feel like they are incapacitated because of nervousness. (See Checkitis, Chapter 28, *SPFM*.)
2826. 1. ACEG. It's pretty hard to show how you'd handle (B) a structural failure, (D) landing short of the runway, and (F) a midair collision. These are things best avoided.
2827. 4. As noted in *SPFM*, the best insurance against checkitis is to be prepared. Study well for the oral and don't try to bluff. (It won't work.) Follow the instructions as given on a mayonnaise jar. *Keep cool but don't freeze.*

CHAPTER 29—REVIEW OF THE FEDERAL AVIATION REGULATIONS

2901. 3. Part 1, definitions of category and class.
2902. 2. FAR 61.65.
2903. 3. FAR 61.3.
2904. 1. FAR 61.5.
2905. 2. FAR 61.15, 91.11, 91.12.
2906. 3. FAR 61.19.
2907. 2. FAR 61.23.
2908. 4. FAR 61.57.
2909. 4. FAR 61.31.
2910. 2. FAR Part 1, 61.51.
2911. 2. FAR 61.57.
2912. 3. FAR 61.107.
2913. 1. FAR 61.87.
2914. 2. FAR 61.107, 61.109.
2915. 3. FAR 61.118.
2916. 1. FAR 61.83.
2917. 4. FAR 61.103, 61.105. According to some of the choices in this and the last question, *everybody* wants to go to South America.
2918. 2. FAR 91.3.
2919. 4. FAR 91.5. OK, it's stretching it a little to say that a preflight inspection is *exactly* required, but have an accident and try to explain your way out of the fact that you didn't do one.
2920. 2. FAR 91.11.
2921. 4. FAR 91.11. Your personal doctor may not understand the effects of a drug at altitude. The aviation medical examiner has had training in high-altitude and other aviation-related problems.
2922. 1. FAR 91.9, 91.13.
2923. 3. FAR 91.15, 91.71.
2924. 4. FAR 91.22.
2925. 1. FAR 91.24, 91.172.

ANSWERS/EXPLANATIONS TO QUESTIONS

2926. 2. FAR 91.15, 91.71.
2927. 3. FAR 91.22. (You need 45 minutes if the flight is at night, 30 minutes if during the day. Look at question 2924 again.)
2928. 4. FAR 91.32.
2929. 3. FAR 91.79. Over congested areas you need to be 1000 feet above the highest obstacle within a horizontal distance of 2000 feet of the aircraft. Answer 1 covers too large an area.
2930. 1. FAR 91.52.
2931. 2. FAR 91.70.
2932. 3. FAR 91.83d. The tower may get busy and forget to cancel your flight plan. It is *your* responsibility. Also, since most accidents happen in the vicinity of an airport, it's a safer procedure to wait and cancel with FSS after you are on the ground. Don't get busy and forget to cancel it.
2933. 2. FAR 91.81.
2934. 2. FAR 91.83.
2935. 2. FAR 91.85, 91.87.
2936. 1. FAR 91.105.
2937. 1. FAR 91.105.
2938. 4. FAR 91.90, 91.24.
2939. 4. FAR 91.90.
2940. 2. FAR 91.105.
2941. 1. FAR 91.109.
2942. 4. FAR 91.105.
2943. 4. *AIM*, "Basic Flight Information."
2944. 3. *AIM*, "Basic Flight Information."
2945. 2. *AIM*, "Basic Flight Information."
2946. 1. FAR 109. You do need a clearance, but this is issued by ATC (not necessarily by a tower facility).
2947. 1. FAR 91 and FCC requirements.
2948. 2. FAR 91.172.
2949. 2. *AIM*, "Basic Flight Information."
2950. 3. *AIM*, "Basic Flight Information."
2951. 1. *AIM*, "Basic Flight Information."
2952. 4. *AIM*, "Basic Flight Information."
2953. 4. *SPFM*, "Appendix."

INDEX

Accidents, 135
AD. *See* Airworthiness, directives
ADF. *See* Automatic Direction Finder
Adiabatic lapse rate, 177
Advanced Pilot's Flight Manual, 99
Advection, fog, 83
Advisory Circular Checklist, 115
Advisory Circulars, 115, 137
Aeronautical Chart Bulletin, 59
A/FD. *See* Airport/Facility Directory
Ailerons, 27, 167, 170
AIM. *See* Airman's Information Manual
Air
  brake system, 24
  currents, 129
  density, 44, 172
  filter, 18
  lapse rate, 185
  pressure, 84
  stability, 129
  warm, 179
Aircraft. *See also* Airplane
  avoiding, 142-43, 196
  documents, 140-41, 153
  fixed landing gear, 149
  high-performance, 139
  inspections, 140-41
  logbook, 140-41, 188
  overdue, 135
  position, 72-74
  pressure, 84
  registration, 140
  speeds, 142
  stress, 170-71
  types, 149
Airflow
  engine cooling, 14-15
  retarding force created by, 4
Airfoil, 3
Airframe and Powerplant Mechanics Powerplant Handbook, 14
Airman's Information Manual (AIM), 61-67, 110, 112, 137
  airport lighting, 143
  "Fitness for Flight," 140
  "Medical Facts for Pilots," 140
Airman Written Text Application, 116

AIRMETS (Airmen's Meteorological Information), 86, 88
Airplane, 136, 182. *See also* Aircraft
  constant-speed propeller, 98-99
  high-performance, 139, 141
  lighting, 113-14, 143
  performance, computing, 5
  services, 55
  stability, 120
  starting, 14, 17, 21-22, 120, 166
  tricycle-gear, 24, 25, 35, 170
Airport
  civilian, 196
  control zones, 144
  lighting, 113-14, 143
  locating, 52
  military, 125, 143, 196
  noncontrolled, 144
  operations, 132
  radar service area, 146
  symbols, 55
  tower-controlled, 144
  traffic area (ATA), 127, 144, 152
Airport Advisory Service, 78, 103
  frequencies, 184, 192
Airport/Facility Directory (A/FD), 52-53, 55-60, 100
  abbreviations, 126
  operation around airports, 144
  runway lighting explanation, 114
  Unicom frequencies, 183
Airport Radar Service Area (ARSA), 146, 147-48
Air Route Traffic Control Centers, 58
Airship, 182
Airspace
  controlled, 141, 146-47, 152
  limits, 61
  restricted, 143
  sea, 70
Airspeed, 6, 50, 120, 151, 171
  calibrated (CAS), 49, 135, 164, 165, 175-77
  corrected for density-altitude, 5
  corrected for instrument and position error, 5
  equivalent, 164

  indicated, 120
  indicator. *See* Indicator, airspeed
  low, 132-33
  stall, 33
  true (TAS), 5, 49, 50, 165, 175-77
  true indicated, 164
Air Traffic Control (ATC), 61, 76, 79
  control zone clearance, 146
  radar facilities, 75
  system, 74
  tower, 77
  transponder signals, 141
Airworthiness
  certificate, 127, 140, 141, 188
  directives (AD), 141
Alcohol, 140, 148, 150
Alphabet, phonetic, 77
ALS. *See* Instrument Approach Light Systems
Alternator, 6, 17, 165
Altimeter, 84, 128, 143, 152
  encoding, 74
  required, 141
  temperature effects, 5, 86, 186
Altitude, 109, 120
  absolute, 5, 164
  high, 84, 140
  indicated, 177
  loss, 30
  minimum safe, 143, 151
  pattern, 144
  pressure, 49, 96, 175
  reporting, automatic, 141
  stall, 200
  true, 5, 51, 164, 177
  wildlife refuge, 120
  wind, 142
Ammeter, 17
ANDS, memory aid, 165
Applicant's Practical Test Checklist, 131
Area navigation (RNAV), 76, 80
ARROW, memory aid, 140
ARSA. *See* Airport Radar Service Area
ATA. *See* Airport, traffic area
ATC. *See* Air Traffic Control
ATIS. *See* Automatic Terminal Information Service

INDEX

Attitude, 151
  indicator, 17, 40, 165, 171
  instrument flying, 149
Automatic Direction Finder (ADF), 71-72, 183, 192-93
  frequencies, 78
Automatic Terminal Information Service (ATIS), 50, 77, 80
Aviation medical examiner, 140, 200
Aviation Weather, 82, 115, 185
Aviation Weather Services, 82, 115

Backfiring, 166
Baffles, 14
Balance, 115, 131
Ballast, 94
Balloon, 142, 182
Bank, 42, 168, 171, 172
  angle for stall, 37, 170
Barometric pressure, 44
Battery, 17, 21, 141, 165
Beacon
  nondirectional (NDB), 78
  radio, 68, 71, 182
  rotating, 113, 114, 143
Bearing
  magnetic, 71-72
  relative, 71, 78, 192
Biennial Flight Review (BFR), 138
Blimp, 182
Brake(s), 23-25
  dragging, 24-25
  hard, 24
  horsepower, 3, 167
  mechanical, 25
  parking, 23-24
  preflight check, 23
  pumping, 24, 166
  reservoir, 23
  soft, 24, 25
Braking, 172
Breathing rate, 140
Briefing, preflight, 105-6

Call sign, 76
Camshaft, 10
Carbon monoxide, 153
Carburetion, 11-12
Carburetor, 11, 14, 18, 165
  ice, 12, 14, 165, 169
Carburetor heat, 12, 14, 18, 29, 119, 165
  hose, 165-66
  power, loss, 169
  rpm effect, 165
  trainer, 165
CAS. *See* Airspeed, calibrated
CDI. *See* Course Deviation Indicator
Ceilings, weather, 91, 107, 152
  control zone minimums, 144-46
Certificate
  airworthiness, 127, 140, 141, 188
  category, 136
  class, 136
  loss, 138
  medical, 136, 149
  private pilot, 135, 149, 150
  restrictions, 149
  student, 136, 150
  types, 148
Certification
  aeronautical experience, 137, 138
  alcohol and drugs, 140
  category and class, 136, 148

flight instructor, 135-39
flight review, 138
high-performance airplanes, 139
minimum requirements, 137
oral exam, 137
pilot, 135-39
practical test, 137
CG. *See* Gravity, center of
Charts, 52-70, 137
  aeronautical, 144
  sectional, 52-55, 143, 182, 183, 191
  takeoff distance, 2
Check, cockpit and pretakeoff, 26
Checkitis, 134, 200
Checklist, 26, 140
Checkpoint, 50, 100-101, 110, 195
Chocks, 24
Chord line, airfoil, 3
CHT. *See* Cylinder, head temperature
Cigar lighter, 17
Circling, 195
Circuit breakers, 7, 17
Class, 136, 148
Climb, 33, 104, 136
  angle (V_x), 197
  constant-speed propeller, 99
  cowl flaps, 15
  fuel required, 191
  rate, 28, 172, 197
  steady-state, 28
Climbout, 105
Climb speed, maximum angle, 131, 172
Clock, 17, 165
Clouds, 83, 88, 185
  clearance, 142, 152
  cumulus, 85, 152
Cockpit
  check, 26, 166
  instruments, 5-7, 164-65
  lighting, 196
  systems, 5-7, 164-65
Codes
  emergency, 75
  transponder, 74-75
Collector rings, 16
Collision, 142
Combined Station/Towers, 56
Combustion, 12
  chamber, 13-14
  deposits, 13
  detonation, 13-14, 16, 99
  distribution of heat from, 14
  heat, 14
  normal, 13-14
  pistons, 13-14
  preignition, 13, 14
Communication, 76-81, 125. *See also* Radio
  light signals, 81
  sequence of frequencies, 77, 104
Compass, magnetic, 6, 40, 41, 165
  Automatic Direction Finder, 71
  course, approximating, 174-75
  heading indicator, 109
  lag, 171
  Northern Hemisphere operation, 119
  required, 141
Compass heading, 51
Compression, 8, 12
  check, 10
  ratio, 11
  rings, 9-10
Computer, 2, 84, 181
  navigation, 49-51, 194

Cones, 112
Contact, 166
Continental Control Area, 69, 147
Control
  system, 2
  zones, 144-46, 147, 152, 153
Controls, 27, 167
  landing, 36, 170
CONVECTIVE SIGMETS, 86
Coordinated Universal Time (UTC), 174
Coordinator
  turn, 6, 17, 33, 40, 165
  turn and slip, 17, 33, 165
Coriolis force, 84, 184, 185
Course
  approximating, 174-75
  compass, 103
  hemispheric rule, 142
  magnetic, 50, 71, 100, 152
  rectangular, 30-31, 32, 132
  true, 49, 103, 175, 180
Course Deviation Indicator (CDI), 72, 74
Cowled radial engines, 16
Cowl flaps, 14, 15, 44
Cowling, 14, 16
Crankcase, 10, 11, 14
Crankshaft, 8, 10
Crash survival, 195-96
Cross-country flying, 48-111, 137, 194-95
  communication. *See* Communication
  emergency, 110-11, 137
  enroute considerations, 109-10
  fuel, 50, 105, 151
  navigation. *See* Navigation
  passengers, 149
  practical test, 133
  problems and emergencies, 110-11
  radio use, 71-81
  safety, 143
  solo, 137
  test, practical, 133
  time, 105
Crosswind, 46, 71
  landing, 36, 170
  takeoff, 137
Cruise, 96, 104
  constant-speed propeller, 99
  cowl flaps, 15
Cruise Performance Chart, 96
Cruising flight, 29
Cyalume sticks, 196
Cylinder, 8, 10, 11, 12
  brake pedal, 23
  cooling fins, 14
  damage, 13
  displacement, 10-11, 165
  head temperature, 13, 14
  spark plugs, 13

Dead reckoning, 137, 143-44, 174
Density, air, 44
Density-altitude, 2, 44, 49, 164, 173
  determining, 128
  fuel-air mixture, 167
  humidity, 179
  propeller efficiency, 116
  rpm setting, 96
  temperature, 2, 172
Descent, 40, 41, 97, 105, 136
  rate, 29, 103
Designated Medical Examiner (DME), 136
Detonation, 13-14, 16, 99
Direct drive, 8

INDEX

Dirigible, 182
Disks, 23
Distance Measuring Equipment (DME), 75-76, 80
Documents, 140-41, 153, 188
Drag, 4, 164, 168, 200
   cowl flaps, 15
   lift, 3
Drizzle, 85
Drugs, 140, 148, 150
Dry-sump system, 14
Dynamic pressure, 164

EFAS. *See* Enroute Flight Advisory Service
EGT (exhaust gas temperature), 12, 16
Eights, 42
Electrical current, 7
Electrical system, 16-17
Electric shavers, 141
Electronic devices, portable, 141
Elevation, 191
Elevator, 27, 38, 167, 171
ELT. *See* Emergency locator transmitter
Emergency, 136, 150, 169
   codes, 75
   cross-country, 110-11, 137
   flying by reference to instruments, 39-41
   frequency, 184, 192
   high-altitude, 47
   practical test, 134
Emergency locator transmitter (ELT), 127, 141-42, 151
   high-altitude, 47, 174
   in-flight, 127, 140
Endorsements, 127, 136-37, 149
Engine, 8-16, 119
   classification, 10-11, 18
   construction, 8
   cooling, 14-15, 123
   cowled radial, 16
   exhaust system, 15-16
   failure, 32
   fire, 166
   fuel-injected, 16, 18
   heat, 14-15, 123
   horizontally opposed, 8, 11, 14, 16, 18
   idle, 26, 167
   ignition, 12-14
   logbook, 140-41
   magnetos, 12-13
   nonturbocharged, 98-99
   oil breather, 14
   oil system, 14
   operation, 8
   Otto cycle, 8, 18
   overhaul, 11
   power loss, 111
   preflight check, 8-11, 14-15, 26
   radial, 15-16
   rough, 12, 13, 16, 21, 26, 32, 96
   seized, 168
   spark plugs, 13-14
   starting, 21, 120
   strokes, 8, 18
   theory, 8
Enroute Flight Advisory Service (EFAS), 59, 78, 130
Equipment requirements (FAR 91), 141-42
Escarpment, 55, 101, 191
Exhaust
   augmenters, 15
   manifold, 166
   system, 8, 15-16

Experience, aeronautical, 137
External power plug, 17

FAA. *See* Federal Aviation Administration
FAA Private Pilot Question Book, 115
FARs. *See* Federal Aviation Regulations
FCC. *See* Federal Communications Commission
Federal Aviation Administration
   publications, 115
   test, written. *See* Private Pilot—Airplane Written Test
Federal Aviation Regulations (FARs), 93, 115-16, 131, 135-53. *See also* Part 1; Part 61; Part 91
   aeronautical experience, 137
   airport radar service area, 146, 147-48
   airport traffic area, 144
   airworthiness of airplane, 141
   altitude, 143
   carrying passengers, 138
   category and class, 136
   certificate replacement, 138
   certification, 135-39
   controlled airspace, 146-47
   control zones, 144-45
   cross-country flight, 137
   documents, 140
   drugs and alcohol, 140
   electronic devices, 141
   equipment requirements, 141-42
   flight plan, 143
   fuel reserve, 143
   general operating and flight rules, 139-48
   high-performance airplanes, 139
   inspection of aircraft, 140
   lighting, 141, 143
   light signals, 144
   medical certificate, 136
   minimum requirements for certification, 137
   oxygen use, 140
   pilot responsibility and authority, 139-40
   restricted airspace, 143
   right-of-way, 142
   seat belts, 140
   solo flight, 136
   speed, 135, 142
   student certificate, 136
   terminal control area, 146
   VOR receivers, 143-44
Federal Communications Commission (FCC), 140
Fins, cylinder cooling, 14
Fire, engine, 166
"Fitness for Flight," 140
Flaps, 15, 35
Flight
   acrobatic, 151
   hour recorder, 17
   minimum controllable speed, 136
   plan, 77, 103, 143, 151, 152, 195-96
   recorder, 17
   review, 138
   routes, 139
   schools, 137
   slow, 33-34, 169
   straight and level, 27, 137
   time, 137
   visibility, 69
   wings-level, 29
Flight Data Center NOTAMS, 61
Flight instructor certification, 135-39

Flight Instructor's Manual, 99
Flight Service Station (FSS), 56, 76, 80, 103
   communication procedures, 77-78, 81
   search procedures, 152
   weather briefing, 183
Flight Standards District Offices, 58
Flight Training Handbook, 115
Flight Watch, 78, 80, 183
Fog, 83
Forecast, 85, 86, 88, 137
   terminal, 106, 129, 194
   winds aloft, 106
Four Forces, 3
Four Fundamentals, 28-29, 167-68
4096 code capability, 141, 146
Frequency
   emergency, 184, 192
   ground control, 183
   sequence, 77, 80, 104
   Unicom, 81
   VOR, 78
Front, 90, 188
   cold and warm, 82, 83, 184
   stationary, 83
Frost, 84, 129, 185
FSS. *See* Flight Service Station
Fuel, 8, 96, 97, 103, 105
   color, 95, 190
   consumption, 50-51, 96, 180-81, 190
   distribution, 12
   management, 97
   mixing with air, 11
   practical test, 132
   requirements, 127, 151, 191, 193
   reserve, 143
   system, 97, 190-91
   takeoff, 26
   tank run dry, 12, 18, 165
   weight, 131, 190
Fuel-air mixture, 8, 9, 11, 16, 165
   density-altitude, 167
   leaning, 13
   prop control, 98-99
   rich, 14, 167, 190
Fuel injection, 12, 18, 165
   distribution, 16, 165
   horsepower requirement, 12, 16
Fuel-to-air ratio, 21
Fuse, 7, 17, 141
Fuselage, 4, 167

Gap, spark plug, 13
Gauge
   cylinder head temperature (CHT), 13
   engine temperature, 141
   exhaust-gas temperature (EGT), 12
   fuel-flow, 12
   manifold pressure, 141
   oil pressure, 6, 17, 21, 165
   oil temperature, 14, 17, 165
   required, 141
   suction, 18
General Aviation District Offices, 58
General Operating and Flight Rules, 136
Generator, 17
Glide
   angle, VASI, 69
   distance, 174
Glider, 136, 142, 182
Go-around, 35
Gravity, 4, 164, 168
   center of (CG), 93, 94, 120, 169, 189

Ground
  control, 192
  effect, 95, 190
  objects, maneuvering by, 132
  references to, 52
  roll, 43, 116, 173, 174
Groundspeed, 50, 75, 105, 168, 172, 180, 193
Gyro instruments, 17, 18
Gyroplane, 142

Hail, 83, 85, 185
HALT, memory aid, 5, 178, 186
Heading, 180
  compass, 103, 104, 105, 180
  hemispheric rule, 142
  indicator. *See* Indicator, heading
  magnetic, 25, 71, 78
Headwind, 45, 46
Hearing aids, 141
Heat
  carburetor. *See* Carburetor heat
  combustion, 14
  engine, 14-15, 123
Heliports, 56
Hemispheric rule, 142
High pressure, 82, 184
Home base, 137
Homing, 71, 78
Hood work, 133
Horsepower, 3, 98, 164
  brake, 3, 167
  thrust, 29, 167, 172
Humidity, 179
Hydraulic system, 23
Hyperventilation, 140
Hypothermia, 196
Hypoxia, 140, 151, 153, 185

Ice, 83
  carburetor, 12, 14, 165, 169
  crystals, 85, 185
  fog, 83
  pellets, 85
  preflight check, 14
Icing
  aloft, 130
  induction, 12
IDENT switch, 75
IFR. *See* Instrument Flight Rules
Ignition
  lead, 166
  preflight check, 12-14
  switch, 17
ILS/DME, 75
Incidents, 135
Indicator
  attitude, 17, 40, 165, 171
  heading, 17, 71, 109, 165, 194
  landing gear position, 141
  turn and slip, 6
  visual approach slope, 69, 81, 113, 132, 143
Indicator, airspeed, 5, 40, 120, 131, 171
  dynamic pressure, 194-95
  required, 141
Inspections, 140-41
Instrument Approach Light Systems (ALS), 113
Instrument Approach Procedures, 61
Instrument Flight Rules (IFR), 58, 74
Instrument Landing System (ILS), 75
Instruments, 137
  cockpit, 5-7

flying by reference to, 39-41, 133, 171
  rating, 148
  turns by, 133
Isobars, 83, 185, 188

Key Position, 47
Knot, 174

Landing(s), 1-2, 35-36, 43-46, 172-74
  crosswind, 36, 170
  elementary forced, 32, 168-69
  ground roll, 45, 116
  lights, 17, 110, 127, 141, 165, 197
  magnetic heading, 25
  without nosewheel, 27
  off-airport, 43
  required to carry passengers, 138
  requirements, 137
  sequence of frequencies, 77
  solo endorsement, 136
  test, practical, 133-34
  wind, 116, 123, 137
Landing, short-field, 43, 44, 45, 133-34
  endorsements, 137
Landing, soft-field, 134, 137
Lapse rate, 5, 177
Latitude, 48, 52, 53, 174
Leaning, 12, 14, 16, 96
  prop control operating, 99
Legend
  Airport/Facility Directory, 55-56
  sectional chart, 55
License, radio, 140
LIFR. *See* Low IFR
Lift, 3, 93, 167, 185, 189
Light(s), 196
  aircraft, other, 121, 196
  anticollision, 113, 141, 143
  approach, 113-14
  electric landing, 141
  landing, 17, 110, 127, 165, 197
  lighted position, 113
  position, 141, 143, 196, 197
  runway, 113-14, 143
  signals, 81, 132, 144
  taxiing, 17
Lighting
  airplane, 113-14, 143
  airport, 113-14, 143
  cockpit, 196
Light trainer
  electrical system, 17
  oil system, 14
Limit load factors, 38, 171
Line
  hold, 25, 166, 195
  isogonic, 191
  primer, 166
  taxiway, 110, 166
LLWS. *See* Low-Level Wind Shear
Load factor, 93, 115, 168, 170
  limit, 189
  measure, 188
  ultimate, 189
Loading
  airplane stability, 120
  span, 170
LOC/DME, 75
Logbook
  aircraft, 140-41, 188
  engine, 140-41, 188
  pilot, 136, 137, 138, 149
Longitude, 48, 52, 53, 174
Low IFR (LIFR), 187

Low-Level Wind Shear (LLWS), 187
Lubrication, 14
Lycoming Flyer, The, 13

Magnetos, 12-13, 166
Maneuvers
  elementary precision, 30-31, 168
  instrument, 133
  postsolo precision, 42, 172
  practical test, 137
  reference to ground objects, 132
Map, 48-49
Markings, holding position, 195
Maximum power range, 16
MAYDAY, 75
Mean sea level (MSL), 135
Medical examination, 136
"Medical Facts for Pilots," 140
Medical Handbook for Pilots, 115
Meridians, 48, 55, 174, 182
Microphone, 76, 113
Miles
  nautical, 50, 55
  statute, 50, 186
Military Operations Areas (MOA), 143
MOA. *See* Military Operations Areas
Moment, 94, 131, 189, 190
MSL. *See* Mean sea level
Multicoms, 78
MVFR, 85

National Transportation Safety Board, 116
  Part 830, 135
National Weather Service telephone numbers, 58
Navigation, 48-51, 174-81
  night, VFR, practical test, 134
  planning, 100-107, 191-94
  radio, 71-76, 137, 143-44, 174
  VOR, 73, 79
NDB. *See* Beacon, nondirectional
Night
  flying, 112-14, 121, 125, 134, 137, 138, 196-97
  fuel requirements, 127
  navigation test, 134, 200
  signaling, 196
  taxiing, 17
  VFR requirements, 127, 134
North Pole, 48, 174
Nosewheel, 27, 170
NOTAMS. *See* Notices to Airmen
Notices to Airmen (NOTAMS), 61, 68, 100

OBS. *See* Omni Bearing Selector
Obstructions, 114, 169
Oil, 95-96, 190
  ashless dispersant, 10, 14
  breather line, 165
  consumption increase, 10, 18
  control rings, 10
  cooler, 165
  mineral, 10
  practical test, 132
  pressure, 6, 17, 21, 111, 165, 166
  sump, 165
  system, 14
  system preflight, 14
  temperature, 13, 14, 17, 165
  viscosity, 14, 95-96
Omni Bearing Selector (OBS), 72, 73, 74
Operations
  placards, 140
  search and rescue, 196

INDEX

Otto cycle, 8, 18
Overbreathing, 140, 153
Overcontrol, 34
Overhaul, 11
Oxygen, 84, 130, 196
   lack, 140, 151, 153
   supplemental, 140

Pacemakers, 141
Parachute Jumping Areas, 59
Parallels, 48, 55, 174, 182
Parking brakes, 23-24
Part 1, FARs, 135
Part 61, FARs, 135-39
Part 91, FARs, 136, 139-48
   aircraft inspection and documents, 140-41
   airplane equipment, 141-42
   Airport Radar Service Area, 147
   avoiding aircraft, 142
   enroute considerations, 143-44
   medical factors, 140
   operation around airports, 144-47
   pilot authority and responsibility, 139-40
Passengers, 138, 140, 149
PATWAS. See Pilot's Automatic Weather Answering Service
Performance, airplane, 5
Pilot
   authority, 139-40
   certification, 135-39
   in command, 127, 140, 148, 149, 150-51
   limitations, 150
   logbook, 136, 137, 138, 149
   privileges, 138, 150
   records, 138
   report (PIREP), 86
   responsibilities, 138, 139-40
   student, endorsements, 149
Pilotage, 137, 143-44, 174
Pilot's Automatic Weather Answering Service (PATWAS), 69
Pilot's Handbook of Aeronautical Knowledge, 115
Pilot's Weight and Balance Handbook, 115
PIREP. See Pilot, report
Pistons, 8, 9, 10, 13-14
   burned, 13
   combustion, 13-14
   rings, 11, 165
Pitch, 171
   propeller, control, 98, 99
Pitot tube, 5, 164
Placards, operations, 140
Plane Sense, 115
Plotter, 2, 48-49, 175
Plug
   external power, 17
   leads, 13
Postsolo maneuvers, 37-47
Power, 10, 16
   constant-speed propeller, 99
   failure, 123, 143
   loss, 13, 26, 32, 111, 169
Precipitation, 84
Preflight
   briefing, 105-6
   requirements, 150
Preflight check, 27, 95, 120, 136, 165-66
   alternator, 17
   brakes, 23
   carburetion, 11-12
   electrical system, 16-17
   engine, 8-11, 14-15
   exhaust, 15-16

ignition, 12-14
oil system, 14
operation, 131-32
test, practical, 131-32
vacuum system, 17-18
Preignition, 13, 14
Presolo, 27-36
Pressure, 49, 90
   air, 84
   altitude, 49, 96, 175
   barometric, 44
   brake, 24
   change, 91
   dynamic, 164
   high, 82, 184
   oil, 6, 17, 21, 111, 165, 166
   pitot tube, 5
   sea level, 82
   static, 164
Pressurization, 84
Pretakeoff check, 26, 166
Primer line, 166
Private Pilot—Airplane Written Test, 115-30, 197
   answering questions, 116
   contents, 1-2, 137
   question selection sheet, 116
Private pilot certificate, 135, 149, 150
Private Pilot—Practical Test Standards, 131, 137
Propeller, 8
   constant-speed, 12, 98-99
   efficiency, 98, 116
   exercising, 98
   fixed-pitch, 39, 96, 98-99
   fuel injection, 12
   pitch control, 98, 99
   throttle, 98, 99
Propping, 166
Pump, vacuum, 6-7, 17-18, 165
Pylons, 42

Radar, 75, 77, 125, 152
   service area, 146
Radar Summary Chart, 130
Radials, 72, 79, 183
Radiation, fog, 83
Radio, 71-81, 141, 183-84. See also Communication
   Automatic Direction Finder, 71-72
   beacon, 68, 71, 182
   crackling, 13
   license, 140
   magneto, 13
   navigation, 71-76, 110, 137, 143-44, 174
Radio Magnetic Indicator (RMI), 183
Rain, 85
Range, 97
Rating, instrument, 148
RCLS. See Runway Centerline Lighting System
Records, pilot, 138
Recovery
   approach to climbing stall, 40
   power-on spiral, 39
   spin, 34, 169
   stall, 33, 40, 136, 169, 200
Registration, aircraft, 140
REIL. See Runway End Identifier Lights
Reports, hourly, 86, 87, 88, 106
Reservoir, brakes, 23
Right-of-way, 68, 142, 182
Rings
   collector, 16

compression, 10
oil control, 10
piston, 11, 165
seating, 10
RMI. See Radio Magnetic Indicator
RNAV. See Area navigation
Rods, 112
Roll, 27, 35, 37, 173, 174
Roll-out, 24
Rotorcraft, 136, 182
rpm, 96
Rudder, 27, 170
   pedal pressure, 24
   top, 168
Run-up, 26, 136
Runway, 25, 109, 116, 123
   lengths, 140
   lights, 113-14, 143
   markings, 109, 110, 166
   right-hand traffic pattern, 125
   traffic, 125
Runway Centerline Lighting System (RCLS), 114
Runway Edge Light System (RELS), 113
Runway End Identifier Lights (REIL), 113

SAE. See Society of Automotive Engineers
Safety, 61, 139-40, 143, 198
Saturation, air, 84
Scales, temperature, 84
Scud running, 54
Sea level
   mean, 135
   pressure, 82
   standard, 184
Seaplane bases, 56
Search and rescue, 196
Seat belts, 140
Sectional chart, 52-55, 143, 182, 183, 191
Services, airplane, 55
SIGMETS (Significant Meteorological Information), 86, 130
Signals, light, 81, 132, 144
Six Cs, 110, 195
Slant range, 75
Smoking, 17, 18, 19, 165
Snow, 85
Society of Automotive Engineers (SAE), 14
Solo, 136, 137
Span loading, 170
Spark plugs, 10, 12, 13-14
Spatial disorientation, 153
Speed, 135
   aircraft, 142
   maneuvering (V_A), 93, 135, 188-89
   maximum angle of climb, 131
   minimum steady-flight, landing configuration (V_{SO}), 46, 135
   never exceed (V_{NE}), 197
   restrictions, 142
   stall, 28, 46, 135, 168, 169
   vertical, indicator, 6
SPFM. See *Student Pilot's Flight Manual, The*
Spin, recovery, 34, 169
Spiral, 169
   power-on, 39, 40
Squall line, 83
SQUAWK, 75, 153
Stabilator, 38, 171
Stage III, 152
Stall, 28, 29, 33-34, 120, 169
   accelerated, 37, 38
   advanced, 37-38, 170

INDEX

Stall (*continued*)
   altitude, 200
   cross-control, 37, 170
   full, 133
   imminent, 132-33
   power-off, 34
   recognition, 136
   recovery, 33, 40, 136, 169, 200
   skidding, 37
   speed, 28, 46, 135, 168, 169
   takeoff and departure, 133
   trim tab, 167
Standard day, 84
Standby, 75
Starting, 14, 17, 21-22, 120, 166
Static pressure, 164
Status of Federal Aviation Regulations, 116
Stoichiometric mixture, 166
Stress, 140, 170-71
Strobes, 143, 197
Student certificate, 136, 150
Student Pilot's Flight Manual, The (SPFM), 1-2, 12
Sublimation, 185
Sunset, 143
Surface Analysis Chart, 188
Survival, crash, 195-96
Switch, ignition, 17
Syllabus, hooded training, 39
System
   Air Traffic Control, 74
   cockpit, 5-7
   control, 2
   electrical, 16-17
   exhaust, 8, 15-16
   fuel, 97, 190-91
   fuel injection, 12
   oil, 14
   vacuum, 17-18

Tab, 167
TACAN. *See* Tactical Air Navigation
Tachometer, 141
Tactical Air Navigation (TACAN), 146
Takeoff, 35-36, 43-46, 170, 172-74
   altitude, 3
   barometric pressure, 44
   constant-speed propeller, 98
   cowl flaps, 44
   crosswind, 137
   distance chart, 2
   engine rough, 26
   frost on wings, 84
   fuel, 26
   ground roll, 43, 45
   nose-up trim setting, 38
   passenger carrying requirements, 138
   prop control, 98-99
   requirements, 3, 137
   roll, 35, 174
   sequence of frequencies, 77
   short-field, 43, 44, 133-34, 137, 172
   soft-field, 44, 134, 137
   solo endorsement, 136
   test, practical, 133-34
   wind shear effect, 185
TAS. *See* Airspeed, true
Taxi guidance line, 25
Taxiing, 23-25, 110, 136, 166
   lights, 17
   night, 17
   wind condition, 120, 166
Taxiway lines, 25, 110, 166
TBO. *See* Time between overhauls

TCA. *See* Terminal Control Areas
TCH. *See* Threshold crossing height
TDZL. *See* Touchdown Zone Lighting
Technical Standard Order (TSO) transponders, 141
Telephone Information Briefing Service (TIBS), 69
Temperature, 44, 190
   altimeter, 5, 86, 186
   cylinder head, 13, 14
   density-altitude, 2, 172
   exhaust gas, 16
   inversion, 127
   oil, 13, 14, 17, 165
   scales, 84
   standard, 5, 97
   takeoff, 3
   true airspeed, 49
   vaporization effect, 12
   viscosity of oil, 14, 95-96
Temperature/dewpoint spread, 194
Terminal Control Areas (TCA), 141, 142, 146, 147
   rules, 152, 153
Terminal Radar Service Area (TRSA), 77, 146, 152
Test
   practical, 131-34, 137, 150, 197-200
   written. *See Private Pilot—Airplane Written Test*
THP. *See* Thrust horsepower
Threshold
   crossing height (TCH), 69
   displaced, 195
Throttle, 12, 13, 14, 29, 166
   propeller operation, 98, 99
Thrust, 167
   horsepower (THP), 29, 167, 172
Thunderstorms, 83, 88, 111
   Automatic Direction Finder, 72
TIBS. *See* Telephone Information Briefing Service
Tie-downs, 24
Time, 105, 120
   flight, required to be certified, 137
Time between overhauls (TBO), 11
Time, Fuel, and Distance to Climb Chart, 96
Timing, magneto, 12
Topography, sectional chart, 54-55
Torque, 3, 169
Touchdown Zone Lighting (TDZL), 114
Tower
   air traffic control, 77
   light signals, 144
   talking with, 76-77
Tower Enroute Control routes, 58
Track, 71
Tracking, VOR, 79
Traffic
   airport, 144
   pattern, 123, 132, 136, 170
   runway, 125
Transcribed Weather Broadcasts (TWEB), 77-78, 125
Transition areas, 147
Transponder, 74-75, 80, 125
   4096 code capability, 141, 146
   maintenance, 153
   Model C, 146
   requirements, 141, 151
   Technical Standard Order, 141
Trim
   pitch, 171
   tab, 167

TRSA. *See* Terminal Radar Service Area
TSO. *See* Technical Standard Order transponders
Turbulence, 84, 88, 121
   wake, 36, 115, 136, 170
Turn, 136
   around a point, 42
   bank of, 30-31, 42
   coordinator, 6, 17, 33, 40, 165
   power, 30
   radius, 195
   reference to instruments, 133
   slipping, 6, 165
   standard rate, 7, 40, 165, 171
Turn and slip
   coordinator, 17, 33, 165
   indicator, 6
TWEB. *See* Transcribed Weather Broadcasts

Unicom, 81, 120, 183
Upslope, fog, 83
UTC. *See* Coordinated Universal Time

V_A, 93, 135, 188-89
V_{NE}, 131, 197
V_{NO}, 197
V_{SO}, 46, 135, 170
V_X, 197
V_Y, 197
Vacuum
   pump, 6-7, 17-18, 165
   system, 17-18
Valves, 8-10, 13
   throttle, 12
Vaporization, 12
Variation, 174
VASI. *See* Visual Approach Slope Indicator
Vectors, wind, 51, 182
Venturi, 12, 17
Vertigo, 146, 153
VFR. *See* Visual Flight Rules
VHF/DF, 126
VHF frequencies, 183
VHF Omnirange (VOR)
   accuracy check, 74
   bearings and, 71
   cross bearings, 195
   dual system, 74
   equipment, 72, 78
   frequencies, 78
   navigation, 73, 79
   phantom station, 76
   receivers, 143-44, 183
   tracking, 79
Viscosity, oil, 14, 95-96
Visibility, 91, 107
   control zone minimums, 144-46
   minimum for VFR, 127
   statute miles, 186
Visual Approach Slope Indicator (VASI), 81, 113, 132, 143
   glide angle, 69
Visual Flight Rules (VFR), 74-75, 85, 127, 135
Voice recorders, 141
VOR. *See* VHF Omnirange
VOR/DME, 75, 76
VORTAC, 75, 76
VOR Test (VOT), 74, 80, 183
Vortex strength, 170
VOT. *See* VOR Test
V speed, 131, 135

Wake Turbulence, 115

WCA. *See* Wind, correction angle
Weather, 82-92, 100, 137, 140, 184
   analyzing, 105-8, 131-32
   briefing, FSS, 183
   broadcasts, 77 78, 125
   continuous transcribed briefing, 130
   expected at arrival, 129
   factors, 142
   forecast. *See* Forecast
   fronts and pressure systems, 90
   hourly reports, 86, 87, 88, 106
   temperature inversion, 127
Weather Depiction Chart, 91-92

Weight, 94, 115, 131, 167
   basic empty, 94
   fuel, 131, 190
   maximum, 94
Weight and Balance, 140
Weight and Balance Envelope, 94
Wet-sump system, 14
Wind, 85, 90, 103, 109
   altitude, 142
   components, 174
   correction angle (WCA), 180
   deflection, 82
   drift, 168

   effect, 194
   landing, 116, 123, 137
   relative, angle of chord line, 3
   shear, 185
   surface, 47
   taxiing, 120, 166
   vectors, 51, 182
Winds Aloft Forecasts, 106, 130
Wings, 4
Wingtip vortices, 121

Zilch's Law, 112

NOTES

NOTES

NOTES

NOTES

NOTES

NOTES

NOTES